Sheila Bennett, Don Dworet with Ken Weber

Special Education
in
Ontario Schools

Sixth Edition

This book is dedicated to the Memory of Don Reilly
a tireless advocate for students with special needs
throughout the province

The authors of *Special Education in Ontario Schools* are grateful for the advice,
assistance and support from many caring professionals in special education.
Thanks are due particularly to Bruce Drewett and his colleagues at the Special Education
Program and Policy Branch, Diane Book, Cheryl Duquette, Marg Harrison, Randy Hill,
Andrea Jack, Kimberly Maich, Robert Maich, Cheryl Missiuna, Susie Palumbo,
Lynda Petrie, Laura Reece, Kelly Anne Russell, Tracy Sacco, Elizabeth Starr

Highland Press
Box 496, St. Davids, ON L0S1P0
Telephone (905) 685 5568
Fax (905) 685 4327
E-mail hldpress@cogeco.ca

Design and cover photo: Fortunato Aglialoro
Editor: Cecile King and Norma Pettit
Indexer: Paula Pike
Project Coordinator: Kaari Turk

Canadian Cataloguing in Publication Data
Bennett, Sheila Marie, 1961–
    Special Education in Ontario Schools / Sheila Bennett, Don Dworet / Ken Weber
6th edition.

Editions 1-3 written by Ken Weber, 4-5 by Ken Weber and Sheila Bennett.
Includes bibliographical references and index
ISBN 978-0-9693061-9-1

    Special Education—Ontario
I, Weber, K.J. (Kenneth Jerome), 1940– II. Dworet, Don, 1950– Weber,
K.J. (Kenneth Jerome), 1940– Special Education In Ontario Schools IV. Title

LC3984.2.O5B45 2008   371.9'09713   C2008-900399-3

Printed and bound in Canada

2 3 4 5   12 11 10 09

Table of Contents

Foreword / 4

CHAPTER 1 Special Education: Then and Now / 5

CHAPTER 2 Continuing Issues in Special Education / 21

CHAPTER 3 The Special Needs Population: Categories and Numbers / 32

CHAPTER 4 Service Delivery: the Infrastructure of Special Education / 40

CHAPTER 5 The Individual Education Plan (IEP): A Team Approach / 57

CHAPTER 6 Identification and Placement: How the IPRC Works / 71

CHAPTER 7 Assessment: Identifying Strengths and Needs / 75

CHAPTER 8 Students With Learning Disabilities / 89

CHAPTER 9 Students With Behavioural Exceptionalities: Students With AD/HD/ 109

CHAPTER 10 Students Who Are Gifted / 133

CHAPTER 11 Students With Intellectual and Developmental Disabilities / 149

CHAPTER 12 Students With Autism Spectrum Disorders / 165

CHAPTER 13 Students With Neurological Disabilities: Chronic Health Needs, Musculoskeletal Impairments, Acquired Brain Injury / 179

CHAPTER 14 Students Who Are Deaf or Hard of Hearing / 191

CHAPTER 15 Students Who Are Blind or Partially Sighted / 204

CHAPTER 16 Students With Speech and Language Disorders / 214

Appendix / 221

Definitions and Categories of Exceptionalities in Ontario / 221

Some Assessment Instruments Popular in Ontario / 222

Ontario Legislation and Policies Affecting Special Education / 229

Subject/Context Index / 231

Author/Resource Index / 237

Foreword

Classroom practices, administrative procedures, and Ontario government policies in special education are built around the ideal that it is possible to respond to the strengths and needs of every student with an exceptionality. Legislation in the province guarantees access to public education for all students regardless of their needs. Further, it assures that students with exceptionalities will have access to programs and resources to meet their special needs. Individual boards and schools are set up to deliver special education services and support, ranging through simple modification and/or accommodation of a student's program to allocation of complex specialized resources, and even to changes in building design. Ministry regulations reinforce ideal professional practices such as the development and monitoring of Individual Education Plans.

Over the past four years, the attention paid to educating students with exceptionalities has received almost as much attention as in 1980 when the province passed legislation requiring all boards to provide programs and services to students with exceptionalities. This attention has led to increases in funding, greater emphasis on parental involvement, refinement of the IEP development process, publication of Ministry of Education Resource documents focusing on inclusion of students with exceptionalities in the regular classroom and attention to helping students with exceptionalities complete their secondary school graduation requirements. Educators in this relatively new century are not questioning whether or not students with exceptionalities should be in their classrooms but rather how should these students be taught in the most effective manner.

On the front lines so to speak, classroom teachers and educational assistants draw on training in special education, and on their own resources and talents and creativity to bring everything together for students with special strengths and needs. Ontario educators have long been recognized, not just in their own province but elsewhere, for their leadership and commitment in matters relating to students with exceptionalities. These qualities are a main reason why special education has been implemented so successfully as a fully functional and vital element in the province's broader system.

Like all systems put together by human beings, Ontario's special education reveals occasional faults. But the system is dynamic. It responds to evolving needs and philosophies; it develops; it adapts. And most of the time it improves. In any case, special education will only be as effective as the people at every level who make it work. Ultimately, special education can only succeed as a concept, as a principle, and most important as a practice, through the actions of professionals who are committed to the belief that every student has a right to the best that schooling can offer. Ironically, the ideal of special education is to put itself out of business. The goal for which it strives is a system of education in which adaptation and accommodation for the needs of every student is automatic, and in which the very idea of special education is unnecessary.

CHAPTER 1

Special Education: Then and Now

December 12, 1980, was a landmark day in the history of education in Ontario. On this date, Lieutenant-Governor John Black Aird signed Bill 82, the Education Amendment Act, into law. This act dramatically changed how students with special needs were going to be educated by Ontario's publicly funded school system. With the signing of this document it was no longer *optional* for boards of education to accept students with special needs into their schools. Rather school boards would now be *required* to provide education to all students regardless of

Dateline 1957 — The Case of Ruthie

It was not until she was almost eight years old that Ruthie began attending school. To begin with, her parents knew she was, in her father's words, "something behind the other young ones." Then there was the long walk down the concession and across the sideroad to the one-room school. She'd have to do this walk alone, and everybody knew Ruthie had this habit of wandering off.

Even at age eight, Ruthie's future as a student was uncertain at best.

"We don't have to take this child in if you don't want," the chairman of S.S. #12 School Board had said to the brand new teacher in August. "It's going to be hard enough in your first year without having a retarded child to look after. The regulations are clear. We don't have to take her. It's up to you."

But the teacher welcomed Ruthie and made her feel part of the tiny student body at S.S. #12. Two girls in grade 8 took her outside to the toilet every day just before recess and noon hour. One of the older boys built her an extended desktop so she could more easily enjoy her favourite activity: colouring on the back of discarded rolls of wallpaper. The younger children, a bit perplexed at first because Ruthie didn't speak, soon learned to ignore her strange noises. And every day after lunch, Ruthie crawled happily into the teacher's lap for the reading of the next sequence in "the afternoon story." By the end of the school year, Ruthie could recognize her own name in print; she understood and followed routines, could count up to ten and, most important in the teacher's view, she no longer wandered away.

The next year might have shown even more development, but Ruthie got caught in a swirl of events that even her parents didn't quite follow. S.S. #12 was closed in June, along with all the other one-room schools in the township. Students were now to be bused to a brand new central school. Ruthie's teacher got married that summer and moved to the other end of the province. At "Central," the school inspector told the staff in primary/junior that no one was obligated to take in Ruthie, but if anyone volunteered, she could be admitted.

There were no takers. Ruthie never went to school again.

Note: In this chapter and throughout the book, the term "parent" represents parents, guardians, and appropriate caregivers.

any disability they may have. Disability would no longer be a barrier to entering or participating in the regular school system. Within a very short time, special education became an integral part of Ontario's system. It did so with such relative ease that it's tempting to believe Bill 82 was a law just waiting to be passed. Yet the long journey to special education as it is today was anything but simple and smooth. This chapter outlines a few of the bumps.

Long Ago and Far Away

Just Survival

Until relatively recent times, society's concern for people with special needs was minimal. Even in cultures like the Greek and the Roman, which we generally view as more enlightened and sophisticated, people with disabilities did not fare very well. Under Solon's law, for example, the weak and children of Athens with disabilities were placed in clay vessels and abandoned. In Rome, children with disabilities were customarily thrown into the Tiber River. And it was not unusual for wealthy families to keep a person who was mentally handicapped for entertainment. No less a personage than the moralist philosopher Seneca reported that his wife kept a "feeble-minded dwarf," ostensibly for that purpose. Even Aristotle, whose writings dominated western thought for more than a thousand years after his death, described people who were deaf as "incapable of reason, no better than the animals of the forest" and "unteachable."

There were some exceptions to this almost universal attitude. The Talmud offered enlightened instructions regarding people who are blind and deaf, and Hippocrates' investigations into epilepsy and intellectual disability suggested that scientific curiosity about special needs was not entirely absent. However, the impact of these exceptions was very limited.

In the Middle Ages, there were a few bright spots. Saint Nicholas Thaumaturgos, fourth-century bishop of Wyre in England, became known as a protector of people who were feeble-minded, but there is little evidence of what he accomplished. (Thaumaturgos was also the patron saint of sailors and pawnbrokers—and the prototype for Santa Claus!) Some monasteries and other clergy established hospices. However, the superstitions of the day, along with a powerful belief in demonic possession and the sheer demands of mere survival, meant that persons with disabilities were very much on their own.

A few strides were made in Europe in the post-Renaissance Era, but they, too, were isolated, short-lived bursts of change, the accomplishments of individuals with will and drive, rather than the product of a general amelioration in attitude. When these individuals died, the fruits of their efforts died with them. Most special educators today, for example, recognize the name Ponce de Leon (1529-82), the Spanish monk who taught children who were deaf to speak and read (although he is often confused with the explorer who visited Florida in 1513). De Leon's techniques were apparently very successful, but his techniques are lost and unknown to us largely because there was no general impetus after his death to continue their use.

> *Every child has a claim on the community for the best means of moral and mental cultivation.*
>
> Harvey Peet, President, New York Institution for the Deaf and Dumb, 1855

Attitudes Begin to Change

Louis Braille (1809-1852) had more lasting success with an alphabet for people who are blind that he adapted from a cipher system invented by Napoleon Bonaparte's staff. By Braille's time, attitudes had also begun to shift. British philosopher, John Locke (1632-1708) had impressed the intellectuals of the western world with his philosophy of "sensationalism," which, among other things, took issue with the long-held view that children are born with innate characteristics imprinted by God, nature, or the devil. Instead, Locke argued that newborns are a tabula rasa, a blank slate waiting to be written upon. Ever so slowly, this idea, given further impetus by scholars like Voltaire, Rousseau, and Goethe, began to chip away at the notion that people with disabilities are the unfortunate product of some Great Plan and should therefore be left alone.

Still, the march toward enlightenment was slow, and innovation was actively discouraged. Jean Marc Itard (1775-1858), who discovered and tried to teach Victor, the wild boy of Aveyron, and Frederick Treves (1867-1923), who rescued John Merrick, the Elephant Man, are among the better known personalities who broke new ground, but their humanism was too radical for their contemporaries. The level of general indifference to people with disabilities, or perhaps just inertia, is evident in the fact that carnival shows continued to display physically unique persons like John Merrick well into the mid-twentieth century.

Canada Moves Forward

Though strongly resisted in the United States, there was some progress in education for people who were deaf and/or blind in Canada. In 1831 in Quebec, Ronald Mcdonald, a reporter with the *Montreal Gazette*, opened a school for people who were deaf in Champlain, Canada's first formal special education project. Similar schools opened in Halifax in 1856, in Toronto (1858), and Winnipeg (1884). A school for people who were blind opened in Toronto in 1872 and one in Halifax a year later. In Ontario, the vigorous work of John Barrett McCann brought about the founding of two residential schools: The Ontario Institution for the Education and Instruction of the Deaf and Dumb, at Belleville, in 1870, and the Ontario Institution for the Education and Instruction of the Blind, at Brantford, in 1872. These schools were followed soon after by the first Canadian residential institution for people

Dateline 1965 — The Case of Leo

No one was more exasperated by Leo's lack of language skills than his mother. A former teacher, she had sent his two older sisters off to grade 1 so well prepared they both skipped a grade. Not Leo. To be sure, he appeared to be just as bright. Certainly he was charming, and so what if he had a few odd speech patterns? That was nothing unusual in a youngster. Yet no matter what she did, Leo's mother just couldn't teach him to recognize letters.

Not that she pushed him to frustration. She was too wise and experienced a mother and teacher. But Leo—she'd never seen anything quite like it. Take the letter "A" for example. He'd willingly trace it, colour it, find "A's" hidden about the kitchen, and sing the "A" song. Yet, though he'd then recognize the letter without a prompt for maybe two or three days, after a week on "B" and "C," the letter "A" would be gone. And it would be really gone! That was part of the exasperation. Re-introducing "A" to Leo was not a simple matter of stimulating recall. It was as though he'd never ever seen it before!

Of course, Leo's printing was disastrous. Nor did it improve as he got older. At the end of grade 1, Leo's principal boldly left the "Printing" mark blank on Leo's report card so he could pass into grade 2. But the problem was still there. So was his letter recognition problem and lack of progress in learning to read. Friends of Leo's mom tried to console her with the explanation that boys are almost always slower but Leo just didn't get any better. Nor did anybody have an explanation, although the grade 4 teacher had seen another boy like Leo once before, and he'd become a real problem because no one seemed able to do anything for him.

Still, the situation was not all bad. Leo's father ran a successful plumbing business where Leo helped out on Saturdays, and as long as the boy was given only one instruction at a time, no one worked harder or more reliably. In fact, it may have been the plumbing business that provided an out for everyone, because by grade 5, Leo's behaviour was changing. He'd already repeated two grades, was facing failure again, and reading was still torture and writing an agony. By grade five, Leo was no longer getting headaches and stomach pains during language arts; but he was now acting out in progressively alarming ways. That was the main reason Leo's mother reluctantly agreed to the arrangement that allowed him to leave school to work for his dad. Even so, one of her worst fears came true some years later. When Leo's dad retired, he had to sell the business, for although Leo was willing and handy, he never learned to read and write well enough to run things.

who were developmentally disabled, which opened in Orillia in 1876. These institutions reflected a growing sense of social responsibility in the general population, as well as a developing interest in people with special needs. Although some of the teaching methods used in the institutions seem odd today, and although the language and terminology make contemporary educators wince, the mere existence of residential schools for people with special needs was a striking development for the time, especially in light of the fact that educating the so-called "normal" population was still far from universal.

Some Help But Much More Needed

Despite the operation of the schools mentioned above there was much more that needed to be done. Due to a combination of economics, geography, and limited concern, comparatively few children with special needs were served, relative to the actual needs in the population with disabilities. Resources were aimed at the most overt and visibly obvious exceptionalities. In addition, the curricula for these students were very much biased toward industrial training. The idea was, in the words of a contemporary, "to make something of the students" so they might find gainful employment. To be fair, that mission very much followed the wishes of the students' own parents and families who, perhaps understandably, felt that "making something of the students" at least offered the students some hope of independence.

Not even this much support was held out to students with exceptionalities whose needs were less obvious, and, were, as a consequence, harder to understand or even to acknowledge. Consequently, students with a learning disability (the term did not even exist until 1963) or those with what we see today as behaviour problems, were usually early dropouts. Right through to the final quarter of the twentieth century, dropouts were regarded—and also saw themselves—as poor educational material in any case. Assembly-line industry absorbed these students into fairly low-level employment and reinforced the perception.

Even established schools designed specifically to serve students with special needs were not always secure, especially if their faculties attempted to be innovative. The Ontario School for Crippled Children (now part of Bloorview MacMillan Children's Rehabilitation Centre in Toronto) had quickly established an international reputation for its programs. As early as 1890, faculty at the Orillia institution had developed quite advanced school programs for its clientele. Yet both had to struggle to keep their programs going in the face of widespread criticism. Students with serious profound needs were often seen as poor candidates for education on the premise that educating them served little purpose, and offered only minimal return to society. In light of that hypothesis, it is more than a little ironic that the societal benefit factor apparently played no role at all in discussions of special education for students who were especially able. Public education for gifted students was almost unheard of until the 1970s.

Acceptance of Responsibility

For many years prior to the end of the Second World War, there was a prominent philosophy called "eugenics." This philosophy believed that society needed to be protected from genetic contamination and argued that "unfortunates" should be protected in institutions, thereby protecting society as well. In 1918, a coalition of medical doctors, social workers, and influential citizens had formed the Canadian National Committee on Mental Hygiene to pressure the government to expand custodial facilities for people who are feeble-minded, whose spread was the result, in the Committee's opinion, of "procreation by unsound stock, the numbers of which were being accelerated by the government's admittance to the Dominion, of degenerate immigrants" (sic!). Under a principle of concern for the public good, and a seemingly well-intentioned concern for the less able, supporters of eugenics were successful in effecting a policy that not only segregated people with special needs, but in practical terms, isolated them.

> *Individuals with disabilities should be served whenever possible in general education classrooms in inclusive neighbourhood schools and community settings.*
>
> Council for Exceptional Children, 1993

On the agenda at the county school board meeting, item no. 5 appeared innocuous enough.

It read:

Approval of funds to install elevator, renovate main entrance,
washroom, fire exits and classroom doorways as outlined in Report 995A.

To Pete and his family, and to three other families with sons and daughters who had severe physical disabilities, item no. 5 was full of implications. Pete had Muscular Dystrophy. Over his years in elementary school, the condition had developed to a point where he could no longer walk for more than a few metres without risking a serious fall. The walking itself was accomplished with the help of crutches which Pete used in alternating wide swings. Increasingly, he was spending longer and longer periods in a wheelchair, and now required some assistance when using the washroom. In a few months, Pete would be eligible to attend the secondary school in his community. But it was an old building where he would not be able to get around, much less get in or out, unless some major structural changes were made. There would also need to be some kind of arrangement developed for Pete's personal hygiene needs. Nothing in either education or civil law obligated the board to do these things, but because it was a fairly small community where Pete and his family were well known and active, the local trustees agreed to consider the matter.

The motion was defeated, but so narrowly that Pete's family was encouraged to press for another possibility. Since 1974, Ontario's Education Act had permitted school boards to provide special education services if they chose to, and by now, some boards in the province were doing that. A few had renovated some schools to accommodate students with physical disabilities. Thus Pete's family, supported by an advocacy group, began urging the local board to arrange—and bear the cost—for Pete to enroll at one of these. Once more the trustees listened carefully and sympathetically, but because there were a number of students in a situation similar to Pete's, they approached the proposal with caution. So cautiously, as it turned out, that the motion kept being tabled. Pete's parents, wary of the outcome, reluctantly sold their home, moved out of the community, and relocated in another part of the province near a school that was modified for students with special needs like their son's.

However, by the end of the Second World War, what was already a trickle of doubt about eugenics became a flood, largely because of the role eugenics had played in Fascism. In the 1960s, the swell of concern for the individual rights of all persons led governments to enshrine those rights in law. Ontario, for example, established its first Human Rights Commission in 1962. By the end of the decade, any notion of racial or cultural superiority or indeed any kind of exclusive human purity had become anathema. Western culture was ready to listen to the idea that every human being has worth.

An Era of Positive Change

In Ontario, special education as we know it today began to come of age in the past 50 years. Although as early as 1950, the Hope Commission had recommended expansion of special education programs, the watershed, the point at which the march to Bill 82 got under way, was in the 1960s. This decade saw things shift from episodic, disconnected attempts to somehow improve the lot of students with exceptionalities, to a goal-directed, coherent movement aimed at educating children with special needs according to those needs. The change occurred around this time for a number of reasons. Throughout the 1960s the civil rights movement in the United States advocated that all people regardless of race, creed, or colour be treated equally. This mantra was taken up by those concerned with people with special needs who argued successfully that physical, emotional, or cognitive disabilities should not in themselves be a barrier to equal treatment. In 1975, the Congress of the United States passed the

Americans with Disabilities Act, Public Law 94-142, a law that mandated that all students be provided a publicly supported education in the "least restrictive environment." Under this law, children with exceptionalities were given the right to a free and appropriate education and their parents were given the right to due process and confidentiality. Boards of education were also mandated to provide a range of educational services and were required to provide an individual education plan for each child deemed exceptional (Winzer, 2008).

The Normalization Principle Comes to Canada

Although separation by ability was still prominent well into the middle of the twentieth century, by the time Ontario enacted Bill 82 in 1980, this notion was succumbing to the principle of *normalization* developed in Scandinavia by Nirje and championed in Canada by Wolf Wolfensberger. In essence, normalization argues against institutionalization and contends that persons with special needs should be viewed more by the points on which they are similar to others, rather than by those on which they differ. The philosophy of normalization holds that once persons with exceptionalities are integrated into mainstream society, they will take on the behaviours of the norm because they will have more normal models to follow. It is a concept that suggests unlimited growth and improvement instead of ceilings and limitations, and it struck a powerful chord, not just in Ontario, but throughout Canada and North America. In only about twenty years, government policies across the continent changed from building and expanding care-based facilities to strategies that saw these centres being closed and the residents being included in their communities.

Dateline 1989 — The Case of Justin

A flurry of October transfers meant that Justin's grade 3 class acquired a new teacher only a week before his situation was scheduled for special review by an Identification, Placement, Review Committee (IPRC). The new teacher wisely allowed the full-time educational assistant in grade 3 to work with the school's resource teacher in putting together documentation for the IPRC. The assistant was experienced and held in high regard in the school, and she had worked with Justin for the past two years. More important, she was one of the few adults who understood and managed his behaviour effectively.

Over the past several years, Justin had been variously diagnosed as Autistic, ADHD, Learning Disabled, Cerebrally Dysfunctional and Mentally Disabled, by a variety of clinical psychologists either in private practice, or employed by the school board. While Justin was still in kindergarten, an IPRC took the unusual step, for a student so young, of identifying him "exceptional: behavioural." Justin's mother signed on to the identification only because it would allow the school to bring in extra resources. However, she served notice she would appeal any move to take her son out of a regular class, and she maintained that position through reviews in grades 1 and 2 in the face of growing evidence that a regular class might not be the best place for him.

The special review in grade 3 was arranged by the principal who, for everyone's sake, planned to make one more stab at modifying Justin's class placement. If that failed, she planned to initiate a rarely used process which could declare him "hard-to-serve" and thereby excluded from the school. Fortunately, everyone, including the boy's mother, agreed to an adjustment. Justin would begin each day in the grade 3 class and then, with the assistant, join a small resource class. He would, depending on his mood and behaviour, return to the regular class as frequently as possible and for as long as possible. Above all, it was agreed that flexibility would prevail and both the assistant and the teachers would be free to make ad hoc decisions as necessary.

For Justin—and everyone—the long-term outcome was very positive. He spent increasingly more time in the regular grade 3 class but there was always a friendly, secure home base to go to if the need arose. Perhaps most telling: the annual IPRC review in grade 4 lasted only ten minutes.

Decisions in the Hands of Educators

Before the 1960s, the predominant approach to providing services for students with special needs was a medical one, that is, focusing on what was wrong with the student. Educators in the 1960s, and even more so in the 1970s, began to set aside this popular view and replace it with a wider, more *ecological* view incorporating the whole person. The ecological perspective takes note of what an exceptional student can do in addition to what is hard or impossible for that student to do. At the same time, teachers and paraprofessionals also began to recognize their own strengths, and the potential power of their own contributions to a student with exceptionalities's case. Whereas in the medical model approach, teachers or educational assistants are expected to defer to some greater, outside expertise, the ecological focus grants them the right to exercise their considerable intuition, knowledge, and experience. An important consequence of the latter approach is that students with special needs are seen as people who can be educated, not as people who should be in custody, medical cases for whom intellectual development and learning are secondary to coping with a handicap.

Perhaps more important, ultimately, is the effect of this perspective on the way special education service is delivered. In a medical model, expertise is visited upon the classroom from above and afar. But in a model that requires empiricism, hypothesis, flexibility, and constant program modification, the decision-making and the delivery of services are likely to be much more current, not to mention appropriate, if they take place on site. By the time the Education Amendment Act was only a decade old, therefore, the trend in Ontario was moving toward management of special needs in the local community school, and specifically in the regular classroom.

Political Advocacy Becomes Prominent

The protest movements of the 1960s were not only successful in improving the social and legal situation for visible minorities, they were also a time when the parents of students with special needs found that they could achieve more for their sons and daughters by acting collectively rather than singly. The result was that political activism by parents and other advocacy groups began to have, and continues to have, a powerful effect on governments. The strength and sophistication of lobbying efforts by groups like the Learning Disabilities Association, the Association for Bright Children, the Association for Community Living, among many others, has been instrumental for decades now in motivating educational jurisdictions to improve the lot of students with exceptionalities. In fact, there were many participants in the process that eventually gave birth to mandatory legislation in Ontario, who acknowledge quite candidly that, were it not for the activity of advocates, the legislation may not have come about as soon as it did. An important consequence of such powerful advocacy was that by the end of the twentieth century, it became accepted, indeed required practice, to involve parents or their representatives in any educational decision-making involving their child.

Bill 82: Major changes to Ontario's Education Act

Five years after the passage of U.S. Public Law 94-142 and after Nova Scotia and Saskatchewan had passed similar legislation, Bill 82, the Education Amendment Act, was passed in December 1980 by the legislature of Ontario. Once this act was passed, special education became a normal, functioning part of Ontario's education system with remarkable speed. Teachers still active today can point to a time only a decade before 1980, when the idea of sending students with special needs to a regular school was not even considered by most jurisdictions in the province. Yet within a decade after 1980, special education was as integral to the system as notebooks and chalk. Although the legislation itself is extensive, the elements most immediately affecting students and their families, and teachers and their schools and boards are these:

- All students resident in the province of Ontario are entitled to a publicly supported education. Every school board in the province is required to provide special education programs and services for its exceptional pupils. If a board cannot provide programs and services, it must pay another board to provide them.

- School boards are to establish Identification, Placement and Review Committees (IPRCs) whose chief function is to identify whether a student is exceptional, and then decide upon a placement for him or her. (For more on the IPRC see chapter 5.)

- Parents of a student with an exceptionality are to be included in the IPRC process. An appeal process is available if the parents are dissatisfied with identification or placement decisions.

- Every school board is required to establish a Special Education Advisory Committee (SEAC) to advise on matters of special education programs and services.

- A comprehensive special education plan must be developed and maintained by each school board in which its programs and services are outlined for public and Ministry examination. The "Plan" is to be updated and amended as necessary to meet the current needs of exceptional pupils. Currently discussions to include the special education plan as a part of the overall school board plan, rather than a separate document are underway.

- School boards are required to implement procedures for early and on-going identification of students' learning abilities and needs.

> *School boards must be held accountable for the academic achievement of all students and for reporting that achievement to parents.*
>
> Bennett and Wynne, 2006,
> *Special Education Transformation*

Implementation Occurs

At the Board Office

Even critics of the Ontario legislation agree that the expectations it raised were met for the most part in the immediately ensuing years. When the bill was passed in 1980, the province's school boards were given five years to establish their plans and systems. Yet in the majority of boards, special education policies and practices were fully operational well before the deadline. More subtle, but certainly crucial to rapid implementation, was the relative ease with which special education became a natural feature in every school board. And it came about in the face of major challenges. Prior to the legislation, for example, separate school boards did not provide programs and services for what were called in 1980 "trainable retarded pupils," and thus most separate boards had to build services from scratch in a very short time. Many smaller school boards, both public and separate, had to develop special education systems with little or no existing base on which to build. Even boards that already had some services before 1980 did not offer the comprehensive systems one could find almost anywhere in the province only five years later. All boards have now established offices of special education with staff who provide consultative and administrative assistance to schools and teachers to help ensure that students with special needs receive appropriate programs and services in whatever classroom they may be placed.

In the Classroom

Still another challenge was finding front-line staff to make the systems work on a daily basis. In 1980, very few teachers in the province undertook special education as a career path. Yet a combination of teachers' inherent skills and ready willingness to learn on the job, supported by a mass professional development drive on the part of the Ministry and of the province's universities, soon addressed this vital component. Within a decade, provincial authorities were able to point to a large cadre

> ### The Special Education Plan ✍
>
> Under Regulation 306, each board of education must establish and maintain a master plan in which it sets out programs and services it will provide. The plan must be reviewed yearly, and every two years the board must prepare a report for the Ministry of Education. In 2000, the Ministry issued a policy document setting standards for these plans.

of teachers clearly committed to the field. Today, over twenty-five years after the passage of Bill 82, most, if not all, Ontario teachers willingly accept students with special needs into their classrooms.

Equally urgent was the need for resource and support personnel, most especially educational assistants, whose role soon took on ever more importance as schools began to deal with a variety of special needs never before encountered in schools. Ontario's colleges were quick to show leadership in developing effective education programs for paraprofessionals, a response that paid dividends immediately, for the graduates soon proved their value in classrooms. It is important to note, however, that in many instances teacher education in special education at the preservice level continues to struggle with preparing educators to meet the complexity presented in today's classrooms. The level of diversity in classrooms is greater than ever before and educators need to have a thorough understanding of assessment and intervention strategies for a wide range of students with varying educational, social, intellectual, physical, and developmental needs.

At Home and School

Parents can play a crucial role in educating children with special needs that is qualita-

Dateline 2000 — The Case of Onisa

Given that, in grade 2, Onisa regularly brought clippings from the *Globe and Mail* and the *Economist* to "show-and-tell," no one in her school was the least bit surprised when in grade 6, she won a UN-sponsored trip to Geneva, Switzerland, for her essay on the meaning of democracy. Still, during the promotion and placement meetings that were held at the end of the school year, both Onisa's regular grade 6 teacher and her "Challenge Program" teacher were uneasy.

Onisa had been identified "gifted" for some time, and her academic achievements were remarkable, especially during her earlier years at the school. But a standardized achievement test administered just before the end of the year in grade 6 hinted at somewhat more modest abilities. Onisa still was clearly in the superior range, but if the language and general awareness categories were factored out, and only her results in math/science were presented, she was actually below the mean for her class. What intrigued both of Onisa's teachers was that this confirmed an unevenness they had noticed: a contrast between what appeared to be her giftedness in language, and her quite ordinary ability in math and science.

It was a dilemma for the teachers because in their board all students left for new schools after grade 6. For Onisa to continue in the "Challenge Program" and be able to develop her unique abilities, her identification as "gifted" would need to be confirmed by the annual IPRC review. However, whereas the "Challenge Program" from grades 1 to 6 was an individualized, in-the-regular-class, enrichment offering, from grade 7 on, students identified "gifted" were generally placed in self-contained classes for an across-the-board enhanced curriculum (including advanced level math and science).

Happily, the school board's resources and the professionalism of its staff were brought to bear on Onisa's behalf. The head of the gifted program was aware of several other students with a similar math/science vs. language imbalance, students who shared Onisa's interests. Accordingly, they were each recommended for the same grade 7 class. It would not be in a school designated for the specially enhanced curriculum, but Onisa and her peers would retain their identification so that if, in the future, it appeared any of them would be better off with the enhanced curriculum, then arrangements could be made with a minimum of fuss.

After six months in her new school, Onisa declined to make the switch when it was offered (although one of her peers accepted). After twelve months had passed, she was eligible once again to compete in the UN essay contest. This time her first step in the process was to write and request an appointment with the federal Minister for External Affairs.

tively and quantitatively different from the one generally required in supporting the education of other children. Although the idea of parent support for education was hardly a novel one in 1980, the manner and extent of parental involvement that grew as a consequence of special education was a new experience. A few senior administrators found the experience more of a challenge than they were hitherto accustomed to, but for the most part, the outcomes proved to be positive. Since the passage of Bill 82 there has been a gradual increase in the amount of parent participation required in the development of the educational program offered to a student with special needs. Currently, Individual Education Plan (IEP) forms ask parents to indicate that they were involved in the plan's development and to sign off on it. (For more about IEPs see chapter 5.)

Outstanding Issues

Role of Parents

After many years of establishing the IPRC process, many boards of education found it more effective to work closely with parents in the development of their child's program as soon as concerns for the child's progress were identified. As a result of these cooperative efforts, boards found that the need for IPRCs diminished. Though the regulatory requirements are still in place (such as the appeal process) many boards, as a result of the cooperation between parents and professionals in the development of the Individual Education Plan (IEP Resource document, 2004) found IPRCs to be unnecessary. Though still in place in a large number of boards, the child's educational program is not dependent on IPRC decisions.

In addition to the personal role of parents in their child's program, the Ministry of Education also reinforced the parent's role by first establishing, then strengthening, the Special Education Advisory Committees (SEACs).

SEACs

Every Ontario school board is required to establish a Special Education Advisory Committee (SEAC), usually with membership taken principally from various parent associations in the community. These groups play a key role in educating the public about special education in general. They have input in decisions about special education finances. They have strong involvement in all aspects of the Special Education Plan, and are often an effective liaison between parents and board in potentially difficult situations. Some boards in the province were already working with parent and advocacy groups as a matter of course, prior to the official setting up of these committees. Still, the fact that this very important role was enshrined in provincial policy suggests that parental involvement is conceived as beneficial in many ways.

In 1997, the Ministry of Education reissued its regulation governing SEACs (Reg. 464)*, further strengthening parents' role. In 2003-4, the Ministry established information and training programs for SEAC members.

Role of Educational Assistants

With the increasing population of students with special needs being taught in schools came the need for more educational assistants (EAs) in both regular and self-contained classrooms. The Ministry of Education suggested in the Individual Education Plan Resource Document (2004) that the EA's role is to assist the teacher by helping students with their learning activities, monitoring and recording their achievements in these activities and assisting with providing appropriate activities as described in the IEP while maintaining ongoing communi-

• • • ⎯⎯⎯⎯

* The Ministry of Education periodically issues regulations that, essentially, have the force of legislation. These are numbered, with the year of issue following. The regulation dealing with SEACs, for example, is O.Reg.464/97. The Ministry also issues Policy/Program Memoranda, which are more explanatory than regulatory but are still considered to have administrative authority. PPM 89/90, for example, describes the role and workings of the province's residential demonstration schools for students with learning disabilities.

• • •

cation with the student's teachers. Though principals and teachers have some discretion in how EAs will be utilized, the IEP document referred to earlier offers some guidelines to the role that EAs can provide in the delivery of educational programs and services to students with special needs.

The Appeal Process

Parents dissatisfied with an IPRC decision can take their case first to an appeal board, and then if matters are unresolved at this level, to a special education tribunal. Concerns about the fairness of appeal boards (which are put together on an ad hoc basis for each appeal) were raised on the premise that the boards were weighted in favour of the school board. Indeed, some school boards did not help matters by frequently appointing representatives who might be seen to lack objectivity. Although an early 1990s study of appeal board hearings showed that the process gives parents a fair and effective hearing, the province subsequently modified this stage of the process to minimize perceptions of unfairness by giving parents a greater voice in choosing members of the appeal board. Parents choose one member of the appeal board (out of three) and jointly participate in choosing the chair.

The tribunal stage, too, weathered a rigorous examination in the 1990s in a legal action that ended in the Supreme Court of Canada. (See The Eaton Case, on page 16.)

The Move to Inclusion

At first it was fairly standard practice in most jurisdictions to place students with special needs in self-contained* classes according to their particular needs. Sometimes these students were placed in these classes in their neighbourhood schools. More often the students were placed in such classes in schools quite a distance from

• • •

* At one time, both special educators and advocates freely used "segregated class" (and sometimes "dedicated class") for the special, separated classes created for students with exceptionalities, but this term was soon euphemized to "self-contained," the term used in ministry documents.

• • •

their homes. The service delivery of putting students with special needs in self-contained classes within schools was not only considered normal but beneficial for all concerned. Enrolling students with special needs in their neighbourhood schools was generally known as *mainstreaming* or *integration*. The philosophy driving the choice of self-contained classroom placement was called *least restrictive environment*. This term was drawn from U.S. legislation requiring multi-disciplinary teams to place students with special needs in an environment as close to a regular classroom in a regular school as possible.

In only a very short time, however, the special education agenda was effectively overwhelmed by pressure from some parents and professionals to place exceptional students into *regular* classes, full time. These parents and professionals pointed out, with the support of quite powerful empirical evidence, that what happened in many, if not most, cases of mainstreaming was that schools hosted two parallel groups, a regular one, and one with students with special needs alongside it looking to get in. Students with exceptionalities were in the school but not really *of* it.

In response, the Regular Education Initiative emerged in the mid-1980s. This iniative was a metaphor more than a strategy, but one that had considerable impact, and that went a long way toward shifting the educational mindset from the subtle parallelism of mainstreaming toward a fuller, more natural integration of students with special needs into the school system.

The next, almost simultaneous step was advocacy in favour of *inclusion* or *inclusionary schooling*. In many ways this approach, too, was but a shift in vocabulary, but it put even more emphasis on the principle of automatically placing students with exceptionalities in the classrooms they would normally attend if they did not have a special need. Inclusionary schooling is now the predominant Ontario model of service delivery, with the expectation that all students with special needs are accepted into, and can benefit from, regular classroom placement.

In tandem with the pressure for full inclusion was the shadow cast by legal concerns: whether or not a school board's decision to place a student in a separate, special class can be a violation of his or her equality rights under the *Canadian Charter of Rights and Freedoms*. The 1997 Supreme Court of Canada decision in Eaton vs. Brant County Board of Education did much to put this issue to rest.

Eaton v. Brant County Board of Education

In 1994, an IPRC review determined that after three years in a regular class, experience and common sense made clear that the subject child, an eleven year old with extensive special needs, was not benefiting from inclusion and that her best interests would be served in a special class. The parents appealed this decision first to the civil court where the situation was directed back to the appeal process established by provincial legislation. The IPRC was then upheld by an appeal board and subsequently by a tribunal. The tribunal decision in turn was upheld by a judicial review, but then it was overturned by the Ontario Court of Appeal, which held that a placement without consent is discriminatory under Section 15 of the *Charter*.

The Ontario Court's position was emphatically rejected by the Supreme Court of Canada in a 9-0 ruling. The original decision was restored, thereby making clear there is no *Charter* presumption in favour of inclusion. The Supreme Court's decision also had the effect of affirming Ontario's special education legislation. In its written judgment, which quoted large parts of the tribunal decision verbatim, the High Court reinforced the notion that placement of children with special needs should be decided on a by-case basis, with the principal determiner being a child's best interests. This outcome did much to diminish the litigiousness that had been growing around special education legislation, and also had the effect of motivating parties on all sides to search for compromise and for "on-the-ground" solutions to the needs of exceptional students. This willingness to compromise has led to a greater emphasis on the Individual Education Plan and to program development accomplished through cooperative efforts of school personnel, parents and, if the student is 16 years of age or older, the student.

Inclusion: The Preferred but Not the Only Option

Accommodating Inclusion

Even before the Eaton case began, the provincial government had taken steps toward accommodating the inclusion issue and amalgamating this point of view with other, usually more eclectic positions taken by many teachers, school boards, and academics. While most people agree on the moral and philosophical merits of full inclusion as an objective, the practice does not always follow the principle with absolute success. Research to support the idea of inclusion is, unfortunately, notoriously hazy. Perhaps more important, results in the classroom sometimes prove ambivalent at best. The ideal implied by inclusion is that when placed with regular students, a student with an exceptionality will also be taught with them; yet irrespective of the effort and support brought to bear, sometimes instruction of students with special needs in the regular classroom doesn't quite work out that way. As a consequence, although full inclusion remains a fundamental goal of special education, on the ground things are generally more fluid.

Thus, as early as the spring of 1991, the Minister of Education declared to the Ontario legislature that integration of pupils with exceptionalities into local community classrooms would be the norm wherever possible, but went on to say that inasmuch as an integrated setting may not be appropriate for every child, school boards would be encouraged to offer a full range of alternative educational placements. This position seemed at once reasonable, educationally sound, and politically astute, and has become, in effect, the way most special education works in the province today.

In 2006, the Ontario Ministry of Education issued a report entitled *Special Education Transformation*. The report presented the results of discussions of a working group composed of teachers, principals, ministry officials, students with special needs, advocacy groups including parents, and members of faculties of education. This report stated that "The first consideration regarding placement would continue to be the regular classroom. A range of options would continue to be available for students whose needs could not be met within the regular classroom. These placements would be duration-specific, intervention-focused and subject to regular reviews." (Bennett and Wynne, *Special Education Transformation*, 2006, p.8). Currently, the majority of students with exceptionalities are in neighbourhood schools being educated with their peers, but because inclusion remains an adaptable concept, a minority continues to be accommodated in other ways.

Turning to Mediation

It is important to recognize that although appeals and litigation are popular avenues in Ontario, legal struggles have figured into just a very tiny number of situations since the passing of the Education Amendment Act. There have been thousands of IPRC decisions since 1980 but only a handful of tribunals, suggesting quite strongly that the process does the job it was designed to do. Another more recent, and positive, trend, which as yet has no basis in the legislation but is actively encouraged by the Ministry, is the use of mediation to resolve impasses. Both parents and boards are finding this technique far less costly and time-consuming than formal appeals, and usually, one that minimizes post-adversarial residue. The recent *Special Education Transformation* (Bennett and Wynne, 2006) report, referred to earlier, further promotes mediation as a preferable approach to dealing with special education disagreements between parents and board rather than using the appeal board/tribunal avenues.

Dateline 2004 — The Case of Teodor (Teddy)

Until the day in late September when Teddy set fire to the hair of a girl seated in front of him, not one teacher in his new high school had paid attention to the special education department's description of Reactive Attachment Disorder, and the advice that might counter its effects. The fire, however, raised Teddy's profile significantly, and when he vandalized several cars the very next day, staff awareness spread quickly.

Like most educators, few of Teddy's teachers had ever heard of Reactive Attachment Disorder. Among the paraprofessionals at the school, only one had knowledge of it; she had dealt with a similar situation at an elementary school. Teddy's case, everyone soon learned, was almost a stereotype. He had been born in Romania when perestroika came to that beleagured country and his first three years had been spent in an ill-kept, underfunded, and grossly understaffed state orphanage. His adoptive parents—Canadians from Ontario—had devoted the next three years to helping him overcome the effects of severe malnutrition, and a mild but correctable spinal deformity. Yet, by the time Teddy began senior kindergarten, the parents were painfully aware that the boy's problems went far beyond his stomach and his back.

Like many children with this syndrome, Teddy had never felt love or experienced bonding in his early, formative years; indeed his very survival day-to-day was uncertain. Had he been born in Canada, there is little doubt that similar treatment would be categorized as child abuse. Thus, despite the efforts of the loving and deeply caring couple who adopted him, Teddy's developing years were marked by low self-esteem, profoundly manipulative behaviour, aggression, defiance, and—a key element in the syndrome—a pronounced lack of capacity for remorse or of what our culture sees as moral perspective.

Although Teddy—not to mention his parents and teachers—had barely survived his elementary school experience, his two years of senior public with the same teacher and under a very watchful and ready-to-intervene principal, had been, by comparison, relatively peaceful. But now, in high school, the worst of Teddy's behaviours were front and centre, a fact confirmed in a behavioural checklist his special education teacher asked staff to complete in advance of an IPRC review. Clearly, steps would have to be taken.

The Current "State" of Special Education

Continual Change and Adaptation

Overall, the education community, students, and parents have adjusted well to the sweeping changes in the educational provisions for students with special needs effected by Education Amendment Act and its related regulations and policy memoranda. Indeed, much of what has been altered has gone barely noticed except by administrators, and by parents with a specific area of interest. Typical of the latter group were parents of children who were developmentally disabled in 1993, when the provincial government in what was known as Bill 4 removed the term "trainable retarded" from the Education Act. The same bill removed the "hard-to-serve" section. This was a complicated, never-used set of clauses that allowed a board to exclude a pupil.

Significant modifications to official policy and practice were introduced in 1998 when the province re-issued the regulation concerning the IPRC process. The new regulation (Reg. 181) expanded the responsibilities of the committee in a variety of ways, required a written Educational Plan for the exceptional student, and generally strengthened the role and rights of parents. In the immediately ensuing years, the written plan, known as the Individual Education Plan (IEP), took on more and more importance, and its development and use for exceptional students was subject to increasingly intense scrutiny, especially by the Ministry. In 2002, a voluntary template was made available by the Ministry, thus providing a theoretically ideal format against which individual boards and schools could compare their own. It is important to note that in the 2003-4 school year almost one-third of students in Ontario receiving special education programs and services were not formally identified by an IPRC, but received these services as a result of an IEP being developed to meet these students' specific needs. Additionally, during this time, 81 per cent of students receiving special education programs and services were placed in regular classrooms.

Further developments include the Co-ordi-nated Services Unit set up in 2001 to establish improved service coordination across several provincial ministries, the Ontario Disabilities Act, 2002, which placed specific accessibility obligations on public sector groups such as school boards, and a pilot program on standards for Autism in 2003. The Special Education Project (an ongoing venture) deals with development and implementation of policies and programs. Other fine tunings include the amount and quality of support materials now available from the Ministry of Education. A good example of this is the *Special Education Companion* (http://www.ocup.org/resources/documents/companions/speced2002.pdf) available on the Ministry of Education website. This work provides extensive programming suggestions to assist teachers in delivering appropriate programs and effective instructional approaches to students with special needs

In 2005, the Ministry of Education issued *Education for All, The Report of the Expert Panel on Literacy and Numeracy Instruction for Students with Special Education Needs, Kindergarten to Grade 6* (Ontario Ministry of Education, 2005). This report further emphasized the importance of acceptance of students with special needs into the regular classroom, and provided approaches (*Universal Design for Learning and Differentiated Instruction*) to help teachers effectively instruct these students along with their classmates.

Regardless of the activities outlined above, the fact that there have been relatively few major alterations in Ontario's official special education policy and practice reinforces the impression that the system works well. When modifications become necessary, experience has demonstrated that teachers and individual boards and schools, with the support of the Ministry of Education and university and college faculties, are more than competent in bringing them about.

The Situation Today

For Ontario students with special needs, universal access to education is guaranteed. The definite first choice of placement is the regular class. And perhaps most important, students with special needs are just that: *students*. In short, special education has become a normal, integral, and functional part of the system. Not that change and development and improvement will no longer be needed; adjustments will always be necessary and will continue to happen. But special education in Ontario is positioned now so that changes to it occur in the larger context of all educational development. As education itself adjusts to social change, to technology, and to general needs, special education will adapt with it. In that context, future developments in special education are likely to be expressed in positive refinements of gains that have already been made.

Dateline 2008 — The case of Jamie Edwards

Jamie Edwards has not had a lot of success in school so far. Now in grade 2, Jamie has had difficulty both academically and socially in senior kindergarten and grade 1. In both years teachers brought him to the attention of Ms. Markesh, the school's learning resource teacher, due to his spontaneous outbursts and slow academic achievement. Ms. Markesh suggested that much of his developmental difficulties may be due to Jamie's age (he was the youngest student in the class having been born on January 2,) and that as he matures his social and academic ability will improve. His new teacher, Ms. Singh, believes that Jamie's difficulties are more than just a question of maturity and believes that a change in Jamie's program may be needed in order for him to have greater success throughout the school day. She discussed this with Ms. Markesh and together they decided it was time for Jamie to be brought to the attention of the in-school team. In addition, Ms. Singh has met with Jamie's parents to discuss the situation and they have agreed to permit Jamie to be assessed. In the meantime and with Mr. and Mrs. Edwards' enthusiastic support Jamie has begun to meet with the learning resource teacher twice a week. During these sessions Jamie works on his regular class assignments, allowing him some 'wiggle room' to complete work as well as playing catch up on some skills that both Ms. Singh and Ms. Markesh have decided he needed help with. Almost immediately Ms. Singh noted that Jamie's outbursts have become, for all intents and purposes, non-existent a fact that pleases both Ms. Singh and his classmates who are now more willing to work and play with him. Ms. Singh, working collaboratively with Ms. Markesh is quite comfortable adjusting her program and taking Jamie's (as well as her other students) strengths and needs into account as she develops her lesson plans for the day. Having become comfortable with both universal design for learning and differentiated instruction, both professional development topics she has learned considerably about over the past two years, she habitually designs lessons that provide for a variety of learners.

Discussion at the in-school team centered around the behavioural and academic skills that have already begun to improve and while there was consensus that, while Jamie is not currently in need of identification, that assessment will still be a useful tool in planning his continued success. Both Ms. Singh and Ms. Markesh have happily accepted the task of deciding on and administering the necessary assessments.

Note: For in-depth detail on provincial legislation, regulations, policy/program memoranda, funding guidelines, and a range of information and services from the Ministry of Education see *Special Education: A Guide for Educators* (2001) available from the Ministry's publications branch or downloaded at

**http://www.edu.gov.on.ca/eng/general/
elemsec/speced/guide.html**

Bennett, S., & Wynne, K. (2006) *Special Education Transformation: the report of the co-chairs with the recommendations of the working table on special education.* Toronto: Queen's Printer for Ontario.

Bunch, G., & Valeo, A. (1997). *Inclusion: recent research.* Toronto: Inclusion Press.

Carrier, J.G. (1986). *Sociology and special education: differentiation and allocation in mass education. American Journal of Education, 94,* 281-312.

Council of Administrators of Special Education (1997). Position paper on delivery of services to students with disabilities. *Keeping in Touch.*

Eaton vs Brant County. SCC#24668, 7 Feb., 1997.

Foerter, J., et al (1991) *Special Education: Bridging the centuries,* (Ontario Teachers' Federation).

Itard, J.M.G. (1806). *The wild boy of Aveyron* (G. Humphrey & M. Humphrey, trans.) (1962). Englewood Cliffs, NJ: Prentice-Hall.

Lupart, J.L., McKeough &Yewchuck, C. (Eds.) (1996). *Schools in transition: Rethinking regular and special education.* Toronto: Nelson Canada.

Oderkirk, J. (1993). Disabilities among children. *Canadian Social Trends,* pp. 22-25.

Ontario Ministry of Education (2005). *Education for all: The report of the expert panel on literacy and numeracy instruction for students with special needs, kindergarten to grade 6.* Toronto: Queen's Printer for Ontario.

Ontario Ministry of Education (2002). *Special Education Companion.* **http://www.ocup.org/resources/documents /companions/speced2002.pdf)**

Smith, D., Luckasson, R. & Crealock, C. (1995). *Introduction to Special Education in Canada.* Scarborough: Allyn & Bacon.

Smith, W. J., & Lusthaus, C. (1994). Equal educational opportunities for students with disabilities in Canada: The right to free and appropriate education. *Exceptionality Education Canada, 4,* 37-73.

Winzer, M. (2008). *Children with Exceptionalities in Canadian Classrooms* (8th edition) Toronto: Pearson Prentice Hall.

Wolfensberger, W. (1975). *The origin and nature of our institutional models.* Syracuse, N.Y: Human Policy Press.

CHAPTER 2

Continuing Issues in Special Education

*"My kid's handicapped. He needs somebody to fight for him and that's me.
I'm a taxpayer too and if your kid can get an education so can mine.
I'm going to do what I have to do. Get used to it."*

Laney G., parent of a child with multiple disabilities

The Paper Chase

Bill 82 stated that a special education program is a program based on and modified by the results of continuous assessment and evaluation and includes a plan containing specific objectives and an outline of educational services that meets the needs of the pupil with exceptionalities. The plan referred to in Bill 82 has led the Ontario Ministry of Education to establish the Individual Education Plan (IEP) and a procedure for how this plan should be created. This process, outlined in a Resource Guide published in 2004, describes the steps board personnel should follow to ensure that the plan is cooperatively developed between education personnel, parents, and the student if the student is 16 years of age or older.

This plan may be one piece of paper among many that the assessment and programming demands of a student with special needs may generate. Students with special needs often require a wide range of personnel who not only make their individual reports but must exchange their reports with the reports of others. Funding mechanisms tend to stir up a paper flurry, especially if unusual equipment or specialized instruction is necessary. Fundamental to teaching exceptional students is the need for extensive adaptations in curriculum and teaching methods, adaptations that need to be recorded for pre-post evaluation, and for dissemination to interested parties. And looming over the whole planning process is the need for a collating plan or file to make sure the various parts work together and toward the same purpose. The consequence is a great deal of paper, and for all parties, a serious task: just how much is necessary and who is responsible?

There is no question that written education plans have beneficial effects, especially if the plans detailing students' needs include descriptions of how, where, and when the needs will be addressed, and accounts of when and how the success (or failure) of these efforts will be evaluated. On the surface, the logic behind the practice is unassailable, for a specific plan brings focus and coordination to meeting a student's needs. It helps to satisfy the need for accountability: viz., if funds are being spent, personnel assigned, and effort expended, so at the very least, everyone involved can follow the tracks. A plan also offers a common basis for discussion should the need for accommodation and/or modification develop, and, far from least in importance unfortunately, a plan provides a documented paper trail should legal issues arise.

There are potential drawbacks, however. One is that a plan can easily become more important than the subject for whom it is designed. Once a plan becomes dominant, then flexibility diminishes and creativity disappears, and without these components, the very essence of "special" education is lost. Granted, the evaluation phase should preclude such an outcome, yet once plan supremacy is established, changes to that plan become very difficult to bring about, especially if the students with exceptionalities are complex. In addition, if the IEP process suggested by the Ministry of Education is followed, the time it takes to make the changes can delay the implementation of appropriate instruction for several weeks. The more complicated a case may be, the greater number of personnel there are to consult, the more resources must be shifted to effect a change—all with paper attached. Then there is the professional time taken up by record keeping. Many Ontario boards have developed on-line IEP forms with "pull-down" menus to assist in indicating accommodations. Though these menus may be helpful in many cases, they may also inhibit the initiation of an appropriate approach that may not be listed on the pull-down list.

As valuable as the detailing of information may be, it is rarely more important than the time spent interacting with the student being recorded. Nevertheless, experience has shown that to make a significant impact on an exceptional student's situation coordinated and recorded planning is essential. Finding the elusive balance between the logical boundaries of a specific plan, and the art of creatively and intuitively responding to a student's needs, will always be a challenge in special education. The fact that teachers and administrators continue to search for it is to their credit.

Inclusion: No Longer an Issue but Certainly a Concern

The controversy over whether students with special needs should be educated in regular classrooms is now, relatively, a non–issue. The vast majority (81% in Ontario) of exceptional students are in regular classes. Teachers, educational assistants, and principals—the people who deal with inclusion on a daily basis—have pretty much discarded the notion that inclusion is still a controversial issue. Even in academic journals, in administration offices, at professional conferences, and among advocacy groups, where the topic of inclusion was once guaranteed to brew up a storm, the winds are now relatively calm. There are a number of reasons for this, the most obvious being that inclusion today is a dominant reality, and in cases where alternatives are chosen, it is usually with the agreement of all parties involved. As an issue for debate therefore, inclusion no longer has much profile. What most educators are concerned with now is making inclusion work.

> *Why are we still arguing about inclusion? The first consideration for every child automatically is regular classroom. There are more urgent issues today. Like funding, delivering service.*
>
> *And keeping up—there's always something new in special ed!"*
>
> Patricia M., elementary school principal

Among those for whom the issue of inclusion still resonates, the arguments have pretty much reached a default stage in parallax positions.

One side tends to argue that all students with special needs, no matter how unique or demanding their needs, should be placed in regular classrooms of neighbourhood schools. Supporters of no-exception inclusion contend that the mere availability of alternative settings can make integration fail for the very simple reason that it does not have to work. To a significant extent, this position is argued as much from a stance of moral superiority as it is from one of superior educational outcomes.

Ranged apart from this view are those who do not see the matter quite so unconditionally. This group contends that, whereas integration should indeed be sought as a first solution, some students might be better served if at least a portion of their program were delivered in a more specialized environment. They argue that to be so rigid is unrealistic, that out of sheer practical necessity, certain cases demand at least some form of special placement from time to time. Although this side leans toward practicality, its supporters, if pressed, will also claim that to deny such an option is in its own way, morally offensive.

Arguments Used to Support Full Integration	Arguments used to Question Full Integration
⇒ Less likely to stigmatize; more natural and reflective of the real world	⇒ Environment too manipulated to reflect the real world
⇒ Develops more positive attitudes and positive relationships	⇒ Student relationships are often unilateral, artificial, and in-class only
⇒ More opportunity for interaction	⇒ Opportunities for intense instruction are reduced
⇒ Age-appropriate models are more readily available	⇒ May not be able to teach and reinforce crucial special skills
⇒ Equal opportunity implies equal rights	⇒ Equal rights do not necessarily imply equal opportunity
⇒ Teachers prefer full integration	⇒ Teachers prefer range of settings
⇒ Parents prefer full integration	⇒ Parents prefer range of settings
⇒ Students, exceptional and otherwise, prefer full integration	⇒ Students, exceptional and otherwise, prefer a range of alternatives

What has made the debate so enduring is that there does not appear to be any absolute answer. Research—a great deal of it over quite a long period of time—has been of regrettably little help, since for practically every research outcome demonstrating support for one view, an opposite result is readily available. Classroom experience is usually very case-specific, so it can be misleading to generalize from the success or failure of one, or even several situations. And empirical evidence demonstrates repeatedly that it is impossible to separate the success or failure of anything that happens in a school from the skill and commitment of individual teachers and assistants.

Fortunately, much has happened over the past decades to wind down the debate. The provincial government has long declared the integration of students with special needs to be the norm in the province's schools, a principle that continues to be affirmed by the Ministry of Education. As mentioned in Chapter 1, the recently issued Special Education Transformation report reaffirmed this view and also recommended that when a special class placement is made it should be duration-specific, and intervention-focused. Though not in regulation, these recommendations provide guidance to IPRCs and IEP developers. Educators and parents of students with special needs in regular classes now know that placing a student in a regular class is not as difficult as once thought, and usually produces significant benefits for all. Likewise, experience has demonstrated that there really are some students who benefit from an alternative setting, no matter how extensive the resources in a regular classroom, nor how adapted the curriculum, nor how allegedly ideal the setting. Ultimately, since proponents on both sides have always had the same objective: to achieve what is best for exceptional students, it is not surprising that the ardour that once prevailed has dissipated considerably.

The Power of Profile

The rapid expansion of special education in the final quarter of the twentieth century was marked by dramatic surges in awareness of certain special needs. No example serves better than that of learning disabilities. As recently as the 1970s, only a small number of teachers and parents, along with a sprinkling of academics, were deeply interested in the type of student who seems to experience serious problems in school despite apparently normal intelligence. Although the number of concerned people was growing, and the problem had acquired a name ("learning disabilities" was first proposed by Samuel Kirk in 1963), this special need still had a low profile in education and in the media. Initially, only a handful of students in publicly supported schools were actually called, or even believed to be, "learning disabled." Now, 45 years after the term was first suggested, approximately one-half of all students officially identified for special education in the province, are identified "learning disabled."

The raising of a profile for a special need seems to follow a pattern. Initially, an advocacy group, consisting mostly of parents with first-hand experience in dealing with the need, succeeds in getting the attention of the media and—not always simultaneously—teachers and the school system. Usually, this parent advocacy is followed by a sharp rise in interest from academics. (Bureaucrats in education, interestingly, are often quite ahead of the game. For example, the learning disabilities issue had wide support among Ontario's Ministry of Education officials well before the school system at large came on side.) A final stage in profile development is to have the special need officially recognized administratively, thereby assuring it a permanent place on every school and school board horizon. The pattern does not end here, for once a significant profile is achieved, the advocacy group instrumental in getting things started usually commits to a program of reinforcement through lobbying, information workshops, production of information literature, etc. An essential difference at this stage, however, is that the group now becomes more a partner in meeting

The Case of Parnell

On the surface, this case seems simple enough. Parnell lags behind his peers in achievement, by at least three grades. Most serious is his apparent inability to read. The problem might be accounted for by Parnell's own explanation that he "didn't go to school much" before coming to Canada three months ago, although the teacher of the grade 5-6 split class where he is placed, reports that the boy frequently manifests "learning disability-like characteristics," adding by way of illustration that he is frequently off-task, rarely follows instructions in proper sequence, seems easily confused, and regularly loses his personal property (and the school's). A preliminary assessment has only reinforced what everybody already knows: Parnell can't read.

On the other hand, the (half-time) assistant in the class points out that when she is able to instruct Parnell one-on-one, in skills like phonics and letter/word recognition, he grasps the material quickly, and retains it. A special reading program is not a viable option. The school's junior reading program was deleted two years ago owing to budget issues and staffing reallocation. The primary program is entirely over-extended and depends to a large extent on volunteers.

The classroom teacher is meeting with the school's learning resource teacher to discuss Parnell and while there is agreement that an IEP needs to be developed there is still discussion about whether or not he should be referred to an IPRC for possible placement in an alternate setting. An issue of some delicacy is related to this situation. Only a month ago, the senior public school that shares a campus with Parnell's school was the focus of obsessive media attention after an advocacy group accused it of "dumping" children of colour like Parnell into special education. A subsequent investigation agreed that the number placed in special education is indeed significantly disproportionate to the number in the general school population.

the special need than an agent for awareness. Two good examples of the effect of this advocacy is the attention paid to students with learning disabilities in the 1980s through the 1990s and the positive result of advocacy efforts by parents to obtain treatment for their children with autism in the the early 2000s.

Many educators acknowledge the necessity of intense lobbying to raise awareness of special needs. Yet an elevated profile is not without potential risks, especially for administrators and, by extension, for the classroom. Cynics point to the possibility that intensive media fascination may actually create a "disability du jour," a charge that in the early years of this century, rightly or wrongly, is directed at the number of students identified with forms of autism. Further, there is always risk that a single issue may capture disproportionate space on the administrative agenda, such as occurred over the matter of inclusion. As well, there is always strong potential that a high profile may cause an overreaction. For example, despite the fact that awareness of learning disabilities was long overdue and that the high profile has generated very positive results, there has never been an entirely satisfactory answer to a legitimate question: are there really that many students with learning disabilities in our schools, or is the identification sometimes convenient for administrators under pressure?

On balance, the benefits brought to the field by increased awareness outweigh the possible drawbacks, provided teachers, assistants, administrators, and advocates behind the thrust keep in mind the need for a rational perspective. Education in general is extremely susceptible to cycles—fads, the cynics would say. Everyone involved with students who have special needs has a responsibility to guard against the backlash that invariably attends this phenomenon.

The Problem of the Purse

Concerns about funding for special education coalesce around several recurring issues, but the most basic one is, simply, adequacy: how much is enough? Unfortunately, no matter what funding is offered by the public purse, it will never be seen as enough. The need (demand?) always seems to outpace the number of dollars allotted. Governments have never managed to resolve this issue, which may be one reason why they pursue accountability with such rigor. While accountability is a laudable goal, not to mention one that attracts positive attention from taxpayers, it is rarely achieved without significant impact on the system receiving the money. For example, a common method of funding special education, one that Ontario adopted in the late 1990s, is a system of incremental grants based on documented needs of individual students.

This system has now been abandoned in favour of an overall amount provided to school boards beyond their basic per pupil grant (used for regular education). These funds must be used for educating students with special needs. Additional funds are also available to assist boards in providing education to low-incidence, high-need students. These funds, commonly known as "Special Incident Portion (SIP)," must be applied for by each school board, with documented evidence of student need.

It is very encouraging that the Ontario Ministry of Education has continued to emphasize that the education of students with special education needs is deserving of a category of funding separate from the per pupil funding provided to boards of education. This protected "envelope" must be spent on providing service to students with special needs. Ontario has tried to ensure that this funding category remains a priority. One issue currently under discussion is the disparity of need among different boards throughout the province. It could be argued that boards that are geographically remote and/or have a large French-speaking population may have need for a different level of funding to service their students with special needs than a board with a large urban socioeconomic and culturally diverse population. A "one size fits all" model may not be appropriate for Ontario but the search for the development of an equitable system is ongoing.

Against Labels	For Labels
⇒ A single label, for example, "gifted," cannot sum up the complexity of a human.	⇒ Academic discussion, professional development, teacher training, research, all need a common frame of reference to be effective.
⇒ Labels often stigmatize by emphasizing weakness and dysfunction.	⇒ Specific vocabulary permits more precise communication in hands-on situations. Caregivers especially must work from the same text.
⇒ Labels often mislead; someone labelled "deaf" may only be hard of hearing.	⇒ Identification of a group's unique needs raises its profile.
⇒ Labels propagate confusion and varied interpretation (as in developmental disabilities).	⇒ Differentiated categories facilitate differentiated responses.
⇒ A labelled person is seen in the label's terms, rather than as a human being with a special need, thereby provoking lowered expectations.	⇒ Accountability requires a mutually acceptable taxonomy of description.
⇒ Labels tend to be life long.	⇒ Experience shows that abolishing one set of labels simply produces another.

Labels, Categories, and Definitions

One of the most divisive issues in special education has long been the question "To Label or Not to Label?" In 1972, Reginald Jones in an article entitled "The Labels and Stigma in Special Education" described the difficulties encountered by students who have a special education label. This oft-cited article brought this issue to the attention of parents and educators and the move toward de-emphasizing labels has continued ever since. In Ontario, however, we maintain a categorical approach with labels such as Behaviour exceptionality, Intellectual exceptionality, and Physical exceptionality. These categories are further divided into definitions which are provided in the Appendix.

There are school districts in North America that have already abandoned contemporary descriptors like "developmentally delayed" because of the gradual acquisition of negative connotations. It seems the need to search for ever more euphemistic vocabulary will never end, for as new and sensitive identifiers age, they take on overtones, thereby provoking need for yet newer ones.

There are indications that in this new century, the matter of labels and categories and definitions has declined significantly as an issue for debate. As we have moved toward accepting diverse learners in our classrooms, the definition of "diverse" now expands not only to include students with racial, language, and cultural differences, but also those with differing learning needs as a result of cognitive, behavioural, physical, and communicative differences. More and more generations are growing up with people with exceptionalities in their midst as a matter of course. Parents and professional educators recognize descriptors simply as a convenience for discussion and administrative procedure. Still, it is unlikely that the vocabulary of special needs will ever be entirely free of controversy for the simple reason that the meaning of words changes over time. Also, when categories of special need broaden, as they do from time to time (case in point: the field of autism now referred to as Autism Spectrum

Disorder), a whole new battery of terms is added to the lexicon, any one of which can raise the level of debate, and provoke another round.

Identification and Placement Concerns

A major criticism of placement in special education classrooms is the disproportionate number of students from low-socioeconomic backgrounds and minorities found in these classrooms. For very real reasons, it is easy to see why the special class is often regarded as an appropriate placement. Children of poverty and some cultural minorities often have a high frequency of serious health and physical problems that affect their education. Conductive hearing loss (usually otitis media), for example, and eye infections affecting sight, occur at a much higher average rate in Aboriginal children in Canada than in the general population. Children of minority groups sometimes experience linguistic difficulties that impinge on their learning in a major way, leading to academic difficulties requiring greater intervention than normally provided. In addition, assessment procedures that do not allow for cultural anomalies may lead to inappropriate placement or label. It is not unusual for children from lower-income families or from recently arrived immigrant families to have difficulties simply because they are confused by the demands of the school culture. Sometimes a family's lack of precedent for educational experience, as well as lack of support for

---

The Case of Vanessa

Of the five students still placed in the "junior resource class" at the end of the school year, Vanessa and one other have been deemed ready by an IPRC to spend part of the school day in a regular grade 5 class. The other three will remain in the resource class come September, where a teacher and two educational assistants will continue to emphasize appropriate behaviour and socialization.

Vanessa's gains after two years in the class have been considerable. She no longer screams at maximum pitch when dissatisfied. She has developed appropriate toileting skills (instead of using the floor, wherever and whenever). Biting, scratching, and hairpulling seem to have been discarded as communication methods. And experimental sessions in the regular grade 4 class indicate that, with a little help from her favourite EA, Vanessa can sustain an age-appropriate relationship with a peer group. Interestingly, what most pleases the adults dealing with Vanessa more than anything is that most of the time, with supervision, she can be trusted to take a regular recess without incident. Still, hers is a situation that will bear careful watching. A similar attempt at reintegration in grade 3 failed utterly, although all agree that this attempt was made too soon, and that the change was too drastic.

Two assessments suggest Vanessa is of average intelligence, and there is no indication of any physical or learning disability despite the experience of her early years. From the time she was a baby until age eight—when Children's Aid took over after her mother was jailed for voluntary manslaughter—Vanessa had moved seventeen times, had known six stepfathers, and had been treated for both TB and malnutrition. Her present school (from grade 2) is the first one she attended with any regularity, although her behaviour was so extreme initially that the principal had to arrange for one-on-one supervision. (Three EAs, the school's full complement, spelled one another over the course of the day.) A possible complication has recently developed. Vanessa's birth father, whom she had never seen until a few months ago, has applied to the family court for custody. Both the court and the Children's Aid Society agree that he is a responsible, mature individual (he is married with two other children) and a good parent. However, he proposes to enroll Vanessa in the same school as his other two children. This school is in a different board in a different community and has a full and absolute inclusion policy, with no designated resource or withdrawal classes. The family court judge has agreed that the father can obtain custody of Vanessa and she is now enrolled in a regular grade 5 classroom. The in-school team is meeting next week to discuss Vanessa's program.

it, can have a serious effect on a student's performance. Very often, heads of families do not manage a child's case by dealing with the school, the education system, and support agencies (or confronting them if necessary), either because they choose not to, or because they lack the sophistication.

In schools, the issue is one of delicate choice. From an educational perspective, these are indeed students with very special needs. And very frequently the needs can be effectively met in a special education mode. However, the educational perspective must be illuminated by consideration of what is morally and socially appropriate. Identification and placement of a student in special education is a major step, one that can be taken with more certainty if the basis of the decision is strictly educational. When the basis is influenced by social, cultural, and economic factors, there is inevitably commensurate erosion of that certainty. It is a hard nut to crack, and no jurisdiction in Canada has yet done so to everyone's satisfaction.

Universal Design for Learning and Differentiated Instruction

The Report of the Expert Panel referred to earlier provides an approach known as "Universal Design for Learning (UDL)." This approach is based on an achitectural premise that improved access for people with handicapping conditions is improved access for all. A ramp, for example, certainly assists a person in a wheelchair, but it also helps the parent with a stroller or a person making a delivery using a handcart. Universal Design for Instruction encourages teachers to take the needs of all their students, academic, social, intellectual, and physical into account when planning for instruction. This consideration occurs at the outset of planning, rather than having adjustments made after the planning occurs, as has traditionally been done.

Differentiated Classroom instruction, according to Carol Ann Tomlinson (1999) is an approach requiring teachers to "begin where students are, not the front of the curriculum guide. They accept and build upon the premise that learners differ in important ways." Teachers

following this approach begin their planning with the needs of all students in mind and present lessons and activities in a manner which effectively captures the needs and abilities of all students in their classrooms. While some would argue that UDL and DI are new ideas for teaching, another equally vocal group would state that educators have been in practice doing versions of this type of planning and implementation for many years. The difference indeed may not be in practice but rather in orientation. While, for many, modifications and accommodations have become commonplace the focus on UDL and DI comes before pencil hits paper. It is an issue of orientation to planning and implementation, a perspective from which to view the individual and class as a whole, a new lens on an age-old practice of instruction.

> *A classroom based on the concept of UDL is specifically planned and developed to meet the special needs of a variety of students, including students who are disabled and those who come from non-dominant cultures. It is flexible, supportive, and adjustable, and increases full access to the curriculum for all students.*
>
> Ontario Ministry of Education, *Education for All*, 2005 p. 10

Assessment and Program

The main goal of an assessment is to provide information from which program planning can be developed. Unfortunately, for several reasons the practice often stumbles clumsily after the theory. Chief among these reasons is a strange combination of expertise and naiveté that seems to prevail on both sides of the assessment/program planning issue. Psychologists, psychometrists, or other assessors, without actual experience in teaching, often have either idealistic or simplistic notions of what actually occurs minute by minute in a classroom. Many classroom teachers, on the other hand, are not confident in their assessment skills, and frequently have difficulty translating results into program. In many cases, much time can elapse between when a student is referred for assessment and when the assessment is actually conducted and the results shared with those who need to know this information. During this period, the student with special needs is expected to receive a program designed to meet his or her needs and it is up to the teacher, confident or not, to provide one

Frequently, teachers and those non-teaching professionals responsible for assessment are obstructed by matters not of their own making, beginning with their own training. Traditionally, neither gets much opportunity to gain more than sketchy knowledge about the other. As well—and probably more important—both sides argue that the gap could easily be narrowed, even closed, by direct communication: that if the teacher(s) and educational assistant(s) of the student being assessed could communicate directly with an assessor, the questions that need answers will at least be put on the table. Yet in many jurisdictions, bureaucracy and systems management impede this very simple expedient. It is common policy for assessors to obtain and report data only to a third party (coordinator, committee, principal, etc.). Then, for a variety of reasons such as privacy regulations, work loads, or in some cases, inefficiency, these data come to the classroom, if at all, in a form that is altered or diluted or summarized to the point of irrelevance. Assessment by non-teachers would also be advanced if teachers were better able to express more precisely why they are referring a student for an in-depth assessment. The better the referral information, the more clearly the assessor will understand what he or she needs to assess and evaluate.

It is the student who falls into the gap this system creates. An assessment may well be competent; the teachers and paraprofessionals may well be effective. But unless there is opportunity for some form of direct communication, the whole point of the procedure is diminished. Fortunately, a very positive outcome of the continuing experience in special education is an increased emphasis on classroom observation and assessment. It stands to reason that competent teachers and educational assistants who are "watching it live," so to speak, are in a crucial position to make perceptive, realistic evaluations of a student's strengths and needs. The fact that their observations are being given increasing

credence in many jurisdictions is a tribute to their professionalism and to commonsense.

Special Education and Research

There is much demand in education today for teachers to use "evidence–based" research approaches to working with students with special needs. In 2005 the Ontario Ministry of Education awarded the Council of Directors of Education 25 million dollars to finance school-based research studies to develop approaches to inclusion that will lead to effective academc, social, and emotional growth in students with special needs. The results of this expenditure is intended to be shared among all boards so that all systems can benefit from this extensive research. It is important, however, to note that drawing firm conclusions from research can be difficult at the best of times. In education, the matter can be especially challenging for the simple reason that the variables in studies involving human interaction—the type of study much pursued in special education—are extremely difficult to control. Unless a study is conducted under laboratory conditions, which paradoxically, would make it unreal at the very outset, researchers, not to mention end-users, can never be absolutely confident about the reasons for an outcome. This weakness means educators are never entirely sure they are dealing with results that would have meaning in their own situations.

Ironically, the two most important components in all of education, students and teachers, are the two most difficult variables to control, a reality reflected in studies of inclusion. Simple logic forces acknowledgement that the personality, the commitment, and the training of classroom professionals have a profound impact on outcomes in their classes. Thus, when a study compares outcomes in two classrooms where all conditions are matched except the element of inclusion, the study is inherently flawed to the extent that it cannot account for the ever-so-crucial spirit and atmosphere that different professionals impart to a teaching environment. Nor can two classrooms ever be found where the collective personality generated by the students is the same. If nothing else, these difficulties explain why there is so much contradictory research on inclusion. Another problem lies in the improper use of results and data. (This is rarely a researcher's error.) For example, it has not been uncommon during the history of special education, for an advocate of one point of view or another to quite blithely use research results about children who are blind, for example, to support a position on children who are autistic. A related abuse arises from the "gee whiz" stories that frequently appear in non-refereed journals and in newspaper columns, anecdotes in which success with a single subject is described in glowing terms. The implications are that a similar outcome can be expected in any student with a similar special need.

Ultimately, perhaps the most unfortunate issue is the reluctance of many teachers to attribute significant value to the role played by research. Many argue, with more than ample justification, that they simply do not have the time to "keep up." A good number insist, again with more than a little justification, that much of the results are irrelevant in any case, at least to their own classrooms. As a consequence, the very people who might have the most to gain from research, and certainly the very people who should have prime responsibility for actually testing the relevance of results, have, in fact, depressingly little involvement. This paradox has been a thorn in the side of education for a long time. Fortunately, teachers are looking for "proven" approaches that will help them teach students with special needs in both their regular and special classes. The *Education For All* (Ontario Ministry of Education, 2005) document, was a major project of the Ministry of Education and the end result was a compilation of effective approaches recommended to teachers to improve literacy and numeracy ability for students with special needs in grades kindergarten to grade 6.

> *Regular classroom teachers in Ontario serve a growing number of students with diverse abilities. According to school board statistics, most students with special needs spend at least 50 per cent of their instructional day in a regular classroom, being taught by regular classroom teachers. It is imperative that inclusion means not only the practice of placing students with special needs in the regular classroom but ensuring that teachers assist every student to prepare for the highest degree of independence possible.*
>
> Ontario Ministry of Education, *Education for All*, 2005 p. 2

READINGS & RESOURCES

Bennett, S., & Wynne, K. (2006). *Special education transformation. The report of the co-chairs with the recommendations of the working table on special education.* Toronto: Ontario Ministry of Education

Council for Exceptional Children (CEC). (1993). CEC policy on inclusive schools and community settings. *Teaching Exceptional Children, 25(4), supplement*

Council for Exceptional Children (1991). "Code of ethics for the CEC," *Teaching Exceptional Children, 23, 2*

Danforth, S., & Taft, S.D. (2004). *Crucial readings in special education.* New Jersey: Pearson Education, Inc.

Friend, M., Bursuck, W. & Hutchinson, N. (1998). *Including Exceptional Students: A practical guide for classroom teachers.* Scarborough: Prentice Hall

Fuchs, D. and Fuchs L.S. (1994). Inclusive schools movement and the radicalisation of special education reform. *Exceptional Children, 60(4),* 294-309

Giangreco, M., Edelman, S., Dennis, R., & Cloninger, C. (1993). My child has a classmate with severe disabilities: What parents of nondisabled students should think about full inclusion. *Developmental Disabilities Bulletin, 21(1),* 77-91

Gutkin, T.B. (1996). Core elements of consultation service delivery for special services personnel: Rationale, practice, and some directions for the future. *Remedial and Special Education, 17(6)*, 333-340

Harry, B. (1992). *Cultural diversity, families, and the special education system: communication and empowerment.* New York: Teachers College Press

Jones, R.L. (1972) Labels and stigma in special education. *Exceptional Children 38(7)*, 553-64

Kliewer, C., & Bilkin, D. (1996). Labeling: Who wants to be called retarded: In W. Stainback & S. Stainback (Eds.), *Controversial issues confronting special education: Divergent Perspectives (2ⁿᵈ Ed., pp. 83-95).* Boston: Allyn & Bacon

Lupart, J. L. (1998). The delusion of inclusion: Implications for Canadian schools. *Canadian Journal of Education, 23(3)*, 251-264

Minke. K.M., Bear, G.G., Deiner, S.A., & Griffin, S.M. (1996). Teachers' experiences with inclusive classrooms: Implications for special education reform. *Journal of Special Education, 30*, 152-186

Ontario Ministry of Education (2005). *Education for all, The report of the expert panel on literacy and numeracy instruction for students with special education needs, kindergarten to grade 6.* Toronto: Queen's Printer for Ontario

Palmer, D.S., Borthwick-Duffy, S.A., & Windaman, K. (1998). Parent's perceptions of inclusive practices for their children with significant cognitive disabilities. *Exceptional Children, 64*, 271-282.

Peterson, J.M., & Hittie, M.M. (2003). *Inclusive teaching: Creating effective schools for all learners.* Boston: Pearson Education

Reynolds, M.C. (1991). Classification and labeling. In J.W. Lloyd, N.N. Singh, & A.C. Repp (Eds.), *The regular education initiative: Alternative perspectives on concepts, issues and models* (pp. 29-42). Sycamore, IL.: Sycamore

Salisbury C. L., Palambaro, M.M., & Hollowood, T.M. (1993). *On the nature of change of an inclusive elementary school. 18,* 75-84.

Snow, J.A. (1989). Systems of support: A new vision. In S. Stainback, W. Stainback, & M. Forest (Eds.), *Education of all students in the mainstream of regular education* (pp. 221-231). Toronto: Paul H. Brookes

Tomlinson, C.A. (1999). *The differentiated classroom: responding to the needs of all learners.* New Jersey: Pearson Merrill Prentice Hall.

Vergason, G.A., & Anderegg, M.L. (1997). The ins and outs of special education terminology. *Teaching Exceptional Children, 29(5)*, 35-39

Vlachou, A. and Barton, L. (1994). Inclusive education: Teachers and the changing culture of schooling. *British Journal of Special Education, 21(3)*, 105-107

Winzer, M. (2008). *Children with Exceptionalities in Canadian Classrooms, 8ᵗʰ edition,* Toronto: Pearson Education Canada

Wood, M. (1998). Whose job is it anyway? Educational roles in inclusion. *Exceptional Children, 64(2)*, 182-195

York, G. (1990). *The Dispossessed: Life and Death in Native Canada.* Toronto: Little Brown and Company (Canada) Ltd.

Ysseldyke, J.E., Algozzine, B., & Thurlow, M.L. (2000). *Critical issues in special education, 3ʳᵈ edition.* Boston: Houghton Mifflin Company.

Links

Ontario Ministry of Education website: **http://www.edu.gov.on.ca**

Council for Exceptional Children website: **http://www.cec.sped.org**

CHAPTER 3

The Special Needs Population:
Categories and Numbers

Ontario Student Population
Number of Students in Publicly Funded Schools Receiving Special Education Services

Elementary 100 401 (7.12%) (IPRC'd)	75 186 (5.33%) not formally identified but receiving services
Secondary 91 501(12.93%) (IPRC'd)	23 637 (3.34%) not formally identified but receiving services

Source: Ministry of Ed., Data as of January 2007

Table 3A

The Categories

Agreement on Generalities ...

Teachers, educational assistants, and administrators in a school board usually share a common vocabulary when talking about special education. Sometimes their official terms are those promulgated by the Ministry of Education. However, it is not unusual for a board to popularize terms unique to itself. Academics may use a moderately differing special education vocabulary, especially if they have different fields of interest, say, psychology or medicine. Advocates, especially if they are emphasizing softer terminologies for special needs, may have yet another set of words. Despite the potential confusion arising from these variations, the many branches of special education nevertheless seem able to communicate because there is a general understanding and acceptance of broad categories like these:

- *Intellectual and developmental differences*: includes students who are intellectually gifted, those who manifest intellectual delay
- *Sensory disabilities*: includes students who are blind and deaf
- *Communication disorders*: includes students who have learning disabilities, those who have pervasive disorders like autism, and those who have speech and language difficulties
- *Physical and health difficulties*: includes students who have genetic disorders, problems that arise from birth trauma, orthopedic conditions, and disabilities caused by disease. Usually, students who have neurological disorders are included here.
- *Behaviour disorders*: includes students who suffer from mental illness, those who are socially maladjusted, delinquent, emotionally disturbed, and those who exhibit conduct disorders.
- *Combinations of the above.*

... but Disagreement on Specifics

The terms above appear in the literature and they are used freely in discussions, but difficulty arises when it comes to defining the terms. After some four decades of in-depth experience, special education has yet to establish a set of clear, standardized categories and definitions that everyone accepts and uses. Part of the difficulty lies in the varying purposes of different stakeholders. Administrators use definitions for identifying candidates and for determining levels of support and resource allocation. Parents, advocates, and community support associations, because they have more immediate remediation objectives, tend to emphasize extensive, symptom-based characteristics. Some support groups argue for no definitions at all because students with special needs simply do not fit into such confines.

Other stakeholders have very individualistic perspectives. Medical professionals have their own view, one that often has limited connection with education. Researchers may develop their own definitions to limit the variables in a study. Teachers and educational assistants want definitions to provide a practical guidance point for planning and practice. Then there is the very notion of special need itself. To anyone who reflects on the fact that *normalcy* is not defined, it is no surprise that departure from normal is hard to describe.

In the Classroom

For those who work with students with exceptionalities on an active, daily basis—teachers, educational assistants, parents—the precision (or lack thereof) in categories and definitions of exceptionality is a minor issue in the grand scheme of things, but it's one that cannot be completely ignored. In the first place, classroom professionals increasingly are expected to become involved with other professionals (medical, for example) within a multidisciplinary team, and it is important that each understand the other. Within a variety of fields, efforts have been made to bridge the gap between disciplines. The Neuro Trauma Foundation of Ontario has, for example, identified education as one of the main priorities for research. There is a growing recognition that for many children a majority of their waking hours, and thus possible rehabilitation hours, are spent in a school setting. Given this fact, the necessity of meaningful communication and collaborative planning between previously separate treatment approaches seems obvious. Secondly, for better or worse there is an unavoidable underlay of politics in special education, so for understanding and productive dialogue, it behooves all parties to be tuned in to all positions. Finally, and perhaps most practically, official categories and definitions issued by a jurisdiction may well be the factor that determines which students are identified exceptional, and what resources can and will be made available for their benefit. For that reason alone, teachers, for example, must be sensitive to categories and definitions.

Ontario's Official Categories and Definitions

When the Education Amendment Act, commonly referred to as Bill 82, made special education mandatory in Ontario, the Ministry of Education issued a set of definitions of exceptionality. The idea was that boards of education would use the definitions when identifying a student as exceptional. Initially, most boards did just that. Over time, some boards began to modify the definitions for their own use, basing their changes within the parameters of the existing Ministry definitions. Others stuck to the Ministry list, but made additions and deletions using terminology that was more suitable and well understood within their own educational context. In recent years, the Ministry of Education has come under increasing criticism for its perceived unwillingness to tackle the issue of revamping the now decades old list of exceptionalities. While changes have been proposed, they have not to date been implemented. Certainly, agreement on the wording of the changes as well as the implications of such a move have been deterrents to decision making and implementation. Organizations that represent groups of individuals with exceptionalities such as attention deficit hyperactivity disorder and acquired brain injury continue to advocate for the recognition of these conditions within the category list. Many feel that as special education matures, and as philosophies, scientific knowledge, and practices change, the categories and definitions should evolve as well.

Despite the fact that many boards of education took on a somewhat "personalized" version of special education categories, the result was not the hodgepodge that one might expect from such independent forays. Granted, in some instances it became possible for a student to qualify for special education in one board in the province, but not in another. But most of the time these were unique cases that, conceivably, would have been problematic anyway. In effect, the relative independence of the province's school boards was simply a reflection of how difficult it is to describe accurately students with special needs. Many fit several definitions; others fall into cracks between definitions; still others resist the confines of qualifiers like "mild," "moderate," and "severe." Then, there is the reality of change. Students with exceptionalities, like all students, grow and develop. Their special needs are not immutable.

Despite these difficulties, there are many useful reasons for maintaining a set of official categories and definitions in a publicly funded education system, not the least of which are issues in resource allocation and other administrative factors. From the time special education first became mandatory in the province, Ontario has maintained an official set of categories and definitions. These are modified from time to time following extensive consultations. The current set, extant at publication, appears in the Appendix of this Sixth Edition.

The Numbers

In 1983, the Canadian Council of Ministers of Education issued data indicating that 15.5 percent of the school-age population in the country was exceptional. That figure, developed at the time by less than rigorous science, became fixed in the consciousness of the general public, not to mention educators who usually have access to more accurate information. Despite the fact that both *incidence data* (number of new cases over a time period) and *prevalence data* (total number of existing cases) are notoriously difficult to collect and collate, there is sufficient experience in special education practice now, along with some useful studies, to suggest that the real figure is not that high. Table 3A at the beginning of this chapter, for example, offers a more optimistic perspective. As well, placement data (see Table 4A in chapter 4) implies that the majority of stu-

dents receiving special education services, both elementary and secondary, are only mildly exceptional. The fact that large numbers of students with exceptionalities receive special education services as part of their regular education, e.g., as resource support or withdrawal assistance, rather than as the central motif of their schooling, e.g., as in specialized fully self-contained settings, suggests that most special needs are neither profound nor severe.

Yet the Numbers Are Growing

In 1986, by the end of the first year of mandatory special education in the province, Ontario's boards had identified 6.5 percent of the school population as receiving special education services. In those earlier days, many boards were still feeling their way through the process. By 1997, the percentage was 9.24, the intervening years having shown a small but steady increase in the number of students identified as having special needs. By 2001-2002, the percentage had continued to rise, with new information indicating that 12.8 percent of the school populations was considered exceptional. This rise in numbers is at least partly a consequence of improved procedures of identification, along with the expansion of special education in areas where it had not previously been offered, such as in the area of autism.

The rise in identification was also linked to a funding model that was connected specifically to a special education diagnosis. Casually referred to as "diagnosing for dollars," monies for special education increased proportionately to the number of students identified. Currently, the percentage of students receiving special education programs and services across the province sits at *13.72%, of which 9.06% have been formally identified through an Identification Placement and Review Committee (IPRC). It would seem that the number of students receiving special education services continues to increase, and that the rate of increase is somewhat greater than the rise in the total school population. There are a number of explanations for this growth, one of which in particular is peculiar to Ontario: the matter of the non-identified special education student.

• • • ⎯⎯⎯⎯

* Ministry of Education 2005-2006 school board reports

⎯⎯⎯⎯ • • •

Non-Identified Students Receiving Special Education Services

Since the inception of Bill 82, it has been common practice that the majority of students who receive special education services in Ontario do so after having first been "identified" by an Identification, Placement, Review Committee (IPRC). Currently, within the province, approximately 81% of students receiving special education are placed in regular classrooms for more than half the instructional day. Partially because of this, partially because of growing trends towards inclusion within the education field, and most likely as a result of the Special Education Transformation Document released by the Ministry of Education in May of 2006 (Bennett and Wynne, 2006, p. 14), the trend toward the identification of students through IPRC may well be on the decline. A memo from the office of the deputy minister to directors of education across the province, dated October 2006, recommended that the IPRC process not be required when both the parents and school agree that the students should be placed in the regular classroom. The Transformation Document itself recommends that the Individual Education Plan (IEP); (see Chapter 5) and IPRC policy be revised to promote effective parent participation, streamline processes, and reduce administrative burden while ensuring a focus on student needs and outcomes.

The move away from the formal identification of services for students with exceptionalities is not without controversy. While in many circles the IPRC was seen as administratively burdensome, and in some cases, a barrier to immediate services, others are concerned that the focus away from the IPRC will in some ways reduce the legislative weight of special education services in terms of parents' ability to appeal decisions. That having been said, the right for any parent or principal to call an IPRC is not in question should the need arise.

Numbers, Numbers and More Numbers?

Hard data to explain the movement in the number of students receiving special education are

---

The Case of Hobie

According to the special education teacher, Hobie is the most loved student in the entire school. No one is certain whether Hobie knows this but that does not matter to his classmates in grade 3 who, in the words of the teacher, "have become twenty-four willing caregivers." Hobie has severe multiple disabilities. He is blind, has no speech, and cannot move any of his limbs. His facial muscles respond to sound stimuli, a fact that convinces his parents—and the teacher and EA—that he can hear. No one has any firm idea at all of his mental capacities.

Hobie has outlived every one of the medical profession's dire predictions and, despite initially grave misgivings about having him in a regular class, the school staff and especially the students have received him enthusiastically. He spends much of his day on a modified skateboard-looking stretcher that can be raised and lowered, and a health aide takes him out every two hours to aspirate him and see to his quite extensive health and hygiene needs. No one has yet figured out how to communicate with him. The students, for their part, go out of their way for Hobie. They vie to roll him into every group situation. They take turns holding his hand during periods like "story time" and "the news." No one ever passes without patting his chest or gently putting a finger to his cheek, and instinctively, they speak to him in peer level language (no baby talk). Everyone interprets Hobie's facial reactions as proof that he is thrilled by what is happening (although recently, a visiting nurse wondered whether the reactions might possibly indicate discomfort or even pain).

Despite the very positive situation, a change looms. Hobie is in this class because the board's "fragile health needs" unit is temporarily housed in the school. Next year, the unit moves to a purpose-built facility in a brand new school and all students currently in the unit move with it, along with the paraprofessionals and aides. When the grade 3 students, on their own initiative, asked the principal to keep Hobie with them next year in grade 4, she was deeply touched, as was upper level administration and the board's trustees. Whether Hobie's thought-to-be-happy situation with the class should outweigh health, safety, and possibly legal considerations, however, must first be resolved.

difficult to come by. The why and how of identification within a schoolboard context is always linked to idiosyncratic practices of that board combined with Ministry mandates. While overall the number of students identified in the province continues to increase, it is within and between numbers that some interesting trends emerge and provide fodder for discussion. A comparison of data collected in 2002 and 2006 indicates that the number of students receiving special education services has shown an increase of 5 percent overall. It is within the secondary school numbers that that increase is most dramatic. Secondary school data indicate that overall there has been a 14.56 percentage increase in the number of students identified as receiving special education services. At the secondary level, since 2002 the number of students identified as receiving services for autism has increased by 175 per cent. A similar, though not quite as dramatic increase was noted in the area of autism at the elementary level, 77.4 percent. It is also interesting to note that in both the secondary and elementary levels, the number of students receiving special education services who were in the category of non-identified also increased, with the largest increase seen at the secondary level, which grew by 74 percent.

Provincial trends towards the recognition and provision of services for students with autism as well as a movement toward the provision of services prior to, or, in some cases, without IPRC identification, certainly seem to be reflected in the numbers provided. Ministry initatives within secondary schools, such as student success programs, to assist educators in recognizing and programming for students with diverse learning needs perhaps also plays a role. Parent advocacy, our evolving understanding of human rights, changes in teacher education programs, shifts in provincial policy, and the introduction of documents such as *Education for All* (Ontario Ministry of Education, 2005) also have an impact on what services are provided for students in the province. The numbers do tell a story but it is not a simple tale and one that cannot be told by numbers alone. Special education continues to be a dynamic field and, accordingly, most explanations are based on some empirical evidence, and to a significant degree, simply on speculation. Ultimately, the simple reality is that the number of Ontario students receiving special education

service has indeed been increasing for some time and may well continue to do so, if only because the field, relative to general education, is still very new. Irrespective of the fact that publicly funded schools have been offering a wide spectrum of special education for several decades now, there is still much to be learned. Tying down the numbers and giving them meaning is certainly part of that needed learning.

Issues Affecting Special Education Data

Getting the numbers right

For many years and across many jurisdictions, the quest for the correct numbers has been an arduous one. Differing definitions, reporting procedures, access to diagnostic expertise, and even factors such as rural versus urban populations serve to complicate the goal of numerical accuracy. Certainly, across the province of Ontario, interested parties have explored a variety of approaches to getting the numbers right. One suggestion, that the number of students with exceptionalities be directly linked to the overall population of the board, has some curb appeal. This approach is often countered, and rightly so, by arguments of geographic factors, the potentially devastating effects of declining enrolments on some boards, as well as the possible dramatic shifts in funding that would accompany such a move. Another possibility might be the adoption of what is termed a proxy measure for identifying the number of students with exceptionalities within a given jurisdiction. A proxy measure would take into account factors such as the average level of income, ethnicity, education level of parents, and access to health support services. The question becomes, do these factors have an impact on the number of students with exceptionalities in a given jurisdiction? To date, the identification of those factors that would accurately identify the number of students with exceptionalities within a given jurisdiction remains elusive.

The Inherent Risks in Comparison

Definitions of exceptionality vary and terminologies differ. Some school systems classify a student's need in terms of the service required, while others do so in terms of a special need. As a result, designations like "learning disabled" and "mild intellectual disability" may be used in different schools for essentially the same case. Comparisons, therefore, must be regarded with wariness at least. In a classic comparison case in 1989, the province of Quebec shocked the field by reporting a prevalence of learning disabilities three times that of Ontario and eight times that of British Columbia. Only after sorting out the fact of differences in definition was the situation understood. (Even in the category "multiple disabilities," which is theoretically subject to more rigorously controlled description, Quebec numbers that year were greater than Ontario's by a factor of 4.5.)

Chronic Problems

Another concern that affects data collection and interpretation in special education is cases of co-occurring disabilities. In some systems, these situations are identified with terms like "multiple exceptionalities" (as in Tables 3B and 3C), but there will inevitably be cases where, although "multi" is an appropriate identification, for a variety of reasons the decision may be taken to classify the individual by what is determined to be a primary special need. (Note that the reported data in Tables 3B and 3C do not distinguish this— and probably could not in any case.) Yet another concern is the potential of certain needs to skew overall data pictures. Serious cases of special needs like blindness or severe developmental dis-

Number of Students Receiving Special Education Services by Area of Exceptionality (Elementary)

Area of Exceptionality	Fully Self-Contained	Partially Integrated	Withdrawal Assistance	Resource Assistance	Indirect Service	Total
Behaviour	1 408	1 088	1 660	1 814	2 194	8 164
Autism	1 498	782	1 174	1 567	1 278	6 299
Deaf & H. of H.	215	165	384	344	412	1 520
Deaf (alt. prog.)	7	<6	21	<6	20	53
Learning Disability	2 191	7 185	13 738	9 425	5 093	37 632
Speech Impairment	42	16	142	123	138	461
Language Impairment	697	1 007	2 290	1 606	1 025	6 625
Giftedness	3 994	2 226	3 071	1 530	2 951	13 772
Mild Intellectual Dis.	2 669	3 013	3 261	1 799	1 045	11 787
Developmental Dis.	3 166	993	866	620	396	6 041
Physical Disability	380	121	282	530	643	1 956
Blind & Low Vision	30	11	97	153	146	437
Deaf-Blind (alt. prog.)	12	0	<6	<6	<6	19
Multiple exceptionalities	1 391	964	1 300	1 060	920	5 635
Sub total	17 700	17 572	28 289	20 577	16 263	100 401
Non-Identified students	1 014	2 990	33 168	22 376	15 638	75 186
(Receiving Special Ed. Programs and Services)						
Grand Total Provincial	18 714	20 562	61 457	42 953	31 901	175 587

Source: Ministry of Ed., Data as of January 2007

Table 3B

Number of Students Receiving Special Education Services by Area of Exceptionality (Secondary)

Area of Exceptionality	Fully Self-Contained	Partially Integrated	Withdrawal Assistance	Resource Assistance	Indirect Service	Total
Behaviour	240	259	1 269	1 345	1 902	**5 015**
Autism	379	257	384	319	250	**1 589**
Deaf & H. of H.	55	31	233	215	313	**847**
Deaf (alt. prog)	<6	9	<6	<6	<6	**15**
Learning Disability	446	2 233	12 722	13 991	16 109	**45 501**
Speech Impairment	0	<6	28	45	60	**134**
Language Impairment	47	193	778	1 287	2 318	**4 623**
Giftedness	336	1 795	1 442	2 751	4 901	**11 255**
Mild Intellectual Dis.	2 041	1 824	3 042	3 064	2 965	**12 936**
Developmental Dis.	2 279	992	293	178	266	**4 008**
Physical Disability	178	87	219	255	362	**1 101**
Blind & Low Vision	12	7	61	82	94	**256**
Deaf-Blind (alt. prog.)	0	0	<6	<6	0	**<6**
Multiple exceptionalities	1 018	800	833	763	805	**4 219**
Sub Total	7 062	8 488	21 307	24 297	30 347	**91 501**
Non-Identified students (Receiving Special Ed. Programs and Services)	124	268	5 970	6 604	10 671	**23 637**
Grand Total Provincial	7 186	8 756	27 277	30 901	41 018	**115 138**

Source: Ministry of Ed., Data as of January 2007

Table 3C

ability are usually identified and added to the data base early on, whereas something like a mild intellectual disability may not become apparent until the individual is in school, and even then, not necessarily until the individual begins to encounter difficulty. This individual may not even be added to a data base at all if it is decided that the need is not serious enough to warrant formal identification, or if the decision is taken to avoid identification in order to avoid stigma.

Nevertheless...Benefits

Notwithstanding the cautions mentioned above, the data made available by the Ministry of Education's Information Management Branch, such as that in Tables 3B and 3C, have significant value. These are data that confirm trends, the identifications in "autism" being a case in point. They force questions, such as why does the total number of students in the "learning disabilities" category increase from elementary to secondary school. The numbers are vital for both long- and short-range projection, for present and future allocation of resources. They are also useful in confirming good news. The clear decline in speech impaired numbers as candidates progress through elementary to secondary school, for example, suggests very strongly that the remedial undertakings in this category have a positive effect. Data like these in the tables permit cautious comparisons and both verify and disprove polemical claims. The data become especially valuable when compared with similar tables from other years. In short, irrespective of the problems inherent in data collection and presentation, and especially in interpretation, without the numbers, the system would be flying blind. Certainly a less appealing prospect.

A Very Special Population ✍

The Ministry of Education has direct responsibility for a number of very special schools in the province. The examples of longest standing, and certainly the best known, are the provincial schools. These are residential schools (with a few day students where feasible) geared to specific exceptionalities. The Ministry also participates in a number of hospital schools and care and treatment facilities at various key locations in the province, as well as schools in a number of correctional facilities. Unlike the provincial schools, where education is the primary mission, in these latter locations the "school" aspect functions in tandem with other purposes.

Taken together, the population of provincial schools and facilities fairly consistently represents about half of one percent of the entire population of publicly funded schools in Ontario, and in most years, just under three percent of the population receiving special education services. (See more in Chapter 4 on Service Delivery.)

READINGS & RESOURCES

Adelman H.S. (1992). LD: The next 25 years. *Journal of Learning Disabilities*, 25, 17-21.

Bennett S. & Wynne K. (2006). *Special Education Transformation: The report of the co-chairs with the recommendations of the working table on Special Education.* Ministry of Education, Ontario http://www.edu.gov.on.ca

Carrier, J. G. (1986). Sociology and special education: Differentiation and allocation in mass education. *American Journal of Education*, 94, 218-312.

Deno, E. (1994). Special education as development capital revisited: A quarter century appraisal of means versus ends. *The Journal of Special Education.* 27, 375-392.

Fujiura, G. T. & Kiyoshi, Y. (2000). Trends in demography of childhood poverty and disability. *Exceptional Children*, 66(2), 187-199.

Johnson, D. R., Stodden, R. A., Emanuel, E. J., Leuking, R., & Mack, M. (2002). Current challenges facing secondary education and transition services: What research tells us. *Exceptional Children*, 68(4), 519-531.

Lipsky, D. K., & Gartner, A. (1989). *Beyond Special Education: Quality for all.* Baltimore: Brookes.

MacMillian, D. L., Gresham, F. M., Bocian, K. M., & Lambros, K. M. (1998). Current plight of borderline students: Where do they belong? *Education and Training in Mental Retardation and Developmental Disabilities*, 33, 83-94.

MacMillian, D. L., & Reschly, A. (1998). Overrepresentation of minority students: The case for greater specificity of the variables examined. *The Journal of Special Education*, 32(1), 15-24.

Ontario Ministry of Education (2005). *Education for all, The report of the expert panel on literacy and numeracy instruction for students with special education needs, kindergarten to grade 6.* Toronto: Queen's Printer for Ontario

Reynolds, M. C. (1991). *Classification and Labeling.* Sycamore, NY: Sycamore.

Ysseldyke, J. & Bielinski, J. (2002). Effects of different methods of reporting and reclassification on trends in test scores for students with disabilities. *Exceptional Children*, 68(2), 189-200.

CHAPTER 4

Service Delivery
The Infrastructure of Special Education

"We've got great teachers, great EAs—and our resources, well, you can always use more resources, but ours are okay. Really, as a principal, my most important special ed. job is getting the right people and the right resources to the right place. And fast."

Jackson T., principal

Accessing Special Education Services: Referral Process

The process by which a student becomes a beneficiary of a special education program and/or service is basically the same in most school boards, although each board has its own policies and procedures. The following reflects what is practised in many boards throughout the province.

Step one: Identify a student who may need a special education program and/or service.

Step two: Discuss the student with the special education resource teacher assigned to your school.

Step three: Bring student to the attention of the in-school team. (An Individual Education Plan (IEP) may be developed at this point.)

Step four: When necessary, refer student to the attention of the Identification, Placement and Review Committee

Step five: Adjust placement when necessary and implement IEP.

Although the sequence seems deceptively simple in a world of procedures and policies, these five steps summarize how special education comes about for a student.

Step One: Identify a student who may need a special education program and/or services.

A small number of students may come to a school with their special needs already assessed and with all or part of a program in place. Those with long-established physical or medical needs are a frequent example. A few others may come tagged, so to speak, for "careful watching," to see whether suspected needs are serious enough to be addressed. Still others, especially the very young, will arrive with extensive information about their needs prepared by parents or a pre-school. Inevitably, there will be students whose special needs, perhaps for the first time ever, will become apparent only during the course of a school year.

Some, or all, of these students will become candidates for special education, a decision that will be made after an assessment and identification of their needs. Assessments vary in extent and formality, depending on the policy and the resources of the school board, and on the particular student being assessed. The purpose is to gain some insight into the subject's intelligence, strengths, needs, health, and behaviour, to predict as much as reasonably possible the likelihood of success in school, and to gather information that will help in developing an Individual Educational Plan should that be deemed necessary. For a few students, an assessment may indicate that special education is not really necessary, and the service delivery process may stop at this point. For candidates who are identified as potential beneficiaries, the steps below are what follow. (See Chapter 7 for more on assessments.)

Step Two: Discuss the student with the special education resource teacher assigned to your school.

In most, if not all, schools in Ontario, a teacher qualifed in special education is assigned the role of "resource teacher." Depending on the size of the school, this teacher may be present in the school for all or part of the day. One of the responsiblities of these teachers is to assist regular class teachers who may have some concerns about the learning needs of some of their students. The resource teacher may provide assistance in assessing student needs, may provide approaches to improving the student's learning, or may suggest that the student be brought to the attention of the in-school team. Please note that students showing abilities indicating possible giftedness are also brought to the attention of the resource teacher.

Step Three: Bring student to the attention of the In-School Team.

Every school will have an in-school team, usually composed of the special education teacher,

---

The Individual Education Plan ✍

The Individual Education Plan, or IEP, is a written plan of action that becomes a road map for everyone involved: student, teachers, educational assistants, parents, and administration. Ideally, the needs highlighted by the assessment are addressed in the IEP. According to the Ministry's *Individual Education Plan Resource Guide* (2004), the development of the plan should involve all concerned parties so that the final result is not a surprise to anyone.

Overview of the IEP Process

1. Gather information.
2. Set the direction.
3. Develop the IEP as it relates to the student's special education program and services.
4. Implement the IEP.
5. Review and update the IEP.

The IEP not only summarizes the student's strengths, needs, and interests (and health and behaviour profile where applicable), it also sets out individualized goals and objectives. These goals and objectives may include simple modifications of the curriculum that everyone else is study-ing. Sometimes, they are entirely unique to the student. As well, an IEP offers ideas and strategies for instruction, elements of scheduling, alternate assessment approaches, environmental adjustments, and other details as appropriate. For students fourteen years and older, a Transition Plan is also developed for post-secondary transition to work, community living or further education. (See chapter 5 for more on IEPs.)

According to the Ontario Ministry of Education, the term *accommodations* is used to refer to "the special teaching and assessment strategies, human supports, and/or individualized equipment required to enable a student to learn and/or to demonstrate learning. Accommodations do not alter the provincial curriculum expectations for the grade" (Ministry of Education, 2004, p. 25). Accommodations can be instructional or environmental (e.g. study carrell, use of headphones, special lighting) or reflect a change in the manner in which the student is assessed.

Modifications, on the other hand, "are changes in the age-appropriate grade-level expectations for a subject or course in order to meet a student's learning needs. These changes may involve developing expectations that reflect knowledge and skills required in the curriculum for a different grade level and/or decreasing the number and/or complexity of the regular grade level curriculum expectations" (Ministry of Education, 2004, p. 25).

Both Sheldon and Jean-Marc were accepted into a pre-school regional centre day program when they were 4.4 years and 4.2 years old respectively. Although both boys presented almost exactly the same behaviours, Sheldon had been diagnosed as autistic while Jean-Marc was diagnosed as having pervasive development disorder. Both boys were totally introverted and engaged in harmful self-stimulation. Neither used intelligible speech, and both were instant runaways if left unsupervised. Happily, the program at the centre was successful in quickly effecting some changes. After about three months, both began to use some meaningful speech, and as well, appeared to understand much of what was being said to them. By the end of one full year, their echolalic habits diminished significantly. Jean-Marc (but not Sheldon) began to refer to himself in the first person (rather than calling himself "he" or "Jean-Marc") and would directly address his favourite educational assistant by name rather than as "she."

In their second year at the centre, Sheldon and Jean-Marc are now enrolled in what the staff calls the "top" group. It took a psychometrist three tries, but she succeeded in completing a pre-school assessment of Jean-Marc and reported him to be of average to just below average intelligence, with speech, although delayed (at 6.4, he is at the norm for 4-year olds), improving at an accelerated pace. Jean-Marc makes eye contact spontaneously about half the time and when directed to "Look at me," will respond appropriately every time. He still exhibits some unusual behaviours (e.g., he will compulsively stroke any clothing that is red in colour, no matter who wears it, and music of any kind will take up his total attention, not only during its playing but after. On occasion he will hum a melody over and over for the remainder of the day). Staff at the centre point proudly to his ability to relate to others. On the thrice-weekly field trips (to shopping malls, parks, etc., anywhere that people gather) Jean-Marc follows directions, takes responsibility, and spontaneously assists with the group.

In Sheldon's case, the field trips are a weak point. Wide open spaces threaten him, as do large numbers of strange adults. While he copes with these situations as long as there is familiar adult support, he still turns to the comfort of repetitive, stereotyped behaviour at these times (alternately patting his cheeks and then his ears; another is spinning round and round, with eyes closed and arms extended; staff has noted several times that he can persist at this indefinitely without getting dizzy.) On the other hand, Sheldon's use of appropriate language has increased dramatically. Although he refused utterly to cooperate with the psychometrist who successfully assessed Jean-Marc, she reinforced—off the record—the opinion of staff that his language usage was at or just below age-appropriate level.

Now, notwithstanding a possible setback incident (after a fire drill, Sheldon was found inside a heating duct in a no-go area of the building; Jean-Marc imitated the alarm bell continuously for several days), both boys are going to go to grade 1 classes in their neighbourhood schools. The receiving principals and teachers have asked for advice on how to best make the transition smooth and what modifications and/or accomodations should be included in these students' IEPs.

the principal and/or vice principal, a regular classroom teacher (perhaps from each division), and any other personnel the principal may believe necessary. If the resource teacher believes that the student's needs or strengths are such that further assessment and/or program strategies are necessary, the teacher will bring the student to the attention of this committee and receive ideas that are designed to help the student achieve. At this point, an IEP may be developed, which permits the teacher to modify and/or accommodate the student's program.

Step Four: When necessary bring the student to the attention of an Identification, Placement and Review Committee (IPRC)

The IPRC may be made up of superintendents (though this is rarely the case) principals, special education consultants and/or coordinators, area resource teachers, regular education teachers, and related professionals (psychologists, social workers, etc.). This committee, after reviewing all assessment data, determines whether the student should be declared exceptional, and may recommend a change in program and/or classroom placement. Once placed, a student so designated must have an IEP prepared within 30 days of placement.

> *I try not to resent the time I spend at meetings and writing reports, but every minute it takes to do that is another minute I'm not where I want to be: helping the kids.*
>
> Arlene Y., special education teacher

Step Five: Adjust placement when necessray and implement IEP.

An oft-debated matter in special education is just where to deliver the service, where to implement the IEP. Most students with special needs are based in regular classrooms and receive all their special education in that setting. Some, especially those whose needs may be more profound, are placed in specialized settings. These settings may be anything from a school where the entire environment is devoted to a particular need (e.g., schools for students who are deaf or hard of hearing), to separate, specialized classes in a neighbourhood school. A quite frequent placement choice will be a combination of the specialized, self-contained classroom, where a student will spend part of his or her day, while for the rest of the day the student is in the regular class. ("Resource room" and "learning centre" are popular designations for special settings used in this way.) In many cases, the appropriate setting may be a regular classroom where resources are brought to the student. The permutations and combinations are considerable. Whatever the choice of setting for the student, the setting is always, within reason, subject to review and adjustment.

Modify and/or Accommodate as Necessary

An essential component of an Individual Education Plan is regular re-examination, for an IEP does not just delineate the student's program. It is also a guide, an evolving benchmark for monitoring the student's progress and development. It is expected that at the very least, the IEP will be reviewed at each report card evaluation period. In most cases the IEP, from each reporting period to the next, is the baseline from which necessary additions, accommodations, and modifications are highlighted. For this reason especially, an IEP is effective in clarifying communication with parents and other significant figures in a student's life.

Range of Placement Options

In Ontario in 2005/6, over 290 000 students were receiving special education programs and services. Table 4A lists the range of options and the number of students receiving each option at either the elementary or secondary level.

Regular Class with Indirect Support

It is not uncommon for a teacher to seek assistance from the special education or resource teacher to obtain instructional ideas on how effectively to teach and/or assess a student with special needs in the regular classroom. In this instance, help is provided in an "indirect" manner, in that no direct assistance is provided to the student by anyone except the regular classroom teacher.

Very often, what becomes "special" about a student's education is a simple and straightforward adjustment in his or her program within the regular class. An example would be a student who has spina bifida and requires a wheelchair for mobility. If this student has learned to manage his or her own condition, as most do, the student will participate in every aspect of the regular classroom in an entirely normal way, but at times, perhaps during a physical education program, there would likely be some accommodations made. For example, the student may not participate in basketball, but would have an alternate appropriate physical activity in its place. Should the student regularly need extra time for things like personal hygiene, a teacher would accommodate by trying to present new or difficult material at times when the student is normally expected to be present.

Number of Students Receiving Special Education Services by Type of Placement				
	Elementary		Secondary	
	2001/2	2005/6	2001/2	2005/6
Fully Self-Contained	19 802	18 714	8 816	7 186
Partially integrated	17 726	20 562	7 563	8 756
Withdrawal assistance	74 813	61 457	24 905	27 277
Resource assistance	42 339	42 953	34 550	30 901
Indirect support	21 672	31 901	24 672	41 018
Total	**176 352**	**175 587**	**100 506**	**115 138**

Source: Ontario Ministry of Education, *School September Report, 2001-0* and Ontario Ministry of Education, *School September Report, 2005-6*. Includes all publicly funded schools, excluding care and treatment facilities. Includes non-identified students receiving service.

Table 4A

Other indirect assistance may be in the form of specialized equipment such as an FM transmitter system for a student who is hard of hearing.

Resource Assistance

"Resource assistance," sometimes called "direct support," is delivered in a variety of ways. It is quite common for the resource teacher to enter the regular classroom and assist the student with special needs while the regular classroom teacher is providing instruction to the rest of the class. This "co-teaching" situation keeps the student with special needs in the regular class thereby assisting in the student's socialization and ensuring that the student doesn't miss curriculum topics presented to the whole class. In the case of a regular class where, for example, a student who is deaf is placed, there may be direct support to the student, ranging from special technical equipment to the presence of a signing interpreter. At the same time, a teacher or consultant with specialized knowledge about deafness may provide support to the classroom teacher in everything from program preparation to in-service training. Another typical example is the situation in which an educational assistant will spend specific amounts of time in classrooms providing remedial support to students in, say, language development. Still another situation is that in which the assistant provides support to a student with behaviour concerns at times in the school day when those concerns tend to manifest themselves.

Resource assistance is sometimes mistakenly construed as relatively low impact, but the assistance can be significant indeed. For example, it is not unusual for a student with intense special needs to have resource assistance in the form of an educational assistant full-time or nearly full-time.

Regular Class/Withdrawal for Assistance

For part of their program, some students with exceptionalities may benefit from an individualized learning experience that is more effectively delivered in a setting less distracting or competitive, or, in some cases, more specially equipped, than a regular classroom. Thus, a student may be withdrawn to a resource room, for example, where a resource teacher or an educational assistant, working in close concert with the regular teacher, will deliver the modified and/or accommodated learning experience called for in the student's IEP. In this arrangement, the student remains a member of the regular class, but part of his or her program is delivered elsewhere on a formally scheduled basis. A fairly typical example of a student who uses this type of placement is one with a learning disability for whom reading and writing pose extra difficulty. Often, the strategies that benefit a student with learning disabilities, as well as others with special needs, can be very effectively delivered in this type of resource arrangement. Taking a student out of a class for one-on-one instruction is by no means a novel idea, especially in the elementary grades. What distinguishes the practice in special education is the specificity of the arrangement, and the guarantee of its regular delivery in a student's plan.

Part-Time Regular Class/Self-Contained Class (Partially Integrated)

The term "self-contained class" refers to a classroom setting composed of students with similarly identified special needs, e.g., learning disabled, behaviourally exceptional, gifted, or developmentally handicapped. Different boards have different policies for the composition and criteria for placement in these classes regardless of the definitions of exceptionality provided by the Ministry of Education (see Appendix). As the designation part-time regular class/self-contained class would suggest, this is an arrangement whereby a student spends time in two settings. Unlike the withdrawal-to-a-resource room choice, this setup is somewhat more formal in that a self-contained classroom is usually more specifically dedicated and managed than a resource room. This approach is used frequently to help students who are making a transition from a full-time self-contained class to a regular class (those gaining control of behaviour issues are a good example) and offers an effective combination of intensive instruction opportunity, together with a normalized experience.

Full-time Self-Contained Class

In order to generate a very specific kind of learning experience, it may be deemed appropriate to place a student with an exceptionality in a self-contained special education class full time. These placements are found in some, but by no means all, regular community schools. Ideally, students with exceptionalities who take their entire program in such classes, participate in general school activities in the same way as other students. The recomendations of the Ontario Ministry of Education Working Group on Special Education suggest that any student's placement in a self-contained class "be duration-specific, intervention–focused and subject to regular reviews" (Bennett & Wynne, 2006, p. 8). When

they are placed in these settings, students rarely remain in these classes 100% of the school day. In most cases, the teacher arranges for the students to spend part of the day in a regular classroom (often with the assistance of an educational assistant) so that they can benefit from interacting and learning with regular classroom students.

Special Schools

A number of dedicated-purpose schools in the province are run under the aegis of the Ministry of Education. In Brantford, the W. Ross Macdonald School, named after a former lieutenant-governor, has programs for students who are blind and deaf/blind. In London, Belleville, and Milton, schools named after former Ontario premiers, the Robarts School, Sir James Whitney School, and Ernest C. Drury School respectively, offer programs for students who are deaf. The ministry also maintains "demonstration" schools at the latter three locations for students diagnosed as having ADHD and/or severe learning disabilities. Each is a residential school with a fairly small population. The schools are known respectively as Amethyst, Sagonaska, and Trillium. In Ottawa, the Centre Jules-Leger offers programs in French for students who are deaf and students who are severely learning disabled.

In addition to dedicated programs for their students, these schools also offer the standard Ontario curriculum. They are resource and training centres for both teachers and the wider community, and play an important role in specialized teacher training. Both the provincial and the demonstration schools enjoy a well-deserved reputation for leadership and for excellence in education. Students are enrolled in the schools through an application process that involves the Ministry and the student's school board.

Specialized, Non-School Settings ("Section 23")

In situations where students are admitted to a care or treatment facility group home or to a custodial or correctional facility, special arrangements are usually necessary to address the students' educational needs. The educational program in these cases is part of a wider program of service that may include medical treatment or service from therapists, psychiatrists, social workers, etc. For the most part, the educational portion of the program is undertaken by a local school board under

The Case of Cassie

Officially, Cassie is 15.2 years old although Family Services acknowledges she may be up to six months younger or as much as a full year older. There are no birth records. Cassie's physical appearance can be interpreted in a variety of ways, and nothing is known of her mother, who is believed to have been a homeless person. Equally uncertain is the origin of Cassie's intellectual disabilities and behaviour problems. Fetal alcohol syndrome is one listed cause, but a large scar over her left ear with an adjacent depression in her skull has also led to a suspicion of acquired brain injury. Nevertheless, both administration and staff at Cassie's school are quick to point out that the cause of her problems concerns them far less than the symptoms.

Prominent among those symptoms are deep-rooted behaviour problems that follow a pattern that her teachers describe as "going on benders." Between episodes of relative calm, Cassie will become aggressive, often violent, for several days. Most recently, in a single day, she scratched a teacher who (unsuccessfully) tried to stop her from beating another student; set fire to clothing in a change room; overturned her desk after failing a test, and then spent an impressive four consecutive hours crying in the arms of an educational assistant in the school's resource room. Academically, Cassie places in the very low percentiles except for mathematics in which she is rated Low Average.

Interestingly, the prime concern about Cassie at the moment relates to service delivery. At the beginning of the current semester, special education in her secondary school switched from a Fixed Resource model to a Mobile Resource model. In the Fixed version, over a four-period (plus lunch) day, identified students attended three regular classes and spent one specifically time-tabled period in a resource room with special education staff. In the Mobile model, identified students take four regular classes, often accompanied by special education staff, with the option to "drop-in" to a resource room as necessary. In theory, "drop-ins" occur after consultation among the student, the regular teacher, and special education staff. In practice, students tend to "drop-in" at will.

Since the adoption of the Mobile model, Cassie has spent almost all her time in the resource room, to be in the company of an educational assistant assigned there. The EA is new but very popular with both students and staff and highly regarded for her skill in dealing with students who act out. Cassie's attachment to the EA and the resource room has generated a number of concerns. One is that sticking exclusively to the EA contradicts the goals of her IEP (not to mention that the EA has become unavailable for other duties). Another arises because the school board is very strongly and publicly committed to inclusion and sees the situation as a potential black mark. Regular teachers, understandably, are relieved that Cassie's presence in their classrooms is limited, but that position puts them in conflict with the special education teachers. At first, no one wanted to stir the pot because Cassie has been undergoing an extended period of calm. But it is expected that Cassie spend more time in regular classrooms and teachers are determing what approaches would be most effective.

---

written agreement with the facility. Funding is a complex matter, for usually several provincial ministries are involved, each with its own priorities, responsibilities, and funding mechanisms. The Ministry of Education describes these settings as "Educational Programs in Government-Approved Facilities for Care, Treatment and Custodial or Correctional Purposes." In everyday parlance, these settings are typically referred to as "Section 23s," this being the number and section of the funding regulation that permits these arrangements to receive provincial dollars. It is important to note that students placed in classrooms in these settings are not officially students registered with a board and therefore do not fall under much of the legislated special education provincial requirements. Students in these classrooms are placed there because they have been accepted or sent to the facility, not because of an IPRC placement decision.

In terms of the placement continuum, specialized, non-school settings, along with special schools, are viewed as quite restrictive settings.

The Cascade or Full Inclusion: The Debate is Over

All school boards in Ontario now accept the premise that inclusion of students with exceptionalities in regular classes should be the normal practice. At the same time, it is Ministry of Education policy that a range of settings (such as those described above) should be available for students whose needs are best addressed under alternative arrangements. For most—but not all—school boards in the province this approach has been pretty much standard practice since special education was first established. The standard practice is based on variations of a long-established placement model known by a variety of names such as the Special Education Cascade, or Continuum Model. (see Figure 4A).

The distinguishing feature of this model is that a continuum of settings for students with exceptionalities is available on a formal, more or less permanent basis. The settings, or learning environments, are progressively more specialized, and students, if it is deemed necessary and beneficial, may be placed in these alternative settings on a short- or longer-term basis. Important philosophical principles of the model are that students always be placed in the least restrictive environment, and that no restricted placement ever be regarded as permanent.

As one might expect, in a province the size of Ontario, geography and budgets have an influence on available placements. Thus, in the case of a setting organized to deal with, say, extremely difficult behaviour, a board might arrange that only one school out of several in an area would offer this special environment. Another school in the area might be chosen to host a special setting for students who are blind. Still another might have a self-contained setting for students with fragile health issues. Each school in the area, however, would likely have its own resource room or similar, moderately specialized setting for part- or full-time placements. No matter how the school board arranges matters, theoretically—and for the most part in practice—in the range of settings model, all students in the board have access, if necessary, to the appropriate setting for their needs.

Placement arrangements built on the principle of inclusion tend to be quite flexible and, sometimes, quite ad hoc (note the looping arrows in Figure 4B). Very often, arrangements are created—and collapsed—entirely according to needs of the moment. Most school boards

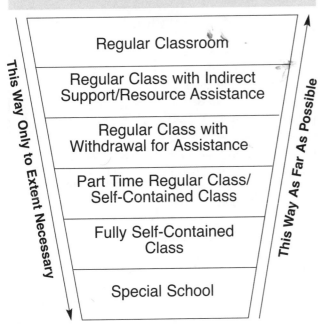

Range of Settings (Cascade) Model

This Way Only to Extent Necessary

This Way As Far As Possible

- Regular Classroom
- Regular Class with Indirect Support/Resource Assistance
- Regular Class with Withdrawal for Assistance
- Part Time Regular Class/ Self-Contained Class
- Fully Self-Contained Class
- Special School

Figure 4A

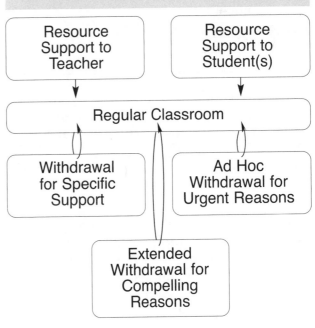

A Descriptive Scheme for Integration

Resource Support to Teacher

Resource Support to Student(s)

Regular Classroom

Withdrawal for Specific Support

Ad Hoc Withdrawal for Urgent Reasons

Extended Withdrawal for Compelling Reasons

Figure 4B

where inclusion is an underpinning philosophy make at least minimal use of alternative settings, if only informally. A board that has every single one of its students with exceptionalities in regular settings, full time, is very rare. Still, the fundamental principle of inclusion is not diluted: a student with an exceptionality, no matter where the student's special education service is delivered, is considered a full-time student in his or her regular classroom. The student is never administratively placed elsewhere. In those instances when a more restrictive setting is accessed, the goal is to return the student to the regular classroom as soon as possible.

Debate over the moral and practical superiority of inclusion versus range of settings raged hotly for several years, but has very much diminished in the light of experience. Most educators in Ontario, even before provincial policy was clarified, were operating from the position that regular class placement should be a first choice as a matter of course. And over time, even the most vociferous supporters of inclusion have acknowledged the accumulating evidence that some students with special needs do indeed benefit from specialized settings. Today, in most schools, it is difficult for an untrained observer to distinguish between the two positions, so similar have they become in practice. What seems to have taken place, then, in the debate over inclusion and range of settings is an amalgamation of the best of both.

Getting Special Education Under Way

Under the regulations implemented after the passage of Bill 82, many boards of education tended to rely almost exclusively on formal procedures to get the process going. Hence most decisions were made by officially constituted Identification, Placement and Review Committees (IPRCs).

A committee would make a determination of exceptionality (if appropriate), decide on a placement, in some cases make recommendations regarding program, and then, if the parents agreed, the student's special education program would begin. As systems and practice matured, schools began to adopt simpler procedures for

some students, reserving the time-consuming and demanding formality of the IPRC for the more complicated cases. The models shown in Situations I and II (Figures 4C and 4D) are reasonably typical examples of the less formal, in-school variety. The model shown in Situation III (Figure 4E) is considerably more formal.

Situation I (Figure 4C) presents a type of case that occurs frequently. It begins when the teacher and/or educational assistant or parent becomes aware of a student's special need(s). When it is possible to bring about appropriate adjustments to meet the needs in the classroom without bringing formal processes to bear, the matter can be resolved quickly, simply, and with reasonable hope of immediate benefit. In Situation I, it is very likely that assessments would be informal and carried out by the teacher, perhaps with assistance from in-school personnel such as the learning resource teacher. In this case, the student is usually not officially identified exceptional, although for school purposes and for data reporting, he or she may be considered a student receiving a special education program and/or service.

Situation II (Figure 4D) is somewhat more complex in that it will likely involve more personnel. This procedure does not formally identify the student as exceptional, but will likely call for somewhat more standardized actions than in

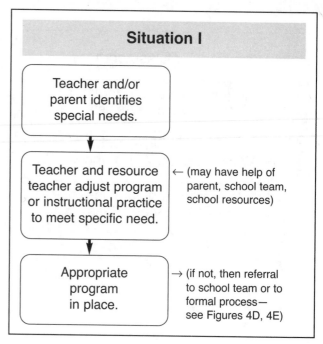

Figure 4C

Situation I. The assessment of needs will usually be more detailed, and may even be supported with formal test results. As with Situation I, the student may now be considered part of the school's special education population. This latter process is becoming a more prevalent practice throughout the province.

As Figure 4E implies, Situation III is more complex. It reflects provincially regulated practice in the province, and is the approach necessary to have a student formally identified as exceptional. Naturally, this process is more time-consuming than Situations I and II, and is subject to standardized procedures required by provincial regulations.

Procedures used by individual schools and boards will differ. These are examples only, and have no official status. In some cases, in order to maintain flexibility and a policy of by-case response, a school will not use standard procedures at all. All schools, however, pay heed to Ministry regulations, and invariably try to proceed with the student's best interests as the top priority.

In those instances where school personnel and parents have difficulty agreeing on an appropriate special education program and/or service for the student, the Ministry recommends that boards put into place an alternative dispute resolution process whereby a facilitator is used to assist the parties reach agreement on a program suited to the needs of the student. The recently released document *Shared Solutions: A guide to preventing and resolving conflicts regarding programs and services for students with special education needs* (Ontario Ministry of Education, 2007) offers suggestions on how this approach could be employed so that the more formal appeal and tribunal process can be avoided (see Chapter 6).

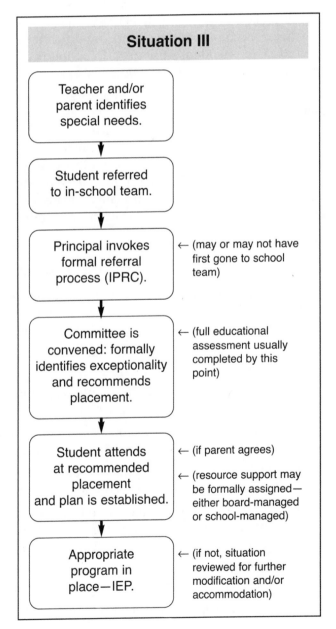

Figure 4E

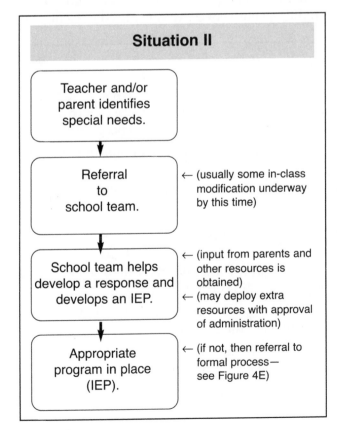

Figure 4D

Service Delivery in Secondary Schools

Because of the structure of a typical high school, special education service delivery is quite different from that in elementary settings. Nevertheless, it is clear from Ontario Ministry of Education Policy documents that students with special needs in secondary schools are entitled to a program and an environment that meets their needs. Though it is recognized that the number of teachers, other students, courses, diploma requirements, and scheduling options that an individual with special needs encounters in a secondary school setting is much greater than in the elementary experience, program accommodations and modifications included on a student's IEP need to be followed by all teachers to whom the student is assigned.

Secondary schools have complex time-tabling. Most are organized on a semester system, and fundamental to that structure is the completion of credits, the basis on which diplomas are awarded. Matching the typically large number of course options with the special needs of a student with an exceptionality means the role of a special education teacher in a high school frequently involves more coordination and consultation than direct intervention.

For a majority of students receiving special education services at the high school level, considerations such as course reduction, careful and strategic course selection, and scheduling of resource room time are common practices, and these must be monitored. Regular teaching staff and other school personnel need to be informed of the contents of a student's IEP and need to ensure that the IEP recommendations as indicated are implemented. Recommendations in an IEP can include:

- no accommodations and modifications: or
- accommodations only, or
- modified learning expectations, with the possibility of accommodations, or
- a non-credit (alternative) course.

Diplomas and Credits

Currently in Ontario, successful completion of a high school program leads to an Ontario Secondary School Diploma (OSSD). This diploma requires completion of 30 high school credits, 40 hours of community involvement, and

---

Student Success/Learning to 18

The Ontario Ministry of Education has developed several strategies to help all students, including students with exceptionalities, succeed in high school. Key to these initiatives are six innovative programs that can be "customized" to suit the needs of the particular secondary school student.

1. Student success teams: Teachers are employed specifically to assist students requiring extra attention and support.

2. Expanded co-op credit: Students can now earn two complusory high school credits through hands-on experience.

3. Specialist high skills major: This program allows students to organize their courses to prepare for specific academic or skilled careers.

4. Dual credit program: Students earn credits that can be put toward both their high school diploma and their post-secondary diploma or apprenticeship certification.

5. Lighthouse project: Innovative local programs can be designed to help students stay in school by providing guidance, support, and alternative learning environments.

6. Grade 8-9 transition: A new initiative to help students succeed in grades 8 and 9 by providing more teachers, intensive professional development, and improved tracking of students having difficulties in these grades.

Source: **www.edu.gov.on.ca/eng/6ways/welcome.html**

---

successful completion of the Ontario Secondary School Literacy Test or course. For those students who fail to meet the requirements of the OSSD, an Ontario Secondary School Certificate, which requires 14 credits, may be issued instead.

Recent changes to secondary school graduation requirements, designed to keep students in school until the age of 18, permit students to take more cooperative education courses and receive secondary school credits for experiential learning. These changes also provided funding to secondary schools to employ additional personnel whose responsibility would be to provide assistance to students having difficulty so that they can achieve and meet secondary school graduation requirements. The "Learning to 18" and "Student Success" initiatives established by the Ontario Ministry of Education in 2005 encouraged all students, including those identified as having special needs, to "achieve their potential and succeed in secondary school" (Ontario Ministry of Education, 2005). These initiatives included:

- *Credit Recovery:* a program designed to assist students to complete successfully courses they had previously failed

- *Alternative Education:* programs designed to "re-engage" students who had difficulty succeeding in high school classrooms

- *Student Success in Grades 9 and 10:* Programs designed to assist students to adjust to secondary school curriculum and environment

- *Program Pathways to Apprenticeship and the Workplace:* designed to permit a combination of courses and workplace experiences to earn secondary school credits

- *College Connections:* designed to permit secondary school students to receive credits for completing courses offered by Ontario colleges

- *Success for Targeted Groups of Students:* designed to assist targeted groups such as ESL or Aboriginal students to succeed in high school

In addition to the above initatives, the Ministry of Education currently requires that all students 14 years of age or older (with the exception of those identified as "gifted") have a Transition Plan in place to assist in program planning. The goal of this plan is to assist these students in making a successful transition from school to the workplace, to post-secondary education or to community living. (For more on Transition Plans, see Chapter 5.)

Secondary School: Modifications and Accommodations

It is certainly the goal of all high schools across the province that as many students as possible successfully complete the high school requirements for graduation. With this goal in mind, a number of programs and options are available to assist students. While specifics may vary, most high schools offer program accommodations and modifications in regular classrooms. In most cases, students are accommodated through arrangements made by the special education department. These students may spend a portion of their day receiving extra assistance in a resource room setting, scheduled either as a regular, daily item, or on an as-needed basis. The same students often have modified programs in the regular classroom. Achievement based on these modified learning expectations is assessed in light of provincial requirements and a decision is made by the principal as to whether to grant a high school credit in the subject area.

- *School—work transition programs:* In these programs, currently referred to as Student Success-Pathways, students at risk for failure as well as those identified with learning problems have an opportunity to participate in school-work programs. These programs vary from board to board and consist of a body of course credits developed to deliver adapted high school curriculum. Course work is delivered at a level suitable to these students and there are strong connections between curriculum and workplace knowledge. Students involved in these programs are not prohibited from obtaining an OSSD. However, some courses developed at the local level referred to as "Essentials" courses (such as a Life Skills courses) do not provide credit toward a graduation diploma.

- *Self-contained special education settings:* Self-contained classes for students with developmental disabilities that focus on social and life skills are not uncommon, though many high schools make an effort to ensure that, while a population such as this may be in a self-contained program for curriculum delivery, they are not isolated for the social aspects of the day. Given the lack of post-secondary options available to students with developmental disabilities, it is not uncommon that students with such disabilities remain in school for a longer period of time than most other pupils. Many stay until the compulsory leaving age of 21.

- *Supervised alternative learning for excused pupils programs (SALEP):* At age 14 or 15, students may be considered for an alternative school environment, which may include workplace placement, life skills, or other activities that the school board deems beneficial to the student's needs. Approval for such a program must be obtained from a SALEP committee set up in accordance with Ministry requirements. Students may remain in this program until the age of 16. During that time, these students are considered registered in school and may apply any credits obtained toward an OSSD.

The Service Providers

The number and type of personnel involved in delivery of service to students with exceptionalities usually depends on the nature and extent of the needs. Naturally, service can only be delivered if personnel are available, if the system is organized to flow the service to the need, and if the ever-so-crucial element of cooperation prevails. Fortunately, the combination of professionalism among educators and members of related fields, and the natural disposition to ameliorate the situation of students with special needs, means that, most of the time, the right things happen.

The list of personnel—of service providers— who work with students with exceptionalities in an exceptional setting can be as varied as there are variations among students. By far the most deeply involved in every educational situation are combinations of the following:

- classroom teacher
- educational assistant
- special education teacher (There are many local terms for this role.)

- special consultant

with input from:

- principals
- parents
- school teams
- advisory groups
- advocacy groups
- social agencies
- specialists

"Outside" people typically become involved when a response to special needs requires a particular expertise. They include members from fields like psychiatry, psychology, psychometry, social work, health, speech, physical and occupational therapy. Some boards of education, particularly larger ones, employ members of these professions directly. This is most frequently the case with professionals in the speech area, and with what is often called "psycho-educational services" (or a variation thereof)—usually people who specialize in assessment and counseling. The latter are more involved at the assessment and program planning stages, although sometimes they will also participate in ongoing delivery of service in situations where exceptional behaviour, for example, is a factor.

Deploying the Personnel

An abiding concern of administrators is to get the appropriate resources into the appropriate settings as efficiently and effectively as possible, all with a view to cost, cooperation, and availability. To accomplish this goal, schools and boards generally organize deployment models, or service models—schemas for managing the various elements in delivering service. Once it has been decided that a student is exceptional and is to receive support, there are management factors that must be decided such as:

- How much support will be needed?
- Are the needed resources available?
- Who is providing support?
- How long will the support continue?
- Where does the support take place?

- Who has primary responsibility for the student?
- When and with what frequency will the case be reviewed?

Who Controls the Resources?

Although resource management policies differ across the province, the most common style is a combination of board-wide control of service delivery and individual school responsibility. Schools within a board will typically have a number of resources allocated, often according to a formula based on population but that also recognizes unique school needs. Thus, within a school, one or more special education teachers will have responsibility, under the principal, for allocating available resources and personnel as needed. If there are needs that go beyond a school's allocated resources or unique situations demanding a response, the board will—ideally—enhance the allocations (an outcome, however, that is inevitably shaped by availability and funding). School-based management, because it circumvents time-consuming bureaucracy, can bring service to bear quickly and flexibly, along with a greater likelihood of informal but immediate cooperation and approval from parents. Special needs that require very specialized expertise—blindness for example—is often more effectively managed at the board level, even though the resources will likely be delivered in a neighbourhood school. The combination of board-wide and individual school service delivery seems not only fiscally reasonable and responsible, but also addresses issues of immediacy, flexibility, accountability, and optimum use of resources.

The School Team

A most significant development in the late 1980s and early 1990s was the gradual realization that the mystery of educating students with special needs is not all that different from the mystery of educating any student. Experience has taught that many educational matters that at first glance imply an elaborate response can actually be addressed "in-house." No one denies that expertise continues to be important, and there is no question that dealing with certain types of exceptionality such as, say, hearing loss or blindness, often requires specialization of some kind. Nevertheless, the needs of most students with exceptionalities can usually be met through a healthy application of common sense, the kind of approach that effective teachers use in all of educational practice. At the same time, teachers have found that cases of special need are almost always more effectively addressed when they are the focus of broad concern, of general cooperation and support, rather than the sole responsibility of a single individual. In many schools, this combination of insights has borne fruit in a more or less formal arrangement sometimes referred to as the In-School Team, the Teacher Support Team, the School-Based Support Team, or similar title.

The School Team Concept

A support or assistance team is a committee of staff members organized to advise and consult with individual teachers who request assistance regarding students perceived as having special needs. The team neither precludes nor replaces formal special education nor diminishes it in any way. Rather, it supports special education, and helps it function more effectively in a school, and more efficiently. In many schools, the team is a forum of first resort to which teachers and parents may bring concerns about the special needs of particular students, without formally invoking special education procedures. This practice not only tends to keep students in the mainstream, but also, by offering this pre-referral opportunity, a team helps to free its school's special education personnel to bring resources to bear where needs are greatest. A team can also enhance service delivery simply by offering broader involvement. Perhaps most important—to teachers and students equally—a team can be a vital instigator of professionalism: the kind of drive that leads a staff to seek solutions. (For more on the school team see Chapter 5.)

The Multidisciplinary Team Concept

For particularly demanding exceptional cases, service delivery is sometimes managed by a multidisciplinary team in which educators share membership with professionals who have specialized expertise. The situation, for example, of a student with multiple needs, such as severe physical disabilities along with fragile health and possibly behavioural or developmental problems, may require the services of a variety of personnel. For this student, a multidisciplinary team may come together only once or twice on a more or less ad hoc basis, usually in an advisory capacity and most often at the initial stages when the student's placement and programming are being established. Ongoing delivery of service will usually be the responsibility of only certain members of the team.

An area of difficulty with the multidisciplinary team approach in educational settings is management and organization. Since the approach is used almost exclusively in cases of extensive need, there is sometimes disagreement over priority in meeting the needs (education? social? physical well-being?). Also, the mere task of bringing together a team of otherwise occupied, diverse professionals is awkward and time-consuming, and usually requires the authority (i.e., for budget, for freeing personnel from other obligations, etc.) of someone in an upper-level administrative role. As well, because there is such wide involvement, ultimate responsibility for the student—even legal responsibility—may become an issue. Difficulties like these often force serious consideration of a quite restricted placement like special day school or residential facility simply because the situation is easier to manage in such a setting.

The Expanding Role of Educational Assistants (Paraprofessionals*)

> *Something you'll notice right away is there's a lot of teachers who don't know what to do with an EA! Not their fault really, any more than it's ours but it's an issue you have to work out.*
>
> Kana V. graduate of an EA program speaking to undergraduates

When special education first became mandatory in Ontario, support personnel, if any such existed at all in a school, were usually found in self-contained classrooms or in a special school where students with extensive needs were placed. Rarely were they found in regular classrooms. That reality changed dramatically over time so that today educational assistants play a role in regular classrooms as a matter of course and, indeed, are much sought after as important contributors in the delivery of service. Their role expanded significantly once inclusion became established as the normative style in the province's schools so that it is not unusual now for both teachers and parents to expect that if students with special needs are placed in a class, an EA will be there too.

What Do EAs Do?

Both the assistants themselves and the teachers they work with, as well as principals and parents, tend to answer this question with "Anything and everything!" A central role, or at least an ideal one, is active teaching of special education students under guidelines established by the teacher and the Individual Education Plan. The teaching takes many forms from direct instruction to remediation to supervision of repeated practice. Very often an EA's instruction of a student with special needs is one-on-one in order to expand or reinforce a concept or skill that other

* As a professional designation, support personnel in classrooms are sometimes described as "paraprofessionals" like their counterparts in medicine and law, "paramedics" and "paralegals". In education, the term "educational assistant" (EA) continues to be popular.

students in a regular classroom have grasped more readily. This will be the case especially in larger, busy classes where demands on the classroom teacher are multiple.

Assistants may observe and record data for a variety of purposes, particularly for assessments wherein recorded observation plays a key role. They may be involved in things as complex as helping develop an IEP, or as straightforward as responsibility for classroom supplies. Among other contributions, EAs tutor, help manage general classroom conduct, modify educational materials, become part of a school team, provide health needs support, and—often a very important role—provide behaviour management support. What they do is, in short, anything and everything.

Cooperative Efforts

The practice of teaming teachers and educational assistants is now fully established in most Ontario schools, and many students with special needs and their teachers rely on the involvement of educational assistants to ensure that the student can progress behaviourally, socially, and academically throughout the school year. Unfortunately, in many instances the precise role of the EA is still rather undefined. It is often left to both professional and paraprofessional to establish working relationships in a classroom as best they can. The situation can be fraught with all the risks found in any human interchange. Anecdotal evidence, for example, is reported from time to time of EAs being given (or taking) ownership of a special needs case, particularly a behaviour issue, or of EAs "wasting away" because a classroom teacher—who is highly unlikely to have received any pre- or post-service preparation in working with another adult in the classroom—is reluctant to share or delegate responsibility. Fortunately, the vast majority of teacher/EA relationships work out positively. It takes time and experience to establish that the purpose of the educational assistant role is not to replace the teacher but to support what goes on in the classroom, and to appreciate that by working cooperatively, two committed adults can fulfill the ultimate goal of all educators: helping students to learn and grow.

Qualifications

At time of publication, Ontario had no legislation precisely addressing the qualifications of educational assistants, although many school boards have their own prerequisites, a policy strongly supported by the Ontario CEC (Council for Exceptional Children). A number of colleges in the province offer impressive educational assistant programs.

Demchak, M., & Morgan, C. R. (1998). Effective collaboration between professionals and paraprofessionals. *Rural Special Education Quarterly*, 17(2), 10-16.

Dworet, D., & Bennett, S. (2002). A view from the North: Special education in Canada. *Teaching Exceptional Children*, 34(5). 22-27.

Fisher, D. (1999). According to their peers: Inclusion as high school students see it. *Mental Retardation*, 37(6), 65-69.

French, N. K. (1998). Working together: Resource teachers and paraeducators. *Remedial and Special Education*, 19, 357-368.

French, N. K. (1999). Para-educators: Who are they and what do they do? *Teaching Exceptional Children*, 32(1), 65-69.

Hunt, P. & Gotez, L. (1997). Research on inclusive educational programs, practices and outcomes for students with severe disabilities. *Journal of Special Education*, 31, 3-29.

Jones, K. H. & Bender W. N. (1993). Utilization of paraprofessionals in special education: A review of the literature. *Remedial and Special Education* 14(1), 7-14.

Lusthaus, E. & Lusthaus, C. (1992). From segregation to full inclusion: an evaluation. *Exceptionality Education Canada*, 2, 95-115.

Minke, K. M., Bear, G. G., Deemer, S. A. & Griffin S. M. (1996). Teachers' experiences with inclusive classrooms: implications for special education reform. *Journal of Special Education*, 30, 152-186.

Morsink C. V., & Lenk L. L. (1992). The delivery of special education programs and services. *Remedial and Special Education*, 13, 33-43.

Ontario Ministry of Education (2007). *Shared Solutions: A guide to preventing and resolving conflicts regarding programs and services for students with special needs*. Ontario: Queen's Printer for Ontario.

Pickett, A. L., & Gerlach, K. (1997). Supervising para-educators in school settings: A team approach. Austin, TX: Pro-Ed.

Smith, W. & Lusthaus, C. (1993). Students with disabilities in Canada: What rights do they have? *Education Canada*, 5(9), 45- 46.

Smith, T. E. C., Polloway, E. A., Patton, J. R. Dowdy, C. A., Heath, N. H. (2001). *Teaching Students with Special Needs in Inclusive Settings* (Canadian Edition) Toronto: Allyn and Bacon

Thousand, J., Rosenberg, R. L., Bishop, K. D., & Villa, R. A. (1997). The evolution of secondary inclusion. *Remedial and Special Education*, 18(5), 270-284, 306.

Wang, M. C., Walberg, H. J. & Reynolds, M. C. (1992). A scenario for better—not separate-special education. *Educational Leadership*, 50, 35-41.

Winzer, Margret. (2008). *Children with Exceptionalities in Canadian Classrooms*, 8th edition, Toronto: Pearson Prentice Hall

Ontario Ministry of Education (1999). *Ontario Secondary School, Grades 9 to 12*, Toronto: Queen's Printer for Ontario

Ontario Ministry of Education (2005). *Strategies for Student Success*. Toronto: Queen's Printer for Ontario

Links

Authors' note: Many Ontario school boards have developed modified programs for students with exceptionalities, especially in secondary schools. The substance of these programs, along with descriptions of service delivery methods, can usually be found on board websites. School board websites can be accessed via **http://sbinfo.edu.gov.on.ca/**

Ontario Ministry of Education Website **http://www.edu.gov.on.ca/eng/parents/speced.html**

Special Needs Ontario Window

http://snow.utoronto.ca

CHAPTER 5

The Individual Education Plan (IEP)
A Team Approach

*"Special education cannot be defined in a single statement. It is a process,
a journey that takes different shapes for different students at different times
in their educational careers. An IEP provides the roadmap for
the completion of that journey."*

Andrea J., principal

The Case of Ms. Kumar

When Ms. Kumar found out she would be having a grade 2 class in September (her first job since graduating), she immediately began to develop and collect materials for the new school year. She came into the school early to decorate her class and make the room feel welcoming. Ms. Kumar learned from her principal that she would be having 18 grade 2s, all of whom had had little difficulty in the grade 1 program.

During the first two weeks of school, despite a few minor adjustments and the establishment of classroom practices, Ms. Kumar's class seemed to settle into an active and productive routine. At the beginning of the third week of school, a new child moved into the neighbourhood. Joey was of grade 2 age but had not yet attended regular school. He had spent senior kindergarten and grade 1 in a day treatment program for children with social/emotional difficulties. His mother had not informed the school of Joey's history and he began school on the Monday in Ms. Kumar's room.

Within the first hour it became obvious that something was wrong. Joey had become very frustrated at journal writing time and got out of his desk frequently. At one point, Joey decided that another child was bothering him, got out of his seat and spat on the child's desk. When Ms. Kumar reprimanded him, he responded by swearing at her and running from the room.

When Joey's mom came to get him at the end of the day, she confessed that she was extremely worried about her son. She had been afraid to tell the school too much about Joey's background in the hope that perhaps a new school meant a fresh start. The principal explained that Joey was now a member of their school and that in this school both teachers and she were willing to do everything in their power to plan and implement a program that would meet Joey's needs.

While Ms. Kumar agrees philosophically with the ideal espoused by the principal, she feels ill equipped to deal with a child with such complex problems. What she feels would be helpful is some form of written guide with specific directions and ideas.

A Roadmap

Planning is an integral component of effective teaching practice. As a matter of course, teachers carefully consider how new learning is to be presented and absorbed, and develop lesson and unit plans to meet that end. For a majority of students, those who fall within what, for lack of a better term, is considered to be the normal range, lesson plans and goals are usually not differentiated to any significant degree. But in the case of students with exceptionalities, planning becomes more complex because their needs, learning characteristics, and abilities are more diverse and challenging. A different, more individualized planning approach is usually necessary. Experience in special education has taught that this differentiated approach is best achieved in what educators know as an Individual Education Plan, an "IEP." For students with exceptionalities, an IEP encompasses both the goal of the teaching enterprise and the directions needed to meet that goal. A popular metaphor for the IEP—*roadmap*—seems apt, for without such a map, the educational process can get off track and both students and educator can become lost or find themselves in a place not intended.

A properly constructed and executed IEP provides consistency, continuity, and clarity of purpose. It allows educators to act within the requirements of their job, but permits them flexibility to adjust curriculum activities and assessments in a planned and systematic way to support their student. An IEP provides specific guidelines for the direction of a student's program, but always allows for the day-to-day adjustments required for any teaching-learning situation. And as a roadmap, an IEP ensures that everyone knows the destination, knows what direction to take, and is in agreement on how to get there.

The Roadmap as Policy

Until the late 1990s in Ontario, the development of an Individual Education Plan for every exceptional student was not required (albeit implied in a Ministry document called *Schools General*). Yet for most Ontario teachers, as with their colleagues in other jurisdictions, using IEPs in various forms and designs had become pretty much standard practice by this time. Therefore, when the province revised and reissued its regulation governing the identification and placement of students with special needs in 1998, making IEPs a clear and official requirement, most educators in the province were already experienced with them.

The Policy Requirements*

Ontario's *Regulation 181/98* requires principals to ensure an Individual Education Plan is developed for every student identified "exceptional" by an Identification, Placement and Review Committee (IPRC; see Chapter 6). It is also the case that an IEP may be developed for students who have not been through the IPRC process but are experiencing difficulty meeting learning expectations, and are deemed by the school board to need special services or educational programs.

In each of the situations above, an IEP must include

- stated reason for developing the plan
- specific educational expectations
- an outline of the special education program and services to be provided to the student
- a description of the methods that will be used to review the student's progress

When an IEP is the part of the IPRC process, principals must ensure the plan is developed within thirty school days after the student is placed in a special education program, *and must ensure it is completed in consultation with the parent* (and the student if 16 years or older). The plan must take into account recommendations by the IPRC that identified the student. A copy of the completed plan must be forwarded to parents (and to 16-plus students) within the 30-day time frame. A copy of the plan must also be included in the student's Ontario Student Record (OSR). In those cases where an IEP is not the result of an IPRC process the timelines are less well defined.

• • • ⎯⎯⎯

* For specifics see *Individual Education Plans, Standards for Development, Program Planning and Implementation* (Ministry of Education, 2000).

⎯⎯⎯ • • •

What an IEP *is...*

✔ a written plan of action for a student whose needs require modification of a regular school program

✔ a document containing a summary of the student's strengths and needs, a statement of goals and expectations, and essential information regarding resources, program, teaching strategies, personnel, etc.

✔ an ongoing, flexible document, developed by school staff, in collaboration with parents and the student where appropriate, usually under the leadership of one or two persons supported by a team

✔ a document made available to teachers, assistants, resource personnel, administrators, parents, and the student where appropriate so that all concerned can direct their energies to the same purposes.

What an IEP *is not...*

✘ a detailed account of every minute of a student's day. An overly detailed and minutely controlled plan would be impossible to implement in a classroom.

✘ an individual effort on the part of the special education teacher to fulfill Ministry requirements. An IEP created in isolation, without the input of personnel and family directly involved with the student, risks becoming merely a superfluous bureaucratic necessity rather than an effective and meaningful document.

✘ a document that, once completed, sits in a file unexamined until the next review. For an IEP to be effective it must be utilized and monitored. It is a living document that requires ongoing development and examination by everyone working with the student.

IPRC and IEP Are Both Needed?

As noted earlier, when an IPRC is in place, an IEP must be developed within a required time frame and shared with parents. In 2007, the Ministry of Education released a recommendation that school boards consider dispensing with the IPRC process in cases where students spend a majority of their time in the regular class and where things were progressing well. In those cases, the IPRC can be seen as administratively burdensome and redundant to a process that is meeting the needs of the student and skipping the procedure. This allows schools and parents to act quickly in a collaborative manner to meet the needs of the students.

It is in those cases where the situation may be more complex or perhaps acrimonious that an IPRC is an essential. Currently, the IPRC process is the only legislative vehicle for ensuring the timely development of an IEP as well as the inclusion of parents, and students 16 and older, in the decision-making process. The IPRC process also allows for appeals by the parties involved and for decision-making that goes beyond the level of the school and school board

should difficulties arise. It is important to remember that parents and principals within the province of Ontario can at any time call for an IPRC when either party deems it necessary for the success of a student.

Preparing IEPs

All IEPs, both those that result from an IPRC process as well as those that are created collaboratively at the school level, follow a well-defined set procedures for development. For all students, the implementation of an IEP is a serious undertaking and must never be confused with the types of accommodations and/or adjustments that educators as competent and caring professionals do on a day-to-day basis for students within a learning environment. The adjustment of a desk, flexible time frames for production of work, repeating, or individually instructing a student on a particular concept are all parts of what would be considered normal teaching practice. It can be difficult for educators at times to see the clear line between what is acceptable adjustment and when that adjustment becomes a need for the development of an IEP. The reason that this determination is difficult is because the line is seldom clear! As with almost every aspect of the teaching endeavour, which is by nature a dynamic process, decisions have to be made in complex and ever-changing circumstances. That is why the development of an IEP must be a team process that takes place over a period of time that looks at existing data, collects information that is needed, communicates with stakeholders, and is monitored throughout. In the steps that follow there is always flexibility in who is involved, what information is collected, and when or if the process needs to be continued or stopped.

Steps in the Process

The sequence presented here represents a pattern suggested by the Ministry of Education. For the most part, although individual boards in the province frequently add their own variations, all of them generally follow these steps.

I. Gathering information

II. Setting the direction

III. Developing the IEP

IV. Implementing the IEP

V. Reviewing and updating

I. Gathering information

From the OSR: For each student in the province, a continuing record called the Ontario Student Record (OSR) is maintained and continually updated. The OSR, then, is a logical place to start gathering details for preparation of an IEP. Information such as previous report cards and reports by teachers and other professional staff, medical information, and—very important—*school history* are customarily available in this file. Especially useful documents often found in the OSR are a student's previous IEPs.

Among other details to be gathered in order to develop an IEP will be the reason(s) an IEP is needed in the first place. This information may come from a recent or even a past IPRC, from a special education teacher, a parent, or school team. Additional information, e.g., whether the student requires specialized health support services, will also be included if appropriate. Information on specialized equipment if applicable, listings of dates of consultations with parents, etc., may also be included. The information will vary case by case, and will range from specific details such as those recorded in an OSR to current, ongoing contributions like the following.

Insights from key persons: Information from people who have different insights and perspectives on a student is valuable in the development of the IEP. The classroom teacher and in many cases the educational assistant have the most contact with a particular student and the information that they can provide is essential. Yet neither of these individuals works alone and will not have all the answers. Parents, principals, special education teachers, previous teachers, other professionals, and indeed students themselves, where appropriate, can and should contribute. Parents, most of the time, have an in-depth understanding of their child. Having seen progress (or lack of it) from year to year, they have a picture no one else has. That picture will most likely have important features such as updated medical information, likes and dislikes, other community involvement, relevant family information, etc.

Formal tests: If the appropriate professionals are available to administer standardized assessments (e.g., an IQ test, standardized achievement tests, etc.) and if the results from such tests will help inform the process, then these are a useful resource. In most cases, test results will not be as important, at least initially, as the careful, daily, in-the-classroom observations of teachers and educational assistants. Formal tests tend to be more important in situations that are at the relatively

> *A team is everybody and that is why we have such a diversity of people: so that they will come from different backgrounds in their teaching. I know I don't know everything and I don't think there is any one person who knows everything, but if we have a group, we can pool our knowledge and come up with the best for the student.*
>
> A. Walsh, special education resource teacher

complex or intractable end of the scale. Indeed, it is not unheard of for students to be trapped in a sort of testing limbo where the school and parents see the need for differentiated programming but waiting lists for standardized assessments are staggeringly long. Therefore, it is important that the use of formal tests be judicious, and administered in a timely fashion so that development of an effective plan does not stagnate.

Classroom observations: For many years, special education suffered from an image as the realm of experts and specialists. Nowhere was this mystique more prevalent than in the area of assessment. Surprisingly, the perception persists. Special education teachers, just like teacher-librarians or computer specialists, do indeed possess some expert knowledge and training, but it does not replace the essential role that regular classroom teachers or educational assistants play in gathering crucial information. Front-line personnel can assess things like the students' interaction with text, how they respond to new tasks, whether they work best in groups or individually, their response to authority and routines, and their response to environmental conditions such as lighting and noise level. Information like this may be recorded in a variety of formats: anecdotal records, checklists, interviews of students and others, even audio/visual recordings. No matter where or in what form this information is recorded, it is most valuable.

Student's work: Samples of a student's previous and current work reveals strengths, needs, and rates of progress. Portfolios of student work, test papers, journal entries, assignments, and artwork all contribute insights. Comparing samples of individual student's work throughout the year not only provides valuable information but much needed validation. In teaching, because the work is in such small units, progress is hard to discern at times and the perception that "we are getting nowhere" persists. A cumulative representative sampling of a student's work over time can not only demonstrate progress but also point out the direction to proceed.

In most cases, the types of information above will offer enough substance to develop an IEP. Naturally, there are situations where it is necessary to return to the sources and dig deeper or wider. In some cases, additional personnel and resources may be needed to conduct other types of assessments (e.g., diagnostic tests). As well, especially in the case of students with special physical or health needs, a school may seek information from medical professionals (although this is almost always done with the help, and certainly the permission, of parents).

II: Setting the Direction

The Strength of Team

Ideally, after the basic information is gathered, a collaborative approach involving staff, parents, and the student (where appropriate) comes into play to establish the plan itself, for the simple reason that involving more than one person in the development of an IEP almost always produces a more thorough, relevant, and creative plan. Most schools in Ontario already have in place some form of active school team* that meets on a regular basis to share information about students with special needs. Accordingly, these teams, with members added on an ad hoc basis (i.e., people with a stake in the case, like the classroom teacher, assistant, parent, etc.), are commonly used to shape and give direction to IEPs.

A school team generally includes the principal (or designate), certain classroom teachers, educational assistants, appointed by the principal, and the school's special education teacher(s), along with ad hoc members. The principal (or designate) is usually responsible for the establishment and maintenance of the team approach to IEP development, but all members of the team play an important role. Each one has a perspective in terms of the information he or she can offer and the support or services he or she may be able to provide. This is where collaboration finds its strength. Once the different perspectives are aired and consolidated, with both the professional and the personal insights that everyone has to offer, the results invariably generate a more complete picture of the student's strengths and needs, along with a more informed and more creative set of strategies and actions for implementation.

• • • ──────

* Also known by other titles like In-School Team, School Support Team, Special Support Team, or just School Team.
────── • • •

Mr. Pickett has taught English to grades 9, 10, and 11 for some years now, and has always felt he does a good job. His peers would agree and note that Mr. Pickett always seems well prepared for his classes, has innovative ideas, and students seem to enjoy being in his class. In the past, under the direction of the previous principal, any students receiving special education support were withdrawn from Mr. Pickett's class and programmed for solely by the special education resource teacher. While Mr. Pickett has never objected to implementing some of the special education resource teacher's suggestions in his class, he has always been comfortable in the knowledge that the primary responsibility for a student's program rested elsewhere. This year, under a new principal, the focus of special education service delivery has shifted, with the primary responsibility of the programming for students who are exceptional now placed squarely on the shoulders of regular classroom teachers, assisted by the special education resource teacher.

This year, Mr. Pickett has two students identified as learning disabled. Both read far below grade level and require a great deal of assistance in completing any written work. He has been reluctant to take ownership for their program and is very resistant to altering his teaching practices in any significant way to accommodate their needs. Although he does not share this with the rest of the staff, Mr. Pickett has grave doubts about his ability to program for the two, fearing he lacks the necessary expertise. He is willing to help them, but does not feel he has the skills.

An in-school team meeting has been called this week to discuss the students. Mr. Pickett, while not a regular member of the in-school team, has been asked to provide in advance some information about these students and then attend the meeting to discuss the students. He is unsure of what kind of information he should provide; nor is he sure about how much he can or should tell the team about modifications and accommodations he has already tried with the students. Mr. Pickett is feeling very hesitant and would like some guidance.

Alternative Styles

Notwithstanding the creative power of a school team for developing IEPs, there are schools in the province where this style is not used. Although Ontario provincial policy specifically requires an IEP be prepared for all students identified exceptional, it does not stipulate that a team be used anywhere in the process (even though it is clear, in its support and explanatory materials that the Ministry of Education strongly supports the team principle). Therefore, in some schools the entire IEP process is begun, developed, written, implemented, and monitored by one or two persons. Most frequently, where this approach is taken, that responsibility rests with the school's special education teacher(s). Nevertheless, because this teacher will be running a number of IEPs, what happens in practice is that he or she works very closely with the classroom teacher and educational assistant of the student concerned. And since the parent is involved too, in many cases, and possibly one or two supporting professionals (e.g., speech and language) even this "single-responsibility" style is, in effect, collaborative.

III: Developing the IEP

After the information is consolidated and checked for accuracy, and after any gaps are filled and possible discrepancies resolved, the material is then summarized on the IEP form that the board or school uses. Many school boards develop and use IEP forms tailored to their own practices. In Ontario, by far the majority of these forms follow the format suggested by the Ministry of Education. Recently the Ministry of Education completed an audit on existing forms of IEPs across the province and discussion is underway for the development of a mandatory provincial template. Formats are continually being tweaked but the most current information can always be found on the Ministry of Education web site at **www.edu.gov.on.ca**. (The authors recommend that teachers and educational assistants be familiar with both the Ministry form and the form currently utilized in their own school board.) Whatever form a board uses, an IEP will almost always be developed with attention to the following essential components.

List strengths and needs: (Much of this part will come from the observations gathered in the first phase of the process.) Including the student's strengths and needs is a prelude to understanding the program modifications that need to be set up. A strength might be expressed as "…has creative ideas for stories and has good story comprehension." A need might be expressed as "…to develop an understanding and application of mathematical concepts." Strengths listed in an IEP must reflect areas where a student has effective learning skills as well as those learning modalities or styles that contribute to the student's success in learning. Stated needs should be drawn directly from assessments and related directly to the areas for which the IEP is being developed. (In those cases where a student has been through an IPRC, strengths and needs listed in an IEP must be consistent with those listed in a student's IPRC statement.)

Establish goals and expectations: Goals state what a student would reasonably be expected to achieve by the end of a school year within a particular curriculum area or skill. *Goals* are considered more global targets for students (e.g., "The student will develop basic computational skills in mathematics."). *Expectations,* on the other hand, are more specific about what the student will be doing (e.g., "The student will be able to recite subtraction facts between 1 and 18."). Expectations should reflect what a student is expected to attain within each reporting period and be written in a way that is observable and measurable. Both goals and expectations should be based directly on the Ontario curriculum when academic performance is being modified. Reporting on the progress of these expectations must be linked with the provincial report card and the progress or lack thereof will serve as a guidepost for both educators and parents as to the necessity of tweaking or continuing the goals and methods set out in the IEP. Alternative goals and expectations for such things as addressing the physical or behavioural needs of a student are also listed in IEPs and reviewed regularly.

Specify strategies and resources: Once goals and expectations are outlined, the task then becomes one of choosing strategies and identifying resources, including personnel, that will be used to help the student and teachers meet them. This section of an IEP stipulates what materials will

---

What's On an IEP Form?

Official forms vary, sometimes quite widely, from board to board, even from school to school. Fortunately, the majority of school boards now follow the template provided by the Ministry of Education. It requires the following information, even though headings may differ.

✓ reason for development of IEP
✓ student profile
✓ assessment data
✓ special supports and services required
✓ student strengths and needs
✓ accommodations (common to all subject areas)
✓ annual program goals
✓ current level of achievement for specific subject areas
✓ learning expectations for specific subject areas
✓ teaching strategies for specific subject areas
✓ assessment methods for specific subject areas
✓ personnel involved in the development of the IEP
✓ Transition Plan (if required)
✓ human resources
✓ review and update information

Except for demographics, not every section of a form will be filled in every time. The abiding problem of *available time* that confronts all teachers means that in practice emphasis will likely be given to the issues that are most relevant in a particular case.

---

be used, what programs and teaching methods will be employed, and who will work with the student, how often, and where.

Monitor the results: A crucial step in the development of an IEP is establishing the features of a monitoring cycle: student progress must be reviewed at least once every reporting period and the results of that progress indicated on the provincial report card. Decisions such as who will track the student's progress, how the record keeping will be handled, who will be responsible for communicating to whom, and what is the time frame for accomplishing the goals, need to be addressed.

> *An IEP is not a pristine piece of paper filed in the OSR and referred to only on occasion. Rather, it is a working document to be filled with crossed-out expectations and remedial attempts, scribbled revisions, and Post-it reminders. It resides on the teacher's desk providing easy access to all concerned during the instructional day.*
>
> R. Daigle, superintendent

Special Case: The Transition Plan

For students 14 and older, with the exception of students identified as gifted, regulations require schools to include a Transition Plan in his or her IEP. The plan is designed to allow for a smooth transition from school to school and/or school to workplace or training centre. It must include specific transition goals and actions required to achieve those goals (e.g., in the case of a student who is deaf who plans on post-secondary education, a plan would identify those institutions especially geared to meeting that special need; in the case of a student with a developmental delay, the plan might identify work and community living options). Under the regulation, the principal is responsible for consulting with appropriate community agencies and/or post-secondary institutions for purposes of completing a meaningful Transition Plan. For more information and samples of Transition Plans, access the Ministry of Education website **www.edu.gov.on.ca** for the document *Transition Planning: A Resource Guide 2002.*

IV: Implementing the IEP

Implementation of an IEP centres around communication and practical application. Teachers and/or educational assistants who will be delivering service to the student need to be informed and prepared for upcoming changes (although, if a collaborative process has been used, it is very likely that key personnel will have been involved in the plan from the beginning). Parents need to be informed of changes and adjustments. The plan itself is translated into the day-to-day operation of the classroom with all practical considerations being taken into account. At the same time, a monitoring system is established, because even though an IEP will be updated at least once every reporting period, it must always be viewed as a working document, one that evolves and develops as new information arises. There are very few IEPs that do not require some modifications early on.

Once again, it is important to point out that the IEP does not cover every minute of every day in the student with an exceptionality's school life. It is a document that records generally how a modified-from-regular program will be conducted and monitored.

V: Reviewing and Updating the IEP

A student's IEP needs to be reviewed each reporting period. Considerations in such a review would include:

- Does the plan still reflect the student's needs?
- Are the strategies and resources still effective?
- Is the student progressing at the rate expected?
- Should changes be made to the assignment of responsibility?
- Has any new information emerged that means the plan should change?
- Is the student displaying responsibility and commitment to the learning process?
- Are family/student commitments in the plan being carried out?

Assigning Primary Responsibility

In most schools, IEPs are developed collaboratively, ideally by an "In-school Team" or "School Team" under the direction of the principal. However, because of the inevitable time constraints in a typical school, and for reasons of efficiency, the primary responsibility for preparation of an IEP is often undertaken by one person, or sometimes two. Very often, that primary person is the classroom teacher of the student under consideration, or one of the school's special education teachers (often called resource teachers), or the two of them in concert, along with the educational assistant. The teacher(s) having primary responsibility will almost certainly have been central in gathering the basic information and also, after consultation with the in-school team, will likely take responsibility for writing the plan, for seeing to its implementation, and may oversee or perhaps actually perform the monitoring of progress. In a well-run system, however, the primary persons do not work unsupported, for the school team is always there for consultation, assistance, and an insertion of fresh ideas.

Dangers and Trouble Spots

Despite the appeal of IEPs, and even though experience has proven their value, there are some potential difficulties to be aware of, both in preparation and implementation. Some teachers feel they are ill equipped to develop what they consider a radical departure from their normal planning. Even teachers with training in special education may have little experience in coordinating a team and developing plans. There can often be confusion, if not tension, over who has responsibility for the various components of the process. And, even though a multidisciplinary approach is useful, a lack of systematic training for school personnel and sporadic attendance at meetings can make the approach difficult to maintain.

Some educators are concerned that the relatively formal nature of the IEP creates yet another level of bureaucracy, and thereby moves education even farther away from its intended recipient, the student. The use of computer programs to develop IEPs, and programs that spin out computer-generated strategies to complete a plan, have raised legitimate concerns over weak paper compliance to the very important IEP process. Yet paper compliance is a natural response for teachers faced with increased workload, heavy demands from administration and parents, excessive paperwork, insufficient support, and lack of training. One entirely legitimate criticism of the IEP form recommended by the Ministry of Education is that, notwithstanding its theoretical excellence, it is too demanding a document for the typically overwhelmed teacher to maintain well.

Ultimately, an IEP is only a tool. A proven one, but a tool nevertheless. To put it to effective use requires the same skills, resources, and above all, *willingness*, that any other educational tool requires. One way to circumvent possible problems with an IEP and to ensure a more beneficial outcome is to manage its preparation and implementation through the power of a school team. Experience proves that a team approach to the IEP not only enhances the quality of an IEP, it also offers greater likelihood that its contents and its ideals will take effect.

The In-School Team

The Role a Team Plays

The role and the style of an in-school team vary from school to school and board to board. Some schools have teams that meet on a regular, scheduled basis; others meet only when a certain number of students have been referred for discussion. Some teams meet to help a teacher with ideas for students who are having only mild difficulty, while other teams meet only if a child is already identified as exceptional or at risk of being so. Team style and function depends on a variety of other factors, too, like the expertise, experience, and beliefs of the staff, the nature of the student population, and the needs of the school. There are some schools, for example, that organize the team role quite bureaucratically, making it official policy that any student being considered for presentation to an Identification, Placement and Review Committee or for the development of an IEP must first be presented to the team. Other schools involve the team only after an IPRC has identified a student as exceptional and therefore in need of an IEP. Still others use a combination of these two approaches. Still, although there is wide variation in the types of in-school teams at work in Ontario, and an equally wide variation in the way their strengths are put to use, one very important, widespread, and effective role for this group is the collaborative development of Individual Education Plans.

Who Is On the Team?

Usually, a team has a relatively permanent core of people, e.g., the principal (or designate), classroom teachers, and special education teacher. Other teachers, professionals, parents, and advocates may be added to suit the needs of an individual case. The group works as a team, but each member usually has a particular role in the team process, a role defined by a variety of factors: their knowledge base, their experience with the student under consideration or, in general, their capacity to provide information or support at a particular level.

❖ *The principal* (or designate) is nominally the head of the team. From a purely practical perspective, administrative power is needed for scheduling, and for making personnel and resources available. Usually, it is the principal who assigns one team member to carry primary responsibility for a particular IEP. The principal is also officially responsible for meeting provincial requirements (time lines for developing a plan, notifying participants, storing information, etc.). Research on effective in-school teams suggests that strong administrative support is a key factor in the success of any in-school team.

❖ A *special education teacher* in a school is often the person assigned the responsibility for scheduling, chairing, and maintaining the records for team meetings. Usually, he or

she is the teacher on the team with skills and training in assessment, as well as the person with the readiest access to a multitude of program modification ideas and additional resources. In most cases, the special education teacher plays a direct role in the implementation of strategies, or else arranges for implementation. It may be the special education teacher who describes and models a new technique for a classroom teacher, arranges for support personnel, works with the student directly, etc. The special education teacher is also a gatekeeper of sorts. He or she communicates regularly with other professionals (e.g., speech and language pathologists, counsellors, assessment services) and is usually the one who can access these resources, depending on the decisions of the team.

At the high school level where students attend multiple classes and can face complex schedules and demands, the role of the special education teacher is somewhat different than in an elementary setting. In many high schools, the special education teacher, sometimes called the SERT or special education resource teacher, has additional responsibilities of coordination with regard to ensuring that all teachers are kept up to date with the important information they need to work with students who have difficulties. Also at the high school level, interventions, such as student success classrooms which are set up slightly differently from board to board but whose fundamental task is working with students who are at risk, have entered the landscape. Initially, the relationship between these types of classrooms and practices and special education was relatively unclear but over time and with Ministry direction there is now an understanding that school success classes and high school special education services are fundamentally linked. After all, in any logical world it would seem clear that in many cases the same population of students (with the exception of those with more serious cognitive and physical difficulties) are being served. Perhaps there are some lingering confusions over who is in charge, so to speak, but given that the student is at the

> *It's not so much that I shell out advice, because if that were the case we would not hear the expertise of others. I more or less stimulate the discussion, try to encourage suggestions from other members of the team, bounce ideas off them. They bounce ideas off each other, so, in a way, I am a facilitator.*
>
> Joan C., special education resource teacher

centre of what we do as educators, including anyone who can contribute to the overall success of the student is essential to the discussion.

❖ Many teams have *classroom teachers* as regular members who attend every meeting whether or not the student being discussed is in their class. Their role is to help generate solutions for students in difficulty and to provide support for implementing these solutions. Regular classroom teachers provide information about curriculum expectations in particular grades; they are aware of combinations of students who may be appropriate for social interventions with students having difficulty; classroom teachers have the best line into school sports and clubs and other activities. They are also a creative source of ideas. Representation from each school division on an elementary team, or from subject areas in the case of secondary schools, provides a better-rounded pool from which to draw information and solutions.

The Case of Ms. Wall

The grade 4/5 split that Ms. Wall was assigned this year presented quite a few challenges in classroom management. Like many experienced teachers, she has a repertoire of strategies to maintain class attention and, while they are effective for many of the students, the behaviour of one student, Audrey, has led her to seek extra support and ideas from the in-school team.

Audrey first came to the school at the beginning of grade 3. She had been identified as developmentally delayed but had always been in a regular class. During the grade 3 year, many discussions were held with concerned individuals, including the parents, as to how to best meet Audrey's academic needs. A suggestion that she move to a segregated class was considered but rejected. Now, with the increasing academic demands in the grade 4 setting, Ms. Wall is seeing what she considers a dramatic change in Audrey's behaviour. Audrey has become extraordinarily quiet and withdrawn. She does not participate in class discussions and spends much of her time staring out the window. In music class, which used to be her favourite subject, Audrey keeps her head down and does not seem to have learned any of the songs.

At the first team meeting, attended by the principal, special education teacher, two regular classroom teachers, and Ms. Wall, it was decided that Audrey's curriculum expectations be decreased with a focus on basic instruction. This instruction would be delivered in part by the special education teacher in a resource room but, for a majority of the program, Audrey would stay in the regular class with Ms. Wall getting planning help from the special education teacher. It was also decided that Audrey would join the grade 1 class for music as an assistant to the teacher and to help the students learn and sing the songs. The immediate result was that Audrey seemed to regain her interest in music. She relishes being "assistant teacher" and in her grade 4 class, Audrey has begun to participate, not just in music class, but in her other subjects as well.

As the team meets to review her case, there are several concerns. Ms. Wall is making every effort to incorporate the curriculum changes but sees a broadening gap between Audrey's achievements and what is expected of the rest of the class. Audrey's parents are encouraged by the progress but are also concerned about Audrey's ability to fit in academically and socially. They have accepted the school's invitation to attend the meeting, called to come up with what everyone feels would be the best plan to meet Audrey's academic and emotional needs.

❖ *A classroom teacher who is an ad hoc team member* because the student under consideration is in his or her class, will have similar, but slightly more onerous responsibilities. Usually, this teacher will collect much of the assessment data, often in collaboration with the special education teacher. He or she will bring in observations of the student's behaviour and work habits across a variety of settings and subject areas, samples of work, results of teacher-made tests, and information gathered through discussions with family members or other involved persons. Perhaps most important, the regular classroom teacher will likely be the person to carry out instructional plans generated by the team, and he or she must, therefore, make sure the rest of the team understands clearly what can be accommodated reasonably in the real world of the teacher's classroom. One real world factor is that the teacher will probably do most of the communicating with the parents.

❖ An *educational assistant* is often an ad hoc member in the case of a student he or she may know better than most, and can play a crucial part in the formation of an IEP. In the implementation of the developed plan, the educational assistant, under the direction of the teacher, may be responsible for particular types of instruction or assistance within the classroom setting. Along with the classroom teacher, the EA often takes on responsibility for monitoring.

❖ Other important team members may be the *parents* of the student being discussed, for they have a wealth of information to be considered. The reasonableness and practicality of interventions such as a behaviour plan that would require home support, is far easier to discuss productively if a parent is present. Perhaps most important, parent participation helps foster bonds of trust and communication. Naturally, parents are almost always ad hoc members. Experience has shown that parents often find it difficult to get to meetings, but the provincial regulations, not to mention effective teaching practice, means they are to be kept informed and consulted.

❖ By regulation, *students who are 16 years and older* may participate in a team meeting in which an IEP is being developed. If the student is a participant in the actual meeting, he or she may play a very special role in describing needs and perspectives, at the very least offering some insights into what is possible and realistic.

❖ *Support personnel* may be involved in a team meeting, but usually are not permanent members. These individuals, physiotherapists or attendance counsellors for example, attend meetings where their information, expertise, and intervention may be needed. Their role, as with all members of an in-school team, is to act as an information resource. Especially with secondary school students, who have considerably more independence and a wider circle of activity that is not necessarily known to their parents or classroom teachers, support personnel may be vital to the implementation and monitoring elements in a plan.

When Educators Collaborate

Educators collaborate naturally. Before and after and in-between classes, in the hall, over lunch, they share strategies they have found useful, seek opinions about their concerns for a student at risk, borrow materials, plan mutual projects for their classes; the exchanges are part of their day (and beyond). But a team situation is more formalized, and the process, as a consequence, requires a somewhat more formal structure. To put together an IEP, most teams follow a variation of this problem-solving technique.

1. identify/clarify the problem
2. formulate a plan
3. initiate the plan
4. assess the success of the plan
5. revise as necessary

Yet even these steps can be more effectively and efficiently realized if members of a team consult and collaborate with some appreciation of team dynamics.

What Makes a Team Succeed?

For collaboration to be successful, all members of the team must, at the very least, share a common focus, a sense that they are each trying to achieve the same goal. But by itself, a mutually understood purpose is still not enough. Realistically, members of a team must be voluntary participants, with a sense of voluntarily shared responsibility and accountability. Above all, to function truly without impediment, team members should have parity. The latter issue can be awkward, particularly given the fact that educators exist in a hierarchical structure in which parity, even on a philosophical level, can be difficult to establish. On the plus side, however, educators are members of a profession, and as a team, they are professionals united to achieve a goal for which they are better equipped than any others.

There is a practical side too. No matter how professionally a team may approach its tasks, there are some simple but fundamental requirements to apply its collective strength effectively. Schools that have been benefitting from the team concept in special education for some time now unanimously attest that to succeed, a team must

✔ have administrative support
✔ meet at regularly scheduled intervals
✔ keep group size manageable
✔ receive pertinent information prior to meetings
✔ set time limits
✔ follow an agenda
✔ set review dates
✔ keep records
✔ share accountability and responsibility

Some Issues in Team Practice

Collaboration with colleagues in a school setting is sometimes a complex dance, and ensuring that everyone is in step can prove difficult. Here are a few of the issues that must be kept in mind.

Personal beliefs: In any group of individuals, there is bound to be a variety of perspectives and beliefs. This indeed is one of the strengths of a team: the multiplicity of perspectives. But perspectives and absolute commitment to an idea or ideal, if held to the exclusion of all else, can interfere with the problem-solving goal of an IEP. It is important to be aware and respectful of the beliefs of team members, and to remember that it is the needs of a student, not the power of a principle, that ultimately must rule.

Dealing with conflict: Ideally, when discussing the important issue of how best to assist students within an educational setting, one would hope that conflicts are rare. While this may be the case in many interactions, elements such as passion, anxiety, hope and optimism, which can be part of any educational discourse, can become more pronounced when issues surrounding students with exceptionalities are at the centre of the discussion. There is a growing recognition within the province of Ontario that educators and families alike need assistance in terms of how best to communicate with each other and thus avoid what may be more difficult and acrimonious discussions later. In the fall of 2007 the Ministry of Education published a document entitled *Shared Solutions: A guide to preventing and resolving conflicts regarding programs and services for students with special education needs.* This document provides information and strategies to allow parents, educators and students with special education needs to resolve conflicts and work together in a more productive and meaningful way.

Administrative support: Administrators, whether at the school level or at the school board level, hold the keys to a variety of resources and decision making powers that are not generally available to other members of the team. Within a school, the principal sets the tone for discipline and the delivery of curriculum. In team meetings, a principal's active participation as a member of the team lends a status and aura of responsibility to that team that it would otherwise not attain. Without administrative support from within the school and at the board level, in-school teams may continue to function, but do so with their hands tied.

Time: As any teacher will attest, there is never enough time—for anything! Thus team meetings can often be viewed as an unwelcome extra in a teacher's schedule. This is even more strongly the case when a team is run inefficiently, decisions are not made or followed up, communication is poor, procedures are not well established, and there is no support. Given that time is a precious commodity, it is essential that team time be seen as worthwhile and, in the end, a time-saving activity. When teams are run well and teachers are given the opportunity to work with their colleagues in an effective way, the benefits to the school far outweigh the time spent at the meeting.

Adams, L., & Cessna, K. (1991). Designing systems to facilitate collaboration: Collective wisdom from Colorado. *Preventing School Failure, 35(4)*, 37-42.

Cole, E., & Brown, R. (1996). Multidisciplinary school teams: A five- year follow-up study. *Canadian Journal of School Psychology, 12*, 155-168.

Cook, L., & Friend, M. (1993). Educational leadership for teacher collaboration. In B. Billingsley (Ed.). *Program leadership for serving students with disabilities* (pp. 421-444). Richmond, VA: Virginia Department of Education.

Dettmer, P. A., Dyck, N.T. and Thurston, L. P. (1996). *Consultation, collaboration and team work for students with special needs.* Toronto: Allyn and Bacon.

Evans, S. B. (1991). A realistic look at the research base for collaboration in special education. *Preventing School Failure, 35(4)*, 10-14.

Friend, M. & Cook, L. (1992). *Interactions: collaboration skills for school professionals.* Toronto: Copp Clark Pitman.

Fuchs, D. & Fuchs, L. S. (1996). Consultation as a technology and the politics of school reform. *Remedial and Special Education, 17(6)*, 386-392.

Idol, L., Nevin, A., & Paolucci-Whitcomb, P. (1994). *Collaborative Consultation* (2nd ed.). Austin, TX: Pro-Ed.

Jordan, A. (1994). *Skills in collaborative classroom consultation.* New York: TJ Press Padstow Ltd.

Mills, M. (1994). The consultative role of school based resource teachers. *B.C. Journal of Special Education, 18(2)*, 181-189.

Napier, E. (1995). *Integrating students with special needs: Effective strategies to provide the most enabling education for all students.* Vancouver: EduServ.

Ontario Ministry of Education and Training (1998). *Individual education plan (IEP) resource guide.* Queen's Printer for Ontario.

Ontario Ministry of Education (2000). *Individual education plans standards for development, program planning and implementation.* Queen's Printer for Ontario.

Ontario Ministry of Education (2001). *Special Education: A guide for educators.* Queen's Printer for Ontario.

Ontario Ministry of Education (2002). *Transition planning: A resource guide.* Queen's Printer for Ontario.

Ontario Ministry of Education (2004). *The Individual Education Plan (IEP), A Resource Guide.* Queen's Printer for Ontario.

Ontario Ministry of Education (2007). *Shared Solutions: A guide to preventing and resolving conflicts regarding programs and services for students with special education needs.* Queen's Printer for Ontario.

O'Shea, D. & O'Shea, L. (1997). Collaboration and school reform: A 21st century perspective. *Journal of Learning Disabilities, 30(4)*, 449-462.

Pugach, M. C. & Johnson, L. J. (1995). A new framework for thinking about collaboration. In *Collaborative practitioners collaborative schools.* Denver, CO: Love.

Safran, S. P., & Safran, J. S. (1996). Intervention assistance programs and prereferral teams. *Remedial and Special Education, 17(6)*, 363-369.

Shea, T. M., & Bauer, A. M. (1991). *Parents and teachers of children with exceptionalities: A handbook for collaboration.* (2nd ed.). Boston: Allyn and Bacon.

Sheridan, S. M., Welch, M., & Orme, S. F. (1996). Is consultation effective? A review of outcome research. *Remedial and Special Education, 17(6)*, 341-354.

Stanovich, P. (1996). Collaboration—The key to successful inclusion in today's schools. *Intervention in School and Clinic, 32(1)*, 39-42.

Westby, C. E., & Ford, V. (1993). The role of team culture in assessment and intervention. *Journal of Educational and Psychological Consultation, 4*, 319-341.

Whitten, E., & Dieker, L. (1993). Intervention assistance teams: A collaborative process to meet the needs of students at risk. *B.C. Journal of Special Education,17(3)*, 275-283.

Wiener, J & Davidson, I. (1990). The in-school team: A prevention model of delivery in special education. *Canadian Journal of Education, 15(4)*, 427-445.

CHAPTER 6

Identification and Placement
How the IPRC Works

This schema outlines main features of Ontario Regulation 181/98, Identification and Placement of Exceptional Pupils, which came into force on September 1, 1998 (amended by Ontario Regulation 137, in 2001).

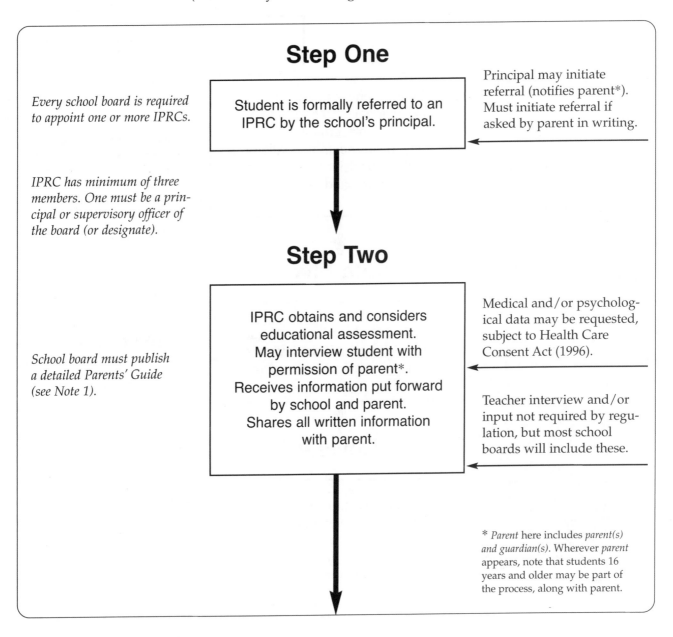

Step One

Every school board is required to appoint one or more IPRCs.

Student is formally referred to an IPRC by the school's principal.

Principal may initiate referral (notifies parent*). Must initiate referral if asked by parent in writing.

IPRC has minimum of three members. One must be a principal or supervisory officer of the board (or designate).

Step Two

School board must publish a detailed Parents' Guide (see Note 1).

IPRC obtains and considers educational assessment. May interview student with permission of parent*. Receives information put forward by school and parent. Shares all written information with parent.

Medical and/or psychological data may be requested, subject to Health Care Consent Act (1996).

Teacher interview and/or input not required by regulation, but most school boards will include these.

* *Parent* here includes *parent(s) and guardian(s)*. Wherever *parent* appears, note that students 16 years and older may be part of the process, along with parent.

Step Three

IPRC must consider all information and proposals for special education programs and services.

Parent may present proposals in addition to those from school board.

Parent entitled to have a representative of choice present.

Parent and representative may participate in all discussions except decision making.

Step Four

IPRC decides student is not exceptional.

Process ends, unless parent appeals, or requests follow-up meeting.

or

Decision statement must list placement, category(s) and definition(s) of exceptionality, and student's strengths/needs.

Written decision of IPRC goes to parent, referring principal, school board.

IPRC identifies student as exceptional, and decides on a placement. May make recommendations (but not decisions) regarding programs and services.

Placement to be regular class if it meets needs, and if parent wishes. IPRC must give reasons if special class is chosen.

Parent may request IPRC meet again to reconsider.

Within 30 school days principal of school where student is placed must see to development of IEP and for 14 year olds and older, a Transition Plan. (See Note 2.)

Step Five

Student is placed according to IPRC decision. IEP is developed and implementation begun.

If parent signs consent or if consent is not signed, but parent does not appeal.

- - - - - - -> Step Five stayed if parent appeals.

Rights and requirements as in Steps One to Five.

Identification and Placement
How the IPRC works
A memorandum in the fall of 2006 from the then Deputy Minister outlined what for some school boards across the province would be a shift in practice with regard to IPRC. The memorandum suggested that school boards re-examine their procedures around IPRC and consider dispensing with a formal IPRC process in those cases where the board and parent were in agreement that the students' placement be in the regular classroom.

Review

Student's situation to be reviewed at least once every school year by an IPRC. Parent may request review after three months.

Reviews confirm existing situation, or may make changes. Principal to review and update IEP.

In Cases of Appeal
Step One (A)

Parent may appeal identification as exceptional, or placement or both.

School board convenes a three member Appeal Board to review the IPRC material and decisions.

One member chosen by board; one by parent; the two select a third as chair (in case of disagreement, chair is chosen by MoE).

Parent and/or representative entitled to participate in all discussions except decision making.

Step Two (A)

Appeal Board agrees with IPRC and recommends its decisions be implemented,
or
disagrees with IPRC and makes recommendation to school board about identification or placement or both.

May interview anyone whom Appeal Board chair feels has information to contribute.

Written recommendation to parent, principal, school board and chair of IPRC.

Written reasons must accompany written statement of recommendation.

Step Three (A)

School board considers recommendation and decides what action to take.

School board is not limited to recommendation of Appeal Board.

Written decision of school board goes to all parties.

Step Four (A)

School board decision is implemented.

If parent signs consent
or
if consent not signed but parent does not appeal.

Step Four (A) stayed if parent appeals.

Final appeal stage is to Special Education Tribunal (see Note 3).

Note 1: Each school board must prepare a parent's guide explaining all elements of the IPRC process, including rights of appeal and the steps involved. The guide must be available at every school in the board, and, if requested by a parent, must be made available in braille, large print, or audio form. The guide will also identify organizations and associations from which parents may seek advice and help.

Note 2: The Transition Plan requirement does not apply to students who are identified "gifted." See chapter 5 for a full explanation of IEPs and Transition Plans.

Note 3: The Special Education Tribunal (Section 57 of the Education Act) is a provincially appointed body that hears appeals from decisions of IPRCs upheld first by an Appeal Board and then by the school board. Tribunal hearings are complex, adversarial in structure, and are conducted under the Statutory Powers Procedure Act of Ontario. A Tribunal decision is final and binding. *The vast majority of IPRCs end at Step Five. Appeals are infrequent and Tribunals are rare. Where either is imminent in a student's case, the Ministry of Education encourages parents and school boards to attempt mediation before going forward.*

Also of note…

- The regulations set specific time limits on steps in the IPRC procedure; e.g., appeals, response periods, etc.

- With a parent's agreement, adjustments are sometimes made to an identified student's situation without a formal IPRC meeting. Also a formal Review is generally not convened to modify a student's IEP unless major change is requested or expected.

- IPRCs were governed originally by Regulation 554, issued in 1981. The procedure was modified by Regulation 305 in 1990. Fairly significant modifications were made in 1998 by Regulation 181, its current form. Regulation 137 in 2001 made a small change to Step Five, specifying a time frame for an IEP and Transition Plan. There have been no other changes.

- For the complete versions of the IPRC regulations and other documents, see **www.edu.gov.on.ca**, or the Ministry publication: *Special Education, A Guide for Educators* (2001), available in government bookstores, public libraries, school board offices.

The Case(s) of Luis and Estella

Although Luis and Estella are almost nine years old, their mother continues to dress them in clothes with matching material and designs. It is her contention, as she explained to an IPRC, that the more Luis and Estella are perceived as "cute," the more readily they will be "welcomed by normal society." The two children are fraternal twins and are developmentally disabled. Luis has Down syndrome, while Estella sustained serious brain injury at birth. Although both speak in a baby talk style, they are otherwise quite socially adept. Their mother has devoted her life to their care and to integrating them into society. The twins attended nursery school. They were enrolled in clubs and sports; and from kindergarten to grade 3 were placed full time in the same regular class in their neighbourhood school.

No one has questioned their placement until now. With two months to go in grade 3, the school has requested an IPRC review. Although the majority of their class reads and writes at an age-appropriate level, neither twin writes his or her name as yet. Luis can recognize his, but Estella does not. Luis can identify about half the letters of the alphabet; he counts to one hundred by rote but does not appear to associate numbers with amounts or quantities. Estella, when asked, will count to five or six and then, as she always does when challenged, will produce a totally engaging smile. The school board psychologist feels that Luis especially, but Estella too, has far greater ability. Experience shows that both learn from very structured teaching and frequent repetition. However, the regular grade 3 class does not provide much opportunity. It is a large, busy class, with one EA who also shares responsibility for the health needs of a girl with cerebral palsy.

Next year presents even more concerns. The school's junior division places several classes into one large, pod-style room, where individual study is emphasized and small group projects prevail. Some, but not all, of the school team believe it would be a disservice to place Estella here, and possibly Luis too. The alternative, at least part time, would be placement either in the school's primary resource room, or the junior one. Current enrolment in the primary room is six. There are three children with severe developmental disabilities, two with physical disabilities, and one child identified autistic. Only one of the six has normal speech. The resource teacher and full time EA emphasize language development. The junior room is almost a mirror image of the primary. The twins' mother objects to placement in either setting.

CHAPTER 7

Assessment
Identifying Strengths and Needs

"Assessment is a process of collecting data for the purpose of making decisions about individuals and groups, and this decision-making role is the reason that assessment touches so many people's lives."

Salvia, Ysseldyke & Bolt, 2007, p. 4

The Purpose of Assessment

When students are assessed, relevant information is gathered and interpreted from a variety of sources that may include teacher-made tests, observation, curriculum-based assessment, peer evaluation, portfolio development, and commercially available standardized test instruments. The results, at least theoretically, reveal some insights into the abilities, intelligence, strengths, needs, and behaviours of the students in question. The discoveries help in making informed evaluations about the students' present status and informed decisions about future instructional practice. Without a way to measure the progress of students, it would be impossible to program effectively within a school setting.

For students deemed exceptional in some way, the path of assessment, while similar to that taken for all students, can be more complicated and far more influential in determining program and placement. The assessment instruments used, the personnel required, indeed the depth and breadth of the assessment process itself, will vary from that used for more general evaluations. Ideally, the assessment process collects information, refines insight into exceptionality, and then sets the table for both programming and follow-up evaluations.

Once regarded as the exclusive realm of specialists, assessment has moved toward a more team-oriented approach with participation, responsibility and accountability being shared by a number of key people, especially the classroom teacher who is most likely to deliver the program. Others involved include the student's parents (and occasionally, in the case of some adolescents, the student himself or herself) the teaching assistant, the school's special education teacher (who may be responsible for some of the more formal investigations) and, if need demands and the personnel are available, various individuals with special expertise such as psychologists and speech and language pathologists.

Assessment: A Very Educated Guess

No matter how keenly we may seek specialized information about students, and no matter how acculturated we may be to the belief that such truth can be revealed, the simple fact is that the very best an educational assessment can produce is a kind of loose probability. However loose though, it is still an important probability. Education itself is not an exact science, and effective teaching is a combination of both art and science leading to effective instruction. An assessment provides information gathered in an organized way that, at the very least, confirms in a presumably unbiased way, the view of the people working with the student. At the very best, it reveals factors that no one had known or possibly even expected.

Granted, there are reasons to harbour doubts about some of the procedures and components in an assessment and, quite possibly, reasons to be wary of the results if they differ significantly from the student's day-to-day performance, but to ignore the possible contribution of an effective assessment to an exceptional student's case would be a disservice indeed. Assessment has an important role to play. What shapes the quality of that role is the quality of the assessment procedures, and the way the results are interpreted and applied.

When Are Assessments Completed?

Arguably, assessment happens at every moment in a school day. Whether they are monitoring a student's behaviour in the halls, or observing while a student shoots baskets in the gym or writes a spelling test, teachers are always presented with opportunity to collect data that will identify needs and strengths. Assessment, quite simply, is an integral part of teaching. Choosing when to assess, what to observe, which piece of work to add to a portfolio, or whom to listen to in reading—these are all part of the daily challenges for classroom teachers.

Almost without exception, every student in every school setting will be subject to a screening at some time or another. A common practice, screening is a relatively formal but broad procedure that determines if more intrusive testing is needed. Usually, groups of students are screened via an achievement test or test of cognitive abilities or other instrument. (Some boards have their own systems of screening to be used along with or in place of, commercially published tests.) The purpose is to discover, in a general way, whether there are any students at risk—or potentially gifted. These students are usually assessed then, in a more formal and extensive way to confirm (or dismiss) their suspected risk or giftedness. Screenings often take place at the preschool level where children entering school are assessed for vision, hearing and general readiness. Further along in the school grades, screening helps to identify students who fall outside what is judged

to be normal performance criteria. These students are tested further to assess the nature and possibly the basis of the discrepancy.

Assessing Students with Special Needs

In the case of students who may be exceptional, the assessment process is more extensive. Initially, a teacher who has concerns about a student may choose to seek assistance through the forum of the in-school team. At this level, often referred to as the "pre-referral intervention level" because the student has not yet been referred for more formalized assessment and identification, the teacher is seeking assistance and direction from colleagues. Generally, the teacher will prepare for a pre-referral by conducting an initial assessment based on observation, classroom performance, samples of the student's work and, possibly, a rating scale/checklist (especially in potential behaviour cases). It is not unusual for the teacher to do a curriculum-based assessment, gathering information over a period of time of the student's performance in a particular curriculum area (like reading, or mathematics). In many boards a "pre-referral form" completed by the teacher requests specific information about the student's achievement and/or behaviour that the in-school team can consider when a particular student's situation is under discussion.

With the assistance of the team, a number of suggestions may be attempted within the classroom setting. This type of intervention, e.g., moving the student to a different reading group, chunking work, allowing for differing modes of information presentation, is often described as "intervention focused assessment." Intervention-focused assessment examines the effectiveness of an intervention: Did the move to the front of the room work? Can the student complete a task better if done orally? Does the introduction of frequent breaks reduce the incidence of misbehaviours?

When a student's situation is more complicated or demanding, then in addition to the assessment described above, more intensive, formal, and specialized procedures (perhaps an IQ test or standardized achievement test, or even in some cases, a diagnostic test) will be carried out. One point when a fairly extensive assessment is usually carried out is prior to the development of an Individual Education Plan (IEP).

Kyeesha's parents call her their "divine gift." She was born to them when they were in their mid-forties after they had experienced several unsuccessful pregnancies over a period of years. Both have successful academic careers (in art history and microbiology) and their home is intellectually and culturally stimulating.

When Kyeesha was four years old, the parents had her assessed for intelligence and general ability in a private clinic. The clinic's test results placed Kyeesha in the Very Superior range intellectually, and for the next two years her parents enrolled her in a private pre-school. Prior to enrolling her in grade 1 of their neighbourhood elementary school, the parents requested an IPRC. The committee, having little information available to it except the clinic's test results as provided by the parents, along with anecdotal accounts from them, quite readily accepted their opinion that Kyeesha should be identified gifted and placed in a primary gifted program.

After considerable success initially, Kyeesha began to lag behind her colleagues in achievement seriously enough that by the end of grade 2, the school requested, and was granted by the parents, permission to conduct an assessment. The school board's chief psychologist somewhat reluctantly reported his conclusion that, intellectually, Kyeesha is in the Average to High Average range. Not unexpectedly, her parents find this difficult to believe. Because they are naturally disposed to cooperate, and no matter what, wish to make decisions that are in their little girl's best interests, they have asked for a meeting with the school. What they want to have explained to them is: how can results of two assessments of the same child differ so greatly; is there other information the school can provide that would help make clear to them what Kyeesha's real status might be and what academic program will be provided.

In cases where a student is formally identified as exceptional, assessment tends to be very thorough and includes assessment data obtained not only by the teacher but by assessment personnel (e.g., psychologist, assessment counsellor) social worker, physiotherapist, speech therapist etc.

Usually, information is collected through a number of sources and a variety of assessment strategies are used. The data aid in the identification of the student as exceptional, help to decide on program and placement, and will be utilized in the development of the IEP. At the follow-up or review stage, the data will be used again with more current and perhaps additional information being added.

Who Does Assessments?

The process, quite naturally, begins in the classroom. It is the teacher who can best observe a student's response to text, reaction to physical environment, and relationship to peers and adults. Teachers collect samples of student's work: journal entries, recordings, tests, and portfolios to name a few. These are the materials that, along with the teacher's own professional opinions and views, establish the initial, basic, and often, most important information. Further testing (and observation) may then be done by a special education resource teacher. The combination has distinct advantages in that the two (or more) teachers can then cooperate in the next step: designing the program implied by the assessment.

At the school board level, there is often a separate unit responsible for assessment, known by descriptors such as psychological or support services. This unit does almost all the assessing for special education outside the classroom setting. Psychologists, or personnel (often referred to as psychometrists, assessment counsellors or psychoeducational consultants) working under their guidance and direct supervision, conduct standardized assessments measuring cognitive strengths, for example, or analyzing behaviour patterns. In jurisdictions where psychological services are not directly available, outside expertise may be hired and, where possible, classroom and special education resource teachers may be given more responsibility in conducting formal types of assessment. Most boards though, even the smaller ones, have formal assessments done by a person for whom this is a primary role.

Some larger school boards may employ speech and language pathologists to assess children with language difficulties Assessments done by physiotherapists and occupational therapists are also outside the jurisdiction of the school boards, though schools may, with the cooperation of the parents, request such assessments. Parents sometimes obtain an assessment privately, even though, by law, they have access to any data the school has. If they choose, they may offer these data to the school.

Components of an Assessment

A majority, if not all of the assessment information collected about a student, revolves around

- what the student is seen to be doing (observation)

- a systematic collection of student work products

- discussions and information sharing by key persons (including parents)

- and finally, testing.

Historically, in special education, emphasis has been placed on the latter element. Indeed, the mystique of testing has often overshadowed and even delayed action on behalf of a student with an exceptionality. The phrase "We are getting him tested" was—and still is— an oft-heard one, and it's not unusual for a teacher to be caught in the frustrating position of waiting on results before modifying or accommodating a program. The benefits of more formalized types of testing can indeed inform the process of program planning. But for some time now, the experience of special education has made clear that formal tests are but one component in a much more complex process; one that starts with teachers in the classroom suspecting something, acting on that suspicion, and trying out possible strategies to ameliorate the difficulty before more formal steps are taken.

The "Battery"

Curiously, the pieces that make up a formal assessment are often described collectively by an artillery term: "assessment battery." What follows here is a description of components that may be used in a battery, although certain of them will almost always be included. (It is difficult, for example, to conceive of an assessment being useful and valid without the observations of the teacher and educational assistant.)

The decision regarding what components to use is typically governed in part by school and board policy. For example, many boards have complex and stringent requirements for identifying students as gifted and specify that certain test instruments be used as part of the identification procedures. Some boards discourage or even forbid the use of certain components. However, once the school and board policies are met—and on the matter of components these matters are flexible for the most part—how an assessment is actually conducted, and what is used, will typically be the choice of the professional personnel involved. That choice will vary according to their knowledge, competence, and personal preference.

Informal (Teacher Made) Tests

A growing awareness of the benefits of assessments conducted by someone working directly with the student on an ongoing basis has led to an increasing acceptance of informal measures designed by classroom teachers to meet their own immediate purposes. A disadvantage to these measures is that there are no norms for them so they usually do not have acceptance beyond the immediate situation. But then, that is not their purpose. Their advantage is that they can be truly tailored to meet specific needs. For example, an informal test can be designed to reveal the presence or absence of a very specific skill, and may well provide a picture of why and when a student fails to grasp a skill (like subtraction) instead of simply confirming that the student has not grasped it (which the teacher already knows in any case).

Informal measures may include a teacher using parts of rating scales and checklists so that he or she can be more certain to have covered all the points. Informal inventories are used here as well. Still another practice (albeit of questionable legality and efficacy) is to use parts of different formal tests to put together the desired information about a student.

Formal Tests

Intelligence tests

Generally, tests measuring intelligence (IQ tests) give a relatively accurate assessment of what an individual has been taught (and what he remembers) and of what the student has been exposed to thus far in his or her life. In this sense, an IQ test is a measure of current performance. What continues to be hotly debated is whether the test measures intellectual potential and can thereby be legitimately regarded as a predictor of future school performance. Despite this concern, these instruments continue to be used for the purpose. Among the several commercially available IQ tests, the most widely used one by far in Ontario has been the Wechsler Intelligence Scale for Children IV (2003) known colloquially as the "WISC IV."

Tests of Academic Achievement

These are the most widely used formal test instruments of all. There are achievement tests for large groups, e.g., the Canadian Achievement Tests, 3rd Edition and there are individual tests as well, e.g., the Peabody Individual Achievement Test, Revised (1998), Wechsler Individual Achievement Test II (2001). Administrators of achievement tests can be anyone from a classroom teacher to a professional psychometrist. Publishers provide detailed administration manuals and recommend that examiners attend training seminars. Very often in special education, achievement tests are used as screening tests.

It seems that our students living in families with complex needs get missed as they move through the education system. Students who have been enrolled in ten or more schools by the time they enroll in high school have often been missed for assessment of their special education needs. That missed diagnosis because they were not in a school long enough to wait for their educational assessment is a tragedy. Over and over again in my twenty-two year career, I have had to sit at meetings and tell a parent of a 14, 15 and even an 18 year old that they were now diagnosed as developmentally delayed. This information is devastating for everyone involved and is very harmful to the esteem and well-being of the teenager. We have to find a better system to help diagnose children at a younger age and reduce the waiting lists for assessment to prevent a late diagnosis of a child. We owe it to them!

Tracy S., principal

Other uses include general comparison, since individual test results are calculated in terms of the results—called norms—developed across a wide, randomly selected population. In other words, the test takers reveal where they stand in terms of the test, compared to a general population.

Diagnostic Tests

The term is misleading. These tests do not diagnose in any absolute sense but rather, present specific information about a student's performance in a specific area. Their true purpose is to suggest areas for remediation. The Woodcock Diagnostic Reading Battery, for example, deals with specific areas like "phonological awareness" and "oral comprehension," presumably giving indication about the extent to which a student is competent in these areas. Critics of this and other similar tests question the value and even the validity of this kind of sub-skill breakdown in an area like reading. However, they acknowledge it may have value in areas like mathematics, where steps in the process of subtraction, for example, can be broken down and illuminated more clearly.

Tests of Cognitive Ability

Judgments about cognitive strengths and needs are inferred from a student's response to items on these tests. Memory, problem solving, and reasoning are examples of the types of skills these tests attempt to measure; the inference being that the better developed these cognitive skills are, the more successfully a student will perform in school-related tasks. The jury is still very much out on the issue of whether or not testing for cognitive abilities is any different from testing for intelligence with the IQ instruments already in use. Cognition is about thinking. Whether testing for thinking is any different from testing for IQ is moot. In Canada, supporters of the distinction generally opt for the Canadian Cognitive Abilities Test, Form K (1998).

Developmental and Readiness Tests

These are primarily administered by classroom teachers, especially teachers of primary grades, to determine the level of ability of students. For exceptional students, their purpose is generally for screening. Very often these instruments are used along with checklists and skill inventories. Two popular examples in Canada, are the Boehm Test of Basic Concepts—Revised (2000) and the Brigance Inventories (1976-99).

Rating Scales, Inventories, and Checklists

These instruments offer descriptive statements about areas like attitude, self-esteem, behaviour, self-care, etc., in lists. Each item in a list is followed by a frequency ranking like "almost all the time, frequently, sometimes, occasionally, rarely," or sometimes just by "yes" or "no." Responses are entered by the student's teacher, educational assistant, parent, social worker, or childcare worker (sometimes all of these for comparison and time/place/situation diagnosis). A reasonably popular example of this type is the Achenbach Child Behavior Checklist.

Some rating scales are designed to be completed by the student. The Coopersmith Self-Esteem Inventory (1983), for example, presents statements to the student like "I often wish I were someone else" followed by "like me ____' and "unlike me ____."

Keys to an Effective Assessment

For reasons of economy, availability of personnel and appropriate instruments, and because of politics and the chronic problem of special education, lack of time, not all educational assessments will meet every one of the following criteria every time. But when these criteria are not met as a basic standard, the results of any assessment should be weighed accordingly.

1 Has the assessment used a broad spectrum of sources (e.g., teacher, parents, other professionals if appropriate, test instruments if appropriate)?

2 If test instruments have been used, are they known to be valid and reliable? Is the examiner adequately trained in the administration of the tests and the interpretation of the results?

3 Was the assessment individually tailored: did it take into account matters like the subject's culture, his or her language, age, school experience, physical abilities?

4 Was the assessment ecological: did it examine the whole student in relation to his or her whole environment, his or her program, classroom situation, home situation?

5 Does the assessment imply or recommend responses: avenues of remediation or enrichment (as opposed to presenting only an enumeration of deficiencies)?

6 Do key persons in the life of the subject—teacher, educational assistant, parent—acknowledge that the assessment has sampled genuinely representative factors?

Most often, the results of these scales are used to determine a developmental profile from which educational or social or self-care objectives are developed. Occasionally, the information may be used to indicate a developmental level and sometimes decisions about placement will be influenced by the level indicated. The AAMD Adaptive Behavior Scale: School Edition (1981-93) often called an adaptive behaviour "test," is frequently used this way. Rating scale instruments invite considerable subjectivity and are both praised and criticized for this factor.

Interviews and Informal Commentary: Teachers and Parents

Any effective assessment procedure will seek opinions from the responsible adults who associate with, and have responsibility for the student most directly. Most school boards invite the classroom teacher, and ideally the educational assistant, to present information. Very often this face-to-face discussion is preceded by written information that may vary from a simple referral form, to anecdotal information, to a fully developed case study. Parents have vital information for an assessment or evaluation team. Their information is invariably current and intimate (if biased sometimes); they also have the advantage of knowing the student's full history. Both Regulation 181 and the IEP Resource Guide produced by the Ontario Ministry of Education require that parents be an integral part of the process in which a child is being considered for special education programming and/or placement.

Medical Information

This becomes part of an assessment only when it is germane, and it often is in the case of a student with special needs. Information may range from data about hearing, sight, and physical ability, to the general health and neurological conditions relevant to a student's situation. These data, if available, will come from the appropriate health professionals; they are almost never prepared by school board personnel. Experience has demonstrated that without cooperation and impetus from parents, medical information, along with useful advice, is often

---

Involve the Parents

What parents have to offer an assessment about a student's abilities is essential for obvious reasons. Answers to the following questions are always useful.

- What are your concerns regarding your child's learning/behaviour at school?

- How does what we do at school affect your child at home (reaction to homework, frustration level, general attitude to coming to school)?

- Has your child had particular success in the past, with a strategy or program?

- What other reports do you have that we may need to be aware of?

- What goals do you have for your child?

- Do you have a preference in method of communication from home to school?

- What questions do you have of us?

- When should we talk again to inform you of your child's progress?

---

hard to come by. Health professionals are understandably wary of privacy regulations, but at the same time, often show a curious reluctance to share more than sketchy information with schools.

Additional Types of Assessment Procedures

Curriculum-Based Assessment (CBA)

Curriculum-based Assessment (CBA) involves measuring a student's performance according to curricular expectations the school has established. Academic abilities and achievement can be systematically examined using this type of assessment. While many different variations exist, two basic components of CBA are probes

Some Important Terms In Assessment

Bands of Confidence: because of the Standard Error of Measurement factor, a test score can never be considered as absolutely correct. Thus some test manuals offer a range around a given score about which there can be some confidence.

Criterion Referenced Test: a number of specific behaviours or performances are stated (e.g., Subject knows the alphabet. Can count from 1-20.) These are the criteria. The subject's ability in this particular area is then assessed.

Grade Equivalent: a subject's raw score on a test is applied statistically to produce the school grade he or she would be in if the student were in the sample groups of students used to determine the norms for the test. (A subject's grade equivalent of 6.2 means that if he were in the group sampled to produce the norms, he would stand at the second month of the sixth grade.)

Norms: the results obtained by representative populations when a particular test was developed. Students who write a test have their results compared to these norms to produce scores like Percentile, Stanine, Grade Equivalent, etc.

Norm Referenced Test: a test which rates a subject's performance relative to the results obtained in a known comparison group (or norm group).

Percentile Rank: a subject's percentile rank of 82 means that the student scored higher than about 82 percent of the norm group.

Reliability: the level of consistency and dependability of a test. (Will it produce similar results over variable conditions?)

Split Half Procedure: involves administering the same subject(s) half of a test instrument (e.g., the odd numbered questions) at a different time from the other half (e.g., the even numbered questions).

Standard Error of Measurement: the extent to which a subject's score is "out." These data are reported (or should be!) in the technical manual that accompanies a test. (See more in this chapter.)

Stanine: a reporting scheme for test results based on an equal interval scale of 1-9 (5 is average; 6 is slightly above etc.).

Validity: the degree to which a test measures what it purports to measure.

See Appendix for more terms.

---

of basic academic skills and content-area strategy assessment. *Probing*, which may be done across subject areas, involves ascertaining the skill and accuracy level of a student's knowledge of curriculum, e.g., letter recognition and arithmetic skills. *Content-area* assessment uses probes to establish knowledge level and also examines learning skills like note taking.

Many observers suggest that curriculum-based assessment, despite the extensive explication and argument that surround it, does not differ very much from the way evaluation in schools was conducted well before special education became commonplace. In the case of a student with an exceptionality, they go on to say, curriculum-based measurement is not really a true alternative since all it really does is confirm that the student is not responding appropriately to the curriculum, a fact already evident. Supporters argue that curriculum-based assessment peers into a student's personal, unique, and complex characteristics as they relate directly to the curriculum, and that this insight is superior to the type of assessment that merely establishes the presence of some disability.

To be effective, curriculum-based assessment must be carried out frequently; it should be specific (i.e., directed exactly at what has been taught); the results should be considered as a reason for possibly adjusting the instruction in addition to just determining how the student is doing; and assessment should consider small, sub-skill gains in addition to the acquisition of more global matters.

Authentic Assessment

Based on the premise that traditional types of assessment instruments fail to measure a student's performance in an authentic way, *authentic assessment* focuses on forming a "complete and realistic" picture of what a child can or cannot do. Authentic assessment allows for a collection of data based on real situations in which the students can be engaged in an interactive way, and during which they can access help from teachers and peers as they supposedly would in any normal situation. This type of assessment is very unlike a formal test situation. The focus is on allowing students to integrate information taught in a classroom situation, and to apply it in a problem solving way. At its best, authentic assessment calls on a learner's best performance based on interaction and practice.

Portfolio Assessment

Portfolios are a collection of student's work that represents growth and development over a specified period of time. Rather than a haphazard collection of work samples periodically collected, a portfolio is a specifically representative sampling. The goal of portfolio development is twofold: first, to provide a vehicle for the teacher to measure progress, and second (and perhaps more important), to allow the student himself or herself to monitor and evaluate his or her academic growth and thereby make informed decisions on how to proceed. Salend (1998) suggests the following guidelines for effective use of portfolio assessment in the classroom:

☞ determine the portfolio to be used (showcase, reflective, cumulative, goal based)

☞ establish procedures for organizing the portfolio

☞ choose a range of authentic classroom products that reflect the objectives of the portfolio

☞ record the significance of items included in student's portfolios

☞ review and evaluate portfolios periodically

Ecological Assessment

This concept includes an amalgam of formal and informal methods, along with careful evaluation of the teaching-learning variables in the student's case. The idea is to examine the context in which the student learns, as well as the student himself or herself. Thus, matters like the teacher's management style, the curriculum, teaching strategies, and instructional materials are examined; work samples produced by the student are evaluated, as is the student's success and error patterns inside and outside of school. *Ecological assessment* is attractive in principle, but management factors make it difficult to do.

Learning Style Assessment

In the 1980s, a proposal that was initially well received offered the idea that by examining how a student learns, by discovering under what conditions or through what style of presentation the student's learning is most natural and effective, remediation then becomes a relatively straightforward case of making appropriate adjustments when the student does not learn. While the idea was successful in promoting attention to individualized programming, as an assessment method it has proven very complex for the rewards it generates. Another problem is that in the development stages of their growth, students' styles are not necessarily stable and thereby accessible to reliable measurement.

Outcome-based Assessment

Outcome-based Assessment requires those professionals working with the student to teach and evaluate those skills that are important in real-life situations. Once these skills, appropriate for the individual, are determined, an assessment is conducted to determine what current ability the student has toward achieving those skills. After this is established, a determination is made about needs to be learned next (similar to Task Analysis, see Chapter 11). An instructional approach is then developed to help the student achieve the outcome determined at the beginning of the process.

Some Issues in the Use of Formal Tests

✦ The power of test *mystique*. Educators, including those who should know better, seem strangely willing to ascribe to tests a kind of mystical capacity to open a window into a student's inner being and the workings of his or her mind. As a result, educators will often defer to test results even if those results contradict their own observations and conclusions arrived at over months of on-site observations and analyses. Ironically, the professionals who administer and interpret the tests are usually the ones who point out that a formal test instrument is just one of several looks at the subject. Yet so strong is the effect of a test result that almost everyone involved in a student's case will, however tacitly, acknowledge its superiority. As a consequence, the relative importance of a test in the general assessment of a student can be strongly, even shockingly disproportionate.

✦ *The aging of published tests* is a serious problem. A quick review of the publication dates of any number of tests still in common use reveals disturbing results. Some standardized tests in use today were developed as early as the 1940s and 1950s—before television! Many were produced in the 1970s and 1980s—before the Internet. Thus, even though some tests are regularly updated*, it is very important for teachers and administrators to be aware of which version is being used. Given that most of the time, the norms of a test are generated at the time of a test's original development, it can happen that the results achieved by students today are being compared against norms established with children who went to school decades ago. It is ironic in the extreme that educators are invariably first to declare that our culture and our children are changing constantly and rapidly; yet these same educators seem to accept test results based at least in part on the performance of people from their parents', even their grandparents' era!

✦ *Bias and tacit discrimination* against lower socio-economic groups and those of diverse cultures persists in testing. In older tests, normed groups may not be representative of current populations so current scores can be misleading. As well, many test items

---

* Publication dates for test instruments typically show the last date an addition or revision was made. However the change (and therefore the date) may indicate only a tiny adjustment to the content or even the layout. A publication date, therefore, does not necessarily mean the year when the instrument was last normed, updated, or otherwise scientifically improved.

Testing Innovation

Within the field of assessment there exists a legitimate and pervasive concern over the aging of both standardized assessments as well as their contents. While many of the 'old reliable' tests are updated regularly there is still the question of how much adjusting can be done before the actual premise and goal of the test need to be reexamined. Fortunately new testing innovations are being worked on. One exciting project that is near completion is the development of a test that has the potential of providing important insights into the field of learning disabilities—The Computerized Test of Information Processing (CTIP), which was scheduled to be released in the Fall of 2007. The CTIP while currently being normed on adults with learning disability/AD/HD, shows great potential to assist both in identification and programming for school age children.

For more information on this test readers are referred to MHS, Multihealth Systems Publishing Company.

suggest that the questions, pictures, expected knowledge base, and required skills do not take into account the diverse nature of many of today's classrooms. Producers of commercial tests claim to have addressed this matter in their revisions, but estimates of their success, as published in academic reviews, are conservative at best.

✦ In tests administered to groups, questions are typically phrased so that answers can be machine-scored, with multiple-choice format being the most popular. Almost every question therefore, must be responded to with a single, confined answer, a structure that invites a great many *dull and simplistic questions* and devotes an excessive amount of space, time, and effort to minutiae. Needless to say, it also leaves little room, if any, for the reflective or creative student.

✦ *Potential for misinterpretation.* It is not uncommon in tests of language and reading

Each of Larry's eight years in the same elementary school has contributed to his reputation as a complete enigma. In fact, he is secretly (and kindly) known by the staff as "What Next Larry" because tales about him invariably attract that phrase.

In kindergarten and grade 1, Larry did not seem to learn to read or write or even print his name. When he returned for grade 2 the next September, he immediately showed language skills well above grade level, and by Christmas was leading the class. By the end of the year he had begun to manifest odd behaviours, the most serious of which was eating chalk. That too, disappeared over the next summer, but when Larry returned in the fall, it appeared he had become an elective mute. Neither his teacher nor an educational assistant of whom he was very fond, could penetrate the mutism. His parents who were, then and now, as baffled as his teachers, reported the same behaviour at home, and that he was being emulated by his immediately younger brother! Like the previous mysteries, this too passed, and in grade 4 Larry took up music. The school has a grade 7-8 band, and Larry showed he could play the clarinet well enough to join this older group and even become a soloist. Again, his parents had no explanation. Larry never had lessons, they reported, and although they kept a clarinet in the attic, no one (except Larry, now) could play it.

Grade 5 saw sports enter the picture. Rather, sportscasting. Larry's teacher scheduled a part of each morning for current events and media study, and two or three times a week, Larry, would report—pleasantly, but obsessively and in total detail—all the scoring from the previous night's NHL games. In grade 6, Larry began his novel. He abandoned that venture before completion, but the writing took up almost all his time until winter break. A standardized achievement test that year showed Larry at grade in language but well behind in math. However, he had been completely absorbed in his novel, especially when math was being taught. In grade 7, Larry became officially eligible for the school band but then dropped out. Instead, he got permission to form a chess club. By the end of the year, it had a higher membership than the band.

It is now the first month of Larry's grade 8 year. The principal (who is both fond of and protective of Larry—the affection is returned, fully) has held a meeting of all staff who have taught or otherwise dealt with Larry. What he has proposed, with the strong support of the boy's parents, is that, since Larry will go to a secondary school next year, it would be to his benefit if his arrival there were preceded by a confidential assessment. The principal wants the teachers to suggest to him just what kind of information such an assessment should seek, and how it should be obtained.

to find lists of single words, out of context, to be read aloud (e.g., see the *Wide Range Achievement Test*-3). These lists are often separated in sub-tests under titles like "Word Recognition," with the results interpreted, not just as a measure of word recognition, but as a measure of general reading ability. The practice also assumes that formally testing an unnatural idea like word recognition is possible and worth doing in the first place.

✦ In tests of achievement especially, *each item tends to be scored with the same value* (usually 1 or 0). School tasks typically increase in difficulty; thus also typically, students merit proportionately enhanced recognition for

dealing with these tasks successfully. In most formal, published tests, Student A, who correctly answers only questions sixteen to twenty, earns the same score as Student B, who correctly answers questions one to five. Granted, a careful item by item analysis would reveal that Students A and B attained a raw score of five by different routes, but in practice, consumers of test information rarely see, or have time to see, an item analysis.

✦ Tests are usually *rigorously timed*, with all the difficulties that causes for slow, not to mention deep, thinkers.

✦ *Misunderstanding "standardized."* Over time,

commercially produced formal tests have come to be called "standardized" (distinguishing them from teacher tests which by implication therefore, are unstandardized). Many test consumers have come to accept "standardized" to mean these tests are based on a standard against which students are judged. This is not at all the case. Test results are indeed compared to a scale of values or "norms,", but these norms are not an absolute standard; they are the scores obtained from the population samples used by the test publishers to establish the basis for comparison. Publishers usually contend that the norms they have established represent the range of results (in a perfect bell curve) that could be expected in a normal or typical population. That claim notwithstanding, the comparison is still relative; it is not standard. What is standard in formal tests are the procedures of administration used each time and scoring the same way every time to reduce examiner interference. It is not a standard of evaluation.

✦ Another well-established practice is to *generalize test results*. If student "C" takes test X in reading comprehension and scores a grade equivalent of say 4.2, those results are for that particular test. Yet it is regular practice by educators to make the assumption that the student's absolute reading level is 4.2.

✦ *Ignoring the standard error of measurement.* One of the most misunderstood and ignored features of a formal test is the standard error of measurement (SEM). Because no test is absolutely accurate, a subject's true score is never known. The score that a subject gets—the "obtained" score—is actually only an estimate of a "true" score. What the SEM does is give a statistical reflection of how close to a true score the subject's obtained score actually is. If, for example, the subject scores 110 on a test with an SEM of 3.8, then approximately two-thirds of the time, statistically, the actual score would fall between 106.2 and 113.8 (the score of 110 plus or minus 3.8). The impact of the SEM can be very powerful (not least because it is so often ignored). If students are identified for a program on the basis of a cutoff in test scores, it is easy to see how the looseness implied by the SEM can be significant.

✦ Taken together, the problems with formal tests (not all of which by any means are the fault of the tests or the examiners) have led to a decrease in their use in assessing exceptional students. Although the testing tradition is still quite solidly established, alternative sources are more frequently being used, and tend to have increasing credibility. What still remains for special education, is to narrow the gulf between the conducting of an assessment of an exceptional student and the developing of a program.

The Formal Case Study

A case study is an efficient executive summary that collates information from a number of sources into one document. In situations where an exceptional student's case has become complicated over time—and many do— and when it has involved a variety of personnel, some of whom may not know one another, or have never worked together, a case study brings together history, current status, and needs. If written with some care, it can be the most effective means by far, of bringing a group of professionals with diverse interests up to speed on a situation for which they share responsibility.

Ideally an educational case study is prepared by the teacher nominally responsible for the student in question and is written according to two principal criteria:

✔ succinctness (Effective writers usually aim at a maximum of two pages.)

✔ a non-judgemental, non-evaluative statement of the *facts*

and most often presents information under headings like these:

1. Demographic data
2. Description of the educational issue
3. Family history
4. Physical and health status
5. Social and behavioural matters
6. Supplementary reports
7. Assessment data
8. Current program and placement

9. Recommendations (Most educational case studies do not include a recommendation component until after the meeting discussions etc. for which the case study was initially prepared).

Regrettably, case studies have pretty much fallen into disuse in education today, not because of any flaws in either the idea or the process but largely because our contemporary system seems to deny the time needed to complete them in favour of a reliance on the Individual Education Plan.

READINGS & RESOURCES

Algozzine, B., & Ysseldyke, J. (1992). *Strategies and tactics for effective instruction.* Longmont, CO: Sopris West.

Bagnato, S. J., Neisworth, J. T., & Munson, S. M. (1997). *Linking authentic assessment and early intervention: Advances in curriculum based assessment (3rd ed.).* Baltimore: Paul H. Brooks.

Benner, S. M. (1992). *Assessing your children with special needs: An ecological perspective.* New York: Longman.

Bufkin, L. J., & Bryde, S. M. (1996). Young children at their best: Linking play to assessment and intervention. *Teaching Exceptional Children, 29,* 50-53.

Cole, E. & Brown. R. (1996). Multidisciplinary school teams: A five-year follow-up study. *Canadian Journal of School Psychology, 12,* 155-168.

Gajris, M., Salend, S. J. & Hemrick, M. A. (1994). Teacher acceptability of testing modifications for mainstreamed students. *Learning Disabilities Research and Practice, 9,* 236-243.

Howell, K. W., Fox, S. L., & Morehead, M. K. (1993). *Curriculum Based evaluation: Teaching and decision making (2nd ed.).* Pacific Grove CA: Brooks/Cole.

Kleinert, H. L., Haigh, J., Kearns, J. F., & Kennedy, S. (2000). Alternate assessments: Lessons learned and roads to be taken. *Exceptional Children, 67(1),* 51-66.

Kubiszyn, T. & Borich, G. (1996*). Educational testing and measurement: classroom application and practice (5th ed.).* New York: Harper Collins.

Neisworth, J. T., & Bagnato, S. J. (1996). Assessment for early intervention: Emerging themes and practices. In S. L. Odom & M. E. McLean (Eds.*) Early intervention/early childhood special education: recommended practices.* Austin TX: Pro-Ed.

Paulson, F. L., Paulson, P. R., & Meyer, C. A. (1991). What makes a portfolio a portfolio? *Educational Leadership, 48(5),* 60-63.

Pierangelo, R., & Giuliana, G. (1998). *Special educators complete guide to 109 diagnostic tests: How to select and interpret tests, use results in IEPs, and remediate specific difficulties.* West Nyack, NY: The Center for Applied Research in Education.

Pierangelo, R., & Giuliani, G. (2006). *The special educator's comprehensive guide to diagnostic tests.* San Francisco: Jossey-Bass.

Pierangelo, P., & Giuliani, G. A., (2006) *Assessment in special education: a practical approach (2nd ed.).* Boston: Pearson: Allyn & Bacon.

Popham, W. J. (1999). *Classroom assessment: What teachers need to know.* Needham Heights, MA: Allyn & Bacon.

Reed, L. C. (1993). Achieving the aims and purposes of schooling through authentic assessments. *Middle School Journal, 25(2),* 11-13.

Salend, S. J. (1998). In Assessment (Special Issue) (1998) *Teaching Exceptional Children, 31(2)* Nov/Dec.

Sarouphim, K. (1999). Discovering multiple intelligences through a performance based assessment: Consistency with independent ratings. *Exceptional Children 65(2),*151-163.

Salvia, J., & Ysseldyke, J. E. (1995). *Assessment (6th ed.)*. Boston: Houghton Mifflin.

Salvia J &Ysseldyke, J. E. with Bolt. S. (2007) *Assessment in special and inclusive education (10th ed.)*. Boston; Houghton Miflin.

Thurlow, M. L., Ysseldyke, J. E., & Silverstein, B. (1995). Testing accommodations for students with disabilities. *Remedial and Special Education, 16(5)*, 260-270.

Tindal, G., McDonald, M., Tedesco, M., Glasow, A. Almond, P., Crawford, L., & Hollenbeck, K. (2003). Alternate assessments in reading and math: Development and validation of students with significant disabilities. *Exceptional Children, 69(4)*, 481-494.

Valenca, S. (1990). A portfolio approach to classroom reading assignments: The whys, whats and hows. *The Reading Teacher, 43(4)*, 38-40.

Venn, J. J. (2007). *Assessing students with special needs (4th ed.)* New Jersey: Pearson Merrill Prentice Hall

Weber, E. (1999*). Student assessment that works: A practical approach*. Needham Heights, MA: Allyn & Bacon.

Ysseldyke, J., & Olsen, K. (1999). Putting alternative assessments into practice: What to measure and possible sources of data. *Exceptional Children, 65(2)*, 175-185.

Links

About.com: Special Education
http:specialed.about.com/od/assessment/ Special_Education_Assessment.htm

Alberta assessment Consortium
www.aac.ab.ca

National Center for Educational Assessment
www.ncea.ca

CHAPTER 8

Students With Learning Disabilities

"I always thought that there was something wrong with me. When I was in the early grades my mom arranged for me to take a taxi into the city once a week, a day long journey, just to get an hour in a special reading clinic at the university. For years my aunt Kit read special lessons every day with me at lunch time. When I went to highschool, even though I tried my best I never seemed to be able to do it right. Mr. Critch my home room teacher, told my mom that if I could only say the answers instead of writing them I would have no trouble at all. Unfortunately back then teachers didn't know a lot about LD and oral tests didn't count. I never graduated highschool."

John C, age 42

Misconceptions About Learning Disabilities

1. "Learning disability" is a social invention that excuses failure in middle- and upper-class children.

A large body of research and an even larger catalogue of experience make clear that a learning disability is a genuine special need, and one that knows no social class barriers. As with any exceptionality, however, the effects of a learning disability can be aggravated by socio-economic factors.

2. Heredity plays no role in learning disabilities.

Although the strength and nature of the connection are unclear, evidence points to a pattern of learning disabilities in families. This seems to be the case particularly in the matter of reading acquisition and fluency, where contemporary genetic research has identified linkages with specific chromosomes.

3. Learning disabilities only show up in schools and are therefore a "school problem."

Certain disabilities may remain hidden until the demands of school-based learning reveal them (e.g., language skills, mathematics skills) but other specific disabilities (e.g., memory and attention; perceptual-motor processing) will become obvious independent of schooling.

4. The main cause of learning disabilities is bad teaching.

Not long after the term for this exceptionality was first developed, its critics offered "dyspedagogia" (bad teaching) as the real cause of the syndrome. Although ineffective instruction has negative consequences for all students, decades of experience, careful observation, and research have demonstrated clearly that learning disabilities are a pre-existing set of special needs, independent of the quality of instruction (although the effects of disabilities are usually made worse by poor instruction).

5. Most children will outgrow a learning disability.

With effective instruction, the majority of children with learning disabilities manage their needs, but disabilities usually endure into adulthood.

6. Students who are learning disabled are highly intelligent.

Although many students with a learning disability develop clever coping strategies and what is sometimes called substitution or diversion behaviours, there is little evidence to substantiate the claim of above-average intelligence. In fact, the weight of evidence suggests that on IQ tests, such students' scores run across the same range as the general population, with what seems to be a tendency to fall in the average to below-average categories.

7. Learning disabilities and acquired brain injury are one and the same.

While many of the teaching and coping techniques may be similar for these two populations, they are indeed very different. Suddenness of onset, sensory, pain and fatigue issues as well as the recovery period associated with acquired brain injury make it a distinct condition.

8. Students who are ADHD are learning disabled (and vice versa).

Hyperactivity and learning disability have become very much interwoven over the past several decades. The connection, however, is not absolute. A person with ADHD is not always learning disabled, or vice versa.

9. Students who are learning disabled are more likely to become delinquent or criminal.

This claim originated in the 1960s and, if nothing else, contributed to the high profile that learning disabilities acquired after that time. Some research shows a slightly higher incidence of learning disabilities in prison populations, but definition problems weaken those findings.

10. It is possible to detect the presence of a learning disability by testing.

No test yet available can detect a learning disability in the same way that a hearing test, for example, can specify the nature and seriousness of a hearing loss. A learning disability is identified through teamwork by educators, parents, and sometimes other professionals, using observation, curriculum-based assessment, informal tests, and to some extent, standardized, formal tests.

What Is a Learning Disability?

The answer to the question "What is a learning disability?" may be better answered, at least initially, by another question, that being "What it isn't"? Learning disabilities are not primarily the result of a sensory impairment, emotional disturbance, physical disability, cultural difference, or developmental delay. While these conditions do not prohibit the existence of a learning disability, they must be eliminated as a primary cause of students' inability to learn successfully. Having eliminated these other factors as a primary cause of difficulty, it soon becomes clear that learning disabilities, as an area of disability, can be the most elusive of all areas in special education. In the first place, it is not a global impairment in which all elements of a student's performance are affected. Nor is it a consistent, easily measured, and clear special need. The only criterion that all students with learning disablties seem to share is loosely described as a difficulty in dealing with information, particularly language-based information, despite apparent freedom from any intellectual or sensory handicap or cultural difference. The difficulty may be in taking in the information, or, in integrating it with what they already know and understand, or, in expressing what they now know as a result of taking in and integrating the information. Or— and this is where the elusiveness begins— it may be a combination of the previous three elements (or just two of the three!). Students with learning disabilities may be disorganized, unable to focus attention, forgetful, and disoriented. They may be hyperactive—or hypoactive. They may be highly resistant to changing inappropriate behaviours, or, so compliant that they are easily led astray. One student may manifest all of these characteristics; another student, while functioning at the same low academic level, may manifest only one of them. And either student may demonstrate some of these characteristics on one day, and on another day, show absolutely none of them. Or all of them!

In effect, the exceptionality of "learning disabilities" is a syndrome of a number of behaviours. Unlike students with intellectual disabilities, in which case the impairment seems to be global, affecting all elements of an individual's performance, students with learning disabilities usually have more specific issues to cope with.

Defining the Indefinable?

When the late Dr. Samuel Kirk, former head of the National Advisory Committee of Handicapped Children, proposed the term "learning disability" to a conference of parents seeking information about their "mystery kids" in the early 1960s, the response was immediate and positive. The fact that the term became widespread very quickly indicated the extent to which large numbers of concerned parents were seeking an explanation why their children did not succeed in school, despite what they, the parents, knew was not lack of intellect. (And it was parents, far more than academics, who were responsible for placing learning disability front and centre in education.) The new term was non-pejorative and all-encompassing. It avoided implications of low intellect and ineptitude, and successfully replaced a variety of unsatisfactory general descriptors like *dyslexia, perceptual handicap, minimally brain-injured, maturational lag,* even *slow learner.* The dark side, however, is that the term learning disability is loose enough to permit a variety of interpretations, and although it offered a sense of focus and direction, and put a consensual face on

The Case of Cory

After his parents' separation, Cory lived with his mother in an inner city area. For a period of about four years, his mother regularly obstructed the father's visiting rights, contravening a string of court orders. On the day Cory entered grade 1, his father picked him up from school at lunch hour and the two disappeared. Eighteen months later his maternal grandparents appeared at Pearson Airport with the boy in tow, claiming they had rescued him from an abusive situation abroad. Children's Aid Society (CAS) intervened and placed him with foster parents for six months, after which his mother was again awarded custody. One year later, Children's Aid again intervened and Cory was returned to the foster parents who had maintained him previously. Meanwhile, Cory's father returned to Canada and applied for, and was denied, permanent custody. But contrary to the recommendations of the CAS, the court granted him weekly visitation rights. At about this time, Cory's mother suddenly remarried, abandoned her suit for restoration of custody, and moved to South America. Her parents (the maternal grandparents above) have now applied for custody, and CAS has entered an application to make Cory a permanent ward.

Cory is now almost ten. He is in a split grade 3/4 in his eleventh school, and has missed about a full year of schooling. He takes medication for TB, and he has a slight hearing loss. Cory reads very poorly. Both his printing, and the language and content of his stories can be easily mistaken for that of a much younger child. His math skills are inconsistent. Although his teacher suspects he may have an articulation problem, a speech consultant feels his odd way of talking is a product of mixing English and Spanish early in life. Everyone agrees that at least part of his learning problems is the result of timidity. A psychologist described Cory's manner as "juvenile shellshock."

The social worker responsible for Cory (a former teacher) believes the evidence clearly indicates a learning disability and that if he is so identified, he'll get some of the help he so obviously needs. The School Team believes Cory's status is a result of his personal history and that what he needs is love and above all stability. To identify him as learning disabled, they argue, will add yet one more change. The principal is strongly opposed to what she calls "using the learning disability category as a dumping ground for problems that have alternate solutions." The IPRC considering the case says it will listen to any argument that clarifies whether or not Cory has a learning disability, and will consider any and all recommendations.

an issue that had been running in all directions, making the next step to a clear and widely accepted definition, proved then—and still does today—a challenging task.

A Variety of Explanations …

Many notions and ideas about how to view learning disabilities have enjoyed periods of popularity since the 1960s. Because they continue to crop up in the literature, and because none of them have been effectively and clearly disproven, they are briefly summarized here.

- *IQ score/achievement discrepancy:* Supporters contend that a difference of two years or more between the mental age obtained on an intelligence test, and the grade-age equivalent obtained on a standardized achievement test indicates a learning disability. The flaw of this approach is that it

reduces the complexity of an individual to numbers. Also, a two-year discrepancy has different meanings at various ages and grade levels.

- *Presumption of central nervous system (CNS) disorder:* Much of the early work in learning disability grew out of central nervous system and brain injury research of the 1930s and 1940s. Researchers, because they noted similar behaviours between children known to have brain injury and those in the new subject pool, tended to make a leap of attribution so that students with learning disabilities were seen to have CNS disorder. Although by the 1980s, special education had generally retreated from the belief in brain anomalies as a cause of learning disabilities, new technologies like magnetic resonance imaging (MRI) have now shown subtle differences in the brains of individuals thought to be learning disabled. Although the connection remains vague, and its value to education unclear, that finding has kept the file open.

- *Impairments in psychological processing:* Psychological processing includes such cognitive functions as memory and attention, perceptual-motor processing, language processing, visual-spatial integration, etc. A strengthening conviction that diminished capacity in one, some, or all of these processes distinguishes persons with learning disabilities led a very important support group, the Learning Disabilities Association of Ontario, to give this hypothesis prominence in its definition published in 2001.

- *Exclusion of environment, culture, mental retardation, sensory impairment, emotional health:* If a learning problem is related to one of the above, that problem is usually not considered a learning disability. Unfortunately, the connection between such factors as emotional health and low, generalized academic achievement is well established, so that separating them from the fact of a learning disability is difficult.

- *Classification:* Educators have favoured classifications of degree in dealing with learning disabilities, applying descriptors like "mild," "moderate," and "severe," as well as classifi-

---

Transition to post-secondary ✍

While it is more than reasonable to assume that students with learning disabilities can and should move into post-secondary educational settings, it is important to provide support for this transition. The following suggestions provide guidance for educators at the high school level who will be in the position to assist these students.

- ✦ Begin transition planning early (probably as soon as the end of grade 9).

- ✦ Allow for a wide variety of courses that lead to programs, but focus on areas of strength.

- ✦ Involve students in the processs.

- ✦ Teach self-advocacy skills (the students should know their rights).

- ✦ Be sure that students understand what a learning disability is.

- ✦ Focus on both academic and personal independence.

- ✦ Update assessment information where needed.

- ✦ Familiarize students with the resources available at the post-secondary institution.

cations of type, usually "specific" for those cases where a student's need tends to be singular (e.g., has special needs in language; does well otherwise) and "general" where a student lags behind peers in most areas. Unfortunately, the lack of an adequate, objective testing instrument for learning disabilities usually means that these classifications become pretty much subjective evaluations. As well, the terms transport poorly. What is "moderate" and/or "specific" in one school may not be in another.

... and a Variety of Definitions

• *Learning Disabilities Association of Ontario, adopted 2001*

Learning disabilities refers to a variety of disorders that affect the acquisition, retention, understanding, organization, or use of verbal and/or non-verbal information. These disorders result from impairments in one or more psychological processes related to learning in combination with otherwise average abilities essential for thinking and reasoning. Learning disabilities are specific, not global, impairments and as such are distinct from intellectual disabilities.

Learning disabilities range in severity and invariably interfere with the acquisition and use of one or more of the following important skills: oral language (e.g., listening, speaking, understanding), reading (e.g., decoding, comprehension), written language (e.g., spelling, written expression), mathematics (e.g., computation, problem solving). Learning disabilities may also cause difficulties with organizational skills, social perception, and social interaction. The impairments are generally life-long. However, their effects may be expressed differently over time, depending on the match between the demands of the environment and the individual's characteristics. Some impairments may be noted during the pre-school years, while others may not become evident until much later. During the school years, learning disabilities are suggested by unexpectedly low achievement or achievement that is sustainable only by extremely high levels of effort and support.

Learning disabilities are due to genetic, other congenital and/or acquired neuro-biological factors. They are not caused by factors such as cultural or language differences, inadequate or inappropriate instruction, socio-economic status, or lack of motivation, although any one of these and other factors may compound the impact of learning disabilities.

Frequently, learning disabilities co-exist with other conditions, including attentional, behavioural, and emotional disorders, sensory impairments or other medical conditions. For success, persons with learning disabilities require specialized interventions in home, school, community and workplace settings appropriate to their individual strengths and needs, including: specific skill instruction; the development of compensatory strategies; appropriate accommodations.

• *Ontario Ministry of Education, as published in A Guide for Educators, 2001*

Learning disability is a learning disorder evident in both academic and social situations that involves one or more of the processes necessary for the proper use of spoken language or the symbols of communication, and that is characterized by a condition that:

a) is not primarily the result of: impairment of vision; impairment of hearing; physical disability; developmental disability; primary emotional disturbance; cultural difference;

b) results in a significant discrepancy between academic achievement and assessed intellectual ability, with deficits in one or more of the following: receptive language (listening, reading); language processing (thinking, conceptualizing, integrating); expressive language (talking, spelling, writing); mathematical computations; and

c) may be associated with one or more conditions diagnosed as: a perceptual handicap; a brain injury; minimal brain dysfunction; dyslexia; developmental aphasia.

• *National Joint Committee on Learning Disabilities (USA) as presented, 1988*

Learning disabilities is a general term that refers to a homogeneous group of disorders manifested by significant difficulties in the acquisition and use of listening, speaking, reading, writing, reasoning, or mathematical abilities. These disorders are intrinsic to the individual, presumed to be due to central nervous system dysfunction, and may occur across the life span.

Problems in self-regulatory behaviour, social perception, and social interaction may exist with learning disabilities but do not by themselves constitute a learning disability, Although learning disabilities may occur concomitantly with other handicapping conditions (e.g., sensory impairment, mental retardation, severe emotional disturbance) or with extrinsic influences (such as cultural differences, insufficient or inappropriate instruction), they are not the result of these conditions or influences.

Characteristics of Learning Disabilities

Processing Language

Many students with learning disabilities are challenged by the task of processing language. At the *receiving* stage (when the student is hearing language or attempting to read it) or at the *sending* stage (speaking or writing), or at the *elaboration* stage (when the student attempts to integrate some language with what he or she already holds), a student with a learning disability often has real problems. For some students, it's only at one of the stages; for others, difficulty arises at two or all three stages. For example, a younger student may not be able to process an incoming set of instructions like: "Use your red crayon to colour the robins, and then your yellow one to draw a line under the 'r-r-r-r' sound." The student will hear the instruction all right, but all the linguistic information: robins, crayons, red, yellow, "r-r-r-r" sound, not to mention the activity, may be too much to process. The student may miss the instruction altogether, or miss a piece of it, or confuse red and yellow, or interchange pieces of information. The result will likely be a poor performance or a non-performance.

An older student may have an equally difficult time with something like this from, say, a geography teacher: "If you refer to your maps of West Africa, you'll notice a good example of how Africa was fragmented by decolonialization. Notice how Gambia is literally inserted into Senegal, and then further down the coast you'll see even more examples with Guinea-Bissau, Guinea, Togo, and Benin all sitting side by side." The older student may have more sophisticated language ability than the one colouring robins, but then he or she is expected to deal with more sophisticated language, and, relatively, is going to have just as much or even more trouble.

It is not unusual for an adult working with a student who has a learning disability to confuse the student's weakness in processing of language with weakness in visual or auditory discrimination. For example, unless the student has a vision or hearing loss, this student will have no difficulty visually discriminating the letter A from a picture of a teepee, or the sound of "book" from the sound of "hook." Where the student will manifest difficulty, however, is recognizing the letter A as such, and giving its name (or recalling the word teepee and saying it). It is not distinguishing between the sounds of "book" and "hook" that is hard; it is recognizing the words and the meanings; or, giving the right answers even if the student knows them. A student who is learning disabled may also have difficulty in producing the letter A on paper (or the

A multimedia literacy program in the self-contained learning disability class at Tino's secondary school has had a major impact on him. The program uses video- and audio-tapes, and some single-sheet print material, but its centrepieces are a software program, items downloaded from the Internet, and a "chat line." Tino gives full credit to this program for the fact that he now can read the TV guide, and billboards, and can "get" the jokes that show up on the chat line. Two weeks ago, the second part of a standardized assessment instrument, administered in split-half form, showed that Tino has learned to note periods at the end of sentences; he can identify the correct spelling of previously learned words after three days (but does not yet write the words). And he can follow directions that tell him how to complete geometric figures. Tino could not do any of these things six months ago.

These are the first indications of progress for Tino in a very long time. He was identified "learning disabled" seven years ago (he's now 15) and has been placed mostly in resource classes since that time. According to reading assessments, Tino has never been able to read above a grade 3 to 4 level. Prior to starting on this new program, Tino had been a regular visitor to both the vice-principal and the counselling office, but for the past while he has avoided demerit points.

Tino's situation comes up for annual review in a month, by the IPRC. Although reviews in the past have pretty much rubber stamped a continuation of his identification and placement, Tino's parents have served notice they want a "serious discussion" this time. The problem, they feel, is that the multimedia program, while beneficial, is too much fun and too unrealistic. They argue that clicking responses on a screen to gradually produce a finished product of some sort (e.g., a math problem, a string of short, connected sentences, a drawing—the program also prints out a certificate of accomplishment each time) will achieve nothing in the long run. The parents want some evidence that Tino either can now, or will soon be able to, manage independently. The situation is not without irony, for Tino's teachers have also wondered about this. Yet they are more aware than most that for the first time, he seems to be getting somewhere. The issue is how to wean him from the program, or perhaps even more basic: whether he should be.

words "book" or "hook"). The student may draw a teepee, but it may be disproportionate. On the other hand, the student may be able to draw a beautiful teepee but when instructed to add a campfire at the left and a horse on the right, will have to guess at these juxtapositions.

Variations in Ability

What makes the language-processing deficiency above so insidious is that it is so variable. If there are three students in the geography class who have learning disabilities, one of them might be entirely confused by the concept of "decolonialization" and miss everything else as a result. A second, unless there is a map right before him or her, will be overwhelmed by all the verbal details of the countries mentioned. The third may understand the point perfectly and even be able to hypothesize on it, but three days later on the examination, may be entirely unable to put

together the language that will explain what he or she thinks.

The English Language is a Factor

The subtleties of English may pose a barrier for students with learning disabilities. A teacher for example, who says to a student, "I don't see your answer" may mean a number of different things. She or he may mean the answer is simply not visibly apparent, or that the answer was not completed, or that she/he does not understand the answer, or that she/he disagrees with it. Because some students who are learning disabled not only have difficulty with language, but even further difficulty in reading between the lines of communication situations and social contexts, they may respond incorrectly to "I don't see your answer" or, respond undiplomatically, or just not respond at all.

Language that attempts to capture time and

The Case of Raghubar

Raghubar's mother is fully involved with the stress of learning to live in a new country and a new culture, but even though she has no other children on whom to base a comparison, she has not been too preoccupied to notice that her little boy does things differently. Not that he is hard to control; and he definitely is not deaf, but somehow, he never seems to hear her. Well, not quite that way either. He hears her, but does perhaps half of what he's asked, or starts the task and then wanders away, or more often than not, does it backwards or leaves out a step. Raghubar almost never gets anything exactly right. Except in soccer. In soccer he is so good that older children in the community park stop to watch him. Still, that, too, is a mixed blessing. Raghubar is a natural athlete, a gifted one, probably. But he also has no fear. He puts himself at such risk that his mother is certain that one day he'll injure himself permanently. And that concern ties into another one. Raghubar never seems to learn from the experience of a bad fall or a banged shin or painful cut. The very next day, he'll go out and do the same thing that led to an accident the first time.

Although she has a fairly limited education herself, Raghubar's mom had the good sense to visit her son's teacher-to-be, well before his formal schooling began. As a result, the teacher was on the lookout for what sounded to him like a learning disability, a suspicion that was reinforced when Raghubar lagged the rest of the class when it began to learn letters. After six months now, in the first grade, it is clear the boy is not picking up what his classmates get. He recognizes only six letters, and in counting, gets to ten and becomes confused. Over half his class is already reading more or less independently.

When the teacher suggested to the principal that an assessment/identification might be in order, he got the two responses he expected: one, that Raghubar is far too young and undeveloped for such a major step; and two, that at this early stage the best strategy is to revise the boy's program. The teacher has now turned to his colleagues for help. Is a six year old too young and undeveloped to be called "learning disabled," he wants to know? And, what program steps can he take right away, for a boy who does not count past ten, and recognizes only six letters?

sequence is another of the many stumbling blocks, in part because the language itself can be very complicated, and in part because chronology and sequence are problems all on their own. For example, in the sentence "Only after it first sprouts blossoms, can the tree bear fruit," the words and the syntax used to describe the sequence, set up real complications. The phrase, "only after" is at the *beginning* of the sentence. Yet it sets up a condition and presents a time frame for the rest of the sentence, which then describes what in effect must happen *before* "only after "! Efficient language users can usually comprehend such a sentence. Students with learning disabilities often do not. Still another barrier exists in the pronoun "it." Not only must "it" be held in short term memory until its referent ("tree") surfaces, the listener/reader must perceive that "it" refers to "tree" and not some other idea! (Research shows that the difficulty with pronouns normally experienced by young language learners, aged four and five, is experienced by students with learning disabilities well

into their teenage and adult years.)

Difficulties like those above are compounded by the problems students with learning disabilities have in relating one sentence to others in a passage, or in relating passages to passages, or even stories to stories, whether written or spoken.

Are We On the Same Wave Length?

One of the more unsettling aspects of the problem in processing language, for teachers, parents, and certainly for the students themselves, is the frustration of discovering that a communication that appeared to be successful, has been partly or even completely misunderstood or misinterpreted. (Admittedly, this is a common trait in all children, but what distinguishes students with learning disabilities is the consistency with which this occurs.) Because teachers, parents, and students often engage in a communication knowing that the potential for confusion is high, all parties often take extra care to be sure that the communication has meshed in a way that what was sent is also what has been received. It is not

The term "dyslexia" was first used by a German ophthalmologist in 1877 to describe a phenomenon in which otherwise normal individuals seem to have great difficulty extracting meaning from print. Around the same time, a pair of British doctors noted the disability but called it "word-blindness," a term that was soon discarded. Over the decades since, a combination of genuine academic research, pop psychology and media fascination* have done much to fix dyslexia in the public consciousness. An American organization with international affiliates, the Orton Dyslexia Society, named after neurologist Samuel Orton (whose work dates to the 1920s and 1930s), has done even more to carry the idea forward, so that dyslexia has become completely familiar in our culture.

For teachers and EAs, the issue is not so much whether dyslexia is real. Most professionals agree there are individuals who, although otherwise physically and intellectually normal, are unable to extract meaning from print or to produce written text in a manner that is age appropriate. But confusion arises because dyslexia is regularly used as a synonym for general learning disabilities (as is frequently the case in England, for example). Although for Canadian educators, dyslexia usually means a specific difficulty—i.e., processing the printed word—such use of the term is not universal, so confusion may occur. The simple reality is that dyslexia and learning disability are not really one and the same inclusive term. The former describes a specific special need associated with language development. The latter has a far broader application, incorporating both language difficulties and other, non-language based learning problems. To use the two terms interchangeably does a disservice.

---

* Popular press items on dyslexia, regularly trot out a list of "famous dyslexics" like Alexander Graham Bell, Pablo Picasso, Jay Leno, Cher, John Lennon, and others.

difficult, therefore, to imagine the stress that results when what appeared to be a successful interchange was really two separate tracks of communication that overlapped from time to time but never bonded into that stage of information interchange we like to call *understanding*. The implications of this problem for life in general, and for the classroom especially, are significant. Whether it occurs solely because of faulty language processing or because of memory problems has yet to be clearly established. All that is known for sure is that it happens. Often.

Memory

An apparently poor memory for learning and for new information is another characteristic that distinguishes many students with a learning disability. They may, at the moment of instruction, learn a technique or an idea, or acquire information, or memorize a sequence or a formula at the same pace and in the same depth as their colleagues without learning disabilities. But unlike the latter, they will have difficulty retrieving it the next day.

Accounting for this supposed memory problem has generated considerable speculation. One hypothesis is that the students forget because they cannot transfer learning and information from short-term to long-term memory, or at least cannot do so easily. Another is that it is strictly a result of poor language processing: not a case of simple forgetting but of not getting a correct grasp of the material in the first place. (More recently, there has been argument, particularly from audiologists, that the faulty processing results from imperfections in the central auditory nerve.) None of the explanations is entirely satisfactory. If the students cannot transfer from short- to long-term memory, then why can teachers and parents cite examples of phenomenal long-term memory retention in students who are learning disabled? If the central auditory nerve is the culprit, why does the forgetting occur just as frequently with written language? And if language-processing problems are the sole cause, why do students with learning disabilities so often make the same *social mistakes* time after time? (Students who are learning disabled frequently have difficult peer relations because of a seeming inability to gain from social experience. They continue to repeat social gaffes, seemingly not remembering what happened when a similar situation cropped up previously.)

Whatever the cause, it is essential to be aware that students with learning disabilities may not have retained what everyone else thinks they have—or should have. It inevitably shapes how we relate to them.

Metacognition

Loosely defined, metacognition has been called "thinking about thinking." For a majority of students who attend school, the ability to strategize, monitor their performance, and adjust accordingly come as natural skills. For a student with a learning disability, the understanding of self, awareness of the mind's activity, sensitivity to the strategies available for learning a task, and an understanding of the regulatory mechanisms needed to complete the task, present a real and persistent challenge. Teachers and educational assistants can readily attest to the difficulty a student with a learning disability has with such tasks as studying, remembering class requirements such as homework, or taking on a project and organizing it through to completion. Oftentimes these difficulties can be misinterpreted as lack of interest, laziness, or outright defiance. Strategies as simple as providing more time, using graphic organizers, and posting reminders have proven to be effective in assisting students with learning disabilities be more successful in their learning environment.

Difficulties With Sequence and Order

Students with learning disabilities miss steps in a sequence, get them out of sequence, reverse the sequence, and as often as not, may simply ignore a sequence. Research has not been able to demonstrate clearly whether this is a cognitive or an affective characteristic, but the weight of empirical evidence is in favour of the former interpretation.

Satisfaction With a Peripheral Understanding

An adolescent seeking a credit in chemistry, when asked what is Boyle's Law, might typically answer "Oh it's about pressure and that." The likelihood is that the student knows more: probably a definition of Boyle's Law, perhaps even an understanding of how to apply it in a problem. If this adolescent is learning disabled, the answer "Pressure and that" may well constitute the sum total of the student's knowledge of the law. *Yet the student will quite likely believe he or she has a thorough grasp of it*, and proceed comfortably in that self-assurance until confronted by a request to apply Boyle's Law to a problem. This is the same student who in grade 2 wrote three lines in his or her journal while the rest of the class averaged twenty. And who likely responded indignantly to a comment about such a slim output with something like "I *did* my journal," or "That's all I have to say!" The key feature is the student's satisfaction with a vague, incomplete, peripheral piece of work, *and* the student's conviction that the work is adequate. This is a crucial behaviour for educators to recognize. It's not defiance; it is not shirking; and it is not an utter lack of ability. It is a misinterpretation of what constitutes completeness.

Poor Time Management

It is not surprising that a student who rarely plans ahead and even more rarely accommodates his or her activity to due dates and timetables, is frequently late, or in the wrong place, or in conflict with some time-specific requirement, or is just chronically off-task. Many students with learning disabilities seem to be unaware of time, or at least of time as a concept organized into sequentially discrete units. This page in the LD catalogue accounts for a significant portion of their trouble in school. Because schools are so time-driven, so inflexibly organized into chronological chunks—sequenced, hierarchical, chronological chunks—the student often feels entirely out of place. School bewilders the student not just because of its emphasis on language (and its commensurate de-emphasis of non-language elements like music and art and athletics where the student may shine) but also because of its apparent obsession with time in specified units. Regrettably, the outside world is equally passionate about time, and learning to deal with that is a necessary prerequisite in all of education. It is not unusual for a student with

Some Day-to-Day School Problems Associated with Learning Disabilities

Coordination/Cooperation
- may have difficulty lining up
- often confused or anxious over taking turns
- may bump, trip, or spill far more frequently than peers

Writing Skills
- may confuse letters in writing and in recitation
- mixes upper and lower case letters
- mixes manuscript and cursive styles, or will continue to use manuscript long after age and grade peers use cursive
- frequently distorts letter size and shape
- attempts at continuous text are scratchy, barely legible
- often mirrors or reverses letters
- awkward, even unnatural movement of the pen or pencil

Personal Organization
- forgets, misplaces things
- needs constant reminding (and often has successfully trained others to do this)
- frequently late or in the wrong place
- poor notion of chronological order
- may confuse instructions especially if there is more than one step

Copying/Note-Making
- careless, often reproduces inaccurately
- loses place often
- far-point copying very slow and inaccurate
- overprints, telescopes, omits
- may have difficulty reproducing a shape from memory
- ignores sub-headings and organization cues

Arithmetic
- reverses numbers
- careless about columnar structure
- may not remember rote matters (multiplication tables)
- carries or borrows wrong digit
- skips or omits steps in problem solving

Reading/Language
- loses place regularly
- makes many flying guesses
- does not attempt a new or strange word
- ignores punctuation and other cues
- makes up words, telescopes
- reverses and transposes
- loses meaning of a sentence from beginning to end
- gets events out of sequence
- infers content that is not there
- forgets details
- does not seem to retain a basic stock of spelling words
- often uses creative, phonetic spelling

Work Speed
- very often does not finish
- works slower than age and grade peers
- frustrated under time pressure

Social
- may relate poorly to peers
- often repeats a social error
- may fail to "read" the wishes of others
- often has difficulty keeping friends
- frequently on the fringe of groups

learning disabilities to perform better, both generally and academically, in an environment where the student is liberated somewhat from the demands of time.

Inconsistent and Episodic

What is at once tantalizing and frustrating for anyone who tries to view the field of learning disabilities objectively (viz., teachers, educational assistants, parents, academics, medical professionals, et al) is the knowledge that the profile of a student with a learning disability is never the same day after day, and that a single characteristic of learning disability is never universal. A student with this disability may regularly write "on" for "no" and "b" for "d," yet in the same sentence use all four elements correctly. He may use "on" for "no" consistently for three weeks, and then suddenly and spontaneously use them correctly while simultaneously beginning to write "was" for "saw," even though those had been correctly used hitherto. This is the adolescent who cannot remember a single irregular verb in French, or the formula for calculating the area of a circle, or the definition of alliteration but who, on a warm Saturday, can strip down, clean, repair, and completely reassemble a mountain bike. This is the child who bumps into everyone in the queue, whose shoes are untied and whose shirttail hangs out, but who is the first in his or her age group to earn Red Cross badges for swimming excellence. This is the one who forgets where he or she put his or her clothes, books, and lunch, who confuses his or her telephone number and address, but can recite without error, a T.V. ad or the lyrics of a song.

It is an acknowledged fact by all associated with persons who are learning disabled that no one student will be the same as another, and that no one student's own pattern will ever be consistent and regular. This phenomenon, among other things, makes children's learning disabilities almost completely resistant to positive identification by formal standardized tests. It bears equally important weight for the classroom teacher who must be ever prepared to adjust to the episodic nature of these students' performance. And, of course, for parents, this inconsistency and episodic behaviour is yet one more arrow in the quiver of confusion.

Difficulty Paying Attention

That students who are learning disabled do not attend as well in class as their more academically successful colleagues is a given. What is less clear is the cause. Do they fail to attend because years of confusion have taught the value of avoidance? Or is the habit innate? The question is a continuing debate in the field. Whether the characteristic is inherent or learned, the simple fact is that most students who are learning disabled do not concentrate in school (and often at home) in sufficient depth or for sufficient time to learn or acquire new information or receive instruction effectively. This attention problem is expressed in

forms that vary from simple daydreaming to pervasive, counter-productive activity.

Low Self-Esteem

Of all the commonly occurring traits in persons who are learning disabled, this one is not inherent but acquired. And the cause, at least as far as school is concerned, is fairly obvious. In a system, that not only rewards but celebrates academic achievement, it is easy to understand that a student who consistently fails to achieve at anywhere near the expected standards will develop serious doubts about his or her whole persona. What makes this characteristic so damaging is that it feeds a continuous loop. A student with a learning disability who has become accustomed to low achievement, also becomes accustomed to putting out minimal effort on the quite understandable premise that there is no point if there is no payoff. Therefore, the achievement level decreases even further, both because it may have been affected in the first place by the learning disability, but also by lack of effort. As a result, neither teacher nor parent nor the student gets to see how good the results really could be. Even worse, both sides become so accustomed to poor achievement that on the rare occasions of success they often look first for the fluke that brought it about!

The next link in this chain is invariably behavioural. Students develop personas to divert attention from their disability and their failure and to attract attention to other matters. The class clown, the victim, the super-competent, the I-don't-care, the bad-guy—these are all popular masks that students with learning disabilities wear.

Assessment and Identification

By Teacher-Educational Assistant-Parent Teamwork

Experience shows that classroom professionals, working cooperatively with parents and EAs, and often with the input of other professionals, are in the best position to establish the presence or absence of a learning disability with considerable certainty. In fact, this kind of teamwork, shaped by a few prerequisites, may be the only way to make a diagnosis with confidence. The prerequisites are disarmingly simple.

1. *Understand the exceptionality.* To diagnose and identify a learning disability, one must be clearly aware of the characteristics that make up this special need. Because a learning disability does not yield to a definable set of criteria in the same way that a hearing loss, for example, does to an audiometric assessment, to uncover the presence of a learning disability, one must first know what to look for empirically.

2. *Observe carefully.* Armed with the knowledge of what to look for (and sufficiently informed by that knowledge to go looking), it follows that an effective way of making the identification is to watch for clear evidence of some or all of the characteristics.

3. *Take time.* Since a learning disability is episodic by nature, it is a given that observation must take place over a period of time. Learning disabilities are not revealed in a one-shot assessment.

4. *Use informal aids.* Rating scales, questionnaires, informal reading inventories, and the like can be of assistance, especially in providing specific focus on a student's needs, and in collating the efforts of different observers.

5. *Teamwork.* In the best interests of the student being assessed, everyone involved, classroom teacher, special education teacher, educational assistant, parents, etc., must share findings, and attempt to achieve a consensus. A team is more likely to impose caution on the identification process. Because the presence of a learning disability is difficult to pin down, and because every human being exhibits some LD characteristics some of the time, the broader view available to a team helps to keep things in perspective.

By Standardized IQ and Achievement Tests

IQ tests and standardized achievement tests are too narrow to capture the complexity of a learning disability, at least in ways that would benefit the student or the student's teachers. Often, in a standardized assessment, the testing done pro-

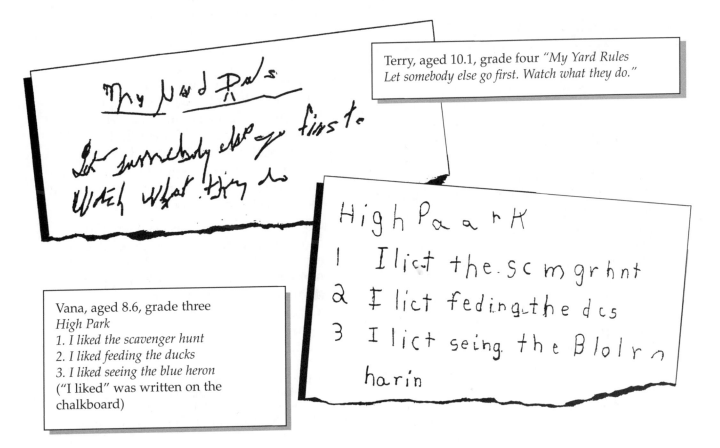

Terry, aged 10.1, grade four *"My Yard Rules Let somebody else go first. Watch what they do."*

Vana, aged 8.6, grade three
High Park
1. I liked the scavenger hunt
2. I liked feeding the ducks
3. I liked seeing the blue heron
("I liked" was written on the chalkboard)

vides the *what* and not the *why* or the *how* that educators need to program for students with learning disabilities. While this type of testing can provide useful information, these instruments simply offer a number. The translation of that number into classroom practice is difficult at best. What the number does reveal is generally what everyone knows already, although a number may have purpose if it is needed to pry loose funds, or to set the table for an administrative action. Another weakness in the use of these tests lies in the episodic nature of learning disabilities, for very often the same instrument will produce an entirely different result on consecutive days, thus diminishing its reliability. Even more important, at least in the classroom, tests do not point to practical, helpful, strategies that classroom personnel can use.

Nevertheless, extensive formal testing to uncover a learning disability continues, possibly because it is a long-established practice (or perhaps because it offers at least a feeling that something is being done!). Therefore, in situations where this type of instrument is used, it is important that the results be seen as only one of several clues.

Some Issues in the Field

✦ *Teacher preparation* for professionals who will be working with students with learning disabilities within the regular class is a growing area of concern. Students with learning disabilities represent by far the largest proportion of students identified with exceptionalities in the province, approximately 43 percent. One could argue successfully that as a classroom teacher, with the increased emphasis on inclusion, that a thorough knowledge of learning disabilities would be an important requirement for successful teaching. Despite this, candidates in teacher education programs express great concern over what they perceive as a lack of preparation to work with students with exceptionalities.

✦ *Universal acceptance of a definition* of learning disabilities continues to elude those who care about this special need. Nor do the many existent definitions, official and other-wise, seem to be coalescing around key points in any noticeable way.

✦ *Assessing* the presence and extent of a learning disability in a manner that produces clear, indisputable results does not seem to be possible.

✦ *Co-occurring disabilities*, most commonly ADHD and behavioural disorders are a constant challenge. Not only is the presence of other special needs difficult to identify and assess*, the very notion is a challenge to administrators charged with service delivery and to those who must address the situation day to day in the classroom. Interestingly, empirical evidence seems to suggest that the issue is a far greater concern at the bureaucratic level, where formal identification, funding, and placement are matters of daily importance. In the classroom, teachers and educational assistants tend to find themselves addressing co-occurring disabilities in a manner similar to that in which they approach students with (presumably) only one special need.

✦ *Integrating* students with learning disabilities into regular classes or educating them in self-contained classes is always up for discussion. The principal advocacy group in the field, the Learning Disabilities Association (LDA), is generally supportive of the idea that schools should maintain the option of self-contained resource placement for some students. Because the trend toward inclusion continues, however, and given the numbers of students identified as learning disabled, teachers of regular classes should always expect to have one or more—usually more—such students in their classes.

✦ *Gender representation* has been a niggling concern for years and is no closer to being explained than it ever was. Data show that males outnumber females by at least two to one in the category of learning disability. Yet, examination of data from any typical

• • • ───────
* McKinney et al. (1993) in "Educational assessment of students with attention deficit disorders" reported that across a wide range of jurisdictions, identification of co-occurrence of learning disability and behaviour varied from 9 to 80 percent! *Exceptional Children*, 60, 125-31.
─────── • • •

> a BlaK roB FaSd the windol wh
> It trd arun , say It had ~ BlaK
> hod SnalKs Kam aut oF th hod

Cameron, aged 15.3, grade nine—opening of a 95 word narrative …
"A black robe faced the window. When it turned around I saw it had a black hood. Snakes came out of the hood."

Canadian jurisdiction will show that this phenomenon is equally true of almost every category of exceptionality.

✦ *Overidentification?* Available data show that students who are learning disabled outnumber their peers in any other category of special need. (This is not an Ontario phenomenon; these data are similar to those in other provinces and in the U.S.) Such numbers continue to provoke accusations of gross misidentification, and of excessive "dumping," viz., underperforming students are simply called learning disabled because that relieves the school system, the parents, and the students themselves of any blame for doing poorly. While there are few educators who would deny that this kind of escape indeed takes place, the accusation is very much unwarranted. Awareness of learning disability is relatively new in education and it follows that there may well have been a rush to identify students who fit so ideally into the category. Evidence that current numbers of identified students with learning disabilities are probably realistic can be found by examining prevalence and incidence data over the past thirty years. The sharp rise in numbers over the late 1960s and through the 1970s began to slow

in the mid-1980s, and numbers have remained quite consistent since.

✦ *Quackery or experimental science?* Even before the term learning disability became popular, there were many unusual therapies, techniques, and teaching methods available to deal with students who, despite apparently normal ability, spoke incomprehensibly, or wrote in most unusual ways, or generally performed in ways that are off the mark for their age. (See the writing examples in this chapter.) It would have been fairly common practice at one time, for example, to engage students like Vana and Terry in extensive calisthenic exercises to—theoretically—develop their "visual-motor integration skills." Very often, popular support for these unusual techniques blossomed as a result of endorsements and "gee whiz" articles in non-refereed journals. Usually, the popularity of a technique declined after it was submitted to careful scrutiny.

Still, it is unfair to dismiss unusual teaching methods out of hand, if only because, given the uncertainty over just what constitutes a learning disability, any response demands at least rational consideration.

(1) Differentiated Instruction: As the movement toward meaningful inclusion of students with diverse learning needs becomes more and more of a reality for educators across Ontario, the challenge of aligning the curriculum content and assignments with the learning needs of students becomes an important focal point for instruction. Differentiated instruction, while providing an enhanced learning environment for all students can be especially effective for students with learning disabilities. Traditionally differentiated instruction has been commonplace in special education settings where Individual Education Plans are the norm. Within the regular class, curriculum planning and design has traditionally been focused on large-group instruction. A move to differentiated instruction takes the focus away from modifying the program after the fact toward planning a program upfront to meet a variety of learning styles and differing abilities.

(2) Empathy and understanding are prerequisite qualities in any person hoping to offer instruction to students with learning disabilities (although this point is likely redundant to an effective teacher). Once one "gets inside" the particular nature of these students, making the necessary steps of accommodation follows naturally. A teacher must set up a warm, supportive climate, without pandering to, or making excuses for, or drawing unnecessary attention to the students' particular needs. The older the students are, the more difficult this task tends to be, for they will likely have well-established and annoying avoidance behaviours, developed over years of practice. Yet, unless a teacher has an appreciation of what his or her students are contending with, and unless there is some sensitivity toward that, all efforts will eventually degenerate into despair and conflict. An environment of mutual trust is crucial for teaching all students with exceptionalities, but for students with learning disabilities there is an added, subtle layer. These students usually do not appear at first to be handicapped in any way; in fact they often seem as though they should be especially successful. But they are not, and most of the time, they do not understand why, any more

than the adults in their lives do. Such is the insidious nature of a learning disability. It is why empathy and understanding on the part of the teacher are so important.

(3) Positive, frequent feedback as quickly as possible, especially on academic matters, is crucial. This feedback helps practically, by keeping the student on task, and more abstractly, by reinforcing momentum, the component so necessary for continuing academic success and achievement. A student with learning disabilities, especially if the student has had a history of failure, is not willing to defer gratification as successful students do. He or she needs reassurance and reinforcement to build self-esteem to a point where the student will put forth his or her best effort. Fortunately, this kind of feedback does not have to be dramatic (although an occasional "celebration" can work wonders). Simple attention to even modest achievement is often all that is necessary to develop self-esteem.

(4) A consistent, systematic approach will help a student with learning disabilities eventually learn to interpret and accommodate expectations. Part of this approach will be a firm insistence on on-task behaviour and thoroughness. Perhaps a more encompassing term would be structure. The very nature of the day-to-day cognitive function of a student who has a learning disability means that not only classroom instruction but such apparently simple things as classroom regulations and expectations must be clearly outlined, with the parameters firmly established. Teachers must remember that a student with a learning disability not only does not learn or manage himself or herself as effectively as he or she might, the student usually does not know how. If the student's teacher establishes the boundaries and points out the steps, both self-management and learning become easier. (And once a structure is established, it is also easier for the teacher to be empathetic and supportive because an operating context has been established that both parties understand.)

(5) Graphic and visual support benefits students with learning disabilities significantly. Use of the

chalkboard, whiteboard, computer, overhead transparencies, pictures, maps, and other concrete supports, helps them to comprehend what might otherwise be a mass of confusion. In fact, many successful teachers assert that it is impossible to teach these students otherwise. A positive note here is that while graphic and visual supports are essential for students who are learning disabled, they are also helpful techniques for all students.

(6) Help in sequencing is important. Teachers must emphasize steps and stages in the proper order as a lesson progresses. The same applies to all assignments, projects, homework, or any other item that requires independent and individual completion. Without guidance in where to begin, and what organization to follow, students with learning disabilities will become confused and likely as not tune out or give up.

(7) Help in dealing with print is important for many students with learning disabilities. Reading, as well as producing legible and coherent text, can be a difficult and time-consuming procedure, so not only must a teacher recognize that challenge and make allowances in time, the teacher may well have to modify the challenge, by simplifying instructions or providing an alternate format.

(8) Awareness of time constraints, one of the realities of school that regular students pick up quickly, is yet another factor that teachers must factor in for their students with learning disabilities. Many of these students do not forward plan, and it may well take their entire school careers before they learn the responsibilities inherent in due dates, appointments, and scheduling. Yet they can and do eventually acquire these skills, however imperfectly, and for that reason it is essential that their teachers persist. (Both parents and teachers attest that this issue is one of the most frustrating, and one that offers the strongest temptation to simply give up.)

(9) "Staying-on-top of things," for lack of a more professional-sounding phrase, may be an apt way of describing all those apparently superficial, but in reality, fundamental behaviours, that a teacher must help his or her students who are learning disabled to exercise. Drawing the student's attention to signal words, counselling about sequence and about time, reminding the student to bring and take materials, cueing things by saying "Watch for the change here," and "This is important"—all these seemingly small things go together to help the student cope with daily life in the classroom.

(10) Making allowances for those skills that students with learning disabilities never ever seem to master is another part of the teacher's role. Correct spelling, for example, is an expectation many of these students almost never meet, and to pursue it relentlessly is counter-productive. It is far more effective both in short and long term to teach the students how to use a dictionary effectively, or to get help via software. Similarly, since these students never seem to master the memorization of multiplication tables, it makes sense to forgo the memorization requirement. Other matters, simple on the surface to most of us, frequently escape students with learning disabilities. Multiple-choice questions, for example, so time-honoured and so commonly used, often have a subtlety that totally confounds. So does convoluted syntax. An attempt to persuade, for example, by saying "Inasmuch as the field day is on Monday and the movie on Wednesday, wouldn't you be better to get the project done this week?" will not succeed like this will: "Finish the project this week, because next week we have a field day and a movie. There will be no time to do it next week".

(11) Simplifying the environment. Within the boundaries of what is practical and sensible, simply by removing distractions a teacher can make a difference. Sometimes the seating arrangement in a room or the adjacent surroundings of a student who is learning disabled can be modified to the student's benefit.

(12) Finally, as evanescent as *hope and optimism* may seem, they are the glue, along with *trust* and *encouragement*, that hold the relationship of teacher and student together. A student with a learning disability, usually far more than his or her peers without learning disabilities, will

TWO SIMPLE ESSENTIALS: Time & Drill

Special education is especially susceptible to allegedly novel instructional concepts often hailed as quasi-"cures." Most of these flare up and dominate the stage for a time before being abandoned or else incorporated into regular classroom practice, usually with more than a little modification. Most of the time, these leading-edge teaching strategies (and the lofty vocabulary that typically accompanies them) are simply elevated re-castings of time-honoured, sound classroom practice. When teachers take a moment to analyze techniques like "scaffolded instruction" or "metacognitive training," or "mnemonic keyword method," for example, they often recognize methods they have already been using, albeit modified to their own purposes. One positive outcome of these models of instruction is that they give special education practices an elevated status. A drawback is that they tend to divert attention from the merit of simple ideas that experience has proven valuable. Two of these simple ideas, long known to be effective with students who are learning disabled, are *expanded instruction time* and *drill*. We draw extra attention to them here, lest they are ignored for lack of apparent sophistication.

Time: Students who are learning disabled take longer to learn, and teaching them a concept, a technique, a set of facts, therefore, simply takes more instruction time. As any experienced teacher will attest, students who are learning disabled often need to be re-taught, or taught the same lesson in a different manner, or with different materials. And they need time to redo and review on their own until the lesson is firm. The following formula illustrates the point.

$$\frac{\text{quality of}}{\text{instruction}} \times \left(\frac{\text{time spent}}{\text{time needed}}\right) = \frac{\text{degree of}}{\text{learning}}$$

For example, if quality of instruction is represented by an arbitrary factor of '5', and if the time needed by the student is also '5', but time spent is '1', the results are modest.

$$5 \times \tfrac{1}{5} = 1$$

Notice that even if the quality of instruction is doubled (to a factor of 10) the effects are still modest if the time spent does not match the time needed

$$10 \times \tfrac{1}{5} = 2$$

But if the time actually spent equates more closely to the time the student needs, the results are significantly different

$$5 \times \tfrac{5}{5} = 5$$

Like any formula laid over something as abstract and individual as learning, this one is guilty of oversimplification. Yet it illustrates the potential impact when a profound need of the typical learning disabled student—*enough time*—is addressed.

Drill: A logical correlation of time is *drill* (or "opportunity to reinforce by practice" if a more elevated description is preferred). Both through research and empiricism, teachers know that practice—drill—plays an important part in learning. Can it be less than reasonable to assume then that learning disabled students, who find learning difficult, require more opportunity to practice until they have something down pat? Granted, going over previously traveled ground is tedious, but no procedure has yet been found, scientific or otherwise, that equals the effect of repeating something often enough until it becomes part of a student's repertoire.

A creative educator can find many ways to make drill interesting through games, and computer and classroom activities.

The sentence by Cameron below is the fifth rewrite of the item that appears on page 103. A resource room EA assisted Cameron with rewrites 2, 3, and 4. This is an independent effort.

a black robe fos faced the window. When it turned around I saw it hada had a black hood. Snakes came out of the hood.

respond to a stimulus, not so much because of a vague awareness that it is part of his or her education, but rather, because the teacher, the one he or she trusts and respects, has asked him/her to. It is a reality that imposes a heavy responsibility on the teacher, but then, without that reality, the art of teaching would not be as exciting. Or as

rewarding. It is trust and encouragement and hope and optimism that lead to the extra steps, the extra efforts, the one-more-times, and ultimately, to the breakthroughs. Realistically, breakthroughs are not all that frequent. What is far more common is plodding progress, but then progress of any kind is worth the effort.

READINGS & RESOURCES

Aylwards, E. H. (2003). Instructional treatment associated with changes in brain activities in children with dyslexia. *Neurology, 61*(2).

Deshler, D. D., Ellis, E. S., & Lenz, B. K. (1996). *Teaching adolescence with learning disabilities: Strategies and methods.* Denver: Love Publishing Inc.

Dyson, L. L. (2003). Children with learning disabilities within the family context: a comparison with siblings in global self-concept, academic self-concept, academic self-perception, and social competence. *Learning Disabilities Research and Practice, 18*(1), 1-9.

Garderen, D., & Whittaker, C. (2006). Planning differentiated instruction for secondary inclusive classrooms. *Teaching Exceptional Children, 38*, 12-20.

Gersten, R. (1998). Recent advances in instructional research for students with learning disabilities: An overview. *Learning Disabilities Research and Practice, 13*(3), 153-172.

Hallenbeck, M. J. (1996). The cognitive strategy in writing: Welcome relief for adolescents with learning disabilities. *Learning Disabilities Research and Practice, 11*, 107-119.

Higgins, E. L., & Raskind, M. H. (1995). Compensatory effectiveness of speech recognition on the written composition performance of post secondary students with learning disabilities. *Learning*

Disability Quarterly, 18, 159-176.

Hinchelwood, J. (1917). *Congenital word blindness.* London: H.K.Lewis.

Hughes, C. A. (1996). Memory and test-taking strategies. In D. D. Deshler, E. S. Ellis, & B. K. Lenz (Eds.), *Teaching adolescents with learning disabilities (2ⁿᵈ ed.).* Denver: Love.

Huntington, D. D., & Bender, W. N. (1993). Adolescents with learning disabilities at risk? Emotional well-being, depression, suicide. *Journal of Learning Disabilities, 26*, 159-166.

Jitendra, A. K., Edwards, C. M., Choutka, C. M., & Treadway, P. S. (2002). A collaborative approach to planning in the content areas for students with learning disabilities: Assessing the general curriculum. *Learning Disabilities Research and Practice, 17*(4), 252-267.

Lewis, S. & Bates, K. (2005). How to implement differentiated instruction? *Journal of Staff Development, 26* (4), 26-31

Levy, N. R. (1996). Teaching analytical writing: Help for general education middle school teachers. *Intervention in School and Clinic, 33*(2), 95-103.

Madaus, J. W. (2005). Navigating the college transition maze: A guide for students with learning disabilities. *Teaching Exceptional Children 37*(3),32-37.

Mavis, L., Donahue, M. L., & Pearl, R. (2003). Studying social development and learning disabilities is not for the faint hearted: Comments on risk/resilience framework. *Learning Disabilities Research and Practice, 18*(2), 2003, 90-93.

McKenzie, R. G. (1991). Content area instruction delivered by secondary learning disabilities teachers: A national survey. *Learning Disabilities Quarterly, 14,* 115-122.

Raskind, M. H., Herman, K. L., & Torgeson, J. K. (1995). Technology for persons with learning disabilities: Report on an international symposium. *Learning Disability Quarterly, 18,* 175-184.

Rea, P. J., McLaughlin, V. L., & Walther-Thomas, C. (2002). Outcomes for students with learning disabilities in inclusive pull out programs. *Exceptional Children, 68*(2), 203-222.

Richardson, S. (1992). Historical perspectives of dyslexia. *Journal of Learning Disabilities, 25*(1), 40-47.

Rose, D., Meyers, A., & Hitchcock, C. (2005). *The universally designed classroom: Accessible curriculum and digital technologies.* Cambridge MA: Harvard Education Press.

Salend, S. J., & Hofsetter, E. (1996). Adapting a problem-solving approach to teaching mathematics to students with mild disabilities. *Intervention in School and Clinic, 31*(4), 209-207.

Sherman, G. F. (1995). Dyslexia: Is it all in your mind? *Perspectives, 21*(4), 1.

Speece, D. L., & Shekitka, L. (2002). How should reading disabilities be operationalized? A survey of experts. *Learning Disabilities Research and Practice, 17*(2), 118-123.

Strong Scott, M., Fletcher, K. L., & Stoyko Deuel L. L. (1998). The effects of intelligence on the identification of young children with learning disabilities. *Learning Disabilities Research and Practice, 13*(2), 81-89.

Swanson, H. L. (1993). Executive processing in learning disabled readers. *Intelligence, 17*(2), 117-149.

Welch, M. (1992). The PLEASE strategy. A metacognitive learning strategy for improving the paragraph writing of students with mild learning disabilities. *Learning Disability Quarterly, 15,* 119-128.

Wong, B. (Ed.) (1995). *Learning about Learning Disabilities (2nd Ed.).* California: Academic Press Ltd.

Links

Learning Disabilities Association of Canada **http://www.ldac-taac.ca/**

LD on line **http://www.ldonline.org/**

National Council for Learning Disabilities **http://www.ncld.org/**

Learning Disabilities Association of Ontario **http://www.ldao.ca/**

CHAPTER 9

Students With Behavioural Exceptionalities
Students with AD/HD

"Working with secondary school students with behavioural exceptionalities causes each day, each moment to be a new unplanned experience. Much of the time is spent trying to develop relationships, community and a safe place so that the students trust me to guide them through the most scary thing of their lives: school. Some days we all feel like failures, but some days, the spark is there and things get accomplished"

Jenessa D. Secondary School Behaviour Resource Teacher.

Misconceptions About Emotional/Behavioural Disorders

1. Youth violence has increased significantly since the mid- to late-twentieth century.

Educators, legal authorities and community workers find it too difficult to establish whether the increase is real, whether data collection is more rigorous, or merely whether perceptions have changed. (A 1999 Canadian study* found that while 56.4 percent in a sample of secondary school administrators believed violence in schools had increased, only 28.1 percent believed this was true in their own schools!)

2. Once a student is identified with an emotional/behavioural disorder in the school system, it is easier to get services in any education system across the country.

Unfortunately, services for students with emotional/behavioural disorders vary across the province, and there is no guarantee that an iden-

tification of an emotional/behavioural disorder will carry over to another board inside or outside the province.

3. Developments in mental health science have made the identification and classification of behavioural disorders simpler and easier for educators.

The dominating schemata for clinical description and classification is the American Psychiatric Association's Diagnostic and Statistical Manual of Mental Disorders IV-TR (DSM-IV-TR** or more commonly referred to as DSM). The DSM, however, classifies disorders as either present or absent. To most classroom teachers and assistants, emotional/behavioural problems are far more subtle.

• • • ──────

* Dolmage, W.R. (1999). Lies, Damned Lies and Statistics: The Media's Treatment of Youth Violence. *Education & Law Journal, 10,* 4-46. (The article describes misconceptions created by media on the issue.)

** At time of publication this is the most recently revised edition of this manual. The next major revison is scheduled for 2011 with periodic additions and commentary posted on the website of American Psychiatric Association.

• • •

4. Bullying is an age-old, natural schoolyard phenomenon and students learn to deal with it as part of growing up.

While educators have long been aware of bullying as a reality of the schoolyard, it is now known that the phenomenon can have long-term consequence for both the bully and the victim.

5. Behavioural disorders are neither age- nor gender-related.

Most studies show identified cases of males outnumber females by ratios of up to 5 to 1. In the last decade of the twentieth century, however, new data began to show significant rate increases for girls over boys, in identified behaviour and in crime.

6. Behavioural disorders are manifested in patterns of aggression and frustration.

There is no doubt that outward-directed behaviour is noticeable and may well be disordered. However, symptoms of behavioural disorder can also be expressed by reticence and withdrawal. The latter is not as easily noticed, particularly in large classroom groupings.

7. Very often a behavioural disorder indicates a student who is bright but frustrated.

Available data suggest a correlation between behavioural disorders and average to low IQ test scores, with the more severe cases even lower.

8. Difficult behaviour is an external manifestation of something deep-rooted.

There is no sound evidence that all the causes of behaviour are rooted deep in a student's psyche, or even necessarily connected to emotional disturbance. Especially in school, inappropriate behaviour is often spontaneous and temporary.

9. A permissive atmosphere that allows students to develop understanding and acceptance of the self is the most effective way to change inappropriate behaviour.

Evidence suggests that a highly structured, ordered, and predictable environment brings about the greatest change in students with a behavioural disorder.

10. Only the behaviour itself should be examined and dealt with, and why the behaviour is occurring is not important.

To deal effectively with a behavioural issue, it is often important to look beyond what is occurring to why it is occurring. This way, motivation, consequences, and rewards, as well as the teaching of new behaviour, can be aligned with the needs of individual students, and positive change is more likely to occur.

Bullies and Their Victims ✍

Bullying behaviour varies among individuals, but three behaviours appear to be common: it is a repeated action over time; it takes place in relationships where there is an imbalance of power; and it is unprovoked. While research—and schoolyard observation—suggests that more boys than girls engage in the behaviour, many teachers insist that more rigorous investigations will inevitably reveal that girls tend to use more subtle, less visible methods to accomplish their ends. Very often, the act of bullying is part of a wider set of behavioural problems. Bullies are often in conflict with authorities, tend to be depressed, are prone to a lifestyle that compromises their health, and often have problems with peer relationships. Victims tend to have lower self-esteem, and some manifest rather disturbed behaviour, although it is not clear whether this behaviour is a condition that arises from the bullying or is pre-existing.

Although a prevailing perception in the early twenty-first century is that bullying has become rampant, it is extremely difficult to establish hard data to support that belief. Nevertheless, research (Mishna 2003, cited in Cummings, Peplar, Mishna & Craig, 2006) indicated that students in self-contained classrooms are stigmatized and more frequently bullied than those in mainstreamed classrooms. Students with behavioural difficulties (especially Attention Deficit Hyperactivity Disorder) have been found to be more involved with bullying, either as the "bully" or the "bullied", than those with more age-appropriate behaviour. Recent legislation is trying to ensure that schools pay closer attention to bullying behaviour and that steps be taken to ensure that schools are a safe place for all students.

Behavioural Disorder, Emotionally/Behaviourally Disturbed or Behavioural Exceptional—What Should It Be Called??

When the topic of behavioural disorders is considered, it needs to be made clear that there is some confusion over what term should be used and which students fall under this category. When Public Law 94-142 was passed in the United States (1975), the term "seriously emotionally disturbed" was used. In 1997, the term was changed to "emotionally disturbed."

In Canada, we also have some confusion over this issue. Some provinces have no term to recognize this population. Others make a distinction among "mild," "moderate," and "severe" behavioural difficulties. In Ontario, the term "behavioural exceptionality" is used to represent students with behavioural and/or emotional issues and is the term that will be used for the remainder of this chapter.

To most people, behavioural exceptionality is behaviour that varies markedly and chronically from accepted norms. In a general way then, the notion is quite widely accepted and understood much in the same way that a general notion of normal behaviour is widely accepted and understood. It is from this point that differences develop, for there seems to be remarkably little agreement as to exactly where on the continuum, from normal to otherwise, behaviour becomes aberrant. Social and cultural conditions are influencing factors. Certain cultures, for example, have very permissive ideas about child rearing, and when the children of that culture, the young particularly, encounter a dominant group where child-rearing values are more structured and restrictive, it is not hard to see why the different values may lead to perceptions of behavioural exceptionality.

Other factors, too, influence perceptions of what one may consider a behavioural exceptionality. Even within a single social setting, such as a school, there can be wide differences, for the same behaviour may be seen as disruptive by one teacher but normal by another. Then there are the realities that all children display varying behaviours and that behaviour patterns increase and decline over time within a single individual. Special educators are especially aware that patterns of conduct are affected by disabling conditions. Students with hearing problems can become extremely frustrated by their inability to comprehend. The same is true of students with visual disabilities (especially younger ones whose condition has not yet been diagnosed) and equally true of those with developmental or learning disabilities.

In order to create a common ground of understanding, mental health professionals, in particular, have attempted to organize behavioural exceptionalities by classification (as in the Diagnostic and Statistical Manual of the American Psychiatric Association). Unfortunately, consensus among this group is still limited. Interestingly, educators seem to have less difficulty with the issue, possibly because they have a more unified perspective and a more clearly delineated set of common objectives. Immediately following is a brief description of the more popular views held by mental health professionals, and of the general view held by educators.

The View From Mental Health

Mental health professionals tend to view behavioural exceptionalities from a particular perspective or theory or enveloping concept, a tendency that affects the research they do, their treatment styles, and the way they attempt to educate others. Listed here is a very brief summary of the more widely held theories.

- *Environmental* Factors in the environment, including diet, air pollution, metals, etc., lead to behavioural problems. (Note that this concept is often held in concert with one or more of the others listed below.)

- *Psychodynamic* People with behavioural exceptionalities are experiencing deep-rooted inner turmoil and their deviations are a manifestation of this turmoil.

- *Psychosocial* An individual's relationship with family and peers may bring on inappropriate or unacceptable behaviour.

- *Psychoeducational* A student's behaviour may be owing to a combination of circumstances that are brought about by stresses in the school, home, or community.

- *Behaviourist* Deviation from normal is the result of having been taught the wrong things or by following inappropriate role models.

- *Biophysical* Deficiencies in genetics, neurology, biochemistry, along with disease and malnutrition, cause deviant behaviour.

- *Combinations* Some or all of the above theories appear in combination.

Teachers' Perceptions of Behavioural Exceptionalities

Given the subjectivity of determining whether or not a student falls into the behavioural exceptionality category, it is important to be aware that most teachers, educational assistants, childcare workers, and others responsible for the students with behavioural exceptionalities accept the value of classifications for mental health purposes, but do not find them very practical on the front lines. Thus, while the classifications used by mental health professionals may be informative, or may have some administrative value, or may possibly be used by a multidisciplinary team, the prevailing style in education is to approach the notion of behavioural exceptionality without terminology or diagnosing. In determining whether or not a student might be behavioural exceptional, an assessment team will almost always consider exclusionary factors: whether or not the behaviour can be traced to specific sensory, social, or health-related causes. Nevertheless, even if a student's inappropriate behaviour can be explained as a direct outcome of some specific, explainable factor, he or she might still be identified as behavioural exceptional, for the simple reason that no matter what the cause, it is still the behaviour—the effect—that the educators must deal with.

When educators identify a student as having a behavioural exceptionality, they generally do so on the basis that the student:

- deviates in a significant manner from the behaviour that is normally expected in the situation

- breaks social or cultural norms that are usually well established for the age level

- shows a tendency toward compulsive and impulsive behaviour that negatively affects learning

- has poor interpersonal relationships, and low self-esteem

- has low academic achievement owing to conduct

(perhaps the most important) manifests any or all of the above characteristics with an intensity, frequency, and/or duration such that additional assistance and/or intervention is likely required to improve the student's ability to maintain appropriate behaviour.

Behavioural Exceptionalities: Concern Over an Increasing Population?

Behaviour that deviates from the norm attracts a disproportionate amount of attention from the media, an interest that leads to a perception that the prevalence of behavioural exceptionalities is on the increase. The increase may indeed be real. Or not. Most of the time, research data simply confirms what teachers and educational assistants already know: that boys outnumber girls, particularly in aggression and hyperactivity; that prevalence rates are highest in the upper grades of elementary school, and first grades of secondary school, and lowest in the primary grades; and that there tends to be a higher rate of aggressive behaviours among children from lower socioeconomic groups. Nevertheless, the value of data collection should never be disregarded.

There was an increase in students identified under the behavioural umbrella between 2001 and 2005—7701 elementary in 2001 versus 8164 in 2005 and 4280 secondary versus 5015 in 2005/6. However, this increase may be attributed to an increase in overall student population with a corresponding focus on zero tolerance policies established by the government of the day. In 2006, under a new government, the zero tolerance policy established under the Safe Schools Act of 2000 was changed to permit principals more flexibilty in their handling of incidents of aggressive behaviour in their schools and, though not yet defined, to put into place "progressive discipline" approaches designed to assist the student with aggressive behavioural difficulties learn more appropriate responses. Time will tell if this change in approach has an effect on the number of students referred to special education because of their behavioural difficulties.

Causes of Behavioural Exceptionalities

Biophysical

The majority of students who are identified as behavioural exceptional appear to be physically healthy. Nevertheless, recent theory and research suggest possible links between biological makeup and behaviour. Sometimes the connection is clearly, if also distressingly, apparent. Children born with fetal alcohol syndrome or fetal alcohol effects are a case in point (see chapter 11 on intellectual disabilities). The causes of pervasive development disorders (e.g., autism, see chapter 12) have become an area of extensive research—and speculation—inasmuch as biology is concerned. Research in genetics is provoking a continuing reassessment of disorders like schizophrenia. As recently as 2003, an Ontario judge sentenced a fourteen-year-old girl to two years probation, after she had pleaded guilty to aggravated assault on a teacher. The sentencing was very much affected by testimony that the girl's behaviour was influenced by a particularly powerful premenstrual syndrome. Biology, it seems, is now being considered in cases of behavioural exceptionality, almost as a matter of course. It is important to note, however that Kauffman (2005) suggests that " biological processes have a pervasive influence on behaviour, they affect behaviour only in interaction with environmental factors (p.165)". It appears, then, that there is a strong interaction between biophysical factors and environmental influences.

Allergies

Allergies, too, are being re-evaluated as causes of disordered behaviour. While the physical effects of allergies on some students are readily acknowledged, a more recent conception of allergies incorporates the thesis that allergenic reactions can generate learning and behavioural problems in a far deeper and more subtle way than the very obvious physical reactions. Though rare, it may be possible that a student has a capacity to tolerate only so much substance in the environment, and in some individuals, a combination of stale air, chalk dust, moulds and fungi in the carpet, and perfume or shaving lotion on the teacher, may exceed that student's tolerance (total load) and cause an allergic reaction expressed both in a physical way (e.g., a rash or watery eyes or sneezing) and in the student's behaviour. These reactions are often far more subtle yet profound than may be immediately apparent.

Speech and Language

Researchers have consistently found a higher incidence of behavioural exceptionalities among students with speech and language impairments than is found in the general population. While there is some debate in the field over whether language impairment is a cause or an effect of behavioural disorders, it seems logical to conclude that a student who has difficulty expressing his or her needs—or frustrations—may choose to act them out. Either way, it is certainly a point that classroom personnel must heed.

Psychological

Psychological explanations for behaviour vary by perspective (e.g., a psychoanalyst sees things differently from a behaviourist) and by setting (e.g., the home, the community, the school, etc.). Two very powerful influences on a child's behaviour are the home and the school. It is difficult to find a single cause for a particular child's behavioural or emotional state. Often the cause is a combination of factors that have led to the child reacting to the environment in a particular way. One major factor, though certainly not in all cases, is the child's relationship with his/her parents. This relationship is crucial to development, particularly in the early years. In homes, for example, where discipline is inconsistent and sometimes harsh, and where there is little reinforcement of affection, children often learn to be aggressive. Empirical evidence, supported by research, has consistently shown that the style of child rearing used by parents will have an impact on the behaviour of their children. Still,

With the cooperation of the district school board, an arrangement worked out by a social worker, the crown attorney, and the family court will keep Scott in custody for the remainder of June, and for July and August. In September he will go to a different school from the one he attended for the past two years. The school will be in a different neighbourhood and Scott will live in a secure group home until it is decided he can be placed with foster parents. Scott is thirteen.

The board has two possible schools for him. One school has a full rotary timetable and a behaviour resource class called the "drop-in room" where students may or may not be counselled depending on need, or work on their academic program, or just relax. If Scott goes to this school, he will be enrolled in a regular grade 6 class. An IPRC has confirmed his "behavioural" identification, and he will be eligible to go to the drop-in room when he feels the need, or, he can be sent there by any of the teachers. The principal of this school, and the staff, openly espouse a nurturing and personal development philosophy. The second school does not have a drop-in room. In fact, the school has no designated class for behaviour, and has only a very limited rotary timetable. If Scott goes here, he will be enrolled in a regular grade 6 class and spend most of his time with the teacher of that class. Whereas the three educational assistants in the first school are assigned to specific classes full time, the three in this school move as needed. The principal here believes strongly in academic achievement and the development of self-reliance, and she has attracted a staff with similar beliefs.

Because of privacy laws, no one knows why Scott is presently in custody. However, it is known that he has a history of aggressive behaviour, especially toward girls, and that the current brush with the courts is the latest in a string. What is also known is that Scott's full-scale IQ score is average; that there is no evidence that he has a learning disability, and that on a standardized achievement test, he was one grade below the age-appropriate level in math and three grades below in language skills. School teams in both schools are discussing Scott's program. What issues and solutions should they be considering?

teachers, especially those who are parents, realize that the causes of a child's behaviour may well be a two-way street, with parents responding to the behaviour originated by the child, rather than the latter simply becoming a product of what the child is taught. Unfortunately for those who work directly with a student, the cause of behavioural exceptionalities is less of an immediate issue than the effects, and is in any case, something they are somewhat powerless to modify: one reason why a multi-disciplinary team, which usually has a member working with the family, can be effective.

Some mental health professionals maintain that schools are a major cause of a student's behavioural difficulties but there is no clear evidence to support this claim. Yet since schools are where students spend a major portion of their wakeful day, it is logical to conclude that what goes on in the classroom, under the direction of the adults there, has a major influence on behaviour. The relationship, therefore, between students and teachers, between students and their classmates, and between students and the school at large can have a significant impact both in causing and correcting disordered behaviour.

Childhood Depression ✍

An often overlooked student is the one who quietly sits at his or her desk, rarely interacts with others, and seems to fade into the woodwork. It is possible that this student is dealing with childhood depression, a disorder whose prevalence has increased dramatically. Students with childhood depression may regularly appear sad, show limited academic gain, may not sleep well, and have feelings of worthlessness or hopelessness. Educators need to recognize these symptoms and refer the student for more intensive mental health evaluation. Treatment for childhood depression usually involves psychotherapy and medication, but teachers can also be very helpful by assisting the student to develop social skills and encouraging an increase in activity level.

Assessment of Behavioural Exceptionality

Unless a student comes to a school already diagnosed and identified, the first step in an assessment is usually taken by a classroom teacher, who calls upon nothing more technical than experience and common sense to recognize behaviour that departs from the norm seriously enough and often enough to be distinguished. In fact, informal screening by teachers and educational assistants has been established throughout education as a fairly reliable first measure.

In most jurisdictions in Canada, what follows formally after this initial phase is governed by a school board's particular plans and procedures. These would include formal assessments, which in turn may be governed by the availability and the expertise of personnel, and the current conceptual model for dealing with behavioural exceptionalities. The teacher and assistant, and often the parents and possibly a social worker or other community service worker, will usually be asked to complete some form of observation instrument like a behaviour checklist or rating scale. (In Ontario, The Child Behaviour Checklist, Achenbach and Edelbrock, 1991, 2001 is very popular.) A declining practice in the assessment of behavioural disorders, although it is still used in some jurisdictions that favour the psycho-dynamic approach, is the administration of projective tests, instruments that purport to reveal the intra-psychic life of the subject. (These tests have come under fairly heavy criticism for their questionable validity and potential for entirely subjective interpretation.) Once sufficient information is gathered, the next phases of program and placement are decided, sometimes by a school team, sometimes by special education teachers, or even by administrative fiat.

Since there is fairly convincing evidence that students who have serious behavioural problems in later grades often had difficulties in kindergarten, there is pressure to identify behavioural exceptionalities early. Doing so is not always possible, however, since disorders often do not emerge until the later grades when personal responsibilities and social and academic demands increase in complexity. Ultimately, the identification of a student as behaviourally

Reactive Attachment Disorder (RAD)

A recent addition to the list of disorders in the DSM-IV-TR is a condition that is believed to arise from an individual's failure to bond with other humans very early in life. RAD (a.k.a. AD) may develop in the very young because of the lack of nurture and attention in places like shelters for abandoned or orphaned children during wars or other crises, or because of deliberate abuse, or even, as some would have it, because modern parents are too involved and time-driven to provide the necessary emotional support for a newborn. According to the description, "RAD Kids" develop a protective shell against what they believe is an unsafe world where no adults can be trusted to care for them. Among the extensive list of symptoms these "unbonded" children are said to present are rage and destructiveness along with frequent lying, cheating, and stealing. They are said to be obsessive, manipulative, unaware of (or unconcerned with) consequences, and have no or limited empathy.

Unfortunately, RAD is easily confused with bipolar disorder, ADHD, Tourette syndrome, even learning disabilities. Advocates of the syndrome insist this confusion occurs simply because RAD is still poorly understood. Critics argue it may be because RAD is not really a separate disorder at all.

exceptional is best accomplished by teamwork, by the collaboration of classroom personnel, parents, and where available and helpful, mental health professionals, operating in an atmosphere of mutual respect and understanding.

Longstanding Issues Still Remain

✦ *As indicated earlier, agreement on an acceptable term for this exceptionality* has long been hard to achieve. Among the more popular identifiers, some of which are still current and overlap several fields are: socially maladjusted, emotionally disturbed, mentally ill, predelinquent, delinquent, emotionally handicapped, socially handicapped, and, of course, most frequently used in education: behaviour disordered or behaviour exceptionality. In the past, labels developed at what seemed to be the discretion of whoever was writing on the subject.

Emotionally disturbed, for example, first appeared (without precise definition) at the beginning of the twentieth century. Since then, many other terms have cropped up from time to time. In Ontario, for example, the term" behavioural exceptionality" is used, but this term is not used in other jurisdictions in Canada. The term behavioural exceptionality is used because it is conceptually inclusive of a variety of problems that warrant professional attention; it is less negative and stigmatizing than many of the other terms (e.g., emotional/behavioural disorder) in use; and it tends to circumvent the suggestion of legal identification. Above all, it is sufficiently comprehensive to have wide applicability.

◆ *Developing a useful definition* has proven just as difficult, for it follows that if the names for an exceptionality are elastic and capricious, describing it would be just as problematic. Definitions are vulnerable to their authors' theoretical perspective: behavioural? psychodynamic?; to their discipline: teacher? psychiatrist? lawyer?; and to their purpose for writing a definition: for research? for education? The effect of these differences is a serious block to practical communication, especially in light of the fact that a multi-disciplinary approach is often necessary, especially in more serious cases. The Ontario definition of behavioural exceptionality (see the Appendix) is based on a variation of what is contained in the United States Individual with Disabilities Education Act. Several groups, such as the Council for Children with Behavioral Disorders for example, have tried to change this definition both in the United States and in Ontario to one that more accurately reflects the behavioural manifestations and the needs of these students. It is believed by many in the field that a more accurate definition could assist

Conduct Disorder ✍

According to Kauffman (2005) 6% to 16% of boys and 2% to 9% of girls under age 18 may have a psychiatric disorder referred to as conduct disorder. This disorder is applied to children who may have great difficulty following rules, throw temper tantrums, destroy property, bully, or regularly act in deceitful ways. Kazdin (1998, cited in Kauffman, 2005) believed that "the term conduct disorder is usually reserved for a pattern of antisocial behavior that is associated with significant impairment in everyday functioning at home or school, and concerns of significant others that the child or adolescent is unmanageable (p. 199)." According to the website of Focus Adolescent Services (www.focusas.com), treatment for children with conduct disorders can be "complex and challenging." Treatment often involves both behaviour therapy and psychotherapy and extends over a long period of time. It is generally acknowledged that the earlier a child with conduct disorder is identified and receives treatment, the better likelihood for a positive outcome and a more productive adult life.

in better identifying these students and lead to more effective intervention.

On the other hand, there may be merit in the argument that this exceptionality, more than any other, should perhaps not be defined at all, that rather, a statement of needs should suffice. Inasmuch as there is no definition of normal behaviour—which would therefore be the referent for behaviour that is not—it is only reasonable that behavioural exceptionality cannot be defined either. Even though behavioural exceptionalities are distinguished by frequency and degree rather than by their nature, these exceptionalities cannot be measured quantitatively. There is no system analogous to the IQ test. And to add to the murkiness, people who exhibit disordered behaviour also behave normally! Above all, behavioural anomalies are exclusive to an individual; there is really no set of symptoms common enough to permit a description, much less a definition, that would be applicable to all cases, and be helpful to those who work with the individuals in question. Thus, unfortunately, the likelihood is that the lack of a useful, universally accepted definition will continue.

✦ *Are needs being met?* An area of concern is the discrepancy between the percentage of the school population that is behaviourally exceptional and the percentage that is actually being served. A Canada-wide study by Dworet and Rathgeber (1990) found that not only are the needs of large numbers of students with behavioural exceptionalities going unserved, this population is getting even less attention than it did in 1981! More recently, a follow-up study with data collected in 2004-5 shows a very uneven rate of prevalence throughout the country. In some jurisdictions, such as the Northwest Territories no reporting of prevalence was possible since they do not identify students with behavioural exceptionalities. Across provinces, Prince Edward Island reported a rate of 6.21%, while Ontario reported a rate of less than 1%, a significant decrease since information was last collected. Hallahan and Kauffman (1994) conclude that over two percent of the school population exhibits disordered behaviour. Yet data show that typically, less than one percent is being served. Recent U.S. Office of Education data show about one percent of students are identified as " emotionally disturbed."

✦ *School standards too high?* There is some evidence that schools illuminate behaviour as unacceptable because they have unrealistic and unnatural standards. Some theorists refer to this as "iatrogenic disorder": i.e., the behaviour arises as a consequence of the way the student is treated, and not out of a natural predisposition. Other theorists advance the idea of psychonoxious behaviours or attention-getting styles that, over time, accumulate a large pool of resentment in peers and teachers so that the student in question is treated as behaviourally exceptional, whether the student actually is so or not.

✦ *Socioeconomics and class distinctions* come into play in this exceptionality. Particularly in the case of adolescents, students from lower-income families report a greater number and variety of penalties for their behaviour. Moreover, certain behaviours by lower-income students are more likely to be regarded as behaviourally exceptional, whereas similar behaviours by students from high-income families are more likely to be seen as legitimate responses to stimuli. A study by Brantlinger (1991) suggests this phenomenon may be owing to inequities in school conditions for lower income students. Her study was conducted in the U.S., however, and in Canada there is ample reason to argue that poorer school conditions in lower socio-economic areas areas are uncommon, and that in fact extensive resources are committed to preventing such inequities. Nevertheless, this is not to deny that different attitudes toward the behaviour of students from lower social classes may well prevail here.

✦ *The stigma* of being identified with a behavioural exceptionality creates a lasting impression. It affects the opinion of teachers and peers, and it can contaminate matters for the student identified. Once placed in the "behavioural" category, exceptional students often find their history hard to escape, and must contend with an atmosphere where expectations govern the way others respond. As a consequence, administrators are often reluctant to apply a behavioural identification, so that some genuine cases of behavioural exceptionality may not be getting the appropriate intervention. This may certainly affect the prevalence rates referred to earlier.

✦ *Legal requirements* regularly complicate the education of a student who has become involved in crime. One of the more significant issues is the disruption of a student's education if he or she is moved through a variety of settings while a case is being decided and a sentence is being served. It is not unusual for an adolescent, particularly, to experience a variety of custodial settings through both the court hearing procedures and subsequent serving of a sentence. These settings will invariably have different educational approaches—if any—and usually, little effort is made to coordinate these approaches. To a student with a behavioural exceptionality such a lack of continuity can aggravate the problem. Another issue that arises out of the legal side is the rigorous privacy stipulations in Canadian law that in some cases preclude a teacher being informed of circumstances surrounding a student's involvement in crime, or even of being informed about a transgression at all. While this law may have no immediate bearing on educational planning, it may require the withholding of information that in some cases could be important not just to the student's program, but also to the well-being of the teacher and other members of the class.

✦ *The use of drugs* to manage behaviour has provoked debate among educators and mental health professionals from the time the very first pill was swallowed. Initially, much of the argument clustered around moral and ethical values that may be violated by chemically altering an individual's makeup and natural function. The debate is unlikely to diminish as long as drugs are used. Other oft-voiced sentiments prevail as well, despite the fact that empirical evidence has weakened many of them. The belief that administering drugs to a child will lead to later drug addiction has not proven demonstrably true. And the argument that drug therapy is an opportunity for parents (and even teachers) to turn their responsibilities over to chemicals, while it may be a fact in isolated, individual cases, has also not found support over time. On the other hand, the jury is still out on the issue of psychological effects: i.e., what impact does regularly taking a pill have on a child's self-esteem? And the accusation that teenagers especially, with quantities of mood-altering drugs available, are often tempted to take illegal advantage of the fact, has evidence to support it.

Overall, however, supporters of psychopharmacology as a method of behaviour management can now point to some positive outcomes. Relatively long-term experience has demonstrated that many children respond positively to medication, most particularly those who are given drugs to reduce impulsivity and improve concentration. There is also fairly clear evidence that drugs are crucial in the treatment of psychotic illnesses like childhood schizophrenia. Yet critics respond that this alleged (and rather narrow) success is a double-edged sword in that it is rapidly accelerating the rate at which drugs are prescribed at the expense of other, drugless therapies. The comment has much evidence to support it. In 1997, for example, Health Canada estimated that over the previous six years, Ritalin consumption had increased by some 460 percent! There is ample reason, in fact, to accept that drug therapy had become a standard treatment regimen, if not the standard. (See also Drug Therapy Approach p. 121, in this chapter.)

Conceptual Models and Their Educational Implications

Although mental health professionals tend to subscribe to a particular, and usually narrow, school of thought when it comes to treating students with behavioural exceptionalities, emphasis on a singular view of behaviour is far less

Although the school board that expelled Suzette six weeks ago has a zero tolerance policy on violence, she was given several chances before the expulsion occurred. On one occasion she pushed and then slapped a teacher. Action on this incident was shelved by mutual agreement when Suzette insisted she had reacted "when he grabbed me." Three student witnesses and one teacher utterly contradict that claim but the teacher asked the principal to drop the matter because, innocent or not, he refused to be, in his words, "dragged through media mud." On another occasion, Suzette scratched another student seriously enough to leave a scar, but an investigation of the incident gave Suzette the benefit of the doubt on the basis of self-defence. The precipitating event for the expulsion was another fight. This time Suzette beat up another girl very badly.

Suzette's exasperated parents have prevailed upon a personal friend, the principal of a large secondary school in a neighbouring board, to accept Suzette, but now he has a dilemma: whether to place her in the school's behavioural resource class. This is an exceptionally successful unit with a highly competent teacher who places almost all her emphasis on academic achievement. There is no scheduled counselling in the class, and despite the fact that all but one of the students has a social worker, the teacher has managed to ban every one of them. The students work hard on a full program, go on field trips, and participate in school events, but their entire program is delivered in this class.

Suzette is sixteen and was designated "behavioural" four years ago. She had been an excellent, high achieving student until, as her mother said to an IPRC "she went teenage-nuts!" Suzette is articulate and has a very powerful personality. At one of her several court hearings, a judge remarked, "After five minutes with you, no one would ever say 'Suzette who?' the next day." What the principal is worried about is a struggle for power if Suzette goes to the behavioural class. He knows her potential for success is very high there, but if a power struggle erupts, the results could be very harmful to both Suzette and the other students. The principal has referred this to the in-school team and is awaiting their input.

common in the classroom. However, it behooves teachers and educational assistants to be aware of some of the current approaches in the mental health field.

Psychodynamic Approach

Although it is a declining force among educators, psychodynamics continues to attract attention in television shows and popular literature. This perspective views behavioural disorders as being within the individual. Thus when this treatment approach is used, the teacher is usually part of a mental health team that seeks to develop a warm supportive atmosphere in which the student will hopefully overcome his or her inner turmoil. Emphasis is placed on acceptance and toleration, somewhat at the expense of direct instruction and acquisition of academic skills. A variation of this style is called the *psychoeducational approach*, in which more effort is directed to practical classroom outcomes. One of the reasons for the decline of the psychodynamic approach is an accumulation of evidence that it does not improve academic achievement, and at the same time, limited evidence that it helps to improve behaviour.

Biophysical Approach

This style emphasizes the organic origins of behaviour, and postulates a direct relationship between behaviour and such things as physical defects, illnesses, diet, and allergies. Advocates of this view have generated a multiplicity of causation theories each with a responsive therapy. Some examples include megavitamin therapy, diet control, symptom control medication, removal of offending substances (like carpets), etc. In the classroom this approach is often combined with a structured, behaviour-based style that emphasizes routine, daily scheduling, frequent repetition of tasks presented in careful sequence, and the elimination of environmental stimuli that are perceived to be extraneous. Available data on the results of this treatment have difficulty separating which aspect, the therapies or the style of instructing, has the most impact.

Environmental Approach

Supporters hold that individuals are a particular collective in a particular space and time, and, as such, must be regarded as the product of an ecological unit made up of themselves, their family, school, neighbourhood, and community. Educational response to students with behavioural exceptionalities, therefore, must necessarily involve the whole of the ecological unit. Where this theory is followed in schools, teachers are expected to instruct the student in social and interpersonal environment skills. At the same time, attempts are made to modify the school's environment to meet the needs of the individual. Family counselling, and, in some cases, counselling of the student's classmates, may be part of the program. The key element is to create in all parts of the unit, an awareness of its reciprocal relationships, and an impetus toward monitoring these relationships to the ultimate benefit of the student identified as behaviourally exceptional. Classroom teachers and educational assistants with experience in this approach, while they attest to its efficacy, at least initially, also point out that the amount of coordination necessary to make it work well, is almost impossible to bring about.

Video Games and Behaviour

Teachers and parents have long suspected that the violence portrayed in some video games has a negative impact on the behaviour of children and adolescents. Although there is inherent logic in that perception, and although it appears to be supported by empirical evidence in the hallways, playgrounds, and even in the classrooms of our schools, it has taken some time to reinforce the suspicion with solid research. In part, this is because the level of extreme violence in some video games is a fairly recent phenomenon, and research that might reveal a potential impact (or not) on players' behaviour must necessarily follow some time after.

It would appear, however, that the research gap is now being filled. A recent review of the literature shows that over forty peer-reviewed studies have been published, every one, without exception, concluding that playing violent video games has an impact on the behaviour of children and adolescents. Several well-executed studies published in the February 2004 issue of the *Journal of Adolescence* (vol. 27, no. 1) make the case with particular clarity. One study (Gentile et al), conducted on a population of over 600 students in grades 8 and 9, concluded that compared to controls, children and adolescents who play violent video games:

- see the world as more hostile
- get into more arguments with teachers
- have more fights
- achieve lower grades

One of the strengths of this study is that it controlled for gender, for amount of time spent playing (average was nine hours per week), and for the possibility of pre-existing hostility in the subjects being studied, all of which adds to the credibility of the results.

Other studies consistently demonstrate effects on violent-video-game players such as lack of empathy for victims, de-sensitization to violence generally, and a greater tendency to condone violence as an acceptable response.

It is important to highlight here the fact that the research work, most particularly the studies conducted since the beginning of the current century, has focused on violent video games that have become available only in the past few years. Teachers and parents who have not reviewed contemporary game materials should realize that the relatively innocuous Pac-Man and Pong type games of earlier generations pale in comparison to more recently available programs that portray indiscriminate mass killings and offer intensely graphic displays of violence. Clearly, video-game violence is a phenomenon that will raise concerns in schools and homes for some time to come. For special education, the problem will be determining to what extent the games may be a contributing or possibly an obfuscating factor in situations where a student is thought to be behaviourally exceptional.

Behaviour Modification Approach

Still seen as the dominant intervention style from an educational point of view, this approach follows the assumption that all behaviour is modifiable by principles of reinforcement. (It is worth pointing out that the dominance of the behavioural approach is at least partly owing to the vast amount of published material it spawns, much of it from American colleges and universities where the theory does indeed dominate.) Educators who adhere to this approach believe that behaviour is controlled by impinging stimuli and that it is possible to:

i)   create behaviours that presently do not exist

ii) maintain and generalize behaviours already established

iii) eliminate inappropriate behaviours

What happens practically is that first, a desirable behaviour or set of behaviours is established. Hopefully, the expected behaviour is within the student's repertoire and, starting slowly, the occurrence of the desired behaviour is increased (or decreased, as the case may be) by the use of a potent reinforcer at the appropriate time. The reinforcer can be concrete, such as food or a toy, or can be more abstract such as checks, stars, or coupons that can be traded for something concrete (commonly known as a token economy system). In every case, the reinforcer should be paired with a social reinforcer, such as praise or a smile, so that when the concrete or token reinforcer is phased out the student can still receive a positively perceived acknowledgement for his or her appropriate behaviour. Educators who use behaviour modification—and many do to a degree, even those who would deny being "behaviourist"—regard every student as a candidate for learning, irrespective of whatever psychopathology may be at the root of behaviour.

Drug Therapy Approach

This treatment essentially means that a student with a behavioural exceptionality is administered psychotropic drugs, most often in pill form, to help control his or her behaviour. Research over the past thirty years suggests fairly emphatically that the medication does indeed succeed in this purpose, implying, therefore, a positive or at least an improved outcome for both the student and

A Caution ...

Teachers and educational assistants are often asked to become involved in the administration and monitoring of prescribed medications. It may be to their benefit, before doing so, to have written instructions from the student's parents, duly co-signed by the school principal or other authority. Some school boards have very specific policies on this issue.

others in his school and personal life. Classroom professionals often become involved in this therapy, first of all to administer the medication during the school day, and secondly—particularly if a drug is being used for the first time with a student—in the monitoring of its positive and negative effects. In the ideal situation, no medication is ever given to a student without its effects being carefully noted and duly reported, so that modifications in the dosage can be made—an outcome that is often necessary. Regrettably, a challenge for teachers and assistants is that necessary modifications, which are always under the control of parents and medical professionals, are not always forthcoming in a timely way. Of possible interest both to parents and educators may be the claim by practitioners of naturopathic medicine that they can treat attention deficit and hyperactivity by means that do not involve administering potentially invasive chemistry.

Whatever medication is administered to a child it must be recognized that the medication alone is usually not sufficient to remediate the academic and social differences a child with a behavioural exceptionality may experience. It is usually a combination of medication and appropriate behavioural and academic interventions that can help social and academic performance improve.

The Classroom Reality: Flexible Common Sense

Teachers and educational assistants who work with students on a day-to-day basis often find it difficult to be entirely faithful to only one of the approaches above when they apply it in the cold (or hot!) reality of the classroom. Most combine a variety of approaches and apply them on an individual basis. For example, all teachers of all

On just her second day in office, the (acting) principal spotted Logan under the secretary's empty chair after morning recess. He was pale, and shaking, and appeared to have been crying. Logan is a month away from his seventh birthday and is in grade 2. The principal, suspecting a playground incident, deliberately ignored Logan for a few minutes, but intervened fifteen minutes later, when he had not moved and began crying hard. In her office, Logan said his grade 2 teacher "touched me here and here and put his hand inside my pants," adding that it had happened several times. Upon consultation with family children's services, the following information was shared. Logan's parents are divorced and have joint custody of him. Last year, he told each of them, on consecutive days, that the other was abusing him sexually. Before the accusations were exposed as completely false, Logan's mother was asked by her professional association to voluntarily suspend her practice (she practises pediatric psychiatry). His father, an attorney with a prominent firm, was asked to take a leave of absence, although the firm denied the request was connected to an interview that Logan gave—on his own initiative—to the tabloid press.

Throughout the investigation the principal learned that in grade 1, Logan had convinced a girl in the class that her parents were separating. She is now in a different school, but according to her parents, still has anxiety attacks even if the two of them leave for work at different times. Also in grade 1, until the teacher discovered it, Logan was quietly talking classmates into destroying their work because it was no good. The same teacher suspects, but cannot prove, that Logan is responsible for a spate of missing materials, and that it was he who ruined the controls of a powered wheelchair used by a boy in the class. At the same time, she acknowledges that Logan is academically superior, that she has never actually seen him do anything remotely improper (the second grade teacher agrees), and that in terms of completing work, obeying routines, and in helping others, Logan appears to be a model student. The acting principal's instinct is to call for an in-school team to discuss the situation. Still, she wonders what that would accomplish.

students—not just those with behavioural exceptionalities—espouse the value of a warm, supportive atmosphere. All teachers recognize the interplay of environmental stimuli, and all are aware of the importance of these phenomena in both learning and social development. Teachers and assistants universally modify behaviour in their students but only some will actually call it behaviour modification. And the view of each student as a dynamic, individual entity is at the very heart of teaching as a profession. Taken together, the practices followed by most educators most of the time, could best be collected under the expression: flexible common sense. While the term may not have definitive intellectual reverberations in the field of behaviour theory, it describes pretty much the route that is followed in the classroom: doing what is effective at the time and what makes sense at the time.

Kauffman (2005) suggested, however, that regardless of the approach used, the teacher needs to establish a baseline of what behaviours are occurring. By understanding the frequency, intensity, and duration of a particular behaviour or set of behaviours the teacher can tell if the intervention that is applied is effective.

Students with AD / HD

Throughout the final years of the twentieth century and on into the next, a confusing and controversial condition has taken a very high profile front seat in special education: Attention Deficit/Hyperactivity Disorder (AD/HD). The condition is being diagnosed with ever-increasing frequency by psychiatrists, psychologists, pediatricians, and family practitioners, especially in North America. As well, AD/HD has captivated the popular press, become a regular subject of educational research, and has been almost completely—and rather uncritically—accepted by the teaching profession. Unfortunately, it is the subject of considerable debate, not just as to the nature of the special needs it represents, but also whether it requires or even deserves distinctive status. Ontario, like most educational jurisdictions, does not list AD/HD as a distinct category of exceptionality. Nor is it included in the Individuals with Educational Disabilities Act (IDEA, 1997) in the U.S. Yet irrespective of its (un)official status, and of the controversy it continues to generate, AD/HD has become a factor in both regular and special education today. The following section attempts to present a perspective for educators and parents.

What Are the Symptoms of AD/HD?

AD/HD, or attention deficit/hyperactivity disorder, is a diagnostic category listed in the *DSM IV-TR of the American Psychiatric Association*. When diagnosing AD/HD, medical practitioners look at three symptoms: the first being inability to sustain attention at age-appropriate level. The student cannot screen out irrelevant stimuli, does not concentrate on tasks long enough to complete them, does not sustain the thought processes necessary to do school work. The second is impulsivity. The student does things without considering consequences, and often repeats the behaviour (does not learn from experience). Work patterns are erratic and scatter-focused. Often perseverates with counter-productive behaviour. Hyperactivity is the third characteristic. The student engages in non-purposeful movement and activity that is usually not age appropriate, and often at an accelerated level. This movement and/or activity usually continues despite intervention. (Interestingly, teachers can often see many of their students in a description like this, or members of their family, or even themselves!)

Are AD/HD Symptoms the Result of Other Factors?

Disruptive or unresponsive behaviour may be the result of anxiety or depression. Regular lapses in attention might be evidence of absence (petit mal) seizures. Fetal alcohol syndrome sometimes produces hyperactive behaviour. An uncooperative student, especially a younger one, may be uncooperative because of a hearing loss, the result of chronic inner ear infections, or an undetected hearing problem. In short, there are many things that can cause the symptoms. To further confuse the matter, AD/HD is most often a medical diagnosis arrived at, supposedly, on the evidence of these symptoms. Yet professional educators see the same symptoms every day in students who are not identified as AD/HD! Supporters of the condition as a separate entity, argue—often with good evidence to support them—that the distinguishing criteria of AD/HD symptoms are high frequency and severity, and that the symptoms are seen repeatedly over extended time.

What Causes AD/HD?

Advocates argue that AD/HD has been around for a long time under other titles like "hyperkinesis" and "minimal brain dysfunction," and "'moral deficit." They posit further, that what makes AD/HD real is a biological or psychological basis, or both. As for psychological cause, proponents argue that there are some individuals who, through no fault of their own, cannot use their human will and self control to manage themselves from within, and that the pace of modern life aggravates this lack of a central control mechanism. The majority of advocates for ADHD, however, see it as a neurologically-based medical condition. Among the causes identified, but not yet widely accepted by both the medical and educational communities, are faulty regulation by a neurotransmitter called norepinephrine, and genetic factors owing to anomalies in certain chromosomes. Recently, specific genes (dopamine transporter gene on chromosome 5 and dopamine receptor D4 gene on chromosome 11) have been discovered that appear to be related to AD/HD. Dopamine deficiency may be a cause of AD/HD, but it is unclear as to whether individuals with AD/HD do not produce enough of it or are unable to properly use what they do produce. Other chemical deficiencies that may be associated with AD/HD are noradrenaline and seratonin. Noradrenaline is a substance that may act on the brain during times of stress and serotonin is a chemical that helps the brain's ability to detect and/or possibly regulate other chemicals (Canadian Attention Deficit/ Hyperactivity Disorder Resource Alliance, **www. CADDRA.CA**).

Just a Confusion with Other Special Needs?

AD/HD has long been associated with learning disabilities because of the inattentiveness factor. The two are not, however, the same thing. Estimates vary, but the literature generally suggests that about one-third of students with learning disabilities may have some degree of attention disorder. Alternatively, the rate of learning disabilities is high in students who are diagnosed AD/HD, possibly because lack of attention and off-task behaviour are detrimental to mastering basic skills. One special need, however, does not absolutely and automatically imply the other. (The same caution applies to combining AD/HD with other behavioural exceptionalities, and with Tourette's Syndrome.)

Another "Modern Day" Phenomenon?

Not entirely, although AD/HD did not capture the public eye until the late twentieth century. A German doctor, Heinrich Hoffman, first described hyperactivity in 1845. In 1902, George Still, a British physician added a moral overlay, a notion that unproductive hyperactivity is somehow associated with evil, a notion that still dogs the issue. (He described "sick" children of average or higher intelligence who had an "abnormal deficit of moral control." Hence the term "moral deficit.") AD/HD was classified clinically in 1968, and acquired its current designation in 1987 (both times an initiative of the medical profession).

When matched against other, more recent types of special need, the time frame in which AD/HD achieved its high profile seems reasonable enough, yet there continues to be intense, sometimes vicious disagreement over whether it should be seen as a distinct clinical entity, or even stronger, whether it really exists! Critics contend that AD/HD has become a label du jour in North America, an invention of a culture that has cast aside its obligation to parent well and now needs an excuse for the result. While such statements are unquestionably harsh, and may be offered more for effect than polemic, they have a powerful impact in the light of two very real factors. One is the accelerated rate of diagnosis. In 1997, the *Globe and Mail* newspaper reported that an estimated half million Canadians, mostly students, had been diagnosed, an extraordinary number for a condition that only got its name a decade before! Subsequent revelations in 2003 and 2004 indicate that the accelerating rate continues.

What Does Having Students with AD/HD Mean to the Classroom?

Teachers and educational assistants have long been used to "antsy" students, particularly younger ones, who find it hard to sit still. And in most classrooms the behaviour is managed successfully most of the time. But where a strongly suspected case of AD/HD is present, teachers can expect a high level

The Case of Hannah

After only a month in nursery school, Hannah was being secretly called "Beagle" by the staff, because of her penchant for running flat out until something or someone stopped her. It was a habit she continued over the next several years. Kindergarten passed fairly smoothly, for Hannah's teacher was a completely unruffled person, committed to letting her students express themselves as much as they wished. Grade 1, however, was a disaster. Not entirely Hannah's fault; the grade 1 teacher was having a difficult year. She had two pre-school children of her own, one of whom was chronically ill, and a husband who worked shifts. But Hannah didn't help things. By this time, running about during story time, quiet time—any time—was an established habit. She regularly blurted out whatever was on her mind during instruction, and seemingly could not keep from interfering with others in the class when they teamed up for an activity. Hannah regularly "borrowed" material without asking, never returned it unless told to, and did not seem remotely aware of how annoying she was to others.

Grade 2 was marked by a field trip crisis when, because of Hannah, the class was asked to leave a petting zoo. Following this trip, Hannah's mother agreed to accompany excursions as one of the parent volunteers supervising a group. Nevertheless, because of some more incidents, and because of an extensive list of complaints from other parents, Hannah's mother eventually kept her daughter at home during all subsequent field trips. Unfortunately, the residue of this move carried into grade 3, when several other parents used it—unsuccessfully—as a precedent for requesting that Hannah be removed from the class altogether.

In grade 3, a pediatrician diagnosed AD/DH and prescribed medication (Ritalin), but Hannah turned out to be one of the minority for whom the side effects, especially sleeplessness, made it impossible to continue. Hannah's mother, a nurse, ruled out a second medication, Cylert, because she'd heard it may cause liver damage. Throughout grade 3, Hannah's impulsive, annoying behaviours worsened. By then it was also evident that she was lagging behind her peers academically.

Hannah is now in grade 4. Her mother reports that she had a "good summer" at a camp for children with AD/HD. Both mother and daughter have new hope because Hannah learned some self-control skills at camp, and because the grade 4 teacher has a reputation for competence in dealing with AD/HD. In spite of this, there has already been an incident. The class is forming groups to put together material for a "time capsule" to be opened in June. Because no group would accept Hannah, she had a tantrum, and then for the first time any one can remember, she began to cry in a deeply heartfelt way. The teacher sees that as a sign the time is ripe for renewed effort to address Hannah's case. An In-School Team meeting has been called to come up with ideas.

of physical activity, inappropriate responses, low frustration tolerance—the list goes on. And each of these behaviours repeat, despite intervention. Whereas it is the student's parent who must bear the ultimate costs emotionally and physically, teachers have a burden all their own, for a student with AD/HD has a concentric effect. The student's lack of restraint and acting out will invariably draw in the student's peers, or distract them, or cause conflict, or interrupt their work, or…

Regrettably, there is no sure remedy in the classroom. Certainly, there is no universally accepted way to deal with AD/HD in school. Behaviour modification is often tried, but offers no guarantees. Isolating the student with AD/HD may be beneficial for the student's peers, but is not a solution for the student himself/herself, at least not long term. Ultimately, the most effective management techniques usually turn out to be those that the teacher and educational assistant work out creatively, often with the parents' help, and these techniques, most of the time, are uniquely successful for that particular student. Chances are slim the same methods will work with the next candidate. Nevertheless, research has found that the most effective treatment is a combination of medication, effective behaviour modification practices and, if possible, individual and family counselling.

Most teachers do find through experience that there are a few common threads in successful management. One is flexibility. There is not much point in banging heads with a student who seems predisposed to repeat wrong behaviours in the first place. Another is setting modest goals, objectives the student has a realistic chance of attaining. Still another is diversion. And all of these must be supported by, for lack of a better phrase, "kind firmness."

✔ STRATEGIES FOR STUDENTS WITH BEHAVIOURAL EXCEPTIONALITIES

Manage the environment: Seat the student away from distracting stimuli like doorways and traffic areas. Try to seat the student so that particularly stimulating students are not in his or her natural line of sight. If possible, seat the student near stable peer models. Periodically utilize a special stimulus-reduced study area like a carrel. Encourage parents to do the same. Experiment with natural light versus fluorescent. Some teachers have reported that natural light is superior.

While instructing: Be simple and concise. Offer one instruction or task at a time, after you are confident you have the student focused and ready. Limit the use of subordinate clauses and embedded phrases, and welcome questions of clarification. Help the student to feel secure by being nearby when the student starts his or her work. While instructing a large group or the whole class, use a technique commonly known as "proximity control" whereby you position yourself near the student frequently so that your physical presence can act as catalyst toward the initiation and maintenance of attentive, appropriate behaviour.

Organization of the day or period: Prepare the student for shifts in topic, setting, schedule, etc. (Again, a teacher's or educational assistant's proximity when these shifts are about to happen, can be very important.) Meet and greet with a few positive one-on-one seconds at crucial points during the day, points when the potential for hyperactivity increases: e.g., transitions such as returning from lunch, gym, recess, etc. When in-class activity is assigned (homework too) help the student get started and then, at first, check back as frequently as you can. Help the student organize his or her output (into notebooks, files, etc.) so that the student gradually accumulates a visible, concrete, cumulative record of his or her efforts.

Other support: Enforce classroom routines and procedures consistently. And have only a few! Too many rules invites disaster! Since planning is never this student's long suit, the adults in the student's life must compensate by planning for him or her, and building in extra time. When a disagreement arises do not argue! You cannot win. Reinforce "good" chunks of time such as on-task behaviour with just-for-her/him, positive eye-contact or other supportive expressions. When your experience tells you an impossible-to-resolve situation is developing, try "antiseptic bouncing," i.e., send the student on an important errand out of the room, or provide some other task that "needs doing now."

Think momentum: Not motivation but momentum. A teacher who only motivates is forever pushing from behind. Eventually, the teacher wears out, or runs out of patience or ideas or most likely, desire. On the other hand, a teacher who tries to build momentum in students, who works at developing in them a sense of personal responsibility, this teacher will not only have a greater and lasting impact on the students but will last longer himself/herself.

Note improvement: Ensure that you have an accurate understanding of the student's behaviour and note when improvements are occurring. In almost every case, a student will revert back to his or her inappropriate patterns, but if this is happening less frequently, with less intensity or for shorter duration, this is a sign of improvement that needs to be brought to the student's attention. Students with AD/HD or behavioural exceptionalities often do not see that they are doing better. Improvement, no matter how small, needs to be brought to the students' attention and to the attention of their parents and the others with whom they may be working.

Teachers and educational assistants who work with students with behavioural exceptionalities are the first to acknowledge that there is no pedagogical magic, no secret formula for teaching success in this area of exceptionality. And those who think there is one and go looking for it are bound to be disappointed. Still, there is one truth, an abiding one that all educators recognize, as do students, parents, and anyone else who bothers to take a second look at classrooms. This is the truth that a teacher who is effective with "regular" students is usually more effective with "behavioural" students. It follows then that to emulate what effective teachers do is at the very least, a practical beginning point for all classroom professionals.

An Effective Teacher's Attitude

There are many human strengths needed to teach effectively. Traits like patience, flexibility, creativity, a sense of humour, a capacity to see all sides of an issue—these are elements that, in the heat of a teaching moment, will outweigh intelligence and scholarship. Effective teachers manifest these characteristics most of the time. However, what they manifest all of the time is not a characteristic at all, but an attitude, a perspective, namely: respect. When teachers', or educational assistants' abiding view is built on respect for students—and on self-respect—the atmosphere in their classroom immediately reflects that attitude in a variety of ways. A place where students feel respected is a safe place to make a mistake, and therefore, an ideal place to learn and grow. Where respect prevails, students recognize that in the eyes of the significant adults there, they have value. Once students feel respected themselves, they are far more likely to show it toward others. And respect for others is fundamental if students are ever to modify their behaviour.

From the instructional end of things, respect, quite simply, infuses everything a teacher does. It smoothes rapport, supports flexibility and patience, and fuels the vitality of faith and hope. A teacher who respects students, plans better, prepares better, and instructs better. A teacher who respects students, instinctively avoids those spontaneous but regrettable and damaging management errors from which recovery is so difficult. Above all, if a teacher establishes genuine respect as the central idiom in a classroom, then everyone shares a behavioural reference point. Mutual respect offers both a stage from which to begin, and an objective to keep in sight.

An Effective Teacher's Style

(1) Recognizing where students are "at": Students with a behavioural problem are often burdened by a history that shapes the expectations that others have of them. And they know it. A second burden, one that reinforces the first, is in-the-classroom helplessness. So many of them do not know how to set about academic tasks, or, how to conduct themselves socially in any way other than in the manner that brought on their problems in the first place. An effective teacher is very much aware of this fact, and begins much of his or her work from inside the student's view. It is a delicate undertaking, for one must purposefully go to where the student is "at," while at the same time continuing to be a separate, adult mentor, with all that the role implies. For a teacher or educational assistant to become a buddy is a deadly mistake. Students don't want that. What they want is an adult who is open, who listens, and who will attempt to understand what they know and do not know, and who will then help them in a face-saving way that produces results, however modest.

(2) Realizing the importance of personal conduct: The manner in which teachers and assistants present their professionalism is a crucial factor in preventing inappropriate classroom behaviour. Ideally, adults who deal with students with behavioural exceptionalities are role models who don't react defensively to challenge, who have the skills to divert a troublesome situation until stability is restored (and then deal with it), and who employ fair and realistic consequences in a consistent way. These are also the people who get to class ahead of time, who are present and visible, responsible and proactive. They are role models of adulthood that communicate to students the possibility that the world does have some sense to it. Naturally, things do not always work out this way, but even the students (or perhaps especially the students, unfortunately)

don't expect things to work right every time. Yet classroom professionals must strive to model this type of conduct if there is to be any hope of modifying their students' behaviour.

(3) Establishing a realistic, consistent and predictable learning environment: This is the sine qua non of an effective teacher's style. Students with a behavioural exceptionality already have trouble making sense of the world, not to mention school. And they are notoriously poor at reading between the lines to determine what is expected of them. These are not students who know how to, much less want to, play the game of school. Teachers and assistants can make things much easier for them—make it more possible for them to behave appropriately—if procedures and expectations are clear, uncomplicated, and predictable. Particularly in the beginning, and until the students develop some confidence in themselves and in their teachers, a predictable pattern is crucial.

This sense of stability and consistency in the classroom develops naturally out of the behaviour of the teacher, but also out of the day-to-day organization. Effective classrooms are not hamstrung by a long list of ironclad rules that students will invariably break, and for which some disciplinary response then becomes necessary. Structure, organization, sequence—these are the important features, and a minimum number of simple, reasonable procedures and routines, not rules, for ensuring that these obtain, makes sense even to students with behavioural problems. There will be some bona fide rules, of course, but most of these are the ones established by the school or the board or other more global entity. And what distinguishes them from classroom procedures and routines is that consequences are applied for breaking them. In the classroom, however, teachers and assistants who organize from a perspective of respect, and who model that attitude themselves, not only have a standard to refer to, but have some room for flexibility when a student pushes against it.

(4) "Catching a kid doing something good": It may be a very challenging task sometimes, but looking for positives and discreetly praising these students will pay dividends. "Discreet" is an operative word here. Students with behavioural exceptionalities, especially older ones, often harbour a profound cynicism that walls them in and protects them from positive reinforcement that they are convinced is insincere. Many of them have had unsatisfactory experiences with so-called "positive reinforcement programs" and, as a result, have well-developed detectors. Praise is important, but it must be proportionate to the accomplishment, sincere, and utterly free of excess. Effusiveness will only embarrass the students and may provoke them into negative behaviour just to restore the balance.

(5) Treating democracy as a very fine line: If given the opportunity, students quite naturally wish to contribute to a classroom's plans, procedures, and even curriculum. Understandably, this is more often the case with older students. The issue is a difficult one for teachers. Anyone who has ever experienced the exchange, "What do you want to do?" "Nuthin!", is naturally wary of a suggestion that students should be consulted. And it is a healthy wariness. To expect students who have been identified with behavioural exceptionalities to involve themselves in productive interchange about procedures and curriculum is something that happens more often in movie scripts than in classrooms. Still it's worth a try. Most effective teachers would never begin a term or a relationship this way, if only because students with a behavioural exceptionality are looking for leadership and order, whether they realize it or not. After some time has passed, however, and once an atmosphere of respect is established, eliciting and then acting upon a suggestion from a student with a behavioural exceptionality can produce real benefits, if only because the student has thereby taken on some responsibility. At the very least, teachers and educational assistants must keep in mind that they are dealing with an exceptionality where, almost always, chaos in various forms has prevailed. That reality must infuse all democratic decisions.

(6) Establishing momentum is more important than motivating Any teacher who operates solely on a principle of motivation quite naturally runs out of ideas over a long school term because the responsibility is always his or hers. Not that motivating is counter-productive or a waste of time, but it is only superficial, and while it may pay temporary dividends, motivation rarely has a lasting impact because it is always the teacher's responsibility (a fact that doubles the potential for an all too common teaching trap: the teacher becomes an entertainer).

More effective is to plan, organize, and teach with a view to getting students rolling on their own. Each teacher or educational assistant will accomplish this in different, personal ways, but establishing momentum has a few absolutes. One is beginning where the student is "at" and then setting achievable goals so that the student can have the delightful (and hitherto unusual) experience of success. Part and parcel of establishing momentum is making those goals short term so the success can come soon. Another is arranging, even manipulating, the goal—especially at first—to make certain the student does succeed. Then, as soon as there is a success, set up opportunity immediately for another, so that the first one can be reinforced and momentum can begin. Still another absolute, a very simple one on the surface, is arranging one's planning and teaching so that students accumulate visible products, like notes, every day. Most students with behavioural exceptionalities have never had the sense of accomplishment that comes from accumulating a set of notes, or of accumulating anything. (Worth pointing out here, is that teachers who are successful in establishing "momentum" in their students, report that they are then much easier to "motivate"!)

(7) Keeping academics front and centre: With the possible exception of cases where the mental health of a student is clearly established as a serious issue, the premier classroom focus should always be on academic learning. Even if the development of social skills is a vital feature of a student's educational plan, the student's own perception should always be that he or she is "here for education." A student with a behavioural exceptionality already feels singled out. To devote the major part of a program to the development of social skills in a transparent, obvious way, only reinforces the distinction. Social skill development can continue to be a principal objective, but its realization should be achieved not just by direct social skill instruction itself, but by learning it during the process of studying what all the other kids are studying. (See Fergie's enlightening comments below.)

(8) Working hard is better than sitting around. Fergie, a fifteen-year-old student in a regular grade 9 class with a "reputation," and in which five students were identified as behavioural (including Fergie), presents this argument much better than we can. See the comment below.

> Some teachers, they don't get much work ready for us 'cause they think we don't care about nothin' right? And they think we don't notice. But how many crossword puzzles do they think we gotta do before we figure it out, right? Don't know why they do that. I mean, we're in school, so why not give us schoolwork? But that's not everybody, now. You take Mrs. P.... Now in her class do we ever have to put out. I mean, she's got work and everything every day! Like there's always stuff on the board for us, and then we get a lesson-thing. And then more work. And we got this huge ton of notes!
>
> What's cool is nobody messes around in Mrs. P.'s class. And like, it's not just that she's mean—like—it's like you're really doin' something in that class, man. It's—it's like you're learning something!"
>
> *Fergie S., aged 15, on audio tape.*
> *(Mrs. P. was in her first year of teaching.)*

Some Habits of an Effective Teacher:

- Establishes and then maintains consistent routines for entering the classroom and beginning the session (the point at which much of the tone for what follows is established), e.g., an effective teacher is always at the doorway to greet, manage, intervene if necessary.

- Sets up and insists on specific seating arrangements (which are then altered as deemed useful in order to reduce or increase opportunities).

- Is highly visible. Interacts with students outside the classroom. Tries to attend anything in the school in which a student with behavioural exceptionality is involved.

- Uses "antiseptic bouncing" when a student is worked up or aggressive. Give the student an errand to run outside the class, or some other activity that may let off steam.

- If demerits are used in the school or class, allows for merits to be earned too.

- Uses proximity control and stands nearby when it appears a situation may develop. Proximity also works in the sense of being available to help and being available to interact. Effective teachers never spend the whole day at the front of a classroom.

- Rarely, if ever, makes the dread mistake of being sarcastic, and always avoids yelling (a profoundly counter-productive behaviour if it's used more than once a term!) or other behaviours that shred dignity.

- Never uses corrosive discipline techniques, e.g., writing out lines, class detentions, using curriculum content like math or spelling drills as a punishment.

- Avoids confronting students with behavioural exceptionalities in front of peers. And does not get into arguments.

- Uses diversions. Younger students, especially, can be distracted from a counter-productive path by giving them alternate activities and goals.

- Lets students know there are high expectations. If necessary, on occasion, an effective teacher will quite willingly, but discreetly, manipulate the components of a task to ensure a positive outcome for a student who needs a boost.

- Sets short-term goals for students who have not yet learned to defer gratification.

- Makes use of reward systems like personal progress charts, and ensures that students accumulate notes and other physical evidence that the time spent in school is producing something of consequence.

Finally, Be Proactive, Plan Ahead

In almost every case, a student identified with a behavioural exceptionality will have behaviours that occur frequently. The teacher can be assured that if a child is non-compliant or aggressive on Monday these behaviours will appear again throughout the week. It is the well-prepared teacher who plans ahead for this eventuality. The teacher either tries to avoid the misbehaviour by setting up conditions that make the behaviour less likely to occur or provides the student with consequences, either positive or negative, if the behaviour does or does not occur. If the behaviour does take place, the consequences are implemented and little discussion (which brings undo attention to the student) needs to occur. Hopefully, over time, the negative behaviour is decreased and there is ample opportunity for reward and/or praise to be offered to the student for his or her cooperative behaviour.

Teachers need to be aware that behavioural change takes time and there will be setbacks. Hopefully, many positive steps will be taken, allowing the student to be "caught doing something good" before the student needs to be in a situation where the focus will be put on something negative.

Aust, P. (1994). When the problem is not the problem: Understanding attention deficit disorder with and without hyperactivity. *Child Welfare, 73(3)*, 215-227.

Barabasz, M., & Barabasz, A. (1996). Attention deficit disorder: Diagnosis, etiology and treatment. *Child Study Journal, 26*, 1-38.

Carbone, E. (2001). Arranging the classroom with an eye (and ear) to students with ADHD. *Teaching Exceptional Children, 34(2)*, 72-81.

Clarke, S., Dunlap, G., Foster-Johnson, L., Childs, K. E., Wilson D., White, R., & Vera, A. (1995). Improving the conduct of students with behavioral disorders by incorporating student interests into curricular areas. *Behavioral Disorders, 20(4)*, 221-237.

Colucci, S. (1993, May). Peer mediation: Creating opportunities for conflict resolution. *Communiqué*, pp. 25-27.

Cummins, J.G., Peplar, D. J., Mishna, F., Craig, W. M., (2006) Bullying and Victimization among students with exceptionalities. *Exceptionality Education Canada 16(3)*, 193-222.

DePaepe, P. A., Shores, R. E., Jack, S. L. & Denny, R. K. (1996). Effects of task difficulty on the disruptive and on-task behavior of students with severe behavior disorders. *Behavioral Disorders, 21(3)*, 216-225.

Dworet, D. H. & Rathgeber, A. J. (1990). Provincial and territorial government responses to behaviorally disordered students in Canada. *Behavioural Disorders, 15(4)*, 201-209.

Dworet, D. and Maich, K. (2004). Canadian School Programs for Students with Emotional Behavioural Disorders: An Updated Look at Canadian Schools, Paper presented at the International Conference of The Council for Exceptional Children, Salt Lake City, Utah

Epstein, M. H. (1999). The development and validation of a scale to assess the emotional and behavioural strengths of children and adolescence. *Remedial and Special Education, 20(5)*, 258-262.

Faber, A., & Mazlish, E. (1996). *How to talk so kids can learn*. New York: Fireside.

Frey, K. S., Hirschtein, M. K.., & Guzzo, B. A. (2000). Second step: Preventing aggression by promoting social competence. *Journal of Emotional and Behavioural Disorders, 8(2)*, 102-112.

Furr, D.L. (1996). Now I understand the rage. *Reaching Today's Youth, 1(1)*, 9-12.

Gentile, D. A., Lynch, P. J., Linder, J. R., & Walsh, D. A. (2004). The effects of violent video game habits on adolescent hostility: Aggressive behaviour and school defiance. *Journal of Adolescence, 27(1)*, 5-22.

Henley, M. (1997). *Teaching self-control: A curriculum for responsible behavior*. Bloomington, IN: National Education Service.

Jenson, W. R., Rhode, G., & Reavis, H.K., (1994). *The tough kids toolbox*. Longmont, CO: Sopris West.

Kauffman, J. M. (1999). How we prevent the prevention of emotional and behavioral disorders. *Exceptional Children, 65*, 448-468.

Kauffman, J. M. (2005). *Characteristics of emotional and behavioral disorders of children* (8th. Ed.) Columbus, OH: Merrill/Prentice Hall.

Lantieri, L., & Patti, J. (1996). Waging peace in our schools. *Reaching Today's Youth, 1(1)*, 43-47.

Lewis, T. J., Heflin, J., & DiGangi, S. (1991). *Teaching students with behavior disorders. Basic questions and answers*. Reston, VA: Council for Exceptional Children.

Lewis, T. J., & Sugai, G. (1999). Effective behaviour support: A system approach to practice school wide management. *Focus on Exceptional Children, 21(6)*, 1-24.

MacDonald, I. M. (1997). Violence in schools: Multiple realities. *Alberta Journal of Educational Research, 43*, 142-156.

Maag, J. W., & Reid, R. (1994). Attention deficit hyperactivity disorder: A functional approach to assessment and treatment. *Behavioral Disorders, 20(1),* 5-23.

Maté, G. (2000). *Scattered Minds: A new look at the origins and healing of attention deficit disorder.* Toronto: Knopf.

Mendler, A. N. (1992). *How to achieve discipline with dignity in the schools.* Bloomington, IN: National Education Service.

Miller, D. (1994). Suicidal behavior of adolescents with behavior disorders and their peers without disabilities. *Behavioral Disorders, 20(1),* 61-68.

Moore, R., Cartledge, G., & Heckman, K. (1995). The effects of social skills instruction and self-monitoring on game related behaviors of adolescents with EBD. *Behavioral Disorders, 20(4),* 253-266.

Newcomer, L. L., Lewis T. J., Powers, L. J.,(2002). Policies and procedures to develop effective school-wide discipline practices at the elementary school level. *Council for Children with Behavioral Disorders*

Oseroff, A., Oseroff, C. E., Westling, D., & Gesser, L. (1999). Teacher's beliefs about maltreatment of students with emotional/behavioural disorders. *Behavioural Disorders, 24,(3),* 197-209.

Reid, R. (1999). Attention deficit hyperactivity disorder: effective methods for the classroom. *Focus on Exceptional Children, 32(4),* 1-20.

Rhode, G., Jenson, W. R., & Reavis, H. K. (1992). *The tough kid book: Practical classroom management strategies.* Longmont, CO: Sopris West.

Safran, S. P., & Oswald, K. (2003). Positive behaviour supports: Can schools reshape disciplinary practices? *Exceptional Children, 69(3),* 361-372.

Shippen, M. E., Simpson, R. G., & Crites, S. S. (2003). A practical guide to functional assessment. *Teaching Exceptional Children, 35(5),* 36-44.

Sprague, J., & Walker, H. (2000). Early identification and intervention for youth with antisocial and violent behaviours. *Exceptional Children, 66(3),* 14.

Wright-Strawderman, C. Lindsay P., Bavarette, L, & Flippo, J. R. (1996). Depression in students with disabilities: recognition and intervention strategies. *Intervention in School and Clinic, 31(5),* 261-275.

Links

American Academy of Child and Adolescent Psychiatry **http://www.aacap.org**

Canadian Attention Deficit Disorder Research Alliance **www.caddra.ca**

Canadian Children's Rights Council **www.canadiancrc.com/bullying.aspx**

Children and Adults with Attention Deficit Disorder **http://www.chadd.org**

Focus Adolescent Services **http://www.focusas.com**

Mayo Clinic **www.mayoclinic.com/health/drug-information/DrugHerbindex.com**

Northern County Psychioatric associates **www.baltimorepsych.com**

Website of Dr. Thomas MaIintyre **www.behavioradvisor.com**

CHAPTER 10

Students Who Are Gifted

"Gifted kids were dealt a bad hand by Galton* with his theory that cream will rise to the top no matter what. That was a century ago and my guess is a century from now we'll still be selling the gifted short, and for the same reason—the silly notion that because of their talents they don't need help. That is utter nonsense. The gifted need support as much as any other exceptional group."

Paul T., teacher of students who are gifted

Misconceptions About Giftedness

1. Students who are gifted always outpace their peers.

The level of achievement for students who are gifted does not always reflect true ability. While some fare well at school, other students who are gifted may underachieve. Cultural differences, gender, and disabilities may affect performance. Some students express giftedness in non-academic ways, or in ways not necessarily curriculum-related.

2. They work harder than their peers.

One of the accepted markers of giftedness is strong task commitment but the trait is not automatic. Commitment may not become evident until it is stimulated by the appropriate conditions.

3. Students who are gifted are bored with school, disruptive, and antagonistic.

They react to neglect, inequity, etc., like any other students.

4. It is common for emotional instability to accompany giftedness.

Students who are gifted usually enjoy good mental health and tend to have fewer emotional problems than the norm. Empirical evidence suggests they may be exceptionally sensitive to matters like injustice, world issues, etc.

5. Students who are gifted are physically inept, self-absorbed, and narrow-minded.

For the most part, they look and act like any other students, although teachers generally report them as above average in health, moral responsibility, and social adeptness.

6. Giftedness is a stable, absolute characteristic.

The evidence, particularly empirical evidence, seems to show that while a highly developed ability in a student seems to be relatively constant, it will express itself with varying intensity over time.

• • • ———

* Francis Galton, a nineteenth century English scientist, eugenics advocate, and one of the first to examine giftedness, proposed that genius would surface no matter the circumstances.

——— • • •

7. Students who are gifted are easy to identify.

They do not necessarily stand out in a group of age peers. Theoretically, a student who is gifted performing at age level is underachieving. Although IQ tests are a frequent means of identifying students who are gifted (and they may often score very high) these instruments are far too narrow as a sole criterion, for they are unable to measure or even highlight characteristics like artistic ability or creativity, for example. Reliance on IQ measures may also discriminate against culturally diverse populations or populations who are disabled.

8. Normally a school system will find 3 to 5 percent of the population gifted.

The percentage identified usually depends on the jurisdiction's definition of gifted, and on its conception of giftedness.

Defining Giftedness

The one consistent factor in defining giftedness is the lack of a consistent definition. For decades, researchers, educators, and parent groups have attempted to settle on one universally acceptable definition but it remains elusive. Even the term "giftedness" is seen by many as too narrow with a preference toward the terms "gifted," "talented," and "creative" gaining popularity. In defining giftedness, there exists a tension between a broad definition that many would argue is necessary, especially when one takes into consideration the underrepresentation of certain groups such as persons with disabilities and ethnic groups versus a narrower and more finely tuned approach that allows for the identification of those students who are "truly" gifted. In 2000, Alberta Learning, a provincial resource for teachers, released a document *Teaching students who are gifted and talented: Programming for children with special needs*. This document describes giftedness as having multiple forms and being diagnostic, developmental, and process-oriented rather than static and narrowly defined through an intelligence test. Giftedness is described as broad in terms of academic ability, talent, social, and interpersonal skills, and even vocational domains. It is also crucially dependent on context. The document notes that giftedness is intimately linked to opportunity and that programming for students who are gifted is essential in their development.

No matter the approach taken, any attempt to describe the characteristics of a student who is gifted reveals just how interwoven are matters like ability and desire in the human psyche, and how crucial are the matters of opportunity, environment, and circumstance. Every classroom teacher, for example, will notice in many of his or her students, from time to time, any or all of the characteristics that appear in the following list. At the same time, the teacher will inevitably reflect on whether the characteristics are situation-related and temporary, or whether they have always been genuinely present in the student, just waiting for exposure by the circumstance. There are other concerns, too, like distinguishing high verbal ability (a commonly accepted identifying characteristic) from mere artfulness and facility; or, distinguishing truly inherent abilities from those that show up in school as a consequence of the student's life at home. The end result is a large body of literature and a wide range of views on just what constitutes giftedness.

Defining by "Characteristics"

Students who display giftedness appear to have characteristics and abilities that stand out from the general run of things. What follows here are many of those most cited by both educators and parents. These are but one way of defining students who are gifted and their use may well prevail more out of tradition than scientific method. However, they are at least a beginning point. The challenge, for educators especially, is to determine not just the presence and the stability of these characteristics in a student, but to decide on their relative importance as standards qualifying a student for specialized instruction.

- wide range of abilities both academic and otherwise
- well-developed attention span, and a deep curiosity; ability to grasp, retain, synthesize, and act upon information
- ability to work independently, and to take responsibility

- capacity to adjust easily to new situations and demands
- superior vocabulary and reading ability
- considerable energy and above-average health
- well-developed capacity for abstract, complex, logical, and insightful conceptualizations
- more interested in questions than answers
- enjoys learning
- self-aware and reflective
- creative and imaginative
- ability to generalize information across settings
- highly developed sense of consequence and forward planning
- motivated and goal oriented
- able to see unusual diverse relationships
- advanced sense of moral/ethical judgment
- thought processes accelerated

Note that along with the positive characteristics above, students who are gifted may also demonstrate attributes that can be considered negative in a learning environment. These include:

- bored and inattentive, particularly when the subject area is not of interest to them
- highly sensitive
- extreme perfectionism
- difficulty changing tasks
- stubbornly prefer certain ways of learning
- overly self-critical and will strive for perfection unrealistically
- unwilling to listen to other perspectives
- insists on dominating discussion

Defining by "Interactions"

Most educators recognize that giftedness is a dynamic exceptionality, really too complex to be confined to a list of static, observable characteristics. Consequently, it has become regular practice now to define giftedness in terms of fluid, overlapping constellations. According to this approach, giftedness is the result of a number of characteristics interacting to achieve a purpose,

rather than being present in the individual in a kind of parallel isolation. One of the first and still very much accepted presentations of this style of identification was offered by Renzulli (1977), which he called the Enrichment Triad Model.

Figure 8A Triad Model

J. S. Renzulli. (1977) *Enrichment Triad Model: A guide for developing defensible programs for the gifted and talented.* Creative Learning Press. (The model has been embellished slightly in subsequent editions.)

Enrichment Triad Model

Sometimes called the "three-ring model" because it is presented as three overlapping circles, giftedness in this schema is seen as an interaction among a high level of general ability, a high level of task commitment, and a high level of creativity. Within the model, all three attributes must be present but will not necessarily be equal.

Students who are gifted, according to Renzulli, are those capable of developing this composite set of traits and applying the composite to any potentially valuable area of human performance. What is significant in this approach is the recognition of both human dynamism and the interplay of key qualities. There are times, quite naturally, when the degree of task commitment glows or fades in an individual. Everyone is more (or less) creative at some moments than at others. And abilities may well be relative to the nature of a task. The Enrichment Triad Model accommodates all of this, which probably explains why it gained very rapid acceptance among educators. Yet it has not led education for the gifted entirely out of the woods. Renzulli himself, in subsequent publications, argued that general ability is less important than specific performance in an operational definition of giftedness. (Which means, of course, that everyone can be gifted at some time: another major consideration for those responsible for definitions.)

Renzulli's later work, *The School-Wide Enrichment Model (SEM)*, which has become a template for school improvement, presents an approach in which the pedagogy of instruction for the gifted is extended to the entire school population. Educators are encouraged to create opportunities for students to develop their talents, participate in enriching activities that appeal to their interests, and allow for a wide variety of student expression. SEM has met with much universal appeal and is used in many countries.

Defining by "Multiples"

An increasingly popular way of looking at giftedness is to recognize that enriched abilities in a human being not only take many inherent forms, but also can be expressed in a variety of ways. Such a point of view is eminently satisfying to educators who accept that academic achievement by itself, and the traditional view of intelligence as measured by an IQ number, are entirely inadequate representations of giftedness.

Triarchic Theory of Intellectual Giftedness

Robert Sternberg (1997), who has published extensively on the nature of creativity, has offered special education two multiple views of what giftedness means. In the first, his triarchic theory, Sternberg posits three kinds of intelligence as necessary for giftedness:

analytic: particularly analytic reasoning and reading comprehension (the intelligence more likely to be measured by traditional IQ tests)

synthetic: creativity, intuition; response to invention, novelty, and coincidence

practical: ability to apply one or both of the above pragmatically

---

The Case of Kyle

Kyle is an only child of professional parents, both very successful lawyers, and both very caring and nurturing to their son. A nanny brings Kyle to the school's day care when it opens, but one or sometimes both parents pick him up (at varying times) from day care after school. Their home and their lifestyle are very much intellectually and culturally enriched. That influence was very obvious when Kyle entered grade 1 with a vocabulary and linguistic ability very much beyond the norm for his age. His identification as gifted was immediately and smoothly effected. (The parents had requested an IPRC prior to his enrollment.)

Throughout grades 1 and 2, Kyle's school performance was equal to that of his also-identified-as-gifted classmates, although there was a glitch in grade 1. Kyle began the year in French immersion, but it became obvious immediately, that it was a most unsuitable program for him. The parents demurred at first, but after extensive consultation with a psychologist they retained privately, they accepted the school's recommendation and Kyle was withdrawn. Early in grade 3, a more serious problem developed. The gifted group, although nominally in regular class, was doing more and more study on a self-contained basis and Kyle had trouble keeping up. By the end of grade 3, the gap between him and his classmates had widened.

It is now June, and the crunch has come. The regular IPRC review requested a full assessment of all students in the gifted primary group, because board policy shifts placements at grade 4 to either full-time special class or full-time regular with enrichment. Kyle and one classmate are below criterion for special class on all markers but one (parent nomination). Board policy gives the IPRC latitude to withdraw Kyle's identification as gifted. The committee declined to do that but did place him in a regular class. His parents are appealing now, on two bases: one that assessments of children Kyle's age (7.9) are unreliable; and two, that separating him from his peers of the past two years is not in his best interests, especially since it was the board that grouped him thus in the first place. The school board says that by its widely accepted standards, Kyle's abilities do not merit special placement. The Appeal Board must now make its recommendations.

Most people have all three kinds of intelligence in their makeup, but a central part of giftedness in this theory is the act of coordinating the three and knowing when to use which one. A person who is gifted, then, is a competent self-manager. Such an individual not only knows what and how better than most, he or she also knows better where and when to use what and how. One reason for the positive reception of Sternberg's position among teachers is its appeal to the notion that creativity, adaptiveness, and old-fashioned common sense and shrewdness play a major role in gifted behaviour.

Pentagonal Implicit Theory of Giftedness

Sternberg presents another theory of giftedness that offers criteria held as implicitly valuable in a culture. The five criteria are excellence, rarity, productivity, demonstrability, and value. (See Figure 8B.) Educators who give credence to this theory are led to consider first what their culture holds

---

A Summary Adaptation of the Pentagonal Implicit Theory

Criterion	Explanation	Example
Excellence	Superior in some way to age peers	Writes narrative fiction much better than peers with same schooling
Rarity	Ability infrequent at age/peer level	Not just better at fiction but usually superior
Productivity	Individual produces	Other writers recognize superior skill
Demonstrability	Proven in a public way	Wins awards of consequence
Value	Ability is valued by society	Recognized by the culture in public ways

Figure 8B

---

dear before they propose to set out a definition of giftedness. If nothing else, this is a theory that goes a long way toward answering a frequent criticism of education for the gifted: namely, that it ignores gifted potential in minorities because of a prejudice in favour of the dominant culture. It also adds background light to the charge that most people interested in education for the gifted, both implicitly and explicitly, limit that interest to elements our society values most. That is to say: in our education system, to be gifted as a writer of poetry, or to be a virtuoso violinist, has more value than to be a gifted cabinet-maker, because that reflects the dominant cultural view.

Multiple Intelligences: The "Gardner Theory"

In *Frames of Mind*, Howard Gardner (1983, 1993) proposes a theory of multiple intelligences: linguistic, musical, logical-mathematical, spatial, bodily-kinesthetic, interpersonal, intrapersonal, and naturalist. (See Figure 8C.) The theory holds that each of these intelligences is independent in function, and that if one intelligence is more powerfully developed than another, it will take over for a weaker or less developed one. (Gardner originally developed the theory while studying stroke patients.) Gardner's very persuasive writings, supported by interesting research, emphasize the multifold aspect of human intelligence, illuminating yet again the inadequacy of IQ testing with its implied notion of intelligence as a single, internal construct. His work has been instrumental in expanding the view that there is considerable development and plasticity in human growth. Further, even though this plasticity may be modulated by genetic constraints, humans are predisposed to certain intellectual operations and styles of operation, all of which can be addressed by education. The Gardner theory has particular appeal to teachers, perhaps because it reflects much more than other notions, the wide variety of abilities they see in a classroom full of students. Not only that, a theory of multiple intelligences reinforces the natural disposition of teachers to promote self-esteem in their students by recognizing that the world has room for many kinds of talent. On the other hand, the theory has also been criticized as a first step in the demise of education for the gifted, for, as the definition becomes broader and more all-encompassing, it has the effect of eliminating any distinction giftedness may have.

Multiple Intelligences (Gardner Theory)

Type	Manifestation
1. Linguistic	Exceptional ability to use words, often prolific
2. Musical	Uncommon sensitivity to pitch, rhythm, timbre, often without training
3. Logical/Mathematical	Rapid problem solving, grasp of underlying principles of causal systems, extraordinary ability to handle long chains of data
4. Spatial	Transforms easily among elements, superb mental imagery, very highly developed perception of pattern
5. Bodily/Kinesthetic	Poise and control of body and movement evident even before training
6. Interpersonal	Capacity to 'read' people even without language
7. Intrapersonal	Very mature sense of self
8. Naturalist*	Sensitivity to nature and ability to recognize and classify natural things

*A recent addition. It has not been accepted as enthusiastically as the initial seven

Figure 8C

Emotional Intelligence

A view advanced by Daniel Goleman (1995, 1997) concludes that star performers owe their superiority to what he calls emotional intelligence. According to Goleman, this intelligence is found in people skills: social radar, political sensitivity, trustworthiness, empathy in personal relationships, and team-building ability to create opportunity out of diversity. The theory was developed out of a survey of personnel in over 500 organizations worldwide. Although it enjoys an exceptionally enthusiastic reception in business and industry, the theory does not have the same appeal to education. Some argue that educators' reticence is owing to the fact that the theory appeared first in the popular press instead of acquiring official sanction by exposure in academic publications first.

The Importance of a Balanced View

The varied explanations of giftedness (there are others beyond those summarized above) both plague and enrich the attempts of educators and parents to define giftedness and properly identify its candidates. Nevertheless, because these views tend to lead away from the notion of giftedness as a single construct (the IQ notion) toward a view of giftedness as an expression of several contributing factors, students are beginning to be more fairly identified. Above all, the idea of giftedness as a construct standing on a number of foundations, gives more credence and importance to creativity, to commitment, and to the expression of ability in ways other than the narrow confines allowed by academic achievement alone.

Some Issues in the Field

✦ *Being practical in gifted identification?*
 Whether one is identified as gifted may, in some cases, be more a matter of pragmatics that pedagogy. A school board with the ability to provide funding for schools for the performing arts may differ in terms of identification procedures from other boards. Strangely, numbers of students identified as gifted in a board have also been known to vary depending on the number of seats available in a specialized setting. One year the cut off may be 130 in terms of IQ but the next year, depending on numbers, it may have to be 135.

✦ *Discrimination and gifted identification?*
 Researchers and educators alike are becoming increasingly concerned about the underrepresentation of particular groups within the category of giftedness. Persons with disabilities, students who are culturally different, females, and students who have low socioeconomic status are often excluded from classes for the gifted in part due to the

narrow identification procedures employed by some school boards. Heavy reliance on IQ measures, for example, can present difficulties for students who have learning disabilities, as well as for those with sensory impairment. The lack of instruments normed on such groups suggests that the scores obtained by students with disabilities may not be representative of their actual ability.

♦ *Separate classes?* How to deal with students once they have been identified as gifted is a continuing debate. At one time, the heat arose primarily over whether or not the students should be placed in separate schools. Proponents of this approach argue that a totally separated (but not totally isolated) environment can offer a much more enriched experience where the students are challenged by interchange with others like themselves, by teachers trained to work with this population, by an atmosphere of intellectual ferment, and by the momentum of exclusivity where elevated goals will obtain. The argument goes further to posit that a congregated environment will offer role modelling less likely to be available in the mainstream. There are reasons to accept the validity of this position. Empirical evidence, particularly, has long demonstrated the stimulating power of high expectations in a specialized, highly charged, intellectual environment.

On the other hand, there are also strong arguments in favour of inclusion. A principal tenet holds that although segregated environments may be successful, they are so specialized as to be unrealistic, and therefore counter-productive. By extension, experience in a rarified environment may mean the student who is gifted will be ill prepared to perform effectively in the real world. Ultimately, like most arguments over this issue, whether to congregate students who are gifted in special schools, or include them, will never be fully resolved, not least because of the politics involved.

♦ *How to program?* When decisions have been taken to maintain students who are gifted in an integrated environment, a next stage of issues inevitably arises over how to provide the proper program. One camp argues for enrichment: providing special activities within a regular class setting for selected students. Proponents say that this keeps the students who are gifted rooted in reality, and that given the premise that every one exhibits giftedness from time to time, there is less risk that potential giftedness will be ignored. Detractors state that enrichment really does not qualify as education for the gifted because students who are gifted in regular programs suffer under the myth that they can easily teach themselves and that what passes for enrichment often means just giving more of the same work, utilizing students who are gifted as tutors, or providing busy work such as crosswords.

A next, more specialized style, *ability grouping*, is also offered in an inclusive environment where the gifted are selected out for differentiated instruction in more or less homogeneous groups. Supporters of this style usually advance the separate classes argument described above, while detractors say ability grouping fosters elitism. A third style, *acceleration*, despite a great deal of uniformly supportive evidence in favour of it, is one of the least used programming methods, usually because of the fear of negative social and emotional consequences for the accelerated student.

Most school boards tackle the program issue by offering a variety of styles for students identified as gifted, on the quite reasonable premise that variety of program is necessary to satisfy a variety of superior abilities.

♦ *Limits to the category?* Advocates of education for the gifted wince at the fact that despite the broadening of the concept, programming for *talent*, unusual ability in, say, music, or athletics, or drama, or the visual arts, continues to be a poor relative in most school boards. Because these abilities are not necessarily accompanied by superior academic achievement, the issue is first: whether to classify them as examples of giftedness; second, and likely far more important: how—even whether—to offer programs aimed at developing talents. An increasing practice in larger jurisdictions now is to develop "arts schools" for talents that come under this rubric. However, admission to these excellent academies is

At a professional development day, one of Lydia's former primary teachers (grades 1 and 2) met the girl's grade 8 teacher in her new school and was surprised to hear that Lydia, one of her brightest ever students, was "just getting by."

"Lydia can certainly handle the curriculum," the grade 8 teacher said, "and she's truly a pleasant young person—wonderful with the little children in our tutoring program; a natural who teaches as well as we do—but yes, just getting by. The work's always done, and on time. Adequate but not much more than that.

"I've always felt she could do better," the teacher continued, "but I've got a big class. The truth is, I'm in my first year and I'm having a busy time. I just can't get around to her as I'd like to, especially with some of the demanding students I've got."

The conversation piqued the grade 8 teacher's curiosity, however, and he soon uncovered the fact that Lydia had been identified gifted in grade 4 in her former school, but neither her placement nor her program changed upon instructions conveyed by the family's parish priest. Lydia's family had emigrated to urban Ontario from a mountain village in southern Europe when she was a little girl. Her parents still do not speak English, and until now their parish priest has been their interlocutor with schools and other officialdom. The grade 8 teacher was also told that Lydia's grade 4 teacher, a committed feminist, had been transferred to another school after she had defiantly attempted to enrich the girl's program.

Without authorization or permission, the grade 8 teacher informally administered an achievement test to Lydia and discovered that, according to the test, she was capable of grade 11-12 work in language and even in math, although she had not yet been exposed to the subject in any significant way.

"A waste," he said to the primary grade teacher a few weeks later. "A shame and a waste. Lydia should have enrichment. Isn't there anything that can be done here?"

often tied to superior academic achievement. Also, distance means students in rural areas may have little opportunity to avail themselves of these specialized settings. (It is an interesting comment, too, on our culture, Sternberg's theory notwithstanding, that exceptional ability in areas like carpentry or design or other trades receive little or no accommodation under the title of giftedness.)

◆ *Survival?* Education for students who are gifted regularly endures accusations of meritocracy and elitism, no matter how egalitarian admission prerequisites may be. For this very important, if somewhat insidious reason, special education for students who are gifted is often in jeopardy. It is not unusual, therefore, for the continuing existence of specialized programming to depend on the vigour and determination of parent advocacy groups, acting in support of determined educators who feel this kind of special education is not just a practical but a moral obli-gation. On the other hand, it is impossible to ignore the uneasiness raised by the overly high number of students identified as gifted.

◆ *Gifted education for primary?* An enduring argument in the field thrives over the issue of offering programs for the very young. Many boards of education are reluctant to formally identify students in the primary grades as gifted, and equally reluctant to authorize special classes, or formal, differentiated program for them. This attitude has taken hold, first of all, because the developmental elasticity so typical at ages 4-5 to 8-9 can make confident identification difficult. Secondly, since primary education is usually very adaptive and flexible, and more individualized, students who are gifted can be easily accommodated in the mainstream. Further, in primary education there is an importance attached to social skills that in some schools takes precedence even over the development of academic and cognitive skills.

Lewis Terman, sometimes referred to as the father of education for the gifted, did much to develop the founding knowledge base for this population. Between 1922 and 1928 Terman and his colleagues, utilizing standardized intelligence testing, identified approximately 1500 children as gifted. Researchers tracked these children (in later years known as "Termites") for three-quarters of a century. The results did much to dispel the myth of the weak, fragile, brainy child. The findings of the long-term studies indicated that while being intellectually superior, the subjects were also superior socially and psychologically, and were more physically healthy.

♦ *Gender?* More males are identified for gifted programs than females, and both educators and parents have had difficulty finding concrete and agreeable explanations for this. There is no conclusive research that points to biological difference as an explanation. Yet, explanations that point to traditions of male dominance in our culture have equally sparse research support. While some efforts have been made to examine whether the learning needs of females who are gifted require a different view of education for the gifted, consensus in the field is that too little has been done to address this discrepancy.

♦ *Building a labyrinth?* The field of education for the gifted is regularly accused of burying itself in complexity, with inordinately interwoven and complicated models for identification, equally intricate models for program, and constant, complicated self-examination. There is empirical evidence to support this accusation. Some boards in Ontario, for example, while recognized for their commitment to educating students who are gifted, have such amazingly intricate and time-consuming patterns of identification—and programs to match—that it is conceivable some students may not be receiving an appropriate program for the simple reason that they (or their parents) lack the will or the means or the stamina to crawl through the bureaucratic web.

How Students are Nominated for Gifted Programs

All school boards in the province, whatever their respective policies regarding the nomination of candidates for education for the gifted, use a number of different methods for making determinations. Usually, a board relies on a combination of elements like the ones listed here.

1. Despite the acknowledged weaknesses of IQ tests, they continue to dominate as a screening device. What is administratively attractive about IQ tests is that they produce a quantified statement, a number, irrespective of whatever else they offer, and in most jurisdictions this number becomes an entry-level border for admission to programs. The established figure varies from one school board to another. (Figures of 135 and 130 Full Scale Score on the Wechsler Intelligence Scale for Children are typical.) The work of such people as Sternberg and Gardner notwithstanding, faith in tradition has not yet been seriously shaken. Rationales for the continued reliance on a number include the presumed fairness of using an objective measure, the high correlation between IQ testing and academic strength, and good old-fashioned test mystique! Detractors argue that IQ tests discriminate against students who are culturally different and students with disabilities.

2. Tests of creativity are sometimes used to identify students who are gifted especially in jurisdictions where creative behaviours are given credence as a major cluster. However, because the validity of these tests is so much in question, their use has less impact, generally, than IQ test scores, and teacher, parent, and peer nominations.

3. Achievement tests are used as initial screening mechanisms for giftedness much in the same way as in the assessment of delayed performance. In typical practice, the student who scores significantly above his or her age level (usually two or more grades) is a potential candidate for programming for the gifted.

4. The development of a portfolio has gained recent popularity with educators as a more comprehensive way in which to assess a student's potential giftedness. Comprised of a collection of representative work, a portfolio can display tal-

These are students whose potential is implied by significant achievement, or by high IQ test scores, but whose apparent abilities are not realized. Not that they are failures, necessarily. They may well work at grade level. However, if an individual is truly gifted, yet produces at an average level, then it may be reasonable to conclude he or she is an underachiever. On the other hand, lest students who are thought to be superior become tarred with the brush of underachievement, it is important for their parents and teachers to evaluate a number of factors before making a judgment.

Has the student learned to learn? Many very able students "coast" in the early grades because they master classroom demands effortlessly. Then, as the level of challenge increases and more is required, they may not rise to the occasion, either because their confidence is eroded, or more likely, because they have not learned consistent, effective work habits.

Do social factors permit success? Some children deliberately underplay their potential because they do not wish to be singled out. Students who are gifted underachievers also tend to have low self-esteem and peer problems, which only exacerbate the underachievement.

Are expectations realistic? Learning is not automatically easy for children who are bright. Sometimes the expectations of the adults in their lives, especially parents, do not match what the children are capable of doing at particular points in their development. Flexibility, communication, addressing skills deficits, and creative programming can greatly assist students who are gifted underachievers in realizing their potential.

Is there a good "fit" between the child and the classroom? An overabundance of busywork, inflexible teaching, low expectations, and an overly competitive classroom environment are factors that contribute to poor achievement by students who are gifted. Some children who are gifted do not fare well in structured environments. Others find it difficult to conform even to the simple demands that are necessary to make a school run efficiently. Such students may well underperform as a result.

---

ents over time and across situations. The information included is generally selected collaboratively between the student and the educator.

5. Teacher nomination is a popular method of screening in the very early grades. Many boards require teachers to use a clearly defined rating scale, or inventory checklist to substantiate a nomination. One problem with this method is that scales usually correlate the academic behaviour of students with what is expected of them academically in the succeeding years (inevitably raising the concern that students who "play the game" are most likely to have an advantage).

6. Parent nomination is used by many school boards, on the quite reasonable premise that parents have the best knowledge of their child's development. Although parent nomination is clearly a beneficial factor in the process of selection, educators must keep in mind that parents often lack opportunity for the wider view when assessing their own child's current and potential success in school. What seems gifted ability at home may not seem so when compared to abilities across a whole class. Interestingly, parents from lower socioeconomic groups seem more likely to report giftedness than parents from higher socioeconomic areas.

7. Peer nomination is yet another method for initiating referral. Although experts in the field have been favourable in their attitude to this style, there is still a serious lack of research to support it.

8. Self-nomination is most effective with older students who display specific types of talents. Very often a self-nomination accompanies a nomination by teacher or parent, and more often than not is presented because the student has been asked to do so by one or both of the latter.

> *The most gifted members of the human species are at their creative best when they cannot have their way.*
>
> Eric Hoffer

The Case of Colin

By the end of the second grade, Colin's pranks had already made him a legend in his school. At first, most of the staff were willing to see the funny side. The upset he caused with his first major foray, for example, by putting what appeared to be soiled facial tissues (he used camembert cheese) on the tables at the school bake sale, was forgiven with chuckles. So was the time he upped the ante with seemingly used toilet tissue in his classmate's lunch boxes. However, everyone was less than amused when, during the return from a fire drill, Colin somehow convinced the entire junior kindergarten class to hide in the janitor's storeroom. Nor was the principal too pleased when Colin attached an inflated condom to the parents' notice board in the entrance hall.

Inevitably, the litany of mischief gradually became more serious. Colin discovered he could bring police to the school by activating the overnight security system with a handheld laser pointer. On one occasion, he pulled the fire alarm at dismissal time and in the ensuing chaos, disabled two school buses by plugging their tail pipes with styrofoam. It was a carefully planned endeavour, for the plugs were precut to size and the chosen vehicles were at the very front and very back of the bus lineup. When a large order of pizza arrived at the school during the first week of school in grade 3, it was widely concluded that Colin was warming up for another year, and something would have to be done.

Serendipity intervened at this point, in the combination of an educational assistant with three year's experience in a class for the gifted, and a teacher with a passion for Renaissance art. In response to a group project they devised for the class, Colin produced a mural which duplicated Da Vinci's The Last Supper, but from a ground level perspective. Thirteen very large pairs of feet exactly paralleled the positioning in Da Vinci's famous work! Among the reactions to this mural was the educational assistant's strong push to have Colin assessed for giftedness. The outcome confirmed her intuition. He was found to be off the scale in creativity and very superior in IQ test results. As well, Colin became caught up in the "Renaissance passion," and the pranks stopped, or at least went on hold.

Where things stand now, Colin qualifies for the highest level of placement for the gifted in the board's Special Education Plan. That would mean a transfer to a nearby school, but both Colin and his parents are opposed to any placement that would take him away from his current teacher and educational assistant. Plans are now underway to accommodate Colin's needs in the regular class with support, but programming is a challenge and Colin's teacher feels overwhelmed. She has referred this to the in-school team. Everyone is concerned that if Colin is unchallenged, the ever-more serious pranks will return.

Organizational Models

Organizing the Students

It is quite common practice for boards to organize students identified as candidates for education for the gifted into differing levels in terms of the provision of services. While terminology may vary, students are usually differentiated by ability so that the majority will likely be identified as Gifted: Level I. A smaller number will be designated Level II and even fewer will be in Level III.

The largest group, Level I, will likely spend most of its time in the regular classroom, but will receive some enriched or differentiated curriculum. This may be in the form of a theme study undertaken independent of, but in addition to, the regular curriculum. The classroom teacher may be helped by a resource teacher, or the latter may have responsibility for the venture entirely on his or her own. (Many schools encourage the teacher and resource teacher to co-operate, and to involve all the students in the class as much as possible, whether they are designated Level I or not.)

Level II students may also be assigned to a regular class, but may be withdrawn more frequently for independent pursuits under the guidance of a resource teacher. These students may also be somewhat more involved in projects that involve several schools at once, and that culminate in special presentations, workshops, etc.

Level III students are more likely to be in separate classes where the entire curriculum is differentiated.

Organizing the Programs

School boards invest considerable time and effort in developing organizational models to fulfill programming requirements for students who are gifted. One immediate outcome is that the programs are thus established on a broad basis, so that there can be a good deal of interaction among schools, with sharing of resources, expenses, etc. To a greater extent, too, than in most other areas of special education, there tends to be more board-wide excursions, cooperative projects, and involvement with what the community at large has to offer. Whether or not a board formally divides its students who have been designated as gifted among levels as described above, it usually designs the delivery of program service around a particular style or model. Following is a list of some of the models that continue in popular use in Ontario. Almost without exception, they are implemented with local variations.

The Enrichment Triad

With modifications, the Enrichment Triad (Renzulli, 1977) continues to be very widely used in the province, indeed throughout Canada. It proposes three levels of activity:

General exploratory activities: designed to expose students to exciting topics, ideas, and fields of knowledge not ordinarily covered by the regular curriculum. There are extras like visiting speakers, field trips, demonstrations, and interest development centres.

Group training activities: methods, materials, and instructional techniques designed to develop thinking processes, research and reference skills, and personal and social skills

Individual or small-group investigations: students investigate real problems and topics using appropriate methods of inquiry.

Twice-Exceptional Learners

A term coined by James Gallagher, "twice-exceptional" refers to students who are both gifted and disabled. Generally, these students show patterns of extreme strengths accompanied by significant difficulties. These students are at risk for underachievement as well as misidentification. Unfortunately, the make-up of school systems can place educators in a position to choose only one type of programming or identification, an unfortunate dilemma for students and educator alike. Students who are twice–exceptional can be inquisitive and impulsive, have high levels of creativity but poor memory, display a superior vocabulary but poor work production. These students need programs that focus on their areas of talent, learning opportunities that are flexible and provide compensatory and remedial assistance as well, and, perhaps most important, a nurturing environment that recognizes their unique way of learning.

An important modification of the Enrichment Triad is the *Revolving Door Identification Model* (Renzulli, et al., 1981). In this model, the resource room teacher is a consultant and the classroom teacher is directly involved in the students' special projects. Students are not permanently in or out of the program, but can apply for special consideration to work on projects of their own choosing. The resource teacher helps the student to frame the area of interest into a researchable problem; suggests where the student can find appropriate methodologies for pursuing the problem like a professional enquirer; helps the student to obtain appropriate resources, provides assistance and encouragement, and helps find appropriate outlets and audiences for the creative work.

Both styles above enjoy more popular use than a third notion developed by the same author called the *Multiple Menu Model* (Renzulli, 1988), which focuses on ways to teach content in efficient and interesting ways.

The Autonomous Learner Model

This is a program developed by Betts (1986)* principally for the secondary school. It adapts to the departmentalized structure of high schools, and anticipates that students will be withdrawn for single periods at specified times of the week. The student progresses through five stages:

i) orientation

ii) individual development: learning the attitudes and concepts necessary for life-long learning

iii) enrichment activities: exploring outside the curriculum; becoming aware of resources

iv) seminars: presenting results of personal pursuits and findings to larger groups for evaluation

v) in-depth study: opportunity to pursue an area of interest on a longer term basis

The Purdue Three-Stage Enrichment Model

This is a half-day or full-day withdrawal program (Feldhausen & Kolloff, 1986) used mostly in elementary schools. The Purdue type of program is quite popular (under names like "Challenge," "Upward Bound," etc.) because it offers enrichment and opportunity without taxing the already scanty resources that typify so many elementary schools. Needless to say, the quality of these programs varies dramatically according to the teacher in charge.

There are three basic components:

i) divergent and convergent thinking, in which the program concentrates on problem solving, decision making, forward planning, etc.

ii) creative problem solving, which offers strategies and techniques in creative problem solving of real problems

iii) development of independent learning, which requires the student to engage in the development of a product through learning and investigation and then share it with an audience

Other Styles

Other responses to the need for educating students who are gifted use more time-honoured approaches.

✧ *Enrichment in the classroom:* A differentiated program of study offering experiences beyond the regular curriculum. This model is delivered by the regular classroom teacher, with or without assistance from a consultant or resource teacher.

✧ *Consultant teacher program:* Enriched instruction is provided within the regular classroom by the classroom teacher with the assistance of an educational consultant or specialist (occasionally delivered by the specialist).

✧ *Community mentor program:* Students interact on an individual basis with selected members of the community to study topics of special interest.

✧ *Independent study program:* projects supervised by a qualified adult

✧ *Learning enrichment service:* Generally, this is a networking system that combines many of the above ideas in an organized way.

• • • ————

*Note that almost all of the models listed here continue to undergo modest revisions (with later publication dates) but in all cases their basic structures are the same. As it is, very few schools or school boards adopt a model without making adaptations.

———— • • •

✔ STRATEGIES FOR THE CLASSROOM

"Achieving potential" is admittedly a buzzword in all of special education, but its use requires no apology for it identifies what special education is all about. The phrase has extraordinary personal and societal significance in the case of students who are gifted.

A program for students who are gifted must be based on the idea of achieving potential, and from that premise alone proceed to accommodate their unique needs. Part of that program—in some cases perhaps all of it—will be met in the role played by the classroom teacher. Each individual teacher of students who are gifted brings to a program, or a class, or a student, his or her own unique nature, as well as his or her own unique talents and interests and skills and background, all of which in the right circumstances, go a long way toward fulfilling the notion of achieving potential. In other words, as with any teaching-learning situation, the teacher is the key.

There are, however, certain absolutes to which teachers should subscribe, irrespective of their own preferences, styles, and areas of interest. These are planning goals that include the following:

(1) *Establish an environment* that shows clearly that intelligent thought, analysis, and creativity are valued.

(2) *Encourage students to discover* and develop their special abilities. Provide the time, space, materials, and opportunities for them to do this at the sacrifice, if necessary, of the laid-on curriculum. (In this sense the teacher is much more of a facilitator than an instructor.) Arrange learning experiences that go beyond the normal acquisition-of-knowledge level. Students who are gifted need to go higher, deeper, and wider in their pursuit of a subject, pushing past the usual limits. Very often the teacher acts as a consultant, using maturity and experience to help the student find a productive critical path, or a method of investigation.

(3) *Provide opportunities* for students to interact with adults, other students, and with various experts so that they will be challenged, not just to know about things, but about people, and so that they will learn to see their own place and their responsibility in the human connection.

(4) *Create an atmosphere where risk-taking*, speculation, and conjecture can be undertaken safely. The teacher recognizes that trial and error are part of learning and that the only real failures in a classroom are those that erode self-esteem. If the teacher takes risks, and fails, the student invariably will learn from this too.

READINGS & RESOURCES

Allen, D. (1995). Encouraging success in female students: Helping girls develop math and science skills. *Gifted Children Today Magazine, 18*(2), 44-45.

Ambrose, D., Allen, J., & Huntly, S. B. (1994). Mentorship of the highly creative. *Roeper Review, 17*(2), 131-133.

Blythe, T., & Gardner, H. (1990). A school for all intelligences. *Educational Leadership, 47*(7), 33-37.

Clarke, B. (2002). *Growing up gifted: Developing the potential of children at home and at school* (6th ed.). Upper Saddle River, NJ: Merrill/Prentice Hall.

Colangelo, N., & Davis, G. A. (1997). *Handbook of gifted education (2nd ed.)*. Needham Heights, MA: Allyn & Bacon.

Coleman, M.R. (2005). Academic strategies that work for gifted students with learning disabilities. *Teaching Exceptional Children, 38*, 28-32.

Davis, G. A., & Rimm, S. B. (1998). *Education of the Gifted and talented. (4th ed.)*. Needham Heights, MA: Allyn & Bacon.

Delisle, J. R. & Gailbraith, J. (2004). *When gifted kids don't have all the answers: How to meet their social and emotional needs*. Minneapolis, MN: Free Spirit Publishing.

Del Prete, T. (1996). Asset or albatross? The education and socialization of gifted students. *Gifted Child Today, 19*(2), 24-25, 44-50.

Feldhausen, J. F., & Kolloff, P. B. (1986). The Purdue three-stage enrichment model for gifted education at the elementary level. In J. S. Renzulli (Ed.). *Systems and models for developing programs for gifted and talented.* Mansfield Centre, CT: Creative Learning Press.

Feldhausen, J. F. & Moon, S. (1992). Grouping gifted students: Issues and concerns. *Gifted Children Quarterly, 36*, 63-67.

Feldman, D. (1993). Child prodigies: A distinctive form of giftedness. *Gifted Child Quarterly, 37*, 188-193.

Fetzer, E. A. (2000). The gifted/learning disabled child: A guide for teachers and parents. *Gifted Child Today, 23*(4), 44-50.

Flint, L. J. (2001). Challenges of identifying and serving gifted children with ADHD, *Teaching Exceptional Children, 33(4),* 62-69.

Ford, D. Y., & Harris, J. J. (Eds.). (1999). *Multicultural Gifted Education.* New York: Teachers College Press.

Friesen, J. W. (1997). The concept of giftedness in First Nations context. *Multicultural Educational Journal, 15*, 26-35.

Gardner, H. (1983). *Frames of mind: The theory of multiple intelligences.* New York: Basic Books.

Gardner, H. (1993). *Multiple intelligences.* New York: Basic Books.

Gardner, H. (1999). *Intelligence reframed: Multiple intelligences for the 21st century.* New York: Basic Books.

Goleman, D. (1995, 97). *Emotional Intelligence. Why it can matter more than IQ.* New York: Bantam Books.

Louis, B. & Lewis M. (1992). Parental beliefs about giftedness in young children and their relationship to actual ability level. *Gifted Child Quarterly, 36*, 27-31.

Maker, J. C., Nielson, A. B., & Rogers, J. A. (1994). Giftedness, diversity and problem solving. *Teaching Exceptional Children, 27*, 4-19.

Masse, L. (2001). Direction of gifted education in the first decade of the 21st century: A step back, continuity, and new direction. *Journal of Secondary Gifted Education, 12*, 170-173.

Matthews, D. J., & Foster, J. F. (2005). *Being smart about gifted children: A guidebook for parents and educators.* Scottsdale, AZ: Great Potential Press.

Montgomery, W. (2001). Creating culturally responsive inclusive classrooms. *Teaching Exceptional Children, 33*(4), 4-9.

Nielsen, M. E., & Higgins, L. D. (2005). The eye of the storm: Services and programs for twice exceptional learners. *Teaching Exceptional Children, 38*(1), 8-15.

Pirto, J. (2001). *"My teeming brain": Understanding creative writers.* Cresskill, NJ: Hampton.

Reis, S. M., & Westberg, K. L. (1994). The impact of staff development on teachers' ability to modify curriculum for gifted and talented students. *Gifted Child Quarterly, 38*, 127-135.

Renzulli, J. S. (1988). The multiple menu model for developing differentiated curriculum for the gifted and talented. *Gifted Child Quarterly, 32*, 298-309.

Renzulli, J. S., & Reis, S. M. (1986). The enrichment triad/revolving door model: A school-wide plan for the development of creative productivity. In J. Renzulli (Ed.). *Systems and models for developing programs for gifted and talented.* Mansfield Centre, CT: Creative Learning Press.

Shaywitz, S. E., Holahan, J. M., Freudenheim, D. A., Fletcher, J. H. M., Makuch, R. W., & Shaywitz, B. A. (2001). Heterogeneity with the gifted: Higher IQ boys exhibit behaviours resembling boys with learning disabilities. *Gifted Child Quarterly, 45*, 16-23.

Shore, B. M., Cornell, D. G., Robinson, A., & Ward, V. S. (1991). *Recommended practices in gifted education.* New York: Teachers College Press.

Silverman, L. K. (1994/1995). To be gifted or feminine: The forced choice of adolescence. *Journal of Secondary Gifted Education, 6*(2), 141-156.

Sternberg, R. J. (2005). WICS: A model of gifted-ness in leadership. *Roeper Review, 28,* 37-44.

Sternberg, R. J. (1997). A triarchic view of gift-edness: Theory and practice. In Colanelo, N. & Davis, G. (Eds.). *Handbook of Gifted Education (2nd ed.).* Toronto: Allyn & Bacon.

Winner, E. (1996). *Gifted children: Myths and realities.* New York: Basic Books.

Links

Association for Bright Children
http://www.abcontario.ca/

Government of BC resource guide
http://www.bced.gov.bc.ca/specialed/gifted/

Kids Source
http://www.kidsource.com/ kidsource/ pages/ed.gifted.html

Mensa
http://www.mensa.org/

Teaching Gifted Children
http://www.canteach. ca/links/ linkgifted.html

CHAPTER 11

Students With Intellectual and Developmental Disabilities

"When I cared for these kids back in the sixties, the goals were so limited. Teach them to feed themselves, how to go to the toilet. ... Stay out of sight! ... that was a big one. 'Course that's when we had 'em at the home. Easy to aim low when you shut them away. Today—well, it's just amazing. There's so much retarded kids can do now. No wonder we don't call them that any more."

Terry B. (retired institutional care worker)

Misconceptions About Intellectual and Developmental Disabilities

1. Developmental disability is a condition like an illness.

Development disability is not something one has, like a heart condition, or big feet, or schizophrenia, but rather a state of functioning characterized by limitations in both intelligence and adaptive skills.

2. An intellectual or developmental disability puts a cap on learning.

An individual's intellectual functioning is not a static thing. (If it were, the role of education would be much different!) Especially for a person with mild disabilities, intensive and early instruction can make a major difference.

3. The disabilities occur equally across class and gender.

Data collected over decades by the American Association on Intellectual and Developmental Disabilities (AAIDD) and others show that, for a variety of reasons, the number of boys identified is greater than that of girls by factors of five to ten. The disability also has a significantly higher prevalence in children from lower socio-economic classes.

4. Developmental and intellectual disabilities are reflected in physical appearance.

Certain groups of students, including many with Down syndrome, do appear physically different from their peers, but the vast majority of students with intellectual or developmental disabilities look just like any other students.

5. Students with intellectual and developmental problems always learn more when they are included with/separated from other students.

It is not possible to lump all special students into a learning environment classification. If they learn much like everyone else, as the evidence suggests, it must be granted that—just as with everyone else—no one environment is consistently and universally superior.

6. A low intelligence quotient (IQ) test score is evidence of at least borderline disability and means the subject's adaptive skills are below normal.

An IQ test may predict academic or school matters, but an individual's level of adaptive skills are more a factor of training, motivation, and social environment, and generally are not tapped by IQ tests.

7. Students with intellectual or developmental disabilities are always compliant/difficult.

Like everyone else, these students experience both happiness and emotional stress and react accordingly. Regardless of a similar label, there is no "always" in the population of individuals with intellectual disabilities.

Definition and Classification

Changes Over Time

For the first half of the twentieth century, significant numbers of people with intellectual and developmental disabilities were housed in large institutions. At this time, the prevailing definition was one established in 1920 by American psychologist H. H. Goddard. Goddard divided the exceptionality into four categories of declining ability, beginning with feeble-minded, followed by moron, idiot, and ending with imbecile. By the 1950s, Goddard's categories were overtaken by the general term mental retardation, with adjectives of degree like "mild," "moderate," "severe," or "profound" added to differentiate. Although in the minds of those who advocated for using the term mental retardation the change represented the best science of the time (and was less offensive than the Goddard terminology), "mental retardation" was nevertheless loaded with implications, for it suggested an incapacity that is both permanent and comprehensive.

By the end of the twentieth century, "mental retardation" was pretty much replaced by the terms "intellectual" and "developmental," usually in combination with a follower: either "disabilities" or "challenged." This change occurred in part out of a gradual realization that classifying people as retarded is a gross over-simplification that ignores the importance of adaptive behaviour, and in part out of passion for political correctness. The result has been, by and large, positive. Although there is some confusion, even among professionals, as to whether terms like "intellectually disabled" or "intellectually challenged" are most appropriate—or whether either term is as comprehensive as "developmental," the language reflects a clear shift in attitude. Not just educators and medical professionals but the public at large now generally view persons with these disabilities as equal citizens in the community, capable of learning, and deserving of an education.

The State of Things Today

Regrettably, there is still no universally accepted definition of intellectual and developmental disability. However, a large body of research, along with intense advocacy by interested parties, and thoughtful application of empirical evidence by educators, has led to a more or less general acknowledgement that three inter-related factors describe the exceptionality. These are:

1. sub-average intellectual functioning
2. problems in adaptive behaviour
3. both of the above occurring during the developmental period

1. Sub-average Intellectual Functioning

This aspect is usually addressed by using IQ test scores to indicate levels. Prior to 1973, it was common practice for school boards to follow the policy of the dominant professional body in the field, the American Association for the Mentally Retarded (AAMR—now called the American Association on Intellectual and Developmental Disabilities [AAIDD]) ,which recommended an IQ test score of 85 and below as the cutoff for identification as "mentally retarded." This is only one standard deviation below the mean, or norm, of 100. In 1973, the AAMR recommendation was changed to an IQ test score of "approximately 70 to 75," or two standard deviations below the mean, thus significantly lowering the barrier. The change recognized the importance of other factors (such as adaptive behaviour), and reinforced the notion that IQ tests are only an aid, not a diagnostic magic wand.

Although there is no "official" set of scores, school boards that use test scores to classify intellectual and developmental disability generally apply the following ranges, each with its own set of general expectations or needs*.

• • • ———

* Some jurisdictions correlate IQ ranges with "classification by degree." The four most frequently used terms are "mild" "moderate," "severe," "profound."

——— • • •

IQ Score	Expectations
Below 25	Student may learn basic self-care and communication skills. Full time ed. assistant or tech. support (or both) likely.
25-40	Part- to full-time support providing instruction for limited independence. Self-help and social skills emphasized. Some life-long assistance likely needed.
40-55	With support may learn independent life skills, self-care and basic academic skills. Supervised independence possible.
55-70	Academic achievement to grade 5 or more is possible with intermittent support. Secondary school academic focused programs may present a challenge.

2. Adaptive Behaviour

Generally, adaptive behaviour refers to how well an individual is able to meet—to adapt to—demands made by his or her environment. It is a dynamic construct, one that is influenced by factors like cultural norms, the demands of a particular situation, and the age-group to which an individual belongs. Including adaptive behaviour in the assessment of intellectual and developmental ability, a practice that began in the 1970s, has proven to be instrumental in shaping a more positive view. Taking adaptive behaviour into account recognizes that many individuals who might score poorly on an IQ test can actually live and learn quite well in a variety of environments. As well, it encompasses recognition of an individual's strengths, not just weaknesses. An assessment of adaptive behaviour, how one fits into his or her academic, social, and family environment, is instrumental in helping to determine the extent and effect of any intellectual and developmental disability and thus the program that will be provided.

The Case of Christina

The annual review of Christina's case took longer to complete this year because she is in grade 8 and the committee requested a full psychometric assessment. It was the first such undertaking since she was in grade 3, five years ago, and confirmed the assertions of the special education resource teacher in the school: that Christina is not only an improved but an improving student. Her IQ test score (both verbal and performance) on the Wechsler scale is Low Average to Borderline (as it was in grade 3). But standardized achievement scores show significant gains in academic skills. Christina reads grade 4/5 material comfortably. (She has had a particularly rewarding experience this year as a "reader" in the kindergarten class.) Creative writing is still a challenge, although this may be a physically related issue; Christina has a disabled left arm and is naturally left-handed. Even with the classroom's several computer programs to help her, however, she has trouble writing even minimally coherent prose. Math gains are significant and measurable. Five years ago, she could not do any basic arithmetic. This year she is working one-on-one with the EA out of the grade 4 textbook.

All the adults who have immediate contact with and responsibility for Christina—her mother, the grade 8 teacher, and the educational assistant who has known her since grade 6—confirm independently that she has had "a very happy year." Everyone agrees this fact is very much a result of efforts to manage her occasional bursts of unusual behaviour, and the fact that Christina's classmates now accept her so completely.

In light of these advances, Christina is going to be promoted to grade 9 and go with her classmates to the neighbourhood secondary school. Christina's mother is very concerned about what the secondary school program will look like and is meeting with the secondary school resource teacher to obtain this information.

3. The Developmental Period

This is the period up to the chronological age of 18.

Defining by Support Needed

In 2002, the AAMR (as this association was called at the time) made yet another major revision to its definition of mental retardation, a change that still includes the intellectual functioning, adaptive behavior, and developmental period factors, but that places new emphasis on the importance of supports. A primary purpose in describing an individual's limitations, the association insists, is to develop a profile of needed supports that, over time, will improve that person's life functioning. Rather than classifying an individual according to a pre-existing diagnostic category—usually one tied to available models of service—a supports approach evaluates the person's needs and then tries to find strategies that address those needs.

Although skeptics say there is nothing new in this approach except the name, and that it is exactly what effective teachers and educational assistants do when they are given the freedom to act in the name of good common sense, advocates point out that at the very least, the approach puts the student ahead of the program and the paperwork.

Ontario's Definition

The categories and definitions of exceptionalities as published in the Ministry of Education's *Special Education: A Guide for Educators* (2001) presents two levels of disability: "mild intellectual" and "developmental" disability, the difference in degree being implicit in the terms. (See Appendix for the complete definitions.) Using both the "intellectual" and "developmental" terms, rather than confusing matters, makes the issue of classification administratively simpler. At the same time, the expansion of each term is worded in a manner that anticipates practical response without adding undue complexity. Such a positive accomplishment is relatively rare in government literature. These terms, however, are open to interpretation by boards of education and there are discrepancies across the province as to which students may belong in a particular category.

> *My first year and I get not one, but two developmental kids in my class! I have to be honest; at the end of September I was going to quit. Sure glad I didn't though. Now that I've had some time, well…it's no different from having any other kids in your class. Not really. But then, these two were pretty good kids. I sure could have used more time on special kids in my teacher training. We never talked about them enough, and well…*
>
> Alexandra P.

Some Issues in the Field

✦ *Terminology.* An abiding concern is what to call an intellectual disability—or whether to call it anything at all! Part of the tension arises out of the desire of administrators, researchers, clinicians, and academics to have a neutral, scientific, and widely accepted term to identify a consonant group for their various purposes. Balanced against this desire is the far less scientific but equally important desire of parents and advocates to expunge terminology from the field for the simple reason that descriptive terms for this exceptionality, no matter how carefully they are chosen, invariably seem to imply limitations, and very rapidly are adopted for pejorative use in popular parlance. There appears to be no simple way out of this dilemma. To professionals, terminology is part and parcel of scientific, educational practice.

In 1993, the Ontario Ministry of Education changed the label for this population. For many years, students with limited intellectual and developmental abilities in Ontario schools were referred to as "trainable retarded" or "educable retarded," depending on the degree of intellectual and developmental limitation. But in the mid 1990s these terms were changed to "developmental disabilities" and "mild intellectual disabilities" (for the specific definition of these terms, go to the Appendix). Recently, as mentioned above, The American

At age seven, Robyn spent several months in a day program at a development centre, but then became ill (she has severe respiratory problems) and remained at home where she was visited daily by a special services at home worker. At age eight she attended her neighbourhood school in a regular grade 1 for three weeks, but with the agreement of her parents, was transferred to a special resource class, full time. This placement continued until grade 4, when she was gradually integrated into a regular class. Robyn moved with her classmates to grade 5 and spent that year with them. She is now in grade 6.

Robyn is identified as seriously developmentally disabled. Her language abilities are below age norms. Her speech is babyish and mostly in the third person, e.g.: Teacher: "Hi, Robyn! How are you today?" Robyn: "Robyn O.K." She does not seem to be able to read, but very much enjoys being read to. She does not participate in any meaningful way in the curriculum; however, she likes to be part of a group when it pursues a task, and very much enjoys being paired with other students when seat work or other individualized tasks are assigned. Attempts to present "parallel curriculum" have been singular failures. Since grade 4, Robyn has never once worked on her own. She seems content only when she is part of others' endeavours. An occasional exception to this behaviour is her willingness to spend time at an art table, colouring with crayons and magic markers. But she tends to have temper tantrums when tired of this activity if she is not immediately diverted. Robyn destroyed a keyboard when she became bored with a computer program.

Until now (February of grade 6) the fact that there is no assistant available to this class (and will not be) has been blunted by the willingness of two classmates, both girls, to befriend, guide, and patiently assist Robyn. But almost simultaneously, the two—in the words of their teacher—"have just discovered boys!" and now actively avoid Robyn, not just inside the classroom but outside too. Robyn's tantrums are now frequent and severe, and her skills have regressed. Motivated at least in part by complaints from parents of other children, the principal has called for an IPRC review. At the committee's first meeting, Robyn's mother made it clear she will not agree to a special class placement. The committee has asked the school, as a first step, to prepare a new IEP for Robyn, working within the present resources available.

Association on Mental Retardation, a highly respected organization representing professionals in this field, changed its name to the American Association on Intellectual and Developmental Disabilities. Though the term "mental retardation" is still used throughout North America, a change of terminology is slowly gaining acceptance.

✦ *Normalization.* The Principle of Normalization suggests that people with disabilities should be seen for their similarities with their non-exceptional peers rather than their differences, and be interacted with in a manner consistent with these individuals' strengths, not their weaknesses or diagnostic label. They should be allowed to thrive in the larger society to the maximum possible extent, consistent with their chronological age and adaptive ability. Though this principle is widely accepted today, in the nineteenth cen-

tury, the gradual development of institutions to care for persons with intellectual and developmental disabilities was regarded as a major step forward. And no doubt it was, for institutions that offered care when the alternative was often abandonment, reflected a degree of social and moral responsibility hitherto unknown. But institutions have a potentially insidious nature. For reasons of economy, ease of management, and sometimes ignorance, the environment in an institution is often impoverished in terms of stimulation and opportunity. Given what special educators now know about human development, it is apparent that many of the behaviours historically associated with a disability are consequences of institutional living. With the growing trend toward deinstitutionalization, individuals with intellectual and developmental disabilities, for the most part, are living in their homes with their families and attending their neighbourhood schools where the necessary supports are provided. When they complete their education, the very large numbers of people with disabilities live in the mainstream, many of them on their own, or with some supervision, many with gainful employment, and acquiring and enjoying the benefits of education.

◆ *Inclusion.* Ontario classrooms are quite diverse, containing students from different cultures, socioeconomic backgrounds, languages, and different learning abilities. The inclusion of students with limited intellectual and developmental disabilities, once thought revolutionary, has now become commonplace. The emphasis on Universal Design for Learning contained in the Education for All document (Ontario Ministry of Education, 2005) clearly supports the principle of inclusion, that is, keeping all students in the regular classroom as the preferred instructional location. Including persons with intellectual and developmental disabilities without reservation in mainstream society is still an issue, in large part because of conflict that seems to arise out of the impatience of the supporters of inclusion, and the guarded hesitancy of the larger society. At the most liberal end of the spectrum are those who argue that all persons should be fully included in society immediately, and most especially in schools. The view is that total inclusion at once is the only possible position that a society can morally and ethically adopt. Regrettably, this position often forces an adversarial context, particularly when educators argue that for some students, empirical evidence suggests a modified school environment may produce better results.

It is not that educators reject inclusion but rather that some prefer a more cautious approach or are concerned that appropriate supports are not provided. Teachers regularly argue that students should be considered on an individual basis, for not all students are ideally suited for immediate inclusion, and that consequences can be potentially disastrous for everyone involved. Unfortunately, the different perspectives often harden because instead of being able simply to recommend this position, educators are made to defend it, and find themselves using arguments that can be interpreted as pro-segregation, whether or not this is indeed what they believe. The risk for students is that the significant developments of the past few decades are sometimes jeopardized by hasty decisions, emotion, polemics, and blanket policies.

Empirical evidence shows that generally children who begin their school lives in inclusive classrooms treat that environment as natural. And most of the time, the inclusion is successful and continues to succeed for all children as they grow. Where success is not universal is in those situations where the inclusion does not start until later grades, and where it is arbitrary.

◆ *Time to learn.* Early theory held that a developmental or intellectual disability implied an absolute limit to potential. This notion was handily reinforced by supposed empirical evidence (especially bizarre behaviours that often turned out to be institutional behaviours) and by notions of incurability. Especially since the success of the normalization movement, it has become evident that with stimulation, support, and direct

---

Prerequisites to Successful Inclusion

A lucid and comprehensive article in the *American Educational Research Journal*, by Scruggs and Mastropieri (1994) offers both a summary of useful research and their own findings on this issue, concluding that seven factors are crucial to successfully integrating students with special needs.

⇒ Administrative Support

⇒ Support from Special Education Personnel

⇒ Accepting, Positive Classroom Atmosphere

⇒ Appropriate Curriculum

⇒ Effective General Teaching Skills

⇒ Peer Assistance

⇒ Disability-Specific Teaching Skills

instruction, there is literally no limit to students' learning capacity. However, the process for some students takes longer. They are learners but they are slower learners. The time factor becomes an issue because many jurisdictions make school enrolment terminal (usually tied to chronological ages of students) either through funding limitations or simply by decree. While continuing education programs go a long way toward circumventing this problem, it is still an issue that has not yet been satisfactorily resolved by school boards and governments.

✦ *Employment and vocational training.* Some adults with intellectual and developmental disabilities have paid employment in industries described as "sheltered workshops," where they are paid for relatively simplistic and repetitive industrial tasks. On one side of this issue is the thought that these adults are thus given an opportunity to contribute to their own support by a gainful activity that is within their capacity under supervision. On the other side, there is opinion that such employment is exploitation, and simply an unsubtle extension of institutionalization. The issue is an awkward and difficult one to resolve in a free economy, and proponents of both sides are able to refer to many practical examples that support their respective arguments. For educators, the disagreement is uncomfortable, since they must resolve for themselves the importance of this potential employment when determining learning objectives for their students. As acceptance of individuals with intellectual and developmental disabilities is increasing in society, opportunities in the private sector are also increasing. Through the development of co-op programs and school-to-work transition programs individuals with intellectual and developmental disabilities are able to demonstrate what they can do in the workforce and therefore, in many cases, obtain gainful employment.

✦ *Greater challenge in the classroom.* Changes in definition, especially the lowering of the "IQ cutoff," changes in placement, especially including students in classrooms

rather than institutions, and the steadily growing awareness that people who are intellectually and developmentally disabled are learners, mean that teachers and educational assistants today encounter greater numbers of students with special needs in their classrooms. Although few would disagree with the premise that these changes have been positive, at the same time the shift has not been without impact. For example, Ontario's category of disability called "educable mentally retarded" now called "mild intellectual disability," (referring to an IQ test score approximately two standard deviations below the mean), were almost always segregated in separate classrooms with separate, dedicated programs. Today, almost all the students who once might have been classified in this way are placed in regular classrooms, thereby expanding dramatically the demands on the professionals who teach in those classrooms. In several school boards, students with more severe intellectual and developmental disabilities are also placed in regular classrooms, often with the support of an educational assistant. Whether an assistant is provided or not, the teacher is ultimately responsible for the student's program and an assessment of how well that program is being achieved.

Should Cause Be a Concern for Educators?

Although insight into the reason for a particular student's disability may satisfy intellectual curiosity and the natural desire to know as much as possible about a student in order to support the student effectively, several factors diminish the value of this knowledge. The amount of hard science in the field, not to mention theory and speculation, is extensive and bewildering even to medical specialists. Causes range from trauma (e.g., anoxia at birth) through chromosomal abnormality (e.g., Down syndrome, tuberous sclerosis, Klinefelter's syndrome) to metabolic (e.g., phenylketonuria, Prader-Willi syndrome) and infectious/toxic conditions in the pregnant mother (e.g., rubella, syphilis, alcohol, cocaine).

More than one name is used for some conditions (e.g., epiloia for tuberous sclerosis), and very often the terms are poorly or incompletely described, or presented in language that is comprehensible only to the thoroughly initiated. Not only can this create confusion, it is also rare that a practical educational response can be inferred from a description of cause. Even worse, it is not unknown for a child's case to be given up as educationally hopeless on the basis of a scientific description of cause. For these reasons, some educators argue that causes should be tendered only for very compelling reasons. (Boards of Education in Ontario, as a matter of practice if not official policy, do not state the cause of a student's disability on the record unless it has treatment implications.)

The Special Case of Down syndrome

One area of disability in which cause may have significance for educators is the chromosomal difference called Down syndrome, estimated to account for 5-6 percent of all cases of intellectual retardation. Students with Down syndrome are often recognizable because of certain common characteristics like a generally smaller stature, thick epicanthal folds in the corners of the eyes, and a smaller oral cavity that results in a protruding tongue. (Less easily noticed but typical are speckling of the iris, a wide gap between the first and second toes, and a single palmar crease on short, broad hands.)

These physical factors provoke an issue of importance when they are juxtaposed with a typical factor that is non-physical. Most persons with Down syndrome are in the mild to moderate range of intellectual limitation, and have generally been shown to have what is called "trait plasticity" (malleable intelligence). Research suggests their early development is normal, particularly in infancy, although it seems to slow as they age. Thus, because the physical aspects of Down syndrome are quite recognizable, it would be a mistake to assume automatically, as many uninformed people do, that a child with the syndrome is intellectually retarded and ipso facto incapable.

A second issue accruing to Down syndrome is the physical health factors of which teachers and assistants should be aware. Persons with Down syndrome are at greater risk for congenital heart defects and upper respiratory infections. Many have hyperflexible joints with a high potential for orthopedic injury. Taken together or singly, these characteristics have implications for what goes on in a classroom or schoolyard.

Instructional Implications

As with all students, students with intellectual and developmental disabilities bring with them to class a variety of characteristics that teachers need to take into consideration when designing their students' program. Students in this category usually require new material to be taught in a variety of ways and then need much drill and repetition (conducted in a motivating manner) to help them retain new information. In addition teachers should also be aware of the following:

Learning and Memory

Problems here, as with other areas, become more marked and more easily observable in tandem with levels of severity, but in almost all students with intellectual and developmental disabilities, learning and memory problems are usually significant. Specific areas of difficulty include ability to pay attention, verbal communication, motivation, ability to generalize, and the ability to understand similarities and differences. Quite typical is difficulty with short-term memory. The students do not tend to use memory strategies spontaneously, although they will learn to use mnemonic strategies if explicitly taught to do so. It is important to point out that once a thing is learned and filed in long-term memory, the students will recall it as well as anyone else when conditions are appropriate.

Learned Helplessness

Poor short-term memory, combined with an apparent lack of motivation and a tendency to be off-task, often leads to a passive pattern wherein the student allows a significant adult (often the EA or sometimes a fellow student) to manage everything. Viewed from the other side, so to speak, the student with disabilities manages to

◉ Consumption of alcohol by an expectant mother, even small amounts, can damage a developing fetus, leading to an organic disorder generally known as fetal alcohol syndrome (FAS). The disorder very often has a major impact on the child after birth, and by extension, on his or her parents and teachers.

◉ FAS usually manifests itself in a combination of physical, behavioural or intellectual problems ranging from minor to very serious. The condition is life-long.

◉ A number of other terms for the syndrome are in use, fetal alcohol spectrum disorder (FASD) and alcohol-related neuro-developmental disorder (ARND) being more recent examples. Perhaps most germane for educators is that medical science now tends to distinguish the full-blown syndrome, FAS, from less severe cases by describing the latter as fetal alcohol effects (FAE).

◉ Characteristics associated with FAS, and to a lesser extent with FAE, are extensive and usually have a major impact on the individual's education and general life style. Physical anomalies are often skeletal, showing up in deformed limbs and growth deficiency, and may appear in a range of heart and urino-genital problems. Individuals born with FAS also have a high rate of epilepsy, especially in the early years. Very often, the more severe cases will have a facial appearance not unlike that associated with Down syndrome. Severe learning difficulties and even the inability to live independently as an adult are possible outcomes of FAS. The learning problems typically found in students are similar to those usually classified as developmentally disabled (poor visual scanning, reading problems, inattentive to or unable to absorb detail, difficulty generalizing and deducing, etc.). Indeed, FAS is now considered to be the second major cause of intellectual and developmental disability in western countries. In addition, significant behavioural problems such as hyperactivity, indiscriminate forming and severing of bonds or attachments, difficulty expressing emotions, low rate of task completion, are common.

◉ Medical science has been certain of the effects of alcohol on an unborn fetus only since the 1970s. Research into FAS, therefore, and experience with the syndrome as a separate condition is still fairly slim. Nevertheless, strong evidence already suggests that for an individual with FAS, or even FAE, the manifestations of the condition intensify rather than lessen as the individual grows older.

◉ Although conclusive data on the prevalence of FAS are still being developed, there is a consensus that the numbers are rising. The impact of increasing numbers has sharp relevance for special educators since it is in their hands where most of the individuals with the condition may end up. Even more frustrating to professionals like teachers and educational assistants who must deal with the effects of FAS is that the syndrome is not a genetic accident but an entirely preventable condition.

◉ For the most part, practical classroom response is similar to the methods applied in the case of other students with intellectual and developmental disabilities (see Strategies for the Classroom later in this chapter).

train a significant adult to do everything for him or her, simply by being universally passive. Educational assistants often report this behaviour as a recurring problem.

Academic Achievement

It requires little effort to recognize that academic achievement is an issue. Achievement deficits seem to be most pronounced in reading comprehension and in arithmetic reasoning and problem-solving. Nevertheless, a steadily growing body of research evidence suggests that time is an important factor. In many cases, students pass through the same phases of cognitive development as non-disabled students, particularly childhood phases, but pass through more slowly and often attain lower levels of achievement. Accordingly, it's safe to infer that many students with intellectual and developmental disabilities may be able to learn much of a standard school curriculum, but will do it more slowly and likely with less efficiency. This fact makes time and regular practice crucial items in the educational planning process.

Speech and Language Problems

Frequency of speech defects are considerably above the norm. Mutism and primitive speech are quite common among those who are severely disabled. Typically, the language level, both oral and written but especially the latter, is below commonly accepted age norms.

Social Adjustment

Many of the students experience difficulty in social interaction because they do not find it easy to "read" a social setting. It is not uncommon for them to participate inappropriately, perhaps by being too loud or too ebullient, for example. Some students in an inclusive setting may at first function in what is called "parallel existence." That is, because they do not know how to naturally ingratiate themselves with their peers, they simply go along in their own world, without really becoming a part of the general social environment. This behaviour occurs most frequently when students with disabilities and so-called normal students interact with one another for the first time, especially if there has been no

---

> ### Genetic Research and the Future
>
> Persons with Williams' syndrome are usually mildly to moderately intellectually limited (typical IQ test scores are about 60), and have profound difficulties with spatial relationships, abstractions, and logical sequences. They typically have elfin-like facial structure, an above-average incidence of heart problems and very often, hyper-sensitive hearing. At the same time, persons with Williams' syndrome have strikingly developed vocabularies, are often warm, compassionate, and outgoing, and—what intrigues researchers most—many have prodigy-level talent in music. What is believed to be the cause of the syndrome was discovered in 1993: the loss of some genetic material on Chromosome 7. Researchers believe this site also influences concentration levels and visual and spatial skills. Discoveries in this type of research may one day revolutionize education.

preparation. (It is very encouraging, however, to observe a class of very young children. The mutual acceptance one invariably sees, forces the conclusion that interaction like this can be natural if inclusion begins early.)

Perseveration

Perseveration is the persistent repetition of a specific behaviour. Some individuals develop behaviours that the rest of the world may look upon as bizarre, and tend to indulge in these behaviours repetitively in times of stress or discomfort. As a consequence, a large part of educational planning is sometimes devoted to teaching self-control. Proponents of inclusion argue—with considerable empirical evidence to support them—that inappropriate behaviours are eliminated more easily and quickly in the mainstream.

Physical

Milestones like learning to walk, toilet, etc., tend to be attained up to nine months or a year later than the norm. There is also a tendency to perform below age-related standards in motor areas, and frequently, features of height, weight and skeletal development are often at the extreme ends of age norms. Persons with moderate (as opposed to mild) disabilities often show even more complex physical differences, and tend to be markedly less able motorically. Very often persons with severe intellectual limitations are part of a multiple set of disabilities with the consequence that simple locomotion and other basic activities become an issue.

Self-Injurious Behaviour

Behaviours that lead to harm of a subject's own body is not infrequent, especially among those with severe developmental disabilities. These behaviours cover a wide range such as headbanging, scratching, pinching, hitting and rectal digging. Unfortunately, research has yet to shed light on the causes of these behaviours or the keys to remediation. Empirical evidence suggests a lack of stimulation and stress as possible causes.

The Importance of Self-Help Skills

For obvious reasons, the most immediate of which is physical health, an important part of an education program deals with items like hygiene, eating and dressing, use of the toilet, physical appearance, etc. While this aspect will be part of an educational plan only to the extent necessary, and that necessity will vary according to the degree of need, learning these culturally significant skills is nevertheless crucial to a student's sense of well-being and sense of self. For students with intellectual and developmental disabilities there is much truth in the old adage that connects feeling good to looking good.

Self-Esteem

Self-esteem tends to be low. A combination of discouraging social experience and of repeated failure often leads to self-expectations of poor performance. When this expectation is overlaid with learned helplessness, it is easy to understand why students with disabilities avoid or ignore challenging tasks. The "if-at-first-you-don't-succeed-quit" syndrome is tempting and comfortable. Educators must avoid the trap of

becoming a controller—the easy route—and instead, by judicious encouragement and behaviour modification, demonstrate to a student that he or she can do an assigned task and should feel proud because of it.

Assessment and Classroom Placement

Individually administered tests of intelligence such as the Wechsler Intelligence Scale for Children-IV continue to play a role in the determination of a student's intellectual and developmental functioning. However, in practice, anecdotal reports by parents, teachers, and EAs also play an important part in completing a picture of needs. So do a range of instruments known as Rating Scales, Achievement Inventories, Personal Checklists, etc. These instruments vary in length and in nature of information sought, but are similar in principle. They are completed by adults who have been able to observe the student in different situations and are able to judge the student's skills in a number of areas. Usually, the skills are rated on a comparative basis (fair, good, excellent, etc.). And most often, the questions deal with areas of general performance like family, community and peer relations, self-care skills, cognitive abilities, and so on. Although these instruments are usually quite informal, and are often constructed locally to meet local needs, there are published adaptive behaviour scales available (e.g., Vineland Adaptive Behavior Scales, Second Edition, Pearson Assessments). In practice, an Identification, Placement and Review Committee (IPRC) will quite regularly accept almost any information about a student with developmental and intellectual disabilities when it is making determinations regarding identification and classroom placement.

As the tables in Chapter 3 indicate, relatively more students in this area of special need are placed in full-time and part-time self-contained classes, despite the vigour of advocates who favour inclusion. Nevertheless, compared to the days before the passing of the Education Amendment Act in 1980, when it was rare for a student with disabilities to attend a regular school, there have been very great changes.

Blaine has just completed his first year at secondary school. He is 18. Although the school is committed to inclusion, three self-contained classes are available on an ad hoc basis. No one is officially placed in these classes full time, but during the past year four students have spent their entire school time there. For the final quarter of the year Blaine became the fifth, mostly because of his overwhelming moroseness and his apparent unwillingness to do anything for himself.

In Blaine's medical report, fetal alcohol syndrome is noted as a primary cause of his disability. He also has chronic health problems and spent three years in a hospital school. Academically, Blaine works at approximately a 9-10 year old level, but every teacher who has had responsibility for him insists that he is significantly more capable than his output indicates. They are unanimous in the belief that the academic performance gap is a product of attitude that—also unanimously—they call "learned helplessness." The school's physical education department has proposed to the in-School team (IST) that next year, the senior football team make Blaine one of the school's "inclusion pals." He would be made an honorary player, attend all practices, and be at all games, dressed in equipment and uniform. Although he would not actually compete, he would be part of every other activity. Football team members would also be expected to invite Blaine to their social events and involve him after school. The coach did this once before with a special student, Mel, and the project was so successful it attracted enthusiastic reviews from the media. Blaine's parents, however, are aware of a dark side. When the football team graduated and scattered to universities, colleges, and employment, Mel was, in effect, suddenly abandoned. So traumatic was the experience that he has still not recovered. Mel was then 22 years of age and he too left the school but now his guardian (a grandmother) reports that "... for nigh on a year now he sits, and eats, and stares. Won't talk. Won't look at me. Won't do anything."

Blaine's parents are willing to do anything for their son but want some assurance from the IST that the football team's undertaking will not end up the way Mel's case did and want more information on what the secondary school program will provide.

Specially dedicated schools for the "mentally retarded," where these students were enrolled—if they went to school at all—have almost all become regular neighbourhood schools. Students with intellectual and developmental disabilities, even though some may be placed in special classes, are part of those neighbourhood schools now, and the majority of students by far are placed in classes on the basis of what their teachers and their parents together believe is in their best interests.

> *I think we accepted early on, my wife and I, that this was a lifetime commitment. Our Sammy's retarded, but he's ours and we don't love him any less. Probably a bit more. Still it's scary when we wonder what will happen to him when we're not around anymore. The schools ... they've done a good job. Really, they have. But he won't be in school forever. And if his mother and I aren't here, what then?*
>
> Hank. S.

✔ STRATEGIES FOR THE CLASSROOM

1. The importance of a positive attitude For teachers and educational assistants working in this area of special need, there is a prerequisite understanding which must be accepted for appropriate educational planning and instruction to occur. The prerequisite, quite simply, requires a positive attitude: recognition and acceptance that these are students like any other, with strengths and needs and likes and dislikes and idiosyncratic behaviours and a capacity to learn. What distinguishes them, perhaps more than any other trait, is that they tend to learn more slowly. The implications of that slower learning speed (perhaps learning rate is better) are significant, but the students can and do learn. Classroom professionals, by nature, accept this, but when they have such students in a class, they need just a bit more of that faith: that quality reflected in the patience, the effort, the flexibility, and the sense of humour that together with enlightened instruction make classrooms successful. Without these intangibles—in liberal quantities—no amount of tactic or technique can be effective. The educator, as always, is the key.

2. A collaborative approach It is common administrative practice to assign educational assistants in classrooms where one or more students with developmental disabilities are enrolled. A principal reason for the popularity of the practice is that, time and again, assistants have proven their immense value. However, doubling the number of adults in a room does not double the achievements automatically. Whether an assistant is assigned to a whole class or specifically to a student (this latter option has come in for serious criticism as a form of de facto segregation), it is crucial that both teacher and assistant work together in an atmosphere of mutual respect and appropriately shared responsibility.

3. Teamwork In a similar vein, teachers and assistants recognize that when students with special needs are in their classes, they are expected to cooperate extensively with other professionals, and certainly with parents. In the case of students with developmental or intellectual disabilities, this support circle often widens considerably. Very active involvement by advocacy groups, for example, often leads to the development of a team of key players in a student's life, who share information, ideas, and concerns about that student and then take some wider responsibility for promoting his or her inclusion in the life of the community. Since school is a major part of a student's community, it is only natural that such a team will often involve and overlap the classroom role. Thus in addition to their responsibility for individual instruction, teachers and assistants often find themselves part of a larger circle of action that includes other students, parents, and interested members of the community.

4. Careful attention to structure both in direct individual instruction and in the general learning environment is another important factor. Experience in both integrated and modified environments suggests that the students are much more comfortable when classroom routines and expectations are regularized. In this case, familiarity breeds not contempt but comfort, and the security engendered by this comfort can usually assure more effective learning. Establishing a structured environment may mean that the teacher or assistant arranges for and continually repeats certain sequences until they are fully assimilated by the students. It may mean temporarily reducing the number of choices a student is expected to make. Very often a great deal of effort is expended on what, in the grand scheme of things, may seem relatively trivial: colour-coded notebooks, for example, with red for one purpose, green for another, etc. Yet these are precisely the kind of arrangements that protect the students from confusing and overlapping demands and allow them to bring their available cognitive strength to bear on a learning task. Without a carefully established structure in which to learn, students tend to expend a prohibitive amount of energy trying to establish it on their own. In an unstructured environment it is easy to seek the comfort of learned helplessness or perseverative behaviour.

The challenge is finding the right balance of structure and flexibility so that organization does not become more important than learning. An additional challenge is finding this balance in an inclusive classroom, where there are many students whose need for a structured and carefully sequenced instruction may not be the same. Professionals in this type of classroom can argue with considerable authority that such a placement for a student with serious developmental or intellectual disabilities, despite its benefits, may also mean having to forgo some of the vital learning support that occurs in a carefully arranged structure.

5. An effective practice for all students, and especially for those with cognitive limitations, is **"drill" and "repetition."** However, it is essential that teachers attempt to design drill and repetition in a motivating manner such as through games, puzzles, or activities. The simple fact is that all students seem to need the opportunity to go over material a certain number of times until it is taken in, and students with this disability perhaps more so.

6. Momentum, or commitment within the individual, is another concern. Students with a disability regularly and successfully invite others to do their work for them, and equally regularly, back away from challenge and opportunity. Encouragement by significant adults is very important therefore. In fact, a teacher who establishes a sense of commitment in a student has usually led him or her through one of the most important steps of development.

7. Use of technology: Students with intellectual and developmental disabilities can be highly stimulated and helped to maintain attention through the appropriate use of a variety of software designed to meet their instructional needs in language and numeracy. Technologies, including voice creation and voice recognition software, may be very helpful in assisting with the instruction of students with limited intellectual ability.

Task Analysis

Task analysis is a method of breaking down a general concept or skill into its component parts. The component parts are then presented in a logical sequence. Particularly for students whose needs are fairly extensive, the method has proven very successful because it is based on sequencing and operant conditioning, and offers a sense of accumulating success.

An example follows. Teaching begins at baseline: the level where the student is functioning prior to instruction (or possibly, one step below, so that success is assured). Each step is taught in a variety of ways until "overlearning" has taken place. Overlearning means practising the concept beyond the point of original mastery—the instructor cannot assume a student has mastered the concept on the basis of a single correct response. Instead the instructor should present the concept on numerous occasions over a time period, expecting the student to respond correctly most of the time before being satisfied the concept has been mastered. (Some instructors determine in advance the criteria for mastery, e.g., four correct responses out of five consecutive trials.)

1st step: state expectation; e.g., tell time to ¼ hour

2nd step: list all steps, operations and pre-requisite skills necessary to do step 1

3rd step: order these in hierarchy or logical teaching sequence

4th step: find out where in this sequence the student is functioning (baseline)

An Example of Task Analysis: (Steps 1-3)

Expectation: Student can read and print in words whole numbers to twenty, using meaningful contexts.

1. Student can attend to task.
2. Student can follow instructions.
3. Student can count from 1-20.
4. Student can read the number "one."
5. Student can read the number "two."
6. Student can read the number "three."
7. Student can read the number "four."

7-20. Same as above, progressing to the number "twenty."

21. Student can print the number "one."
22. Student can print the number "two."
23. Student can print the number "three."

24-40. Same as above, to number "twenty."

41. Student can demonstrate the correct use of numbers "one" through "twenty" when reading or writing these numbers in context.

Note: The final task is a demonstration that the expectation has been achieved.

READINGS & RESOURCES

Beck, J., Brores, J., Hogue, E., Shipstead, J., & Knowlton, E. (1994). Strategies for functional community-based instruction and inclusion for children with mental retardation. *Teaching Exceptional Children* (1994, Winter) pp. 44-48.

Browder, D. M & Spooner, F. (2006) *Teaching Language Arts, Math, and Science to Students with Significant Cognitive Disabilities.* Baltimore: Brooks

Carnevale, A.P., Gainer, L. J., & Meltzer, A. S. (1990). *Workplace basics, The essential skills employers want.* San Francisco: Jossey-Bass.

Cipanni, E., & Spooner, F. (1994). *Curricular and Instructional approaches for persons with severe disabilities.* Needham Heights, MA: Allyn & Bacon.

Crealock, C., & Bachor, D. (1995). *Instructional strategies for students with special needs* (2nd Ed.). Scarborough, ON: Allyn & Bacon Canada.

Cronin, M. E., & Parron, J. R. (1993). *Life skills instruction for all students with special needs: A practical guide for integrating real life content into the curriculum.* Austin TX: Pro-Ed.

Drew, C. J., Hardman, M. L., & Logan, D. R. (1996). *Mental retardation: a life cycle approach* (6th ed.), Upper Saddle River NJ: Merrill/Prentice Hall.

Feldman, M. A., & Walton-Allen, N. (1997). Effects of maternal mental retardation and poverty on intellectual, academic, and behavior status of school age children. *American Journal on Mental Retardation*, 101, 352-364.

Freeman, S. F. N., & Alkin, M. C. (2000). Academic and social attainments of children with mental retardation in general education and special education settings. *Remedial and Special Education, 21(1)*, 3-18.

Goddard, H.H. (1920). *Human efficiency and level of intelligence.* Princeton, N.J.: Princeton University Press.

Graziano, A. M. (2002). *Developmental disabilities: Introduction to a diverse field.* Boston, MA: Allyn & Bacon.

Grossman, H. J. (1992). *Special education in a diverse society.* Boston: Allyn & Bacon.

Hankin, J. R. (1994). FAS prevention strategies: Passive and active measures. *Alcohol Health and Research World, 18(1)*, 62-66.

Herr, S. S., & Weber, G. (1999). *Aging, rights, and quality of life: Prospects for older people with developmental disabilities*. Baltimore, MD: Paul H. Brookes.

Kozma, C. & Stock, J. S. (1993). What is mental retardation? In R. Smith (Ed.), *Children with mental retardation* (pp.1-49). Rockville, MD: Woodbine House.

Meyer, L. H., Peck, C. A., & Brown L. (1991). *Critical issues in the lives of people with severe disabilities*. Baltimore, MD: Paul H. Brookes.

Reiss, S. (1994). Issues in defining mental retardation. *American Journal of Mental Retardation, 99*, 1-7.

Sands, D. J., & Wehmeyer, M. L. (Eds.). (1996). *Self-determination across the life span: Theory and practice*. Baltimore: Brookes.

Scruggs, T., & Mastropieri, M. (1994). Successful mainstreaming: A qualitative analysis of three representational cases. *American Educational Research Journal, 31(4)*, 785-811.

Snell, M. E. (1993). *Instruction of students with severe disabilities* (4th ed.). New York: Macmillan

Smith, T. E. C., Polloway, E. A., Patton, J., Dowdy, C.A., Heath, N., McIntyre, L. J., Francis, G. C. ((2006*), Teaching Students with Special Needs in Inclusive Settings*, (2nd Canadian Edition), Toronto: Pearson.

Weaver, H. R., Adams, S. M., Landers, M. F., & Fryberger, Y. B. (1998). Meeting the life skills of students with developmental disabilities in integrated settings. In A. Hilton & R. Ringlaben (Eds.), *Best and promising practices in developmental disabilities* (pp. 87-106). Austin TX: Pro-Ed.

Wolfensberger, W., Nirje, B., Olshansky, S., Perske, R., & Roos, P. (1972) *Normalization in human services*. Toronto: Leonard Crainford.

Links

Ontario Association for Community Living
http://www.communitylivingontario.ca

Canadian Association for Community Living
http://www.cacl.ca/

Canadian Down Syndrome Society
http://www.cdss.ca

Canadian Centre for Substance Abuse (FAE/S)
http://www.ccsa/CCSA/EN/Topics/Populations/FASD.htm

American Association on Intellectual and Developmental Disabilities
http://www.aamr.org

Council for Exceptional Children
http://www.cec.sped.org

Division on Developmental Disabilities
http://www.dddcec.org

CHAPTER 12

Students With Autism Spectrum Disorders

"Having a child with an ASD has fundamentally changed who I am, from where I live in the country, what kind of home I live in, how I spend money, how I parent, my career path, how I spend my spare time, how I react to stress, to how I view the world and my reactions to it. Having a child with ASD has not-so-gently forced me to put my world into perspective, from the big picture of looking ahead to my child's adult years, to everyday decisions and situations, and how I choose to react to them. He has taught me what is important, what should be let go, and how to struggle and advocate not only for his needs, but for the needs of the children and families I teach and support as a professional. So far, it has been a truly awe-inspiring journey. During the very difficult years, one of my many wishes is that I had more hope—or had someone to give me that hope for the future; that things would get better. They did."

Kimberly M, mother of Robert

Misconceptions About Autism Spectrum Disorders (ASDs)

1. ASDs are a kind of mental illness.

Although ASDs appears in the list of mental disorders presented by the *Diagnostic and Statistical Manual* of the American Psychiatric Association, there are no known psychiatric causes.

2. ASDs are untreatable.

Intensive intervention, especially if begun early, can often make a significant impact on an individual's development. Not all treatments, however, are effective for all children with ASDs.

3. Preoccupied, career-oriented parents are most at risk for causing ASDs.

Although this was once a popular theory, there is no concrete evidence to substantiate it.

4. ASDs are the result of our socially disconnected urban culture.

The nexus of relationships once regularly present in families and communities may indeed be disappearing, but the effects have not been connected to ASDs.

5. ASDs can be caused by vaccinations.

The study that led to this belief, published in *Lancet* in 1998, was retracted by most of its authors and by the journal in 2004. There is no evidence to indicate that vaccinations cause ASDs.

Autism Spectrum Disorders

Autism spectrum disorders (ASDs) is a neurological disorder classified in the *Diagnostic and Statistical Manual—IV-TR(DSM—IV-TR)* of the American Psychiatric Association. It represents a range of behaviours that originally were classified as "autism," a severely incapacitating disability that can possibly affect all aspects of an individual's development, and, if not treated, can be life-long. Autism Spectrum Disorders, however, describes individuals who have characteristics ranging from what was called autism, which can be very severe, to those with characteristics that have less impact (though still quite serious) on social, cognitive, or emotional growth. People with ASDs are believed to have anomalies in both the structure and the chemistry of the brain. The characteristics of behaviours associated with ASDs are not due to psychiatric or emotional difficulties, but rather are linked to neurological and/or genetic causes.

For several decades after autism was first described in 1943, the disorder was customarily known by that single term. By the end of the century, "autism" was seen as too narrow to encompass the many manifestations of the disorder. Both professionals and public alike began to acknowledge a range, or *spectrum*. Hence, the more or less accepted term today is "autism spectrum disorders," although in general discussions, in symposia, and even in academic papers, "autism" is regularly used as a kind of shorthand.

A further development must be noted in that the *DSM* now presents five different distinctions of autism, under the heading "Pervasive Developmental Disorder" (PDD), so this term, too, is now part of the mix.

A simple caveat for teachers and educational assistants is to be aware that terminology used to describe autism spectrum disorders is somewhat elastic, and that explanations of cause, characteristics, and prevalence continue to evolve as well.

The DSM and Pervasive Development Disorder

Recent editions of the DSM divide ASDs into five separate categories, under the heading of "Pervasive Developmental Disorders."

(For practical purposes within the education community, the first three disorders described below represent the spectrum referred to as autism spectrum disorders.) The five contained in *DSM-IV-TR* (the most recent version of the

Diagnostic and Statistical Manual of the American Psychiatric Association) are summarized below.

Autistic disorder: includes impairment in social interaction, communication, and imaginative play prior to age three, with restricted interests and repeated behaviours

Asperger's disorder (syndrome): is usually applied to individuals with speech and average to above average intelligence, but who are impaired in social interactions and have unusually restricted or specialized interests

Pervasive developmental disorder—not otherwise specified: is also called "atypical autism." This is a somewhat vague category that picks up individuals otherwise not classified but who nevertheless have severe impairments of an autistic nature.

Childhood disintegrative disorder: is characterized by the presence of a range of autistic behaviours that appear after normal development for at least two years

Rett's disorder: is progressive and so far seen only in girls. There is a period of normal development followed by the loss of acquired skills. A key symptom is replacement of purposeful hand movements with repetitive movements between ages 1-4.

A note on terms and labels

"It is important to distinguish between the clinical terms and descriptions of ASDs and our understanding and knowledge of people who live with ASDs. We need to understand clinical terms used in medical settings, during diagnosis, and in certain treatment or intervention settings. However, it is wise to keep in mind that these terms may also be seen as limiting labels to some people with ASDs who feel that ASDs have been "medicalized" to the point where individuals who are unique in their skills, abilities, and value to their communities have been forgotten or eclipsed by the 'disorder'." *Used with permission Autism Society Canada*

Characteristics of Autism Spectrum Disorders

Whatever definition of autism spectrum disorders eventually prevails, a reality in the classroom is that students who have the disorder generally present certain characteristic manifestations or symptoms. These vary in style and intensity from individual to individual in one or several of the following clusters.

- *Social interaction:* May find relating to others difficult or even impossible, reflected in anything from lack of eye contact to total withdrawal. May show little interest in making friends or in shared play, and will spend inordinate amounts of time alone. Seeming unawareness of social interplay and an absence of intuition are typical (e.g., student does not read body language of others; talks but does not listen; seems unaware of protocols).

- *Communication*:* Speech may be delayed, diminished, or entirely absent. May use gestures rather than words; often uses words without attaching their usual meaning. Many students with ASDs demonstrate "echolalia"—the repeating of a word or phrase spoken by another person.

- *Behaviours:* The descriptor "bizarre" is often applied. May become obsessed with a theme (e.g., hockey scores) or object (spinning objects are frequent examples among children). Will often engage in repeated ritualistic actions (e.g., rocking in place) and demand absolute adherence to routines.

- *Responses to sensory stimuli:* Reaction to sights, sounds, conversational buzz, the development of a crowd (e.g., as at recess or an assembly) etc. often varies dramatically from what would usually be anticipated in other students; responses may range from extremely acute to nothing at all, and are often bizarre. Tolerance for some stimuli may be fine, while specific noises such as the sound of a ringing telephone may cause great upset.

• • • —————

* The Ministry of Education includes autism under Communication in its definitions (see Appendix).

————— • • •

- *Transitions:* Change of any type is often very difficult for a child with autism spectrum disorder. Modifications in classroom or school routine may be extremely upsetting (e.g., shifting to group work after quiet seat work). Shifts into and out of recess or lunch hour or dismissal time are often difficult. Changes in personnel (e.g., educational assistant or supply teacher) can cause much traumatic response.

Current evidence suggests that autism spectrum disorders typically appear in the first three years of life, especially between the ages of two to three, and is four times more common in males than in females.

Exploding Numbers

Obscure Beginnings ...

In 1943, American psychologist, Leo Kanner, published a paper identifying what he called "autistic children." Not that the exceptionality suddenly appeared in the mid-twentieth century. Rather, what Kanner did was separate out a small group who to this point had been classified as either emotionally disturbed or mentally retarded, or both. Kanner pointed out that the group he called autistic (borrowing the term from Eugen Bleuler, who also coined the term "schizophrenia" in 1912) was not as slow learning as the mentally retarded, and did not fit the pattern typical of the disturbed.

A year later, in 1944, Austrian psychologist, Hans Asperger, independently published what was essentially a similar hypothesis, but unlike the group Kanner described, the people Asperger identified all had speech. Hence "Asperger's syndrome (or disorder)" came to be used to distinguish autistic children who use language.

In the 1980s, prevalence rates for autism were held to be four in every ten thousand. And for the most part, few people had any awareness, much less understanding of this exceptionality, for many identified cases were institutionalized, often for life. By the end of the twentieth century, prevalence rates were being revised sharply upward to ranges of around one in every one thousand births. By 2007, Autism Canada was

Raven, age 15, has spent the past three years in a self-contained classroom with four other students with severe ASDs, where she has made great strides under a dedicated teacher and very patient educational assistant. Because school board officials repeatedly point to this classroom as proof of "what is possible," it has become a popular spot for visitors. Curiously—or perhaps not curiously—despite all the positive features in the setting, what visitors remember most is the sight of Raven's palms. Both her left and right hands have thick scars that match the concentric rings of electric stove elements. One day when she was nine, Raven turned the elements on and put palms down until they—quite literally—cooked!

Six years later, Raven still has an inexplicable insensitivity to physical pain. (She nearly died at age 12 from a burst appendix; an abscessed molar went unnoticed until huge swelling made it obvious.) Yet she is extremely sensitive to other, seemingly innocuous stimuli, especially sounds. Only in the past year, for example, and only if warned in advance, can she tolerate the sound of paper being shuffled or folded. Although music is an important part of her program—the EA discovered some time ago that Raven's tantrums can be calmed by soft classical music—the classroom piano had to be removed because just one note would send her into a frenzy.

Raven still does not have—or does not use—speech, but she will now mouth certain nouns softly if she wants something. She still rocks when bored or stressed or faced with change in her routine or surroundings, but no longer pulls out clumps of hair. She has stopped throwing her food, and waits her turn for the classroom "en suite." Recently, she undertook responsibility for the aquarium. Raven has also learned to acknowledge the presence of others, even strangers, although she will not make eye contact. She now sits in "circle" after lunch each day without prompting. In sum, a comparison of Raven's profile today with the base line established three years ago, shows major, continuing progress.

The IPRC is placing Raven in an inclusive high school with educational assistant and resource room support and is asking that her IEP be prepared.

> *Having Asperger's is like being a coyote in a city park. You survive but it's the wrong environment. You just don't fit.*
>
> Jon K., age 19, diagnosed with Asperger's Syndrome

citing a prevalence rate of one in every 200 births and The U.S. Centre for Disease Control reported that ASDs occurs 1 in every 150. If accurate, that figure means the rate has nearly quadrupled in only a few years! Autism Canada reports that ASDs is the most prevalent neurological disorder or severe developmental disability of childhood.

Why the Rapid Acceleration?

Although such a profound increase in prevalence rate challenges credibility (an issue that will likely confront the field for some time),

there are a number of explanations for it, some satisfactory, some otherwise. Once the *DSM* included autism spectrum disorders, there was an increase in the number of diagnoses if only because a wider range of medical professionals

Red Flags for Parents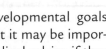

Children do not attain developmental goals according to a timetable. Yet it may be important for parents to seek medical advice if they notice that their child

♦ does not babble at 1 year,

♦ hears but does not respond to his name,

♦ avoids eye contact and cuddling,

♦ begins developing language then stops,

♦ does not point to things or seek attention.

became more enlightened. Educators, faced with the presence of vastly increased numbers of special education students in the 1980s and 1990s, became far more sensitive to the needs of students with ASDs. Increased publicity led to greater awareness in the public at large. With more awareness has come more research, greater attention to empirical evidence, more elaborated definitions, and more informed diagnoses.

The Cause

Science has not yet established the specific cause of ASDs but explanations for ASDs are plentiful. Some theories have appeal, based as they are on attractive empirical evidence, a good example being the current dominance of the genetic cause. Indeed, much of the current research has revealed a genetic basis, the hypothesis reinforced by apparent patterns of ASDs in twins and in families. According to the United States National Institute on Mental Health, recent neuroimaging studies have shown that abnormal brain development beginning in the infant's first months may relate to later anatomical abnormalities often seen in children with ASDs, and may be caused by genetic defects in brain growth factors.

Diagnosis

Diagnosing a child with ASD is often very difficult because there is not yet a biological marker or medical test to definitely determine that a child has an ASD. It is through an understanding of the child's development and behaviour that a diagnosis of an ASD is made by a medical practitioner or psychologist.

In the *DSM-IV-TR*, a list of criteria for each type of pervasive developmental disorder is

---

The Case of Larry

Because his mother has been offered a major career opportunity, Larry's family is considering a move to another community. The stress of relocating is exacerbated by Larry's situation. He is eight years old and has Asperger's syndrome. Although the parents insist he is not a savant, Larry does things that other eight year olds do not. He can, for example, recite an entire weather forecast verbatim, having heard it only once (provided weather is his current passion du jour). When he became interested in the Korean War, he could cite the regimental names and personnel numbers of every country contributing to the UN forces. At the moment, Larry is obsessed with astrolabes, sextants, and compasses. He can describe their origins, history, function, and construction with a degree of accuracy known to only a few scholars.

Larry is also afraid to use any bathroom except the one in the basement of his family home. He has yet to master tying shoelaces and, to prevent anxiety attacks, must be escorted to and from the school bus by an adult he trusts. Although he has an impressive vocabulary and clear speech, Larry cannot—or does not want to—converse with others. And he does not get on well with his peer group. As the EA explained, "It's not so much that his peers can't understand him; it's more that they can't stand him!" Larry, it seems, prefers his own world and actively excludes others from it.

Yet his current situation in a regular grade 3 class shows marked improvement. According to his principal, Larry is placed where both the teacher and the educational assistant are not only qualified in special education but have taken a particular interest in autism spectrum disorders. Together, they have made extensive, if uphill, efforts to create an atmosphere of positive acceptance and community in the class. (Larry is not the only student with special needs included here.) They have been successful in generating a feeling among the other students that human differences are a matter of degree and that "we're all different." They have also made strides in "softening Larry's corners" as the EA puts it, teaching him to respect the feelings of others.

It is apparent that Larry will continue to develop important social skills in this environment. The concern is over Larry moving to a new classroom. What issues and interventions should be considered in Larry's new placement?

included. Diagnosis of ASD is based on a consideration of three areas: the degree of communication impairment, the degree of social impairment, and the degree of the child's repetitive interests and/or activities. Currently, there are a variety of assessment instruments that can assist, but cannot definitively determine, if a child has an ASD. Examples of these assessment instruments include: the Autism Behaviour Checklist (ABC), which is used by teachers and parents as a screening instrument, and the Autism Diagnostic Interview-Revised (ADI-R), which can be used to semi-structure a parent interview. This interview (conducted by a clinician) can help identify characteristics in the child that can be associated with the diagnosis of ASDs and pervasive developmental disorders.

Ideally, a child should be evaluated by a multidisciplinary team, the members of which are familiar with autism spectrum disorders in its various manifestations. Again ideally, the conclusions of the team will be reached only after extensive observation—the sole diagnostic technique with any solid history—and after a collation and comparison of the various results, and then after informed discussion. Needless to say, unless the subject child's case is managed aggressively, an ideal evaluation is less than frequently achieved. In practice, a diagnosis that actually places a label like PDD or Asperger's syndrome on a child is ultimately in the hands of a medical professional. Once that label is attached to a student, the education system may go forward with its own approach to both a placement and a program that accommodates the student's needs.

> *I still remember in the delivery room I had visions of flooding the backyard, skating, shinny. He'd be a right winger; that was my dream. But when Kev stopped talking to us—stopped looking at us—and started all that strange stuff, I knew hockey was going to be the last thing on the agenda.*
>
> Alf R., parent of a child diagnosed with "childhood disintegrative disorder"

Treatment

Taken generally, interventions fall into four principal categories: *biochemical* (vitamin supplements, medications, food allergies); *neurosensory* (patterning, sensory integration techniques, facilitated communication, auditory training); *psycho-dynamic* (holding and body contact therapy, psychotherapy); *behavioural* (intensive behaviour intervention, aversive therapy, and various other forms of behaviour modification).

Treatment Standards ✍

According to Autism Society Canada, an effective treatment program should be one that is supported by scientific research and includes:

◆ Early and intensive treatment and education techniques to help people with ASDs develop and learn new skills

◆ Clear guidelines and expectations for behaviour

◆ Highly structured—specialized and consistent education plan tailored to the individual

◆ Parental and family participation in assessment, curriculum planning, instruction, monitoring, and evaluation. These people know the person best and will have the clearest understanding of the individual's history and learning style.

(Autism Society Canada)

For every treatment style there are vociferous supporters and equally vocal critics, although comparatively few styles are actually backed (or claim to be) by scientific studies. One such approach, Applied Behaviour Analysis (ABA), is an approach based on the principles defined by B. F. Skinner in 1953. In an article reported by Heflin and Alaimo (2007), Baer, Wolf, and Risley (1968) suggested that ABA should contain the following five dimensions:

1. *Applied and effective:* new behaviours being taught to the child should have goals that benefit the student and are valued by the

community. Procedures employed should be minimally invasive and considered acceptable in terms of the outcome; all of the outcomes and procedures should be acceptable in improving the quality of life for everyone involved.

2. *Technological:* this approach represents the strategies employed to change behaviour. Teachers must ensure that the items they use for reinforcement are in fact appropriate and attractive to the student. If the behaviour is not changing or is getting worse, then what is being employed is not a reinforcement. In addition to reinforcment, strategies include "prompting," i.e., providing assistance so that the appropriate response can be obtained. Once the reinforcement and prompting is determined, discrete trial training occurs. This step defines a basic unit of instruction that presents an opportunity for the student to respond correctly.

3. *Behavioural:* This step takes a functional view of the behaviour and requires the teacher or parent to try to determine the function of a particular behaviour. Once it is understood why the child is behaving a certain way, interventions and/or changes in the environment can be made to make it easier for the child to behave in an appropriate manner.

4. *Analytic and conceptual:* It is important that when ABA is being applied that there is an element of accountability taking place: that measurement of changes in behaviour are occurring and that the interventions being applied are working. Baselines need to be established before ABA is applied and data needs to be regularly collected to determine the program's effectiveness.

> "It's annoying. It's difficult. People treat you differently when they know. If they first saw you and they didn't know, they treat you like a normal person, but if they do know, they treat you weird and different. It makes me feel annoyed."
>
> (Robert, An adolescent diagnosed with ASD at age 9)

5. *Generalization:* Once the behaviour is learned, it can be repeated in a variety of settings. This ability to use the newly learned behaviour often does not happen automatically and needs to be included as part of the intervention procedures.

Intensive Behaviour Intervention*

Intensive Behaviour Intervention (IBI) is a highly structured program based on ABA principles. It is designed to develop age-appropriate skills and independence in a child with ASDs (or other disability). Originally, IBI was conceived for and applied to children from the ages of approximately two to approximately five or six, but there is pressure from advocates to expand that target group. The program follows behaviour modification principles and is very intensive and hands-on, typically involving 20 to 40 hours per week of direct service from professionals. Parents and/or caregivers are crucial to its implementation and are expected to follow the regimen faithfully and precisely.

An IBI program is individualized and built around needs in communication, daily living and safety skills, social skills, motor skills, pre-academics, self-management, and attending skills. It is formally administered, supervised, and evaluated by qualified service providers, typically a clinical psychologist in tandem with other qualified personnel. IBI is very effective with young children and when the intervention is early is said to produce dramatic, positive results. Currently, though there is a waiting list, the province of Ontario provides IBI for children with ASDs. For the past several years, there was cutoff once the child reached the age of six, but this cutoff has been the subject of much legal action brought on by parents against the government of Ontario. In March 2005, the trial judge ruled the age criterion discriminates against the children on the basis of age and that the refusal to provide or fund IBI and

• • • ————
* Though not the same, IBI and ABA are often inaccurately used interchangeably. IBI is one form of ABA and represents a very structured approach to teaching individuals with ASDs.
———— • • •

appropriate educational services discriminates against them on the basis of disability. This decision, however, was overturned by the Ontario Court of Appeals in July 2006. This court ruled that the Ontario government's refusal to provide IBI beyond age six was not discriminatory and did not contravene the Canadian Charter of Rights and Freedoms. The parents then applied to the Supreme Court of Canada. On April 12, 2007, the Supreme Court indicated that it would not grant the parents "leave to appeal," essentially upholding the decision of the Ontario Court of Appeals. Despite this decision the Ontario government is continuing to fund IBI beyond age six and has also increased funding to school boards so that students with ASD's can be provided appropriate educational interventions.

Current Ontario Policy

In May of 2007, the Ontario Ministry of Education issued a Policy/Program Memorandum providing direction to school boards on how to support their use of Applied Behaviour Analysis in the school setting for students with ASDs. This memorandum requires school boards to

- offer students with ASDs special education program and services, including, where appropriate, special education programs using ABA methods

- plan for the transition between various activities and settings involving students with ASDs

In addition, The Ministry published a document entitled *Effective Educational Practices for Students with Autism Spectrum Disorders* to provide an additional resource to teachers to help them understand and teach students with ASDs.

Examples of Other Treatment Programs

Behavioural programs in various forms are not new in the treatment of ASDs. *Aversion therapy*, for example, has been in use for several decades, although it has generally been applied only in institutional settings, and often experimentally. In the past, mild electric shock, was once considered effective in curbing self-injurious behaviour. Other aversion methods still in occasional use include water spraying, and denial of food treats.

A program in the neurosensory category that attracted a rash of front-page media attention during the 1990s is *facilitated communication (FC)*. This idea operates on the premise that a child with an ASD (or other person) who does not use speech can peck out words or symbols on a keyboard if a "facilitator" gently props that person's arm above the keyboard. FC continues to be used, although it is heavily criticized for lack of validation. The Autism Society of Canada reports that FC could be "potentially harmful."

Another treatment example is the *Tomatis method,* an auditory integration training concept, in which an individual spends hours a day listening to specially created sounds and classical music, particularly that of Mozart, with the low frequencies filtered out. Over time, the frequencies are added back, along with voices and other everyday sounds. A premise is that children with autism spectrum disorders may overcome extreme oversensitivity to certain sounds, and may be sufficiently soothed to decrease hyperactivity. Like FC, the Tomatis program is criticized for lack of validation.

The TEACCH program (Treatment and Education of Autistic and related Communication-handicapped Children), established in 1972 by Dr. Eric Schopler, has a positive profile in the field, its continuing use after more than thirty years being a tribute to its efficacy. This program begins with an exceptionally detailed assessment to uncover the individual's potential for acquiring communication skills and competencies for independent living. TEACCH is not behaviour modification in that it does not work on behaviours directly (except in the case of endangering behaviours). Rather, it tries to give the student a better understanding of his or her environment to reduce anxiety (and the reactions that develop from that) and emphasizes communication skills so that the student can deal better with the world around him or her.

Picture Exchange Communication System: For many students with autism spectrum disorders, verbal communication is limited. In place of fluent speech, alternative and augmentative communication systems may be used. One of the most popular is the Picture Exchange Communication System whereby pictures are used to represent what a student may need. By selecting appropriate pictures, the parent or teacher can indicate what they expect of the student and the student can indicate his or her particular needs and wants. Sign language and technology can also be used to assist students with autism spectrum disorders to communicate without using speech.

Social Stories: This approach, developed by Carol Gray in 1991, is designed to help students with ASDs better understand the world around them. Social Stories can be used to help the student understand social cues, how to better react to social situations, and help make the student more comfortable in both familiar and unfamiliar social situations. (See the Resource Section at the end of this chapter for further information.)

Do the Treatments Work?

An enduring problem for both professionals and parents is true validation of the many methods proposed to treat ASDs. For parents who, understandably, are interested in almost any proposal that may offer help to their child, whether or not to adopt a particular treatment program can be a real dilemma. Very often they learn of a program through enthusiastic anecdotal tribute, and the impetus to try it becomes almost irresistible. But once launched into a program, they typically face significant costs in time, effort, and money (very few programs produce immediate or even early results) and the ever-present worry that they may not have chosen wisely.

Implications of Specific Treatments for the Classroom

Very often, a student identified with an ASD comes to the classroom with a treatment program already in place. The teacher—and the educational assistant if the classroom is fortunate enough to have one—is then expected to adhere to the tenets of that program, and sometimes even be in charge of implementing it whether or not the teacher or EA agree with its principles or has received training in it. This can be a particular problem because of the amount of time and resource the program may require, not to mention its potential for disruption. Even more troubling to many teachers is that a predetermined treatment program may well deny them opportunities for creative response. As well, in inclusive classrooms especially, a method with laid-on requirements has the potential of denying the purpose of inclusion by

isolating the student, however unintentionally.

On the other hand, teachers can be just as confused and challenged by a student with an ASD as anyone else, and the clear plan of response typically outlined in a treatment program may well be a relief.

Some Issues in the Field

✦ It is not unusual for a bandwagon effect to develop around a treatment. While rational doubt should be enough to make most people view these accounts with caution, a strong wish to believe on the part of some parents, together with a lack of information, can easily subvert natural wariness. A bandwagon effect even accrues to programs where positive results are supported more scientifically. For example, both empirical evidence and investigation now leave little doubt that for the most part IBI can improve matters for a child with ASD, particularly if that child is very young and if the treatment begins early. As well, evidence continues to demonstrate—no surprise—that IBI is more effective with the less severe cases. Yet by the beginning of the millennium, the program was being vigorously pursued by parents irrespective of the type of ASD with which their child was diagnosed. And by the middle of the decade, there was an added twist. The apparent success of IBI with very young children had led parents to advocate for its extension beyond the time (age 5-6) at which the program has typically ended so that IBI intervention can take place in schools. As this book goes to press the position of the Supreme Court of Canada (as indicated above) is that schools do not have to provide this treatment, but there are still cases before the courts challenging this issue.

✦ The cost of implementing a program continues to beleaguer both parents and governments. Not that ASDs is unique on this issue, but the intensity of need that distinguishes ASDs usually requires a response of equal intensity—with heavy expenses attached. The delicacy of the issue lies not in whether the program is worth the price, but in who will pay it. A program like

IBI, which requires 20 to 40 hours of service a week from qualified personnel, along with training, travel, and other supplementary expenses, is way beyond the income of most Canadian families. Although government funding is available in most provinces, Ontario included, those monies are not unlimited. The demand by parents for greater funding and expanded programs has thus led to an increase in litigation and human rights appeals.

✦ The *media* have had a powerful impact on the public impression of ASDs over the past decade or so, and, as usual, the impact comes as a mixed blessing. The performance of actor, Dustin Hoffman, in the popular 1988 Hollywood movie *Rain Man* did much to create awareness of an exceptionality hitherto known only vaguely. Yet the same movie did much to create a false impression. The person with autism spectrum disorder played by Hoffman is typically obsessive, but not so typically, he has competent language, is very charming, and is also a savant. As any special educator can quickly attest, neither charm nor language are always present in people with ASDs, and those with savant characteristics represent only about 10 percent of the population with ASDs.

✦ To include in the regular classroom—or not—is, as ever, an issue that continues to roil. In the case of students whose ASD is reflected in self-injurious or bizarre behaviours, the debate tends to get quite intense. All the standard arguments on both sides of the question apply, although even strong advocates of inclusion acknowledge that the intense needs of severe cases of ASDs are a major challenge to the support usually available in a regular classroom.

> *If you let your students pick their own groups we'll always be picked last. Defeats the purpose of having groups, doesn't it?*
>
> Jon K., age 19, diagnosed with Asperger's syndrome

✔ STRATEGIES FOR THE CLASSROOM

- *Special placement.* Students manifesting quite severe characteristics of ASDs are likely to be placed in special classrooms for at least part of their school day. Typically, teachers and assistants in this setting will implement a predetermined program.

- *Intuition.* With ASDs, perhaps more than any other exceptionality, there is less commonality from case to case and what "works" in one situation often will not translate to another. Thus, in the regular classroom especially, intuition, along with trial and error (and, therefore, good record keeping!) are two essential arrows in the quiver shared by teacher and assistant.

- *Teaching essential skills.* Teachers and educational assistants must be prepared to offer instruction in what for most students would be skills normally acquired in the simple process of growing up. For example, it follows that a student who needs to be taught to pay attention to his or her name (not unusual in ASDs) will likely find it difficult to follow simple instructions. This is not necessarily owing to diminished intelligence, but more to a style of processing information. Usually, a student with an ASD needs more time to switch focus, to attach meaning to the words being tossed at him or her, and to follow through on requests.

- *Understanding the ordinary.* A major challenge is getting a student with an ASD to understand and accept the very ordinary, frequently occurring phenomena that characterize the behaviour of students in a classroom. Getting the student to understand, for example, that a classmate's movement from point A to point B is not necessarily an "invasion of his or her space" or that physical contact among peers is normal, is not something most classroom professionals have to encounter on an ordinary day. At the same time, a teacher or assistant who tries to educate a student with an ASD in these matters must realize that the aversive behaviours are real, not something to be punished, but, rather, a condition to be acknowledged so that alternatives can be taught. The suggestions below offer a few simple procedures that generally are helpful.

- *Provide a safe haven.* The noise and disorder of recess, a pep rally, an assembly, sometimes even normal classroom noise (such as on the day before a holiday break) may overwhelm the student. It may be advisable to have a quiet place for the student to go to, or to develop a routine response (e.g., by having him or her pair with a calm classmate) in these situations. Perhaps more important may be to anticipate and watch for signs that the student is approaching meltdown. At these times, it may also be useful if the student can be taught to recognize the signs himself or herself and to teach the student how to act accordingly. There may be a trusted adult (office personnel? nurse? other teacher, or EA?) for the student to go to. Some students find it helpful to overcome stress by listening to music for a brief period.

- *Prepare for changes in routine.* Until the student develops the appropriate skills, it may be necessary for the teacher/EA to be at the student's side when change is imminent, to quietly coach and help the student through.

- *Structure group work very deliberately.* Ensure that the task, roles, and timelines are clearly understood by all group members.

- *Seating plans are useful.* Because of the potential for intense reactions to stimuli and for unusual behaviours, attention to where the student sits, relative to the entrance, work areas, etc., and relative to who sits near him or her, may pre-empt "situations."

- *The Internet may help.* Some students find the Internet an ideal medium of communication because it offers the opportunity for interaction, cognition, and language use without the impact of nearby human presence. The key for the teacher/EA, of course, is to use the tool judiciously lest it become an escape.

- *Be a positive interlocutor.* The teacher or educational assistant, especially at first, may be the only one in a classroom who understands that the student with ASD lacks the intuition necessary for successful social and intellectual exchange. It will probably be necessary to coach both the student with ASD and the student's classmates in this reality; the special student on what impact he or she is having and the classmates to realize they should not take abruptness personally.

- *Capitalize on special interests.* Having a student with ASD in a class, especially one with Asperger's, may mean that you have a child in the classroom who has become an "expert" on a specific topic. There may be reward for everyone and personal satisfaction for the student, if he or she is allowed to educate others on this personal intense interest.

- *A caring community.* As much as it sounds like an overbeaten cliché, there's no substitute for a classroom where understanding, accommodation, and forgiveness prevail. It takes the professionals in the room to make it happen.

- *Try to determine what precipitates a specific inappropriate behaviour and then design the environment to decrease the likelihood that these precipitating events will occur.* For example: if you notice that a student with ASD acts inappropriately when another student sharpens his or her pencil, perhaps sharpened pencils can be provided throughout the day so that the inappropriate response can be avoided.

✔ STRATEGIES FOR THE CLASSROOM *cont'd*

(The following is from an adult diagnosed with an autism spectrum disorder at age three.)

■ My head is like a video. The only way I learn is to see things. That's why nouns and verbs are easier to learn than other words. When you teach an autistic kid things, show him.

■ You need blocks and sticks and things like that for math.

■ Use art a lot.

■ Phonics is best for reading. So are poems. And music and songs.

■ Autistic kids stick with special things they like. I loved trains. Still do. My best teacher used math trains. We had train records and we read train stories. Ms. King was so cool.

■ When you talk, don't say so much at once. Don't talk slow. We're not idiots! Just don't say so much at once! I wish we had computers when I was in school. With computers you control the information coming in.

READINGS & RESOURCES

Akshoomoff, N. (2000). *Neurological underpinnings of autism (Vol. 9).* Baltimore: Brookes.

Attwood, T. (1998). *Asperger's Syndrome: A Guide for parents and professionals.* London: Jessica Kingsley.

Bauer, S. (1995). Autism and the pervasive developmental disorders. *Pediatrics in Review, 16,* 130-136.

Brownell, M. T., & Walther-Thomas, C., (2001). Steven Shore: Understanding the autism spectrum – what teachers need to know. *Intervention in School and Clinic, 36,* 293-305.

Cattell-Gordon, D., & Volkmar, F. R. (1998). The development of an effective applied behaviour analysis program for young children with autism: A parent's perspective. *Infants and Young Children, 10(3),* 79-85.

Cohen, D. J., & Volkmar, F. R. (1997). *Handbook of autism and pervasive developmental disorders.* New York: John Wiley & Sons.

Donnellan, A. M. (1999). Invented knowledge and autism: Highlighting our strengths and expanding the conversation. *The Journal of the Association for Persons with Severe Handicaps, 24(3),* 203-236.

Dunlap, G., & Fox, L. (1999). Supporting families of young children with autism. *Infants and Young Children, 12(2),* 48-54.

Gresham, F. L., & MacMillan, D. L. (1997). Autistic recovery? An analysis and critique of the empirical evidence on the early intervention project. *Behavioural Disorders, 22,* 185-201.

Gresham, F. L., & MacMillan, D. L. (1998). Early intervention project: Can its claims be substantiated and its effects replicated? *Journal of Autism and Developmental Disorders, 28(1),* 5-13.

Heflin, J., & Alaimo, D. F., (2007). *Students with Autism Spectrum Disorders: Effective Instructional Practices.* New Jersey: Pearson Merrill/Prentice Hall

Klin, A., Volkmar, F., & Sparrow, S. S. (2000). *Asperger Syndrome.* New Haven, CT: Child Study Center, Yale University.

Lovaas, I. O. (1987). Behavioural Treatment of Normal Educational and Intellectual Functioning in Young Autistic Children, *Journal of Consulting & Clinical Psychology, 55:* 3-9.

Lovaas, I. O. (1981). *Teaching developmentally disabled children: The me book*, Baltimore: University Park Press.

Maurice, C. (1996). *Behavioural intervention for young children with autism: A manual for parents and professionals*. Austin, TX: Pro-Ed.

McGee, G. G., Morrier, M. J., & Daly, T. (1999). An incidental teaching approach to early intervention for toddlers with autism. *The Journal of the Association for Persons with Severe Handicaps, 24(3)*, 133-146.

McLaughlin-Cheng, E. (1998). Asperger syndrome and autism: A literature and meta-analysis. *Focus on Autism and Other Developmental Disorders, 13(4)*, 234-245.

Mostert, M. P. (2001). Facilitated communication since 1995: A review of published studies. *Journal of Autism and Developmental Disorders, 31*, 287-313.

Myles, B. S., & Simpson, R. (Eds.). (1998). *Educating children and youth with autism: Strategies for effective practice*. Austin, TX: Pro-Ed.

Myles, B. et al. (2001). *Asperger Syndrome Diagnostic Scale*. Austin, TX: Pro-Ed.

Myles, B. S., & Simpson, R. L. (2001). Understanding the hidden curriculum: An essential social skill for children and youth with Asperger syndrome. *Intervention in School and Clinic, 36*, 279-386.

National Research Council. (2001). *Educating children with autism*. Washington D.C.: National Academy Press.

Ontario Ministry of Education (2007) *Effective Educational Practices for Students with Autism Sprectrum Disorders: A Resource Guide*. Toronto: Ontario Ministry of Education.

Ontario Ministry of Education (2007) *Making a difference for students with autism spectrum disorder in Ontario schools: From evidence to action* www.edu.gov.on.ca/ eng/document/nr/07.02/autismFeb07.pdf

Ontario Ministry of Education, Policy/Program Memorandum No.140 (2007), Incorporating methods of applied behaviour analysis (ABA) into programs for students with autism spectrum disorders (ASD) www.edu.gov.on.ca/extra/eng/ppm/ 140.html

Prizant, B. M., & Rubin, E. (1999). Contemporary issues in interventions for autism spectrum disorders: A commentary. *The Journal of the Association for Persons with Severe Handicaps, 24(3)*, 199-208.

Quill, K. A. (1995). *Teaching children with autism: strategies to enhance communication and socialization*. Baltimore: Brookes.

Rapin, I. (1997). Current concepts in autism. *New England Journal of Medicine. 337(2)*, 97-104.

Rogers, S. J, (1998). Empirically supported comprehensive treatments for young children with autism. *Journal of Clinical Child Psychology, 27(2)*, 168-179.

Ruble, L. A., & Dalrymple, M. J., (1996). An alternative view of outcome in autism. *Focus on autism and other developmental disabilities, 11(1)*, 3-14.

Safran, J. A. (2002). Supporting students with Asperger's syndrome in general education. *Teaching Exceptional Children, 34(5)*, 67-70.

Schopler, E. et al. (1998). *Asperger syndrome or high-functioning autism?* New York: Plenum Press..

Siegel, B. (2003). *Helping children with autism learn*. New York: Oxford University Press.

Wilkinson, K. M., (1998). Profiles of language and communication skills in autism. *Mental Retardation and Developmental Disabilities Research Reviews, 4(2)*, 73-79.

Williams, K. (2001). Understanding the student with Asperger syndrome: Guidelines for teachers. *Intervention in School and Clinic, 36*, 287-292.

Wing, L. (1988). "The continuum of autistic characteristics,, in Schopler E. & Mesibov, G. B. (Eds.), *Diagnosis and Assessment in Autism*. New York: Plenum Press.

Links

Autism Society (Canada)
www.autismsocietycanada.ca

Autism Ontario **www.autismontario.com**

Autism Resources **www.autism-resources.com**

Canadian Autism Intervention Network
www.autism.org

Centre for the Study of Autism
www.autism.org

www.thegraycenter.org
(Social Story Information)

Treatment and Education of Autistic and related Communication-handicapped Children
www.teacch.com

Geneva Centre for Autism
www.autism.net

CHAPTER 13

Students with Neurological Disabilities
Chronic health needs • Musculoskeletal impairments • Acquired brain injury

"What I don't get is, what's with everybody! The way they treat us!
I mean—so I've got tics. And sometimes I hum. What's so bad about that?
So I've got Tourettes. Big deal! And Eddy … he's got CP. So he jerks. So what?
I mean, what's the big deal? Why do people treat us like we're some kind of freaks
or something? It's not like they're perfect either, you know."

Paulo, age 16

Misconceptions About Neurological Disabilities and Chronic Health Needs

1. Students with special health conditions are automatic candidates for special education.

Very often the distribution of intelligence and abilities like hearing or vision among students with health needs is similar to that of the rest of the population. Students with chronic needs may often miss a great deal of school and may benefit from a remedial program that includes special education programming.

2. Students with Tourette syndrome swear and "talk dirty."

The characteristic is known as "coprolalia." Only about a third of individuals with the syndrome manifest this trait, which waxes, wanes, and often disappears altogether.

3. The physical condition of students with cerebral palsy cannot be remediated or improved.

Cerebral palsy is considered irreversible, but therapy, prosthetic devices, and sometimes surgical procedures can make a positive change, especially if intervention is begun early.

4. When disabling conditions are neurologically based, there is always a consequent diminishing of intellectual capacity.

There is a higher incidence of intellectual problems among people with cerebral palsy, but the connection is not absolute. Other conditions such as spina bifida, muscular dystrophy, or convulsive disorders generally have no connection with levels of intelligence.

5. Conditions like epilepsy and Tourettes indicate mental illness.

People with these conditions are no more or less disposed to mental illness than anyone else.

6. People with spina bifida are incontinent.

Lack of bowel and bladder control is a genuine problem that accompanies more severe cases of spina bifida, but milder cases generally do not have this problem.

7. Arthritis is found only in elderly adults.

It is found in all ages.

8. Medical science is reducing the incidence of physical disabilities and chronic conditions.

The number of children with these conditions is increasing because medical advances, particularly in post-natal care, have increased the birth and early year survival rate.

Describing the Needs

The primary characteristics of students with a physical disability or other neurological or health needs are the proper concern of the health professions. Because a majority of students with these types of conditions attend neighbourhood schools, it follows that teachers and educational assistants should be familiar with the characteristics and implications of these types of conditions. From an educational perspective, some bio-medical knowledge can be useful for developing an appropriate program. Certainly, the knowledge can be very helpful in understanding a student's emotional needs and learning patterns. In most cases (with the occasional exception of some neurologically based conditions, like Tourette syndrome), a student with a physical or health need will arrive in class already defined and classified by health personnel, and will have been presented to an IPRC. Thus, classroom personnel should receive a fair amount of information in advance.

It is very important to recognize that a physical or health or neurological condition will manifest itself in a variety of ways. It is even more important, when it does, to remember that the student with the condition is first and foremost, a student. Teachers should approach medical information, therefore, from an educational and cooperative perspective, not from a diagnostic or treatment one. In addition to learning about a particular condition, it is also wise to seek out the specifics of the individual student's case, since epilepsy, for example, or Tourette syndrome or acquired brain injury, will manifest itself in a variety of ways.

The descriptions that follow here are quite brief and offer preliminary information only. The authors have scrupulously avoided presenting a catalogue of the very long list of conditions encountered in the schools of the province, for despite the drama implied by the conditions, they are of very low prevalence, and each case will, inevitably, be significantly different from others.

Cerebral Palsy

Cerebral palsy is a condition caused by injury to the brain before, during, or after birth, and is chiefly characterized by motor disorder. It is not progressive, nor is it contagious. But it is incurable, although therapy can be helpful in improving comfort and mobility.

Approximately fifty percent of people with cerebral palsy have pyramidal (also called spastic) palsy, characterized by slow, laborious, poorly coordinated voluntary movement, stiff, tense muscles, and, in some cases, a degree of involuntary movement. About twenty-five percent have extrapyramidal (also called choreoathetoid, and atonic) cerebral palsy, characterized by regular, involuntary, writhing movements, difficulty maintaining posture, and floppy muscle tone. Ataxic cerebral palsy, characterized by poor coordination, balance, and posture, affects approximately fifteen percent. People with ataxia may be ambulatory; most others generally require a wheelchair. Some people with cerebral palsy have a combination of these symptoms.

Other matters associated with cerebral palsy are intellectual and developmental delays (not an absolute connection, but the incidence is higher than in the general population), speech and language problems, visual and auditory difficulties, and seizures. An ongoing debate over cerebral palsy arises from the fact that IQ test scores for children with this condition tend to be lower than the general average. However, appropriateness of IQ tests, their administration, and interpretation are often suspect in these situations.

Spina bifida

Spina bifida occurs in the spinal column when one or more vertebrae do not close during prenatal development. It is not a progressive condition and generally manifests itself in three basic forms. The resulting condition varies from minor to severe. Spina bifida occulta is the most common form of spina bifida and is the mildest. This form of spina bifida usually does not result in any visible effect and can only be detected by x-ray. Meningocele is considered a more serious form of spina bifida in which the covering of the spinal column protrudes from the defect in the spine, creating a sac of cerebrospinal fluid. This condition is usually corrected shortly after birth and most individuals do not have major difficulties. The most severe condition is spina bifida with mylemeningocele in which a sac containing nerves and parts of the spinal cord protrude. This type of spina bifida usually results in irreversible (so far) disability, the most obvious being lower body paralysis as well as bladder and bowel control difficulties. This form of spina bifida is often accompanied by hydrocephalus, an enlargement of the head caused by an excessive collection of cerebrospinal fluid in the brain that, if not diagnosed and treated in time, can cause brain injury. Usually, the medical response to hydrocephalus is the installation of a shunt (a short tube) in the spinal column to help this fluid drain. Hydrocephalus and the presence of a shunt, indeed spina bifida itself, usually do not preclude a student's normal progress through school.

Muscular Dystrophy (MD)

Muscular dystrophies include a large group of genetically inherited diseases that can affect people at various stages of life. These diseases are characterized by skeletal muscle wasting and weakness to varying degrees. The most common form of childhood muscular dystrophy is Duchenne MD. Affecting more boys than girls, Duchenne MD is generally evident between the ages of three and five and can be seen as the child begins to walk. This disorder, which progresses rapidly, is characterized initially by weakening of the pelvic girdle and progresses to a stage where the child is bedridden. Lifespan estimates for children with Duchenne MD are around 20, although recent medical innovations have prolonged this. Treatments include physical therapy and respiratory therapy as well as medications. Children within a school setting will be assisted by technological and physical adaptation to their learning environment. Muscular dystrophy does not affect the student's ability to learn, but programming for these students must take into account the progressive nature of the disease, and planning for accommodations over time becomes crucial. Also, careful consideration should be given to the socialization aspects of the student's educational environment. It is important that consideration be given and opportunities provided for peers to adjust to the student's changes in health and functioning.

Acquired Brain Injury

Acquired brain injury (ABI) is any type of sudden injury that causes temporary or permanent damage to the brain after birth (or according to some definitions, after two years of age). Motor vehicle accidents, near drowning, violence-related incidents, and sports-related injuries are among the leading causes.

ABI can have a serious effect on a student's cognitive, behavioural/emotional, and physical well-being. The list of potential problems is intimidating. Cognitively, students may experience difficulties with attention, processing, judg-

The car crash that seriously disabled Matt also caused serious injury to three of his friends and killed two others, but Matt is the only crash victim with permanent spinal injury. Although his condition was at first diagnosed as diplegic (legs more involved than arms), after about six months of therapy, Matt had a stroke and went into a coma. Doctors are sure he had another stroke, for he came to having developed extreme choreoathetosis (abrupt, involuntary writhing movements) in all four limbs. This condition was so intense and painful that after three months it was decided to relieve the condition with a non-reversible surgical procedure that has made Matt a quadriplegic.

The accident happened after a weekend field party when Matt was 15 years old in grade 10. At the time, he was identified gifted and had been placed part-time in a self-contained class with gifted peers, and part-time in advanced grade 12 language and math classes. Matt is now 19. He returned to school about a year ago and, to everyone's delight, demonstrated immediately that although his body was largely immobilized, his intellect was unimpaired.

An admirable piece of creative thinking on the part of a special education teacher solved a potentially serious obstruction to Matt's rehabilitation. Bioengineering staff at the hospital had fashioned a "headstick" so that Matt can tap a computer keyboard. (Matt speaks normally; he uses a computer for writing, problem solving, and a range of activities.) But leaning over the keyboard with the headstick exhausted him after a brief time, so the teacher simply mounted the keyboard above the monitor so that Matt's neck brace supports most of his movements.

Matt has done exceptionally well since his return and will graduate with honours. Now he has asked his teachers for some career counseling which they are willing to do. He is considering a liberal arts degree or a career in accounting. The teachers also recognize that they need to support him to prepare for whatever choice he makes.

ment, anticipation, perception, problem solving, transfer of learning, memory initiation, and fatigue. As for behaviour and emotion, students may experience agitation, disinhibition, sudden outbursts of anger, and impulsivity, and have general difficulty controlling their emotions. Students with ABI may become isolated and withdrawn or overly aggressive, difficulties that are often exacerbated by a lack of social awareness and ability to self-monitor. Physical difficulties may include central and peripheral nervous system disruption, as well as orthopedic complications. Students may experience difficulty in other areas such as fine and gross motor, speech, hearing, vision, taste, olfaction, muscle spasticity, contracture, paresis or paralysis, and physical fatigue.

Students who experience an acquired brain injury usually need specialized help in a school setting. Often the period following the injury can be difficult due to the sudden change in the student's functioning, but also due to the variability of performance during what is termed the recovery period, which can last for up to two years. A team approach, involving parents, school, and medical personnel, is the most effective way of meeting the challenges.

Seizure Disorders (Epilepsy)

Epilepsy is not a disease but rather a symptom of a brain disorder that leads to seizures. There are several types of seizure, the two most common being tonic-clonic and absence seizure (formerly called "grand-mal" and "petit-mal"). In a tonic-clonic seizure, an individual loses consciousness, often convulses, and may fall. Breathing may stop temporarily. The individual may lose bowel and bladder control, or bite the tongue. After one to five minutes or so, the person regains consciousness, but may experience confusion and headache and often goes into deep sleep. Absence seizures, on the other hand, are very brief and often go unnoticed. They may occur several times a day, usually when the person is sedentary, and are characterized by what is often called a "clouding of the consciousness," during which the individual's eyes may stare blankly, or the hands move aimlessly. Return to normal is usually abrupt. It is not unknown for teachers and educational assistants to be the first to suspect absence seizures, since one-on-one learning situations are good opportunities for observation, especially if there is an effort to find out why a particular student's style is marked by significant ups and downs of understanding.

Students with idiopathic epilepsy (of unknown origin) seem to function entirely normally between seizures. Those with symptomatic epilepsy (from brain injury) often have to cope with the consequences of a primary condition, of which epilepsy is one factor. Either way, epilepsy itself, is not usually the reason a student is referred to an IPRC. Very often, it is the primary condition, or the side effects of seizure-control medication, that lead to consideration for special education.

Many students who have tonic-clonic seizures seem to be extremely sensitive about the events, and teachers may find themselves more challenged by the emotional than by the physical consequences of seizure. How a teacher deals with a post-seizure classroom atmosphere can have a major impact. Reassurance and emotional support for the student who had the seizure is crucial. Equally vital is how the teacher educates the other students about epilepsy. (The Epilepsy Association has excellent material to assist with this issue. It also has up-to-date information on new medications for seizure control.)

Tourette Syndrome (a.k.a. 'Tourettes' or TS)

Tourettes is a neurological disorder that usually manifests itself in childhood, and is frequently characterized by motor and/or vocal tics. In a small percentage of the cases, the sounds are obscenities or curses (called "coprolalia"). Although the condition was long thought to be limited to these manifestations, recent and more careful study of Tourettes suggests that significant behavioural features may also be involved, such as hyperactivity, obsession, and indiscriminate rage. Although Tourettes seems to be a life-long disorder, symptoms have been known to disappear for long periods or even disappear altogether, with and without medication.

Although it is a neurological disorder, there is no test for Tourettes so that a diagnosis must be determined clinically, i.e., by observation. Most health professionals consider the following criteria as necessary for a diagnosis.

- Multiple motor and vocal tics must have been present for some time, although not necessarily together.

- Tics occur often, usually in bouts, nearly daily for over a year.

- Other causes such as medication side effects are ruled out.

- The effort expended to suppress tics affects other aspects of the individual's life.

While parents and teachers are front and cen-

Finding information on rare conditions and disorders that may have implications for the classroom has become easier in recent years with the use of the internet (though remember that one has to be a careful consumer of internet information). Mobius syndrome and tuberous sclerosis are typical examples. Tuberous sclerosis is marked by lesions in the brain and other organs, often the skin, and is very frequently accompanied by serious developmental delay. Students frequently have seizures, and some manifest obsessive compulsive, and rage behaviours, not unlike those found in students with autism or Tourettes. With Mobius syndrome, first described in 1888 as congenital facial diplegia, the muscles of the face gradually weaken, so much so that the individual cannot make facial expressions, even when crying or laughing. Atrophy of the tongue is common. In some cases, the forehead and eyebrows may even droop over the eyes, making vision difficult. Although there is no clear evidence of intellectual delay, Mobius is a condition that generates special needs both at home and in the classroom.

Although these conditions do not automatically force a need for special education, the circumstances accompanying them may mean that a special education intervention is preferred for a variety of reasons. In such cases, both teacher and educational assistant will often find it useful to contact support groups—if they exist. There is such a group for tuberous sclerosis, but not as yet for Mobius syndrome. Usually access to support groups is available via the Internet or through the community support department of larger hospitals. (See more on support groups later in this chapter.)

tre in pointing out the frequent presence of obsessive behaviour, hyperactivity, uncontrolled rages, etc., in people with Tourettes, some health professionals seem uncertain about whether these constitute part of the syndrome.

Students with Tourettes in a Classroom Setting

Students with Tourettes can have difficulty in getting started (or finished), problems with comprehending verbal instructions, and confusion over space-time directionality. Given those difficulties, it is not hard to understand why Tourettes is confused with a learning disability, intellectual handicap, schizophrenia, and other conditions. No one medication dominates in the way that Ritalin does with ADHD management (although haloperidol is popular). Nevertheless, drugs are frequently used and side effects may have an impact.

The role of the teacher and assistant, as usual, is vital in the case of a student with Tourettes. Understanding, empathy, common sense support, and remediation strategies are obvious needs. Perhaps the most vital matter in assuring the student's security and sense of well being is the way in which classroom professionals manage the effect of the syndrome on the student's peers.

Multiple Disabilities

Students identified as multiple-disabled or multi-handicapped typically have more than one special need. There is limited evidence showing that certain single handicaps are more predisposed to be accompanied by others. In fact, a particularly vicious prevailing myth is that all students with multiple-disabilities are severely intellectually delayed. Another myth is that all students with multiple disabilities have no oral language. Yet there does seem to be a higher prevalence of disability associated with certain exceptionalities. Children with cerebral palsy, for example, have a disproportionately high ratio of visual impairments. About a third of children with significant hearing loss also have additional special needs.

A case of multiple disability often requires considerable administrative attention. Establishing an appropriate placement, for example, may be difficult. A jurisdiction may have only one student diagnosed deaf/blind, physically disabled, and developmentally delayed. And it may have a total of three students who are identified as severely autistic, one of whom also has a visual impairment. The tendency in situations where these students are not integrated into regular classes is to identify them as multiple-disabled and place them together in a single self-contained class. The rationale for such a placement is, generally, that such congregation allows individualized programming and easy access to support services, that it can permit program overlap, and that it is economically feasible. Still, it is not uncommon for students with multiple, severe disabilities to be integrated into a regular class, ideally with the support of an educational assistant or health aide (or both).

Whatever the identification and placement of a student with several distinct special needs, his or her program will usually be:

i) highly individualized; with

ii) a significant amount of specialized support; and

iii) marked by extensive communication and cooperation (at least attempted) with the student's home so that education and habilitation can be coordinated beyond the school day.

Chronic Health Needs

Modern medical science continues to improve the survival, growth, and development rate among children who are born with profound needs. These children go on to attend school, where their special health-care needs must be met, sometimes prior to their learning. Teachers and assistants today encounter students with cystic fibrosis, scoliosis, congenital malformations, muscular dystrophy, diabetes, cancer, allergies, asthma,* and other chronic conditions that preceding generations had never even imagined. As a consequence, among items that distinguish modern classrooms, in addition to learning hardware, are things like oxygen tanks and Epi-pens. And with that reality comes the necessity for some knowledge of health maintenance. Not that classroom professionals should be medical managers, but for obvious reasons it is important they have an understanding of both

• • • ─────
* Most teachers and educational assistants today will readily agree with the claim by V.Q. Getch and S. Newharth-Pritchett that at any given time there are at least two children with Asthma in a classroom. (See *Teaching Exceptional Children*, 1999, 1, 30-36.)
───── • • •

daily and emergency procedures. What makes this an even trickier challenge is that their primary responsibility is still to educate, with all this implies, not to treat. Attending school, simply being in school, is a crucial element in the normalization and growth of all students and teachers and assistants have powerful roles to play in that process.

A chronic health-care need does not automatically predestine a student for special education, especially in terms of placement. If a student's health need can be met in a regular school, there is no reason why it cannot be met as well in a regular classroom, for a chronic health-care situation, of itself, does not usually generate the need for an Individualized Educational Program. However, the effects of the health need (missed time, frequent medical and/or therapeutic interventions) may indeed mean that special programming is required. Either way, chronic health needs have become a factor in neighbourhood schools today.

Some Issues in the Field

While it has been well established that the role of the educational assistant has proven to be extremely valuable in the successful delivery of services for students with exceptionalities, it is within the area of health needs that perhaps this role is the most visible and essential. Many children with complex health needs require a specialized type of knowledge and treatment that is, in general, not within what would be considered standard teacher education. A successful partnership between teachers and educational assistants (or health aides, a term sometimes used) is characterized by mutual respect for the knowledge base of each as well as rapport and trust. With these professionals working together many children with complex needs can be maintained with their peer group and enjoy a successful experience within a school setting.

✦ A particular concern to teachers is how to react in an emergency situation. It is this concern that sometimes leads them to resist placement of high-risk students in their classes. Usually, the resistance can be overcome with information and education about the particular exceptionality. However, a constant—and justified—complaint of front-line classroom personnel is that they are not kept adequately informed about students with health needs. Changes in medication, environmental triggers (e.g., of a seizure incident), crucial times of day: all these factors can be very important to the accommodation of a student with special health needs, and teachers quite rightly argue that poor communication from health personnel, inefficient bureaucracy in a school or larger system, not to mention stringent privacy regulations, make their jobs more difficult and even put the student at risk, all of which substantiates the wisdom of regular, direct communication with parents who, for obvious reasons, will likely be both helpful and informative.

+ Families often experience practical and emotional havoc when they have a child with physical disabilities, or neurological condition, or chronic health need. Such a child inevitably demands a disproportionate amount of the family's resources in love, energy, money, and time. Needless to say, families react in different ways, and their feelings usually have a profound effect on the way the child reacts in turn to the world at large. In whatever way the family—and the child—react, the teacher, educational assistant, and a wide number of personnel in a school are inevitably drawn into this reaction, so that relative to their other students, they almost invariably find themselves expending equally disproportionate amounts of love, energy, money, and time. How these demands are dealt with in a school, morally and practically, can become a matter of serious debate.

+ Responsibility by default is not unusual in the case of students who are severely disabled. Most of the time it occurs when an educational assistant becomes the sole teacher, classroom caregiver, even, unfortunately, sole companion of a student with profound needs. The issue is a particularly difficult one to solve, for the student's needs are usually very demanding and it is both realistic and sensible for the needs to be dealt with by the person most familiar and competent. Often this is the EA. This type of

---

The Case of Tamhana

The grade 4 teacher had met Tamhana two years ago while substituting in a grade 2 class for several months. At the time, the teacher had taken note of the young girl's persistent and unusual behaviour, but followed the advice of a colleague and did not pursue the matter. Now, as the grade 4 teacher, he regrets that decision, for Tamhana's apparent oddities are much more pronounced, and more obsessive to a marked degree. She has continued a grade 2 habit: returning from the schoolyard according to a very specific walking pattern. But whereas she would permit intervention two years ago, Tamhana blows into a frightening rage now, if interrupted. She enters the classroom by a patterned path as well (and her peers have learned not to get in her way). Her lunch is eaten in specific sequence, and she has taken to counting aloud while chewing to ensure an identical number of "chews" each time.

Tamhana's facial tics, very evident in grade 2, have ceased, but she now makes strange sounds when sitting alone (which, regrettably, is most of the time), ranging from growls to oohs and eehs, and on one occasion, the teacher is certain, barking. Lately, Tamhana has taken to impulsively running from the room. She allows herself to be brought back and is very remorseful for causing a disturbance. However, she cannot explain why she runs out, and often, if questioned the following day, denies any knowledge of the event.

The teacher, like many of the staff, believes Tamhana has Tourette syndrome and wants the principal to refer her to an IPRC. Unfortunately, this was attempted in grade 3 and then abandoned after a friend of Tamhana's family told her parents that girls don't get Tourettes. As a result, the parents refused all requests from the IPRC for cooperation. The staff has now learned of an additional complication: that Tamhana's father does not want attention focused on a female child in any way that might bring disgrace on the family. What the teacher knows he must do is somehow convince the girl's parents that some kind of intervention is necessary, for Tamhana's behaviour is intensifying daily.

management runs counter to the purpose of an inclusive classroom placement. It is also antithetical to the objective behind placing a student in a self-contained class in a neighbourhood school, for even in a specialized setting like this, it is expected that the student will interact with as wide a variety of people as possible. The issue is a challenge for educational assistants, for both their inclination and their professional training leans toward a wider use of their talents.

Some Implications for the Classroom

❖ North Americans live in a culture obsessed with beautiful bodies. Health and strength are not enough; we must be well formed and attractive. It is not surprising, therefore, that, especially to the students with physically exceptionalities, there is not only a battle to overcome the limitations imposed by their own bodies, there is also a battle to be accepted by others without stigma. The same phenomenon applies to behaviour. To people with Tourette syndrome, for example, the band of acceptable or so-called normal behaviour in our culture appears very narrow, so that when their condition expresses itself, they feel very much singled out. Therefore, a teacher with one or more of these students in his or her class often finds himself/herself dealing as much with behaviours—that of the students with the disabilities, his or her own, that of other students, the culture at large—as he or she does with curriculum and instruction. Students with exceptionalities can often have negative feelings about themselves, especially if it is obvious that others around them do. Conversely, they may become independent and self-sufficient in response to the expectations of others. Self-acceptance and self-awareness will develop in kind with the open and honest appraisal that significant people in their lives give to them. It is essential that teachers and educational assistants alike are aware of the profound influence their actions and attitudes can have on a class when it comes to interacting with students who are disabled. A look, a turn of phrase, and subtle body language can send clear messages of inclusion or exclusion, a message that will be heard and acted upon by those who look to the teacher and educational assistant for instruction. Working in inclusive settings with students with exceptionalities goes far beyond reading, writing, and math, and ventures well into acceptance by attitude and example.

❖ Treatment of conditions like epilepsy or Tourette syndrome often involves the use of medication that has sedating side effects. Teachers sometimes find they are adjusting, not to an exceptionality, but to its treatment. It is not uncommon for a student to be in need of special accommodation not because of the condition but rather because of the effects of the medication used to control a primary condition.

❖ The normal adjustments that every teacher makes to accommodate his or her students' personal needs are often intensified in cases of chronic health need. The students often miss a great deal of instructional time through illness and absences for therapy, etc. Teachers also have to make allowances in scheduling and in monitoring so that matters of the students' personal hygiene can be addressed. As well, students with particularly serious disabilities often have attendant behavioural, even psychiatric problems, that can call upon the full extent of one's patience and stamina.

❖ A disabling condition like cerebral palsy can affect progress through the natural stages of development, so teachers can safely anticipate that some students may not be working at the same academic level as their peers, and must therefore make adjustments in program and evaluation.

(1) Students in both regular and self-contained classes—most especially younger children—will invariably take their cue from adults when seeking out how to react to and behave toward people with disabilities. Teachers and EAs must play a very positive leadership and modelling role, showing other students tactfully how to be helpful without taking over, how to react with empathy not pity, and how to treat their peer's exceptionalities with common sense.

(2) Where there are no secondary exceptionalities to deal with, such as developmental delay for example, teachers of a student with non-sensory physical limitations, or neurological impairments or chronic conditions, will likely treat a student in the same way as he or she treats everyone else, making allowance only for special needs in day-to-day functioning. These special needs might include help in the administration of medication, help in the effective use of a prosthesis (artificial replacement for a body part), or some other adaptive device necessary for daily living.

(3) Continuing developments in computer technology accelerate far ahead of the capacity of texts like this one to describe them, and, of course, classroom professionals need to stay abreast as best as they can to utilize this progress on behalf of their students.

(4) Because many children with physical disabilities can be absent from school frequently, cooperation in out-of-school assistance can be important to academic success. Some jurisdictions appoint what are called "itinerant" teachers, or teachers of the home and hospital-bound, whose teaching load usually involves on-site instruction at home, in hospital, or in other institutions.

(5) It is rare, but not unheard of, for the classroom teacher or EA to be a catalyst in the discovery of a condition, such as absence seizures for example, that may go unnoticed in a large and chaotic family but in the more structured demands of school become evident. Such relatively unknown conditions like Tourette syndrome sometimes go undiagnosed even through adolescence.

(6) Effective communication among teachers, parents, and health-care professionals is absolutely essential, but such communication is ignored with discouraging frequency. It is often incumbent upon the teacher or EA to initiate the communication, usually by direct and regular contact with the parents.

Help From Support and Advocacy Groups

Support and advocacy groups are helpful in a variety of ways. Members of organizations like The Epilepsy Association, The Learning Disabilities Association, The Tourette Syndrome Foundation, Association for Community Living, The Canadian Hearing Society, The Canadian National Institute for the Blind, and many more are usually well informed and current, and quite aggressive in seeking out information, supporting innovative practice, or dealing with slow-moving bureaucrats, and reluctant, sometimes poorly informed health professionals. All of these are issues that can be faced by classroom professionals, and most of the time, regular contact and help from the appropriate advocacy group can be quite helpful in addressing them. Associations, for example, have education programs in kit form or video that are useful for enlightening both students and adults. It is not unknown for an advocacy group to be prominent in getting service. Advocacy groups are also a remarkably effective first line of emotional support and information to a family who has just learned their child has been diagnosed.

CHAPTER 14

Students Who are Deaf or Hard of Hearing

"Being hearing impaired, it was almost impossible to participate in class the same way as other students. Teachers thought that because I wore a hearing aid that the problem was "fixed," I could hear "normally" and therefore should be able to participate in classroom or group activities like the others were expected to. Nothing could have been further from the truth. I never knew what I missed hearing or heard incorrectly, therefore my responses were more often than not off topic. Even if I could hear what the teacher was saying, I could rarely hear others in class. To avoid feeling ridiculed and stupid because of inappropriate contributions, I withdrew as much as possible."

Lynda P., (45) hearing impaired since birth

Misconceptions About Deafness

1. Deafness diminishes intellectual ability.

The range of intellectual ability among individuals who are deaf is the same as it is for those who hear normally. Nevertheless, students who are deaf may lag academically because of their difficulties in communicating with people who hear and can use spoken language easily.

2. Deafness leads automatically to muteness or to inability to speak.

People who are born deaf or become deaf before acquiring speech (usually called prelingual deafness) sometimes have difficulty learning to speak clearly, but the connection between deafness and the inability to speak is not absolute.

3. People who are profoundly deaf live in a world of total silence.

People with profound deafness can respond to some sounds, particularly to the vibrations.

4. Hearing aids restore normal hearing.

Hearing aids do not restore normal hearing, but the technology has become very sophisticated now and allows for extensive customizing to individual needs.

5. It is counterproductive and potentially harmful for people who are deaf or hard of hearing to socialize almost exclusively with others who are also deaf or hard of hearing.

Some members of the deaf community argue that an exclusive "deaf culture" is entirely natural and should be encouraged. Others argue the opposite with equal vigour. There is as yet no conclusive evidence that the desire of some people who are deaf or hard of hearing to associate primarily with one another is anything but normal.

6. Teaching signing to people who are deaf or hard of hearing will retard their development of spoken language.

There continues to be much controversy about the relationship between the development of spoken language and the age at which sign language is introduced. Teaching of sign language does not, of itself, retard the development of spoken language. However, if a person who is deaf or hard of hearing chooses to learn or to use sign exclusively, the development of facility in spoken language may be affected.

7. Individuals who are deaf compensate by reading lips.

When reading lips the receiver notes facial expression, hand gestures, and other body language in addition to simple lip movement. This skill does not come more easily to individuals with hearing loss than to anyone else. Reading lips alone is often not helpful because of similarities in the words of spoken language, and because of the inconsistencies in the lip movements of speakers. Some experts estimate that only 30 percent of spoken language can be understood using this technique.

8. American Sign Language (ASL) is a universal sign language characterized by a loose style of gesturing primarily used to convey concrete ideas.

ASL is one (sign) language among many. Just as there is no universal spoken language, there is also no universal sign language. ASL is a sophisticated language with its own set of grammatical rules and can be used to convey levels of abstraction just as oral language does. See more about signing later in this chapter.

9. With the increasing movement toward the inclusion in regular classrooms of students with special needs, regular classroom teachers have become better prepared to deal with students who have hearing impairments.

While many schools boards provide both professional development as well as support services and personnel, on balance, within the field of special education, the proportion of students with deafness is relatively small and the time for professional development relatively short. Preparation at the preservice level is at best site specific and at worst non-existent.

Types of Hearing Loss

Most hearing losses are conductive or sensorineural (and sometimes, but not frequently, both).

In the case of *conductive* hearing loss, sound is reduced or blocked before it reaches the inner ear, and may occur as the result of infection, trauma, wax build-up, or other cause. Sometimes, the blockage can be cleared or the sound amplified to reduce the effects of conductive hearing loss.

In *sensorineural* hearing loss, the problem is in the reception of sound in the inner ear or in the transmission of electrical impulses along the auditory nerve. Sound may reach the inner ear, but because of problems in the inner ear struc-

---

Possible Indications of Mild to Moderate Hearing Loss in Children

In primary classrooms especially, children who experience more than the usual frequency of colds, earaches, sore throats, etc., need to be watched carefully for signs of the hearing problems that may follow. The following signs merit attention if a teacher or educational assistant notices them consistently.

- poor articulation, especially consonants, not attributable to factors like age or a different first language
- loud or soft speech that is at an inappropriate level for the environment

- physical signs (like constantly cocking the head)
- trouble following directions or answering simple questions
- unusually frequent requests for repetition
- unusual inattentiveness

The possibility of a hearing loss should always be considered when assessing a student's behaviour problems and/or failure to meet academic potential.

tures, it may not be transmitted meaningfully, even with amplification. There are many possible causes for sensorineural hearing loss, including such apparently simple diseases as mumps and measles, more complex viral infections like meningitis, and a range of congenital disorders and types of trauma. Attempts to correct sensorineural loss tend to be more radical and the results less predictable than corrections of conductive hearing.

Some specialists in the field distinguish a third type of hearing difficulty, which they call *central auditory dysfunction*. This hearing difficulty is described as an inability to interpret correctly (i.e., in the brain) some sounds that travel along the auditory nerve, even though sensitivity to sound may be otherwise normal. Central auditory dysfunction is still pretty much a mystery and is not yet universally accepted as a valid explanation of hearing difficulty.

Classifications of Hearing Loss

Specialists in the field of hearing generally include four markers to classify an individual's hearing loss. These are

- *site of loss:* whether the loss is conductive or sensorineural, or both

- *age of onset:* whether the loss is pre- or post-lingual

- *etiology:* whether the individual's loss was present at birth (congenital loss) or has arisen since birth (adventitious loss)

- *severity:* acuity of hearing, measured by an individual's response to intensity, or loudness, measured in decibels (dB), across a range of frequencies, measured in hertz (Hz). A simple metaphor for the severity measure can be found in the controls on a radio. The volume control of a radio increases or decreases the decibel rating of sound that issues from the speaker, while the frequency or pitch is modified by how carefully the tuner is set to the signal, and also by the degree of clarity achieved by adjusting the tenor/bass setting. Most of the speech in a typical classroom will range from 400 Hz to 2500 Hz, often depending on whether one person is speaking or

whether there is classroom buzz. The decibel rating in a classroom may vary from as low as 30 dB (a whisper) to as high as 80 dB or 90 dB (a shout). In most cases, comfortable human conversation has a decibel rating of around 35 dB to 50 dB, in a frequency or hertz range of about 400 Hz to 1250 Hz. The severity classification is the one most frequently used by educators because it can be structured into functional clusters. Such clusters imply some simple guidelines for the classroom.

A Caution About Severity

It is important to note that the characteristics used to describe the implications of hearing loss are by no means all there is to know about per-

> ### Degrees of Hearing Loss*
>
> Sound intensity is measured in decibels (dB). The faintest sound that a person can hear is measured at 0 dB.
>
> *Mild:* Loss range is 25 dB-40 dB. Subject may have difficulty with faint or distant sounds and with conversations; may have loss in groups, or settings with ambient noise.
>
> *Moderate:* Loss range is 41 dB-55 dB. Subject frequently has difficulty hearing normal speech, especially in groups, class discussions, etc.
>
> *Moderate/severe:* Loss range is 56 dB-70 dB. Subject frequently has difficulty comprehending speech. Voices must be loud or amplified to be understood.
>
> *Severe:* Loss range is 71 dB-90 dB. Subject has great difficulty understanding even loud or amplified speech. The latter may seem faint and distorted. Subject usually requires amplification and intensive speech and language training.
>
> *Profound (deaf):* Loss range is 91 dB+. Subject may be aware of loud sounds and vibrations, but may not even comprehend amplified speech without training.
>
> ---
>
> * A hearing loss is also described as *bilateral* (both ears) or *unilateral* (one ear) with the severity of loss of each ear indicated individually.

Common Sounds	dB Rating	Usual Effect
rustling leaves	20	pleasant
whisper	30	barely audible
2-3 people conversing	40-65	varies
hair dryer on high	70	interferes, disrupts
occupied cafeteria food blender motorcycle 5 m. away	80-95	annoying (85 dB for 8 hrs begins hearing damage)
chain saw, snowmobile jet flyby 300 m. away	105-110	regular exposure without protection can damage
sound system at 100+ watts rock concert or jet takeoff	120 110-140	pain threshold is 125 dB

sons who are deaf or hard of hearing. Just like those who hear normally, people who are deaf and hard of hearing are as completely individual as anyone else, and therefore attend or tune out like anyone else. Another difficulty with classification is that, despite a certain presumed level of function in a person who is deaf or hard of hearing, that function will invariably be affected by the style and expressive quality of the person sending the communication.

Some Issues in the Field

✦ Although several matters have a high profile, the single most overwhelming and consuming issue is communication method or style. On the surface, the issue appears to be a simple one of oralism versus manualism (signing): that is, should a person who is deaf or hard of hearing learn to develop and fully use whatever residual hearing he or she has available in order to communicate with people who hear, or, should the emphasis and energy be devoted to learning how to sign in order to communicate with other signers (who, by and large, will be other people who are deaf or hard of hearing, family members, and teachers).

The Deaf Culture

Supporters of manualism argue that being deaf means being part of a culture that is distinguished by, among other things, its own language. They argue that because experience shows most people who are deaf or hard of hearing do not become comfortable participants in the hearing culture, to deny them their own language therefore denies them their own culture and forces them into one where they are at risk, or at the very least, are not full participants. The phrase *deaf community* is frequently used (especially by those who are deaf or hard of hearing) to describe people who are deaf or hard of hearing as a cohesive group who share their own entertainment, activities—and language. This tendency toward self-exclusion does not prevail to the same degree among other groups with an equally apparent special need.

Supporters of oralism counter that the world is dominated by, and made up mostly of, people who hear, and that persons who are deaf or hard of hearing who do not avail themselves of the opportunity to be part of the dominant culture are denying reality and relegating themselves to what is in effect not a culture, but a sub-culture with all that this implies. Some advocates on this side of the issue suggest that it may be advantageous for persons who are deaf or hard of hearing to develop skill in both styles of communication, either simultaneously or separately, in order that they can make a choice.

The issue of oralism versus manualism can

present parents of a young child with an agonizing decision, for it is advantageous to begin either method as early as possible.

Educators, too, are inevitably involved in this issue, both practically and ethically. Learning to read, for example, can be significantly affected if a student is using ASL as the predominant means of communication. For example, a phrase that in print is written, "Yesterday I went to the store." is typically signed in ASL as "Yesterday me store go." Because sensitivity to syntax is such a powerful component in learning to read, it follows that some children who are deaf and hard of hearing who are using ASL may have an extra hurdle to face when learning to read English text.

Still another matter for educators is sensitivity to the intensity of this debate. While their primary role is to teach, that role can be more complex if the student (or his or her parents) is intensely committed to one side or the other of this communication and culture issue.

♦ Further complicating the matter of educating students who are deaf and hard of hearing is the *intensity of debate inside the respective oralism and manualism philosophies themselves.* Even after a decision has been taken to emphasize one approach or the other, there is the potential for further disagreement over technique. For example, among supporters of manualism, American Sign Language has become an overwhelming, but not unanimous, choice.

♦ In recent years, sophisticated *surgical implantation technology* has generated more possibilities—and difficult decisions—for dealing with significant hearing loss. One of the more vigorously debated technologies is the *cochlear implant.* In this procedure, a receiver is implanted either within or outside the cochlea (part of the inner ear) and an external component transmits signals to this receiver. The present state of cochlear implant technology does not restore normal hearing, but there is evidence to suggest that it can dramatically improve a subject's ability to interpret speech and to make sense of environmental sounds, both natural and artificial. Controversy about the procedure and the technology arises over the suitability of candidates, the type of implant

A personal stereo system at maximum volume has been estimated to have a decibels level of between 100 dB to 110 dB. At a level of 105 dB exposure over 1 minute can risk permanent hearing loss.

to use, and the impact on the subject. Also of concern is what some consider the primative state of the technology and the risk of damage to the cochlear nerve, which might prohibit the use of advanced devices that may be developed with further research.

Somewhat less controversial is an at-the-ear, skullbone-anchored hearing aid system that stimulates the inner ear by transmitting signals to the skull. This implantation technology was initially limited to subjects with conductive hearing loss, and has enjoyed a significant level of success. Research is now being extended to subjects with sensorineural loss.

♦ An issue that plagues researchers, and one that has more than a peripheral impact on educators, is determining the *true prevalence* of hearing loss in Canadian populations. Inconsistent definitions across jurisdictions, differences in the style of collecting and reporting data, and difficulties in assessing hearing loss among individuals with other disabilities (especially if these disabilities are multiple) lead to some confusing numbers in the field. The National Institution on Deafness and Other Communication Disorders reports that 17 out of every 1000 children in Americia under the age of 18 experience some type of hearing loss. This percentage increases with age. A 1991 Health and Activities Limitation study stated that 1 in every 25 Canadians had impaired hearing, but again, lack of a standard definition of what constitutes a hearing impairment is at issue. In a study published in 1994, Schein noted that the prevalence rate in the U.S. is reported as 86 per 1000 while in Canada, it is 41 per 1000. He also showed wide variations among the reported rates in Canadian provinces (e.g., 34/1000 in Northwest Territories versus 61/1000 in Manitoba). The uncertainties implied by these differences in data affect funding, research, and even the degree of importance given to the matter by administrators. The Canadian Association of the Deaf, in a 2002 report, suggests, with great caution as to the reliability of the number, that approximately 310 000 Canadians are profoundly deaf and the possiblilty that 2.8 million are hard of hearing.

Typical School Placements

- *Special residential schools.* There are five such schools in Ontario, each of which offers day programs as well. The Sir James Whitney school in Belleville, the Robarts school in London, and the Ernest C. Drury school in Milton are well known and highly regarded. Also held in high repute is the unique program at the W. Ross MacDonald school in Brantford for students who are blind and deaf/blind, as well as the Centre Jules-Leger in Ottawa, which focuses on students with learing disabilities and visual impairments and deafness. Interestingly, over the past decade and more, the population of students who are deaf at these schools has declined somewhat, leading to the inference that more students with hearing loss are being educated in their neighbourhood schools.

- *Special classes within regular elementary or secondary schools.* Self-contained classes of students who are deaf and hard of hearing are not uncommon.

- *Part-time inclusion programs.* Students may attend some regular classes in a regular school. A signing interpreter or an FM communication system or other support might be used. This type of program may have a resource room component, especially if a trained teacher of students who are deaf is available to work directly with the students and to consult with the regular class teachers.

- *Itinerant teacher programs.* Specialist teachers of students who are deaf offer assistance in classrooms. In this program, students are usually in a regular class full time (and more often than not, have a hearing loss of lesser severity).

Communication Approaches and Supports

Oral Approaches

A child who is deaf or hard of hearing who learns via an oral approach typically is taught to take advantage of auditory, visual, and tactile input. Much attention is given to auditory training, talking, speechreading, and amplification. Usually, oral programs emphasize the development of intelligible speech. Research suggests that significant successes in this type of program tend to occur in fully integrated school programs, and in students with above-average IQ test scores whose parents are fully involved and supportive, and who have above-average socio-economic status. Some of the methods used under the rubric of oralism are described below. Educators and parents who wish to investigate further, usually begin with information available from the Canadian Hearing Society.

Speechreading

This is a process wherein a person receives a message principally by observing a speaker's face, paying special attention to the lips, and expressions and gestures in the face, body, and hands. Speechreading is enhanced if the receiver is aware of and familiar with the context of the speech. Complications such as poor lighting or any instance where the educators face may not be in clear view make this method only one of several avenues for people who are deaf to receive information. Very few people who are deaf and hard of hearing rely on speechreading exclusively.

Auditory Training

This process teaches a child to use what residual hearing he or she has. Also called the auditory method and auditory learning, the process operates on the principle of teaching a child to learn how to listen rather than just learning how to hear. Advocates argue that only a very few children are unable to benefit from this training, especially if it is begun as early as possible. Essentially, the method involves first the development of awareness of sound, then the ability to make gross discriminations among sounds in the environment, and finally the ability to discriminate among speech sounds. Supporters argue for

Frequently in this situation, the interpreter will sit with the class and face the instructor, while the student who is deaf will sit with the class and face the interpreter.

☞ Be prepared for significant distraction at first.

☞ Both interpreter and student will benefit from getting lesson summaries in advance.

☞ Be conscious of the lag between oral speech and its translation into sign.

☞ A visual aid (e.g., a transparency) means the student who is deaf has two stimuli to process with one sensory organ. (Not dissimilar, in the case of a person who hears, to being addressed by two people at once.)

the earliest possible use of amplifications, as well as simultaneous training in speech production.

Specialized Approaches

There are a number of individual and unique ideas appearing in the field from time to time, some of which attract attention because of active support—and active criticism. Two that have attained a high profile, even though they are not widely used, are the *cued speech method and the acoupedic method*. The first uses a combination of oral and manual styles. Attempts to develop the individual's residual hearing capacity and the capacity for speech are supported by eight manual configurations and four hand positions to supplement the visual manifestations of speech. The originator of cued speech, Orin Cornett, claims it can be learned in 12 to 15 hours by anyone of average intelligence. The acoupedic method, on the other hand, excludes all visual clues in order to encourage the individual to use residual hearing to the maximum extent possible.

Manual Approaches

American Sign Language (ASL)

In May 1993, Ontario became the first Canadian province to authorize the use of ASL (and LSQ, Langue de Signes Quebecoise) as a language of instruction for students who are deaf or hard of hearing. Ontario schools for students who are deaf now use ASL *and* written English, *and* allow students opportunities to use and develop their auditory and speech potential.

ASL is a true language in itself, quite different from spoken language and most emphatically not a translation of English into manually communicated words. ASL has its own vocabulary, its own

grammar, its own word order, and its own history. American Sign Language is founded on combinations of symbolic gestures produced by the shape, the location, and the movement of the hands. Whereas methods like *Total Communication* (see below) very often employ iconic signs, in which the shape of the sign encodes English as much as possible, the signs of ASL are unique. Many ASL signs symbolize concepts rather than individual words. ASL has no signs for the grammatical markers, such as "ed" and "ing" that express verb tense and condition. Rather, users depend on facial expression and body language to replace voice intonation and enhance meaning. ASL tends to be learned by children who are deaf or hard of hearing in special settings like schools, rather than being passed on by parents in the way that language is learned by most hearing people. (The predecessor of ASL is FSL, French Sign Language, developed as a one-hand signing system by Abbé Charles Michel de l'Epee, 1712-1784, who founded an institution for people who were deaf in Paris, in 1770.)

Fingerspelling

This method spells out the letters of the English alphabet by using various finger positions on one hand. As a technique, it is often used as one part of the Total Communication method. Members of the Canadian Hearing Society have varied in their endorsement of fingerspelling. Critics generally hold that it is exceptionally inefficient and time consuming and requires an inordinate amount of attention for a style that has large potential for error. Supporters, especially those who are competent in the use of the method, say that it is ideal for "fill-in," those times when a communication doesn't "get through," and the communicator must resort to spelling out a word or words (just as hearing people sometime feel the need to do).

Combination Approaches

Although the communication approach of a person who is deaf or hard of hearing is likely to emphasize one rather than several methods, he or she will invariably avail himself/herself of other sources for information (like facial expressions, body language, etc.) in the same way as a person who hears. Within the taxonomy of communication styles advocated for people who are deaf, there are approaches that operate from this multi-source position both practically and philosophically. Two of these approaches are the *Rochester Method* and *Total Communication*. The Rochester Method uses fingerspelling in conjunction with speech, speechreading, and amplification. Total Communication may be defined as the use of speech, speechreading, fingerspelling, and amplification, along with the simultaneous use of a school-based manual system. In a school-based Total Communication system, signs are usually taught in the same order as language. This teaches the child to communicate manually using English syntax. Also, unlike ASL, the signs tend to attempt to reflect English syntax. Worth noting is that some classrooms use ASL as part of a Total Communication approach. As well, even advocates who strongly support ASL to the exclusion of all else acknowledge the potential usefulness of other support like speechreading and hearing aid technology.

Hearing Aid Technology

There was a time not long ago when fitting someone with a hearing aid meant installing a device that simply amplified incoming sound. While the basic advantage of such a system is obvious, the accompanying drawbacks were often significant. Although straight amplification is still available today and in some cases is entirely adequate for a user, the technology has become far more sophisticated and versatile.

Users of in-the-ear hearing aids (until recently, the most common) often find the technology difficult to accommodate because at the same time as the aids augment incoming sound, they also create a plugged-ear sensation that intensifies the sound of the user's own voice, and dramatically amplifies previously unnoticed cranial noises such as those created while chewing food or taking deep breaths. Not infrequently, this phenomenon causes a new user to reject the technology entirely. A recent and increasingly popular technological development, usually called "open-fit hearing aids," addresses this issue. The "open-fit" places a small receiver behind the ear from which a very small tube leads into the ear. The technology augments sound, but leaves the ear open to receive normal sounds, and does not cause a plugged-ear sensation. Experience thus far indicates that this system works best in cases of high-frequency hearing loss.

In most cases, professionals who assess hearing (audiologists and audiometrists) can not only point to where on the decibel and hertz range an individual has hearing problems, they can identify assistive devices that can be customized to address those problems. This technological step represents somewhat of a revolution for people with a hearing loss, for it means that, in many cases, they are able to acquire hearing aids, although often at significant expense, that compensate for loss without adding new problems by amplifying other sounds unnecessarily.

In the classroom, technology can be generalized across a very wide spectrum. One example, and there are many, is a system that uses FM radio band technology. In this system, the teacher (and/or other students) wears a transmitter and the student(s) who has (have) a hearing loss a receiver. For the student who is deaf or hard of hearing, the amount of classroom ambient noise is usually less obtrusive, with sounds coming principally from whoever is wearing the transmitter. The system—between speaker and listener—is usually wireless. This is only one of many systems recently developed primarily for classroom use. Educators involved in choosing technological support for students who are deaf or who have a hearing loss need to investigate the options thoroughly, particularly in seeking out recent developments, and in seeking out the possibilities for customization of the support. Ironically, in an age that turns readily to technology in almost every facet of life, less than one-third of people who could be helped by hearing aids actually own and use one.

Educational Implications of Hearing Loss

❖ Students who are deaf and hard of hearing often do not have an easy time in school, mostly because of what is, in effect, a language barrier. Studies over several decades suggest that their academic achievement is affected by five specific factors more than any other. These are the severity of the hearing loss, the chronological age at onset, intelligence, socio-economic status of the family, and hearing status of the parents (a deaf student of deaf parents is considered to have a better chance for academic success than if the parents are hearing).

❖ Achievement test scores for students who are deaf or hard of hearing are often significantly lower than the scores of students who hear, even on adapted test instruments. However, it behooves educators to consider whether this lower performance is simply the result of a bad fit between the real abilities of students who are deaf and hard of hearing and the way achievement is measured. Even though students who are deaf may lag in reading and other language skills, teachers must be on guard against interpreting a difficulty with language as an inherent lack of ability. Yet the issue of language development and its effective use is inevitably a principal consideration in any evaluation of ability.

❖ The difficulties students who are deaf have in communicating often lead to exaggerated compensatory behaviours or to frustration that is expressed in ways that cause the students to be unfairly labelled as disturbed, or odd, or even developmentally disabled. In the past it was not unusual to find students who are deaf of normal intellectual and emotional mien placed in segregated classes because of this mistaken label. There has even developed over time a so-called "psychology of the deaf," in which the characteristics of people who are deaf or hard of hearing are sometimes described in very unflattering language. One result of this perception of people who are deaf, no matter what its accuracy or its origins, is rein-

> *It happened in grade 4. I was nine. I was concentrating on math—I love math; the numbers follow a pattern, not like words where the rules always change. I was aware other kids were moving. Nothing unusual about that. Class of thirty. But then the lights went out! I looked up. Everyone, including the teacher, had disappeared! I was so scared! I ran to the door and there was a class monitor waving at me. Probably yelling too. Looked like it anyway. It was a fire drill. Mustn't run, mustn't talk. But when I caught up with the class I was shaking and sobbing. Once again I felt ignored.*
>
> Vivienne T., profoundly deaf from birth

forcement of the isolation that students who are deaf or hard of hearing frequently describe as the worst part of living in a hearing world. Being aware of and responding to this factor is very important for teachers and educational assistants.

❖ Classroom environment plays a major role in accommodating the needs of a student who has a hearing loss. Although matters such as locating the student's desk are always taken into immediate account by most teachers and educational assistants, there are other issues that recent findings have shown to be important. One of these is the amount of echo in the classroom, technically referred to as reverberation (the amount of time it takes for a sound to decrease to 60 dB after it is turned off). Naturally, the more reverberation can be reduced, the less likely a student with hearing loss will experience interference. Interestingly, the impact of reverberation on students with normal hearing can be very significant too, a fact that makes reverberation reduction through the use of carpeting, acoustical ceiling tiles, and drapes (which may introduce allergy considerations; nothing is simple!) a matter for serious consideration.

❖ Yet another issue is signal-to-noise ratio. This ratio is the decibel level of the speaker divided by the decibel level of the ambient sounds in the room. The higher the latter, the lower the ratio and, naturally, the lower the ratio, the more difficulty a student who is deaf or hard of hearing will experience. Signal-to-noise ratio is a powerful argument for advocates who support self-contained classrooms for students who are deaf and hard of hearing.

❖ Whether a student with hearing loss has an interpreter, or has amplification devices, or uses Total Communication—whatever the approach—communicating is very hard work, both as a consequence of the concentration needed to receive information and of the effort needed to send it. Students who are deaf or hard of hearing get very tired, usually more so than their peers who hear, and teach-ers must recognize this. (It is important for people who hear to realize, too, that signing is very tiring work; an interpreter has an intensely energy-consuming job.)

❖ Meaningful cooperation with the hearing world can be difficult to achieve. People who are deaf or hard of hearing often describe their experiences with others in societal control (e.g., police, and other officialdom) as unsatisfactory. An important responsibility of educators, because of their potential for extensive contact with students who are deaf and hard of hearing, is to sensitize the hearing public to this matter.

The Case of Nils

Nils' thirteenth birthday was more dramatic, if not traumatic, than most such days for a young adolescent. To begin with, on that day he boarded a plane in Stockholm, with his mother, to come to Canada. She had accepted a three-year diplomatic posting, with an option of a three-year extension.

On the day of their arrival, Nils and his mother learned their first lesson in Canadian geography. The school for students who are deaf that had agreed to accept Nils was too far away from his new home for him to be a day student. Even more distressing, they learned that the school used a communication style quite different from that which Nils used. From age six, Nils had attended a private, residential school for the deaf that uses sign exclusively. Moreover, the style of signing is one the school has developed, and it is quite significantly different from any form of sign used in any general way in North America. This difference might not have been an issue for Nils in his home country, for the school provides personal interpreters for students who leave to enroll in neighbourhood schools. However, with Nils' move to Canada, the matter has become far more complicated.

Over a series of meetings during the first month of his life in Canada (during the summer vacation), Nils and his mother have decided, and the local (Ontario) board has agreed, that he will enroll in the neighbourhood school. At this point, however, the boy and his mother have a further decision to make, choosing from among one, or a combination, of the following options.

1. The Swedish diplomatic service will provide and pay for a personal, in-class, signing interpreter trained in the signing style used by Nils' former school.

2. Given that Nils has some residual hearing (his loss is severe to profound but he wears two powerful aids) a type of Total Communication can be used.

3. Nils is already familiar with sign; continue sign but use ASL.

One piece of good news for Nils is that the teacher of the class where he will attend is both qualified and interested in special education. She acknowledges that she has preferences in the matter of communication, but has pointed out in meetings with Nils and his mother that she will happily accommodate whatever decision is made.

Nils' school career has demonstrated that he is very bright and very resourceful, and although his language skills are typically lagging behind those of his peers who hear, his superiority in subject areas like mathematics suggest that he would likely respond to any or all of the above. The question to be solved: what is best for him?

The following suggestions are collected from students who are deaf and hard of hearing. They were asked to offer advice to teachers and educational assistants in regular classes.

(1) *Seat the student toward the front* of the room and to one side, with the better ear toward the teacher and class. Otherwise, seat in the second seat from the front, second row from the window, or similar setting, but always with light on the teacher's face.

(2) *Permit the student to move* his or her seat if the teaching centre moves to another part of the room.

(3) *A student who is deaf or hard of hearing needs to see* the speaker's face. Seat the student two to three metres away from the place where you do most of your talking. Keep your hands away from your face.

(4) *From time to time attempt to keep your mouth near the level* of the student's eyes. For example, instead of always standing, sit at your desk at certain times.

(5) *Be sure to have* the student's visual and aural attention before giving assignments or announcements.

(6) *Make a practice of asking both* students who are hearing and hard of hearing to repeat directions for the benefit of the whole class. Ask the student to repeat instructions to ensure he or she understands.

(7) *Do not turn your back while talking*. Do not talk while writing on the chalkboard. A moving speaker is impossible to speechread. Do not walk around the room while talking about important things.

(8) *Don't use loud tones* or exaggerated mouth movements. Use the same tone of voice and the same inflection you use for everyone else. Avoid gestures. Excessive gestures draw attention away from the face and lips. They're embarrassing too.

(9) *Many words sound the same*—blue, blew; tax, tacks. This is confusing enough. But many words that do not sound the same look the same on the lips; e.g., bat, pat, mat look alike, as do bad, pad, mad.

(10) *It may be helpful* to explain to other students that many words look alike. Let the class try to speechread a few sentences. This procedure will help others in the class to understand. Understanding helps eliminate teasing and unfair judgments.

(11) *During a discussion*, ask questions to ensure that the person with hearing loss understands. If student does not understand, restate the material in a different way. Perhaps the student was not familiar with the key words that you used, or some of them may have looked like other words.

(12) *Names of people and places*, especially new ones, are very difficult to understand. It is well to place new words or terms on the chalkboard and discuss new material from this vocabulary.

(13) *A buddy can explain things*. A buddy can be a great fallback, but there may be potential for too much dependence.

(14) *Try rephrasing* rather than repeating, but be sure a rephrase does not add confusion.

(15) *If the person with a hearing loss* is completely lost, say quietly "I'm talking about..." This often gives the student a fresh start. But be discreet!

(16) *If the student* seems to have trouble with certain words repeatedly, use these words often in as many ways as possible.

(17) *Find out* if the student has a good ear and speak to that side.

(18) *If your class* has group discussions or cooperative learning activities, a round table is better for a student who is deaf or hard of hearing than a rectangular one.

(19) *If you have a good relationship* with your student, you can tell the student when his or her voice is too loud or when it's getting on other students' nerves.

(20) *Encourage participation* in extra-curricular activities. Students who are deaf or hard of hearing are like any others. They take their lead from their teachers.

(21) *If a visit is being planned*, or a visitor is coming, prepare for it. Write new and unusual words on the chalkboard; help the student with hearing loss become familiar with the names of persons or objects the student will be seeing. Explain any special rules ahead of time when you can be sure that the student understands them. The brief discussion will help the student associate lip movements with new words and promote understanding of their meaning. By telling the student in advance what unit of activity will be studied, the student has an opportunity to find material on the subject and will be able to follow along much better because he or she will be more familiar with the vocabulary. Always, in history, science, and geography lessons where there will be new vocabulary or new concepts, try to give the student a brief written statement, e.g., "Today's topic is the Introduction of The War of 1812. Key words are Niagara Frontier, Sir Isaac Brock, York, James Madison", etc.

(22) *Students who are deaf tire more easily* than others do. You can help by planning the day's work so the periods when they must pay careful attention are interspersed with other activities.

(23) *Encourage the student* to keep trying. Please be patient. Repeat instructions as often as necessary.

(24) *If possible*, try to help the student learn to use a dictionary pronunciation key.

(25) *Many students hear better* on some days than others.

(26) *Talk with the students who are deaf or hard of hearing every day*. Talk often rather than for a long time. Ask questions about movies, TV programs, hobbies, travel, work, etc.

(27) *A regular hearing aid* makes speech louder, not always clearer. It often amplifies all other noise too. See if some of the other noise can be reduced.

(28) *If it has not already been investigated*, look into the possibility of using an FM system. This system can be more effective in a classroom than a hearing aid.

(29) *There is a lot of helpful computer software* and a computer doesn't get tired of repeating something. If the student controls the keyboard, then the number of repeats will be just what is needed. Not too many. Not too few. While you are at it, most computers with sound capacity will have earphones. Earphones are always better for people with a hearing loss. They concentrate the sound and block out all the background. Half the time it's the background that's the problem.

(30) Author's note: The following is verbatim (orally) from a very bright twelve-year old student with a severe hearing loss.

> "Our teaching assistant this year was the best help I ever had. And she wasn't a hearing specialist. Couldn't sign or nothing. But she was helpful. You don't always need a specialist. Just a good T.A."

Akamatsu, C. Tane, Stewart, David A. & Mayer Connie (2006). Is it time to look beyond teacher's signing behaviour? *Sign Language Studies 2,(3)*, 230-236.

Calderon, R., & Naidu, S. (2000). Further support for the benefits of early identification and intervention for children with hearing loss. *The Volta Review, 100(5)*, 53-84.

Feher-Prout, T. (1996). Stress and coping in families with deaf children. *Journal of Deaf Studies and Deaf Education. 1*, 155-166.

Gaty, J. C. (1992). Teaching speech to hearing impaired children. *The Volta Review, 94*, 49-61.

Greer, A. E., & Tobey, E. (1992). Effects of cochlear implants and tactile aids on the development of speech production skills in children with profound hearing impairment. *The Volta Review, 94*, 135-163.

Holt, J., & Marshall, W. (1994). *Classroom attributes and achievement scores for deaf and hard of hearing students*. Silver Speng MD: Registry of Interpreters of the Deaf.

Luetke-Stahlman, B., & Luckner, J. (1991). *Effectively educating students with hearing impairments*. New York: Longman.

Mayer, C., Akamatsu, C. T. (2000). Deaf children creating written texts: Contribution of American Sign Language and signed forms of English. *American Annals of the Deaf, 145*, 394-403.

Mayer, C., Akamatsu, C. T., & Stewart, D. (2002). A model for effective practice: Dialogic inquiry with students who are deaf. *Exceptional Children, 68*(4), 485-502.

MacDougall, James, C. (2004). Irreconcilable differences: The education of deaf children in Canada. *Education Canada 44*, Issue 1.

Mitchell, Ross E. & Karchmer, Michael A. (2006). Demographics of deaf education: More students in more places. *American Annals of the Deaf 151* (2) 95-113.

Lartz, L. Maribeth & Litchfield, Sharon K. (2006). Administrators' ratings of competencies needed to prepare preservice teachers for oral deaf education programs. *American Annals of the Deaf 150(5)*, 443-442.

Moores, D. F. (2001). *Educating the deaf: Psychology, principles, and practices (5th ed.)*. Boston: Houghton Mifflin.

Roberts, K. (1997). A preliminary account of the effects of otitis media on 15-month-olds' categorization and some implications for early language learning. *Journal of Speech, Language and Hearing Research, 40*, 508-518.

Salend, S. J., & Longo, M. (1994). The role of the educational interpreter in mainstreaming. *Teaching Exceptional Children, 26*, 22-28.

Schein, J. (1994). Deafness in Canada and the United States, *Deaf American Monographs*, 93-99.

Schirmer, B. R. (2000). *Language and literacy development in children who are deaf*. Boston: Allyn & Bacon.

Schildroth, A. N., & Hontto, S. A. (1994). Inclusion or exclusion? Deaf students and the inclusion movement. *American Annals of the Deaf, 139*, 239-243.

Schirmer, B. R., & Woolsey, M. L. (1997). Effect of teacher questions on the reading comprehension of deaf children. *Journal of Deaf Studies and Deaf Education, 2*, 47-56.

Links

FOR FURTHER INFORMATION CONTACT:
The Canadian Association of the Deaf
203–251 Bank Street, Ottawa Ontario
K2P 1X3
(613) 565-8882 TTY   (613) 565-2882 Voice
(613) 565-1207 Fax
www.cad.ca

Ontario Association of the Deaf
http://www.deafontario.ca

Canadian Hearing Society **www.chs.ca**

Hearing Foundation of Canada
http://www.thfc.ca

Goverment of British Columbia
http://www.bced.gov.bc.ca/specialed/ hearimpair/

CHAPTER 15

Students Who are Blind or Partially Sighted

"If there was only one thing about sighted people that I could change, it would be to make them think of me as just a normal person who can't see. So that when I do something normal, like find a CD and slip into the player and turn it on—stuff like that—nobody will say 'Isn't he something?' When we blind people do ordinary things, it's because we're ordinary people. It's not like we should be in a circus."

Corey P-N., age 29, blind from birth

Misconceptions About Blindness and Partial Sight

1. People who are blind have no sight at all.

Only a small percentage of people who are legally blind have absolutely no vision. The majority has a useful amount of functional vision.

2. People who are blind use Braille as their primary method of reading.

The majority use print—often large type—as a primary source of reading. An increasing trend among people who cannot see print is to use audio technology rather than Braille.

3. Individuals who are blind automatically develop better acuity in their other senses.

Through concentration and attention, persons who are blind often learn to make very fine discriminations in the sensations they obtain. This is not automatic but rather, represents a better use of received sensations.

4. Almost any person who is blind would benefit from the use of a guide dog.

While guide dogs can indeed provide much needed assistance, in actuality only a small percentage of persons who are blind use one.

Individuals who use guide dogs must be over 16 and demonstrate that they are able to care for the animal. Given the age restrictions, the use of such an animal would be rare in a school setting.

5. If students who are partially sighted use their eyes too much, their sight will deteriorate.

Only in rare conditions is this true; visual discrimination ability can actually improve through training and use. Strong lenses, holding books close to the eyes, and using the eyes usually does not harm vision.

6. Students who are blind automatically become good listeners.

Good listening is primarily a learned skill. Although many individuals who are blind develop good listening skills, it is the result of effort because they depend on these skills for so much of their information.

7. Instructing children in mobility techniques should wait until elementary or even secondary school age.

The adage of "earlier the better" applies to children who are blind as well as to their peers who are sighted. Even the use of a cane at an early age has been shown to have advantages.

Definitions of Blindness

Legal blindness in Canada is defined as distance acuity of 6/60 m or 20/200 ft or less in the better eye after the best available correction. That means the person must stand at six meters or less to see an object, which would normally be seen at sixty meters. Persons whose visual field is reduced to an angle of twenty degrees or less at its widest diameter are also legally blind. (People with normal sight have a visual field of 180 degrees.) A person who is partially sighted is one whose distance acuity is 6/13 or less in the better eye. It is important to recognize that someone with visual acuity of 6/60 can probably read, or at least see, print. Total blindness, i.e., inability to see anything at all, is actually uncommon.

Prevalence of Blindness

For educators, three important facts underline the matter of prevalence. The first of these is that blindness and visual impairments are both low-incidence conditions. Second, they are conditions that affect adults at significantly greater rates than children and teenagers. A third is that while the conditions do not appear with high frequency in North America, their prevalence in many Asian, African, and South American countries is much greater. Lack of sanitation, vitamin deficiency (particularly Vitamin A), poor sanitation and the high potential for water-borne illness raise the numbers in these countries.

> *Sighted people have all these ways of saying shut up without actually saying it—you know? Like—they turn away, or they stand up suddenly. Stuff like that.*
>
> *I never interpreted that as shut up even when I knew it was happening, until someone told me about it. I'm glad I was told though. Helps to know. That's one of the things about being blind. Everybody treats you with kid gloves. We don't need that. We've got to be told to shut up too just like everybody else.*
>
> Ginny de V. age 17

Classifications

Near normal vision: able to function without special training, but will use corrective lenses.

Moderate functional impairment: requires specialized aids and lighting.

Reduction in central vision: moderate field loss; may qualify for special services as legally blind.

Low vision: even after correction, vision is lower than normal, although correction is usually helpful.

Poor functional vision (and possible poor central vision with marked field loss): Standard correction is of little or no benefit. Usually strong reading aids and other technologies are needed.

Blind: total field loss as well as total detail loss; may distinguish between light and dark.

Vision can be further classified into congenital and adventitious categories. Students with *congenital vision loss* have been visually impaired since birth, while those with *adventitious loss* have acquired it later in life, most likely through illnes or injury.

Some Typical Causes of Blindness

Retinal detachment: The retina can become separated through injury or disease, making the eye incapable of receiving images.

Retinoblastoma: a genetic disease that presents with malignant tumors. Treatment usually involves chemotherapy and localized eye-saving measures. According to the Ontario Cancer Institute, the majority of eyes are saved. The Institute advises genetic counselling for the families involved.

Retinopathy of Prematurity (formerly known as Retrolental Fibroplasia): a condition occurring in babies who are exposed to a greater than normal concentration of oxygen post-natally.

Rubella: a syndrome occurring as a result of maternal rubella infection during the first months of pregnancy.

Sympathetic Ophthalmia: When there is a penetrating wound to one eye, the other eye may reflect the same characteristics as the injured eye.

Although the ultimate diagnosis of a student's visual problem—or even its existence—would naturally be determined by an optometrist or ophthalmologist, teachers and educational assistants can play an important role in early detection. While this is a more common occurrence in the very early grades, teachers of older students should not exclude themselves, since eye disease and poor vision can begin at any stage in life and grow serious rapidly. Any of the characteristics in the Classroom Checklist, especially if observed over time, might indicate real or potential visual impairment.

1. **Appearance of eyes**

   – One eye turns in or out at any time?

   – Reddened eyes or lids?

   – Encrusted eyelids?

   – Frequent sties on lids?

   – Eyes tear excessively?

2. **Complaints by student**

   – Headaches in forehead or temples?

   – Burning or itching of eyes after reading or deskwork?

   – Nausea or dizziness?

   – Print blurs or moves after reading a short time?

3. **Behavioural signs of visual problems**

   – Head turns while reading across the page?

   – Loses place often during reading?

   – Needs finger or marker to keep place?

   – Tilts head abnormally while working at desk?

   – Rereads or skips line unknowingly?

   – Too frequently omits or substitutes words?

   – Complains of seeing double (diplopia)?

   – Misaligns number columns regularly?

   – Squints, closes or covers one eye?

   – Orients a worksheet unusually?

   – Must feel things to understand?

   – Disorderly placement of words or drawings on page?

   – Blinks to clear view of chalkboard after near task?

   – Squints to see chalkboard?

   – Holds book too closely?

   – Avoids all possible near-centred tasks?

   – Closes or covers one eye when reading?

   – Rubs eyes a great deal?

Some Typical Causes of Partial Sight

Albinism: A genetically transmitted disease in which the eyes are light sensitive. Minimum illumination is needed, and tinted glasses are usually prescribed.

Astigmatism: This defect causes an error in refraction. Images are blurred and there is generally poor visual discrimination. Glasses are prescribed, usually with positive results. Good illumination usually helps too.

Cataracts: Any lens opacity is a cataract. Such opacity causes blank areas in what is seen. Depending upon the nature of the opacity, adjustments in lighting are usually necessary.

Colour deficiency (a.k.a., colour blindness): Unable to distinguish colours. More boys than girls are affected.

Glaucoma: a problem caused by increased intraocular pressure. Glaucoma patients require regular medical attention and sometimes suffer headaches. Quite often peripheral vision is poor. Good illumination is recommended.

Hyperopia: The hyperopic eye is far-sighted. A student with this condition usually functions well in gross motor activity, but finds reading and other near work difficult and tiring until correction is provided.

Macular degeneration: The centre of the field of

vision blurs causing most detail to be lost. Some limited peripheral vision usually remains. There are two common forms: "wet," which usually progresses rapidly, and "dry," which develops more slowly.

Monocular vision: Through disease, accident, or defect, a person is left with only one functioning eye.

Myopia: Distance vision is blurred so that gross activities can be difficult. A student with this condition is more comfortable with reading and other close work

Nystagmus: The involuntary movement of the eyeball caused by this problem makes focusing and fixation difficult.

Optic atrophy: The optic nerve sustains permanent loss of its ability to carry clear images to the brain. May result in restricted fields of vision.

Peripheral vision: This is the ability to see only those activities and objects outside of the direct line of vision. Because of defective central vision, the student may have to tilt the head or raise or lower the eyes in order to read.

Retinitis pigmentosa: Pigment deposits in the retina cause loss of peripheral fields resulting in tunnel vision. Major difficulties occur in dim light. Good illumination is needed.

Strabismus: An imbalance of the eye muscles causes failure of the two eyes to focus on the same object. The eyes can cross or deviate upward or downward. Early treatment is vital, or a "lazy eye" condition (amblyopia) can result.

Tunnel vision: The field of vision is so reduced that a child sees only what is directly in front. It creates the same visual image that others see when looking through a tube, severely affecting mobility and the collection of information from the environment.

Some Issues in the Field

✦ A most significant issue for individuals who are blind and partially sighted is successful adjustment to the world at large. This adjustment calls for mobility and a sensitivity to the environment that is natural in persons with sight but not so in those whose vision is limited. Much of a person who is

---

Working with the Resource Teacher for the Visually Impaired ✍

Many students who are blind or visually impaired spend a majority of their day, if not all of it, in a regular class with peers. While many of their learning opportunities need not take a great deal of adjustment, there are certainly specialized interventions and techniques that may be necessary. Because the percentage of students with blindness and visual impairments within a given population can be very low, it is not always a reasonable expectation that all classroom teachers will have the specialized knowledge needed to be as effective as possible. Because of this, it is not uncommon for boards of education to have what would be referred to as itinerant teachers or resource persons for the following types of things.

· Explanation of the student's impairment to educators at the school level

· Assessment of the student's residual vision

· Provision, training (teacher and student), and integration of specialized equipment

· Strategies for instruction

· Provision of Braille

· Socialization and adaptation strategies (student, teacher, and sometimes classmates)

· Orientation and mobility information

· Available resource support materials and organizations

---

blind or partially sighted's energy, life force, education, and time are devoted to this matter, especially when they are young. At the same time, because they are normal human beings in every other respect, persons who are blind naturally wish to live the lives that the rest of the world does. A great deal of the initial social exchange between people who are visually disabled and the people with sight in their lives is devoted to finding a mutually comfortable, appropriate, and effective means of associating.

✦ The failure of individuals and families to have regular eyesight examinations continues

At age three, Lori seemed to bump into things and fall over her playmates far more frequently than seemed normal for her age. Both parents suspected a vision problem. That suspicion was reinforced two years later by a very observant kindergarten teacher and an equally perceptive educational assistant. After the first week of school, both instructors began to keep an "Events Journal" on Lori, noting specifically those behaviours that suggested Lori had impaired vision. Within ten days they were both convinced that their young student was using peripheral vision to accomplish what other students did by focusing face on. A conference with Lori's parents led to a visit with an ophthalmologist and then, confirmation of what the two suspected: that Lori had macular degeneration.

The quick and careful thinking by Lori's kindergarten teacher and educational assistant made a huge difference in her life. Macular degeneration usually means that the individual has blurred or completely obscured centre-of-field vision, while retaining some vision at the edges of the field. Very often it is progressive and intensifies over time. The early intervention in Lori's case meant that she was able to receive special training at a crucial time in her development. Lori's average to above-average ability, and what every adult in her life calls "high-profile spunk," along with this training, meant that she was able to progress quite smoothly through the next years of her school career. She was in a regular class in her neighbourhood school for this time.

Now, in the seventh grade, a problem has arisen. Lori's condition has worsened over time so that essentially, she has lost all of her vision. For several years now, she has been identified as legally blind for funding purposes. None of this has denied her full participation in all class activities, something she and her parents insist on, even though her mishaps have increased in number and seriousness—most recently a broken arm in gym. Other difficulties have arisen as well. Lori is in the school band, but she does not have a natural ear, cannot see the notes, and plays her trombone badly—and loudly. The dropout rate from the band has now reached a crisis level. Because of an incident during a natural science field trip last year (Lori fell over an embankment and pulled two other students down with her; no one was hurt) this year's cross-country skiing trip (an overnighter) can't attract enough volunteer parent supervisors and may be cancelled.

A meeting of Lori's teachers, assistants and parents has been called for next week by school officials. The agenda specifically sets aside the legal issues involved. What the administration wishes to discuss is what is best for Lori and her schoolmates in terms of their education and social development. What should her program be?

to be a nagging concern of health care professionals and educators. Infants as young as three months can now be tested with considerable accuracy. Optometrists urge that all children be examined by three years of age and again at school entrance. This is because many vision problems are more correctable if a response is made early. It is also important to begin teaching visual efficiency early, if visual acuity is poor or weakening. Testing is especially important if there is a familial pattern of such problems as strabismus, cataracts, etc. Despite the logical and impassioned arguments of both educators and health professionals, the response of families and even educational jurisdictions is, surprisingly, less intense than one might expect, given the ease and limited expense with which these examinations can be conducted.

✦ In an-ever increasing technological world it is not unexpected that technological innovations would find a place in the area of disabilities. Computerized programs that automatically scan and enlarge print for students with limited vision, voice-activated cell phones, personal data assistants, and even GPS tracking devices to assist in mobility are only some of the options available for persons with vision difficulties. While technology holds out great promise, it is not without its limitations. Braille users point out that the ability to scan for information, read a speech, and taking notes are far more easily done using Braille than any type of recorded information. Mobility devices that use a method similar to echo location are only in their preliminary stages and should not be used in place of the long cane. There are also concerns about access and affordability of this technology for all persons who are blind. Certainly, technology should not be seen as a panacea, but rather as yet another set of options for persons who are blind to use judiciously and where maximum gain can be achieved.

Some Educational Implications of Teaching Students with Special Visual Needs

❖ Empirical evidence suggests that in the classroom, especially among younger students, cognitive abilities in those who are blind and partially sighted tend to develop more slowly than the norm. There is a good deal of support for the view, however, that this apparent lag is owing more to differentiated early learning experiences rather than to any inherent intellectual difference. Children who are blind simply have not had the opportunity to experience some of the things that children with sight have.

❖ It is difficult for students with serious vision problems to develop a spatial map of their environment. However, it is possible to develop the concept of space with other senses, such as noting the time it takes to walk various distances, or feeling the dimensions between objects. Because the amount of information that can be taken in at one time is limited, the process is understandably slower. This fact makes the time to acquire learning an important factor—as it is with almost all students with exceptionalities.

❖ For students who cannot see, or who see poorly, it is often difficult to understand abstract concepts without the aid of concrete materials. Such students will benefit from three-dimensional models, manipulative games and materials.

❖ Students who are blind and partially sighted are often overprotected by the adults in their lives and treated over-delicately by fellow students. Although this is not an unnatural response, it is important that independence be a prominent and continuing objective in the education of students with vision problems. Fostering this independence calls for frequent and delicate judgments by the teacher and educational assistant.

❖ Students who are blind must be taught social and communicative skills that many persons with sight acquire naturally. Most cultures, for example, attach great importance to whether or not a speaker looks at his or her listener, and many advocates for the blind urge that this habit be taught. However, some so-called natural skills are much more difficult to teach. For example, people with sight make constant use, subconsciously, of body language, important markers that indicate responses like reinforcement, enthusiasm, reluctance, disagreement, uneasiness, etc. Body language can alert a speaker to modify a particular communication and sometimes even indicates whether or not a communication is finished—or should be! For obvious reasons, the very notion of body language, and the means of dealing with it is something that students who are blind and partially sighted cannot be expected to acquire naturally.

❖ The less a person is able to know the world through sight, the more important it becomes that he or she be a good listener. Although it was once assumed that good listening skills automatically develop as a consequence of sight deprivation, it is now known that such skills must be taught.

❖ Professionals dealing with the very young must be particularly conscious of the fact that many children are not aware of a visual problem if they have one. Or if they are aware, they often do not understand its extent or its implications. This is important for classroom professionals, not just in discovering the presence of the problem, but in helping the child to deal with it.

❖ Academic success is more closely related to social, cultural, and familial factors than to degree of visual impairment.

Visual Stimulation

As recently as the 1960s, students with low vision were encouraged to "save" their visual capacity, to keep it from "wearing out." Today, the belief is that the more one's residual vision is used the stronger and fitter it may become. Thus, educators now encourage students with low vision to attend to light and objects, to use tracing and scanning techniques, and to exercise their residual vision in a variety of ways (e.g., a popular technique with younger and even older children is to sort, classify, sequence, and creatively rearrange pictures). With students who have low vision, many of the technical devices mentioned in this chapter can be very useful, but the students must be trained to use them.

Assistive Technology

Braille

This well-known writing system is named for Louis Braille, but it originated in the hands of Charles Barbier, an officer in the army of Napoleon Bonaparte. Barbier devised a system of raised dot writing that could be read by touch in the dark. Braille published his modified system in 1834. Within twenty years this system was adopted by the Paris School for the Blind, but it took another half century for Braille to penetrate North America. By the mid-1950s, more than half of all persons who were blind and seriously visually impaired were Braille users. But by the end of the century, the number had dropped to below ten percent. More recently, there has been resurgence in the use of Braille, partly in recognition of its usefulness as a means of communication.

Braille is a tactile communication method. Cells of from one to six raised dots on paper represent the letters of the alphabet (and numbers). Although it is a direct transliteration of English (or other language), Braille regularly resorts to contractions to save time and space. For example, in English Braille, the letter "r" by itself means "rather." Although it has been established that Braille is easier to read than raised letters of the alphabet, it is still a much slower process than reading print is for the average reader with sight.

Students can begin learning Braille in the first grade or earlier, and have a number of technologies available to them, beginning with Braille books. A brailler is a six key device not unlike a typewriter. (Integrated classrooms where a brailler is used must become accustomed to its noise.) There is also the *Optacon,** which converts print into Braille electronically. Students need intensive Braille instruction over a number of years in order to become fluent in its use.

Computer-Assisted Technology

Computer technology continues to develop at a rate that almost outpaces the capacity of special education to use it effectively. Some examples are the Versabraille II+*, a laptop computer that combines brailler and word processor technology, the Kurzweil Reading Machine,* which converts print to audio output, the DragonDictate,* a speech-activated word processor, and the Braille Blazer,* which prints Braille at 10-15 characters per second.

Optical Aids

Students who are blind and partially sighted and their teachers are assisted by still other devices, which, although they may appear simple in comparison to computer technology, are remarkable examples of technical common sense. These include items like large print materials, embossed rulers and tape measures, Braille watches, three-dimensional maps, hand-held and stand mounted magnifiers, special lighting, etc.

Mobility Assists

The long cane is one of the most effective and simplest devices yet devised for safe, efficient mobility. It's important to note that although the use of one seems simple to people who can see, learning to use a cane effectively requires some training and practice. Guide dogs are reported by those who can use them as extremely helpful in alerting

* * *
* Brand names are used in these descriptions. Further information about these devices and competing brands are available from provincial ministries and from the Canadian National Institute for the Blind. Also, web search engines regularly list both updated and new technologies.
* * *

them to changes in the immediate environment, to potential dangers, and in guiding them through complex situations. Electronic devices like laser canes and sonic guides (worn on the head) are still experimental and very expensive.

Educational Placement

Increasingly, and with marked success, students who are blind and partially sighted are being educated in the regular classroom. Special assistance may be delivered by an itinerant specialist teacher who provides advice on strategy, materials, and, possibly, on curricular modification. Such modification may be intense instruction on how to listen, how to make "mental mobility maps," etc. The assistance may also take the form of one of the educational aids listed above, or it may be a combination of aid from several sources. As they have in all other areas of special education, educational assistants in the classroom have proven to be invaluable for students who are blind and partially sighted.

For some students, a resource room may play a central role in their educational setting. The utilization of this type of setting may offer a more certain guarantee of the specialized instruction the students may need, while still permitting a high degree of integration.

A more specialized placement, used particularly for students whose vision problems are quite seriously disabling, is an entirely self-contained classroom, or even a residential school devoted to students who are blind (and students who are blind with other special needs as well). In these environments, where there are usually very low student-teacher ratios, students receive regular school curriculum adapted to their needs, along with very specialized instruction related to their blindness. While these types of placements can provide certain types of specialized instruction, considerations such as the lack of a diverse social environment and, in the case of residential placements, separation from family, are very real concerns. In recent years, these types of settings have been decreasing in number.

✔ STRATEGIES FOR THE CLASSROOM

(1) *It is usually very beneficial* for a teacher of a regular class with a student who is blind or partially sighted to establish the practice of holding regular, informal, and private discussions with that student to work out special means of communication.*

(2) *It may be necessary for a teacher* to set up the classroom with the expectation that physical arrangements will not be altered, at least for a significant period of time. While this may contradict the style a teacher likes to follow, it may be a necessity for simple reasons of safety.

(3) *At the same time*, there is the student's normal need to be physically mobile, to explore, to

• • • ───────

* A quite loquacious blind student in one of my classes did not sense that her extensive contributions to class discussions often wore out her classmates' receptivity. We worked out a simple and very subtle pencil tap so that she would know when to quit.

─────── • • •

expand his or her capacity, as well as the need to perceive the self as both part of and separate from the environment. A great deal of professional skill is demanded of teachers and educational assistants in marrying this need with the obvious requirements of safety and efficient function described above. The key phrase is responsible independence.

(4) *Common sense.* A student with partial sight, for example, should always be permitted to sit near the chalkboard, to borrow or photocopy notes. (Yet the exceptionality need not be emphasized. If other students are blindfolded in an activity, the student who is blind should be too.) An overhead transparency can be photocopied for someone who cannot see the screen. Students who are partially sighted almost always respond to better lighting. Additional time may be necessary for tests or a variety of other activities. Doors should always be fully open or fully closed. Name students being addressed; if an instruction is given to another child, a child who is blind may automatically follow it with perhaps disastrous results. By the same token, be explicit in giving instructions, particularly those involving movement from one place to another. A student who is blind cannot be expected to compensate for obstacles. If told to "come here," he or she may well come in a straight line regardless of hazards, because of his or her trust in the teacher.

(5) *Teachers, assistants*, and fellow students with sight often have to make allowances for communication style. Students who are blind and partially blind usually do not reinforce others' understanding with eye contact or facial expression—a phenomenon that takes some getting used to. In the same vein, the students often place great interpretive value on the expression and tone of their teacher's voice. This can be very important in some situations. Also, if an individual who is blind responds to a communication with total silence, it may be because he or she is taking in and interpreting available cues. This, too, requires adjustment from the teacher.

(6) *"Blindisms"* are characteristic mannerisms such as rocking, head shaking, hand shaking, and eye poking. Most advocates suggest that teacher and educational assistants adroitly discourage these behaviours, for they may isolate the student as irremediably different in a way that goes beyond merely being blind

(7) *Many people who are blind* have grown to associate physical contact with being guided. Gestures such as patting and hugging may have negative connotations for some students, or may be misinterpreted. When an individual who is blind is being guided, let him or her be the one who maintains and controls the physical contact. Don't grab the person's arm and steer; let the person hold your arm.

(8) *When individuals who are blind* are lost or disoriented, they may need to be repositioned in order to work out direction. If a person with sight has occasion to help in this situation, it is important to make the person who is blind understand where he or she is first. Once the student is oriented as best as possible, then explanation about direction can follow. A subset of this issue is the matter of snow-covered surfaces. People who are blind often describe snow as their fog because the snow covers the surface references they use to orient their position. It follows, then, that they will often need more assistance in winter.

(9) *A tactful classroom buddy* or advocate is always helpful, but this arrangement should never be an unnaturally long-term arrangement.

(10) *Perhaps the single most* important role a teacher plays is being the classroom leader in developing a positive attitude. Students with sight will take their cue from their teacher in determining how to react to and inter-relate with a student who is blind in their midst. An accepting atmosphere for this student, with realistic expectations, will build the student's self-esteem, sense of success, and willingness to deal with the world. It will also contribute in a major way to the maturing of all students in the class.

Bishop, V. E. (1996). *Teaching visually impaired children*. (2nd ed.). Springfield, IL: Charles C. Thomas.

Canadian National Institute for the Blind (CNIB). (1993). *History of the CNIB.*

Chein-Huey Chang, S. & Shaler J. (2002). The views of students with visual impairments on the support they received from teachers. *Journal of Visual Impairment and Blindness,* August 2002.

Davis P. & Hopwood, V. (2002). Including children with visual impairment in the mainstream primary school classroom. *Journal of Research in Special Education Needs*, 2(3).

Donley, P. R. (2002). A touch of Class: Teaching Languages of the blind and visually impaired: Some suggestions. *The Canadian Modern Language Review*, 59 (2).

Erin, J. (1996). Children with multiple and visual disabilities. In *Children with visual impairments: A parent's guide* (pp. 287-316). Bethesda, MD: Woodbine House.

George, A. L. & Duquette, C. (2006). The psychosocial experiences of a student with low vision. *Journal of Visual Impairment and Blindness.* March 2006.

Hallahan, D. P. & Kauffman, J. M. (2006). *Exceptional Learners: An introduction to special education.* Boston: Pearson Education Inc.

Hill, E. W., & Snook-Hill, M. (1996). Orientation and Mobility. In M. C. Holdbrook (Ed.). *Children with visual impairments: A parents guide* (pp. 259-286). Bethesda, MD: Woodbine House.

Kirchner, C., & Diament, S. (1999). Estimates of the number of visually impaired students, their teachers, and orientation and mobility specialists. *Journal of Visual Impairment and Blindness*, 93(9), 600-606.

Minor, R. J. (2001). The experience of living with and using a guide dog. *RE:view*, 32, 183-190.

Sacks, S. Z., & Wolffe, K. E. (1998). Lifestyles of adolescents with visual impairments: An ethnographic analysis. *Journal of Visual Impairment and Blindness*, 92(1), 7-17.

Tuttle, D. W., & Tuttle, T. N. (1996). *Self esteem and adjusting with blindness: The process of responding to life's demands.* (2nd ed.). Springfield, IL: Charles C. Thomas.

Uslan, M. M. (1992). Barriers to acquiring assistive technology. Cost and lack of information. *Journal of Visual Impairment and Blindness*, 86(9), 465-478.

Links

Canadian National Institute for the Blind
http://www.cnib.ca/

American Foundation for the Blind
http://www.afb.org/

World Health Organization
http://www.who.int/health_topics/ blindness/en/

CHAPTER 16

Students with Speech and Language Disorders

"Try this. Just for a day, or even an hour. Stop in the middle of each sentence. But leave your mouth open and make it clear you're trying to talk but can't. Then watch how people look at you. Like you've got two heads. Now think of living your life like that."

Ronnie K., diagnosed with aphasia at age 11

Misconceptions About Speech and Language Disorders

1. Speech and language disorders are synonymous.

While they can often be found together, it is indeed possible for a person to have no difficulty with articulation but still be able to speak in a way that is incomprehensible.

2. Stuttering affects all ages and both genders equally.

Stuttering affects more boys than girls and more children than adults. The child over adult ratio is usually ascribed to the fact that by adulthood, many people with a stutter have been helped by speech and language specialists.

3. Speech and language disorders are not related to intelligence.

Prevalence data show that although the disorders may occur among very intelligent individuals, they are found more frequently among persons with lower intellectual ability.

4. Articulation disorders in very young children especially, are not serious, and correction is rarely worth the effort or the risk of trauma.

Many small children have unique speech patterns but articulation disorders should never be dismissed as insignificant. "He'll grow out of it" is often an inappropriate substitute for remedial action.

5. If an individual has a speech or language disorder, that individual also has a learning disability.

The connection is not an absolute one, although difficulties with language affect both areas. Speech and language disorders also overlap other areas of special need, such as deafness. Some estimates say up to 50 percent of students in special education receive speech and language intervention.

Defining Speech and Language Disorders

For most children, the process of acquiring language, though seemingly complex, follows a relatively straightforward path. From birth, children are exposed to a language-rich environment. Parents and caregivers are responsive, motivating teachers who provide ongoing opportunities for infants and toddlers to develop the necessary language skills to build a solid foundation for future language use. As a result of this early and continuous interaction, for a majority of children language develops naturally. The successful acquisition of language can have a dramatic effect on a child's ability to understand and function in both the social and academic world. Communication, the exchange of ideas, can take many forms: a word, an expression, a movement of the body. When a child lacks the ability to engage effectively in this interactive exchange of information, the child's learning capacity is compromised and socialization potentially limited. Without such learning and socializing opportunities, the acquisition of language becomes more difficult and the opportunities to improve more limited. Because of this, it is essential that students with speech and language difficulties receive some type of structured intervention to assist them in the development of effective communication skills.

An Important Distinction

The distinction between a speech disorder and a language disorder is an important one. *Speech disorders* are characterized by impairments of voice, articulation of sounds, or fluency. In essence, a student who has difficulty with the oral production of language is considered to have a speech disorder. *Language disorders*, on the other hand, encompass both receptive and expressive language and, therefore, may result in a problem receiving information and/or formulating an acceptable and adequate response.

Types of Speech Disorders

Speech disorders, while more common in particular types of populations such as individuals with lower intellectual ability, are not exclusive to those populations and can be found across a wide range of students. Diagnosis and treatment are generally

---

Clues to a Speech or Language Disorder

◆ Does the student follow simple directions?

◆ Does the student understand the meanings of words that others understand?

◆ Does the student have a limited vocabulary compared with age peers?

◆ Does the student understand longer, more complex sentences?

◆ Does the student follow the general rules of grammar?

◆ Does the student have more than normal difficulty finding the correct word?

Articulation Expectations

By age eight, most children have a repertoire of the sounds that they will use for adult speech, and most acquire these sounds in a similar sequence. In a normal population distribution, for example, 9 out of 10 will master these sounds:

By the end of age 3	/m/, /n/, /ng/, /p/, /f/, /h/, /w/
By the end of age 3½	/y/
By the end of age 4	/b/, /d/, /gl, /k/, /r/
By the end of age 4½	/s/, /sh/, /ch/
By the end of age 6	/t/, /l/, /v/, /th (as in then)
By the end of age 7	/z/, /zh/ (treasure) /j/, /th/ (three)

An average three-year-old will say 50 percent of the sounds in English correctly and will be 90 percent intelligible.

---

the province of professionals in the field, in particular speech and language pathologists, although it can often be a teacher or educational assistant who first notices that something may be amiss. Students with speech disorders have difficulty with the production of sound. This can be a result of a number of factors such as inability to manipulate the tongue, lips and jaw, breath irregularities, and damage to the vocal chords. Speech disorders are generally divided into three distinct yet related categories: *articulation*, *voice*, and *fluency*.

Articulation disorders

By far the most common type of speech disorder, articulation disorders are characterized by atypical production of speech sounds in a language. These vary from omissions (e.g., "numer" for number) to substitutions (e.g., "tack" for back), additions (e.g., "sawl" for saw), and distortions (e.g., "thleep" for sleep). For obvious reasons, an articulation anomaly must be a regular and typical element in the student's speech before it is regarded as a disorder.

Voice disorders

Everyone's voice is unique. Individuals may have a quiet or loud voice, one with a nasal quality, or one with variations in pitch. All of these variations of speech can be considered normal. When the variations become so pronounced they cause the speaker difficulty in communicating successfully, they are considered voice disorders. Voice disorders are characterized by atypical production of vocal quality, pitch (high/low), loudness, and resonance, (e.g., a harsh or whispery vocal quality).

Fluency disorder

When a person's flow of speech is unusually irregular, marked by stoppages, repetitions, unusual pauses, and atypical rhythms, a fluency disorder may be present. Stuttering is the most common type of fluency disorder and is characterized by the repetition of a particular syllable or sound of a word, or by the inability to express a word or sound for a noticeably long time. Children who stutter will generally outgrow the disorder but should it persist for more than two years these children run a higher risk for chronic stuttering.

Types of Language Disorders

Language disorders are characterized by difficulty in the use and understanding of language. As with disorders of speech, they are found across a wide spectrum of the population. Students with language disorders can be at risk in the development of literacy. In the very early stages of infancy, children begin to acquire language skills. Small infants respond to voice by turning their heads and smiling. At two to three months, they start to coo, and by the age of four have approximately 1000 to 1500 words. By the time a child starts grade 1, more complex parts of language, such as the use of irregular verbs, are being mastered. Not all children reach these milestones at these times for a variety of reasons. They may have difficulty hearing; some do not have the intellectual ability; others are not sufficiently exposed to language.

Some children may experience difficulty with expressive language (the formulation of understandable speech), as in the use of incorrect tenses: "I go to the store yesterday." Others may have difficulty with receptive language (the ability to comprehend spoken, written, or other symbol systems). A set of directions, for example,

"Get your red jacket from the closet and make sure to put on your scarf and mittens," may overwhelm. In the latter situation, it is not hard to understand why the complication intensifies in a school setting where a student may be told to: "Discuss the impact of urban society as a root cause for the Civil War." Most often individuals with language disorders have some combination of both expressive and receptive difficulties.

Some Common Language Problems

Language is comprised of a variety of components including morphology, phonology, syntax, semantics, and pragmatics. These components, when impaired or not developed in any way, result in language disorders. Someone having a problem with the morphology of language, for example, may have difficulty understanding and using sections of words that have meaning. (The dog bark when the car went by.) With problems in phonology (combining sounds to form words and manipulating sound sequences to form coherent speech) the person may say "bwush" instead of brush. Syntax, the rules that govern the combining of words to form coherent sentences can be a challenge (What he is doing?), while problems with the semantics of a language (combining words and sentences to convey meaning) often mean the individual just doesn't "get it," particularly if an expression is idiomatic or metaphorical. The baseball metaphor, for example, "I'll go to bat for him," in reference to

---

Selective Mutism ✍

Selective mutism is not generally considered a communication disorder. Rather, it is categorized under psychiatric disorders. Formerly known as *elective mutism*, it is characterized by a child's inability to speak in certain social settings. The student may speak with family and/or select individuals at school, but, due most likely to intense anxiety, is unable to speak in a variety of social settings. Students with selective mutism may communicate through facial expression, gestures, and other types of body language, and despite their inability to speak in certain settings are otherwise developmentally normal.

defending a person, may well be interpreted literally as an actual baseball game situation. Problems with pragmatics, using language socially to greet others, to request needs or information, to protest, pretend, and respond mean that an individual may be unresponsive to normal social interchange.

Central Auditory Processing Disorders

Some students seem not to be listening although their hearing may be perfectly intact. More and more professionals in the speech and language field believe this apparent lack of listening is owing to a "central auditory processing" (CAP) disorder, which is characterized by an inability to recognize as meaningful acoustic signals sent to auditory areas of the brain. Normally, people use both ears to fuse information, and to "tune out" auditory distractions (selective attention). People who demonstrate CAP difficulties may lose messages, mix them up, or fail to integrate the information coming in via both ears. Students with CAP disorders generally exhibit the following types of behaviours. (However, it should be noted that these behaviours might also be associated with many students who have other types of difficulties, likely a reason why the notion of central auditory processing disorder has not yet been fully accepted across the broad area of special education.)

- Inconsistent response to oral speech
- Better response to oral speech in quiet environments than in noisy environments
- Poor response to speech in environments that distort speech, such as a gym
- Better response to speech when the speaker is close
- Frequent communication checks such as "what?" or "huh?"

Getting Help

Most students with speech and language diffi-

The Case of Brent

Brent, in senior kindergarten, is the eldest of five children. For the first two months of school, his only form of communication was a slight nodding of the head. Brent seemed unwilling to follow class routines, did not socialize with other children, and refused to comply with direct requests by the teacher. While Brent eventually did begin to speak, his utterances were mumbled and scant. At times, it seemed as though his answers were designed to cause difficulty or mock the teacher.

Following kindergarten, Brent was placed in a self-contained class that emphasized behaviour modification. In the new setting his disruptive and non-compliant behaviour persisted. Brent's special class teacher suggested to the in-school team that he be assessed by the board's speech and language pathologist, a request supported by the principal and Brent's parents. Test results showed that, in both expressive and receptive language, Brent was functioning at the age level of a two and a half-year-old, results with profound implications.

The IPRC review is to be held next week to discuss Brent's situation. Neither the teacher nor educational assistant in the behaviour class has any special training in areas of speech and language, but both are willing to undertake any program to help Brent, as long as they are given professional advice and supervision. The school board has one full-time speech and language specialist with a very busy schedule. She visits the school twice weekly where she works with two children in a regular grade 1 class. If Brent were placed here, she would include him in her twice-weekly sessions. The grade 1 class, though, is a very busy and somewhat noisy setting, in a pod-style room with three other primary classes. The specialist feels that given the intensity of Brent's language needs, this may not be as helpful a setting as the behaviour class where things are much quieter and more controlled. The principal is now seeking opinions from the in-school team.

Students Who Rely on Augmentative and Alternative Communication

We communicate for many reasons each day, such as greeting people, commenting, sharing information, telling stories, making requests, directing others, asking and answering questions, agreeing or protesting, expressing emotions, sharing humour, and for other reasons. Communication enables teachers and students to engage effectively in their roles as facilitators and learners of the curriculum.

Everyone communicates using a combination of many methods. These may include body language, facial expressions, gestures, sounds, spoken words, pointing to objects and people, and writing. Other ways to communicate include sign language, pointing to pictures/photographs/words, and operating speech-generating devices.

For some students with impairment in the production of oral language, speech alone is insufficient to convey what they would like to communicate. These students often rely on *Augmentative and Alternative Communication (AAC)*. AAC refers to using one or more communication methods to supplement speech (*Augmentative Communication*) or replace speech (*Alternative Communication*). Students who rely on AAC utilize various combinations of communication reasons and methods, depending on their unique profile of speech, receptive and expressive language, cognition, and physical capabilities and challenges. The goal of AAC is to close the gap between receptive and expressive language.

In Ontario, individuals who need an AAC assessment can be referred to a multidisciplinary team at a designated Augmentative Communication Services Clinic, Ministry of Health and Long Term Care. An AAC team may include speech-language pathologists, occupational therapists, communication disorder assistants, technologists, and educators. AAC teams work with individuals, their families, educators, and other professionals to develop AAC skills. If equipment is required, funding is available through the Ministry of Health and Long Term Care. AAC teams provide ongoing consultation and/or training to further develop AAC skills, provide training and support for communication partners, and provide consultation regarding curriculum adaptations and inclusion.

Inclusion and programming for a student who relies on AAC will require an exploration of resources including past IEPs, school board therapy reports, and reports from external services such as Augmentative Communication Services. Discussions with the student, his or her family, past educators, therapists, and other involved professionals provide invaluable information for the classroom teacher. Observation of the student communicating using the reasons and methods identified within reports and discussions is also important. By understanding a student's communication reasons and methods, the teacher can incorporate purposeful communication throughout the school day. Strategies to support AAC in the classroom vary according to the needs of each student but typically include modelling, encouraging, and providing opportunities for a variety of communication reasons and methods, giving students enough time to communicate, and responding naturally.

The development of an AAC system is a lifelong process as individuals are constantly learning to communicate more effectively. Teachers have an important role in facilitating this development. Collaboration will help to ensure the student's communication continues to develop as an essential part of his or her life.

This submission was created by: Mary Harrison, OT, Debbie Hayne, AAC Resource Teacher, and Rebecca Shultis, SLP, of the Communication Assessment and Support Team (CAST), Niagara Peninsula Children's Centre.

culties are in regular classroom settings. To assist them and their teachers, many school boards either employ or retain the services of speech and language specialists. The availability of these professionals to provide direct intervention on an ongoing basis varies from board to board. Often, there are just too many students requiring support. Thus, a special education teacher or classroom teacher or educational assistant, under specific direction from a speech and language specialist, may be enlisted to work directly with students. Intervention may involve working on a particular sound, or playing a word game to develop expressive language skills, or other relatively straightforward activities. Where more extensive assistance is required but is unavailable at the school board level, a speech and language specialist may refer cases to support services outside the jurisdiction of the board. Some parents may also choose to get support privately.

Vital Roles for the Teacher and Educational Assistant

Very often, in fact in most cases, a specialist in speech and language will determine and manage the needs of the student. The more severe the case, the more likely the teacher and educational assistant will be part of a team, collaborating to develop programming ideas. However, since nothing in practice is as straightforward as it appears in theory, it will still be incumbent upon regular classroom personnel to provide leadership in several ways. These would include providing extended opportunities for the student to talk, making the classroom an enjoyable place for the student to work on his or her speech and language, and modeling an appropriate response to abnormal language for peers to follow. In short, the teacher's role with speech and language disorders is similar to that which the teacher fills with all students: to be a compassionate professional who takes responsibility for developing the whole individual. An essential difference in the speech and language area lies in the tradition that considerable expert help is usually available.

Strategies for the Classroom

For Listening

- Allow for students to ask for clarification and be willing to repeat instructions.
- Avoid long periods of instruction where listening only is required.
- Gain attention before speaking (eye contact, tap on the shoulder).
- Be aware of your delivery style. Decrease rate of speech; use repetition, simple explanations, and short sentences.
- Use many types of expression other than oral.
- Limit figurative language.
- Check for comprehension by asking the student to repeat what has been said.
- Paraphrase your own ideas after speaking to ensure comprehension.
- Be conscious of noise levels and, where possible, improve classroom acoustics.
- Offer preferential seating, away from pencil sharpeners, open windows, doorways.
- Use visual support to supplement information.

For speech

- Restate a student's phrases in a more grammatically correct way.
- Structure the physical environment to increase opportunities for interaction.
- Be sensitive to the student's current level of language.
- Provide opportunities for interactive games and activities.
- Create situations that promote the use of oral language, e.g., limit supplies for an activity in order to prompt the student to ask for them "Can I get the paint now?"
- Avoid placing undo pressure on a student to use language.
- Reinforce the correct use of language.
- Introduce new words in a variety of contexts and use repetition.
- Be careful of overcorrecting the student's language; doing so may discourage the student from speaking.
- Encourage discussion about things that the student is interested in.

Asher, S., & Gazelle, H. (1999). Loneliness, peer relations, and language disorders in childhood. *Topics in Language Disorders, 19*(2), 16-33.

Battle, D. (1998). *Communication disorders in multicultural populations* (2nd ed.). Boston, MA: Butterworth-Heinemann.

Bauman Waengler, J. (2000). *Articulator and phonological impairments: A clinical focus.* Boston: Allyn & Bacon.

Berstein, D. K., & Bankson, N. W. (1997). *Language and communication disorders in children* (4th ed.). Boston: Allyn & Bacon.

Bobrick, B. (1995). *Knotted tongues: Stuttering in history and the quest for a cure.* New York: Simon & Schuster.

Butler, K. G. (Ed.). (1999). Children's language, behaviour, and emotional problems. (Special issue). *Topics in Language Disorders, 19*(2).

Calandrella, A. M., & Wilcox, M. J. (2000). Predicting language outcomes for young prelinguistic children with developmental delay. *Journal of Speech, Language and Hearing Research, 43,* 1061-1071.

Filla, A., Wolery, W., & Anthony, L. (1999). Promoting children's conversations during play with adult prompts. *Journal of Early Intervention, 22*(3), 93-108.

Hatnes, W. O., Moran, M. J., & Pindzola, R. H. (1994). *Communication disorders in the classroom* (2nd ed.). Dubuque IA: Kendall/Hunt.

Hedge, M. L., & Kaiser, A. P. (1994). *Introduction to communicative disorders.* Austin, TX: Pro-Ed.

Hulit, L. M. & Howard, M. R. (1993). *Born to talk.* New York: Macmillan.

La Blance, G. R. Steckol, K. F., & Smith, V. L. (1994). Stuttering: The role of the classroom teacher. *Teaching Exceptional Children, 26*(2), 10-12.

Morrison, J. & Shriberg, L. (1992). Articulation testing versus conversational speech sampling. *Journal of Speech and Hearing Research, 35*(2), 259-273.

Ownes, R. (1996). *Language development: An introduction* (4th ed.). Boston: Allyn & Bacon.

Palmer, J. M. & Yantis, P. A. (1990). *Survey of communication disorders.* Baltimore: Williams & Wilkins.

Schraeder, T., Quinn, M., Stockman, I., & Miller, J. (1999). Authentic assessment as an approach to preschool speech-language screening. *American Journal of Speech-Language Pathology, 8*(3), 195-200.

Shames, G., Wiig, E., & Secord, W. (1993). *Human communication disorders* (4th ed.). New York: Macmillan.

Stark, R. E., Bernstein, L. E. & Demorest, M. E. (1993). Vocal communication in the first 18 months of life. *Journal of Speech and Hearing Research, 36,* 548-558.

Wang, P. P., & Baron, M. A. (1997). Language and communication: Development and disorders. In M.L. Batshaw (Ed.), *Children with disabilities* (4th ed. pp. 275-292) Baltimore: Brookes.

Ward-Leeper, G. (1991). *Disorders of speech and language.* London, ON: The Department of Communicative Disorders.

Links

AAC Intervention:
www.aacintervention.com

Kids Health for parents
http://kidshealth.org/parent/medical/ ears/ central_auditory.html

Closing the Gap:
http://www.closingthegap.com/

OACRS: **www.oacrs.com** provides links to the Children's Treatment Centres in Ontario.

Ontario Assoc. of S.L.P. and Audiologists
http://www.osla.on.ca

APPENDIX

Definitions and Categories of Exceptionality in Ontario

Exceptional Pupil

An *exceptional pupil* means a pupil whose behavioural, communicational, intellectual, physical, or multiple exceptionalities are such that a committee considers the pupil to need placement in a special education program.

Special Education Program

A *special education program* means, in respect of a pupil with an exceptionality, an educational program that is based on and modified by the results of continuous assessment and evaluation and that includes a plan containing specific objectives and an outline of educational services that meets the needs of the pupil with an exceptionality.

Special Education Services

Special education services means facilities and resources, including support personnel and equipment, necessary for developing and implementing a special education program.

The following five categories included in the definition of an exceptional pupil (see above) was clarified in a memo to school boards on January 15, 1999:

Behaviour

A learning disorder characterized by specific behaviour problems over such a period of time, and to such a marked degree, and of such a nature, as to adversely affect educational performance, and that may be accompanied by one or more of the following:

a) an inability to build or to maintain interpersonal relationships

b) excessive fears or anxieties

c) a tendency to compulsive reaction

d) an inability to learn that cannot be traced to intellectual, sensory, or other health factors, or any combination thereof

Communication

Autism

A severe learning disorder that is characterized by

a) disturbances in: rate of educational development; ability to relate to the environment; mobility; perception, speech, and language

b) lack of the representational symbolic behaviour that precedes language

Deaf and Hard of Hearing

An impairment characterized by deficits in language and speech development because of a diminished or non-existent auditory response to sound

Language Impairment

A learning disorder characterized by an impairment in comprehension and/or the use of verbal communication or the written or other symbol system of communication that may be associated with neurological, psychological, physical, or sensory factors, and that may

a) involve one or more of the form, content, and function of language in communication, and

b) include one or more of: language delay; dysfluency; voice and articulation development, which may or may not be organically or functionally based

Speech Impairment

A disorder in language formulation that may be associated with neurological, psychological, physical, or sensory factors; that involves perceptual motor aspects of transmitting oral messages; and that may be characterized by impairment in articulation, rhythm, and stress

Learning Disability

A learning disorder evident in both academic and social situations that involves one or more of the processes necessary for the proper use of spoken language or the symbols of communication, and that is characterized by a condition that

a) is not primarily the result of impairment of vision; impairment of hearing; physical disability; developmental disability; primary emotional disturbance; cultural difference

b) results in a significant discrepancy between academic achievement and assessed intellectual ability, with deficits in one or more of the following: receptive language (listening, reading); language processing (thinking, conceptualizing, integrating); expressive language (talking, spelling, writing); mathematical computations; and

c) may be associated with one or more conditions diagnosed as a perceptual handicap; a brain injury; minimal brain dysfunction; dyslexia; developmental aphasia

Intellectual

Giftedness

An unusually advanced degree of general intellectual ability that requires differentiated learning experiences of a depth and breadth beyond those normally provided in the regular school program to satisfy the level of educational potential indicated

Mild Intellectual Disability

A learning disorder characterized by

a) an ability to profit educationally within a regular class with the aid of considerable curriculum modification and supportive service

b) an inability to profit educationally within a regular class because of slow intellectual development

c) a potential for academic learning, independent social adjustment, and economic self-support

Developmental Disability

A severe learning disorder characterized by

a) an inability to profit from a special education program for students with mild intellectual disabilities because of slow intellectual development

b) an ability to profit from a special education program that is designed to accommodate slow intellectual development

c) a limited potential for academic learning, independent social adjustment; and economic self-support

Physical

Physical Disability

A condition of such severe physical limitation or deficiency as to require special assistance in learning situations to provide the opportunity for educational achievement equivalent to that of pupils without exceptionalities who are of the same age or development level

Blind and Low Vision

A condition of partial or total impairment of sight or vision that even with correction affects educational performance adversely

Multiple

Multiple Exceptionalities

A combination of learning or other disorders, impairments, or physical disabilities that is of such a nature as to require, for educational achievement, the services of one or more teachers holding qualifications in special education and the provision of support services appropriate for such disorders, impairments, or disabilities

Some Assessment Instruments Popular in Ontario

Titles below appear in alphabetical order, and include the "familiar" name. Each summary is brief. For in-depth reviews and information on test construction refer to the Buros Mental Measurement website (**www.unl.edu/buros**).

Please note that it is extremely important to be aware of the age of both the content and norms of any testing instrument. Results based on content and norms established decades ago may produce misleading or irrelevant information that could affect appropriate programming.

Adaptive Behavior Evaluation Scale-Revised (ABERS-R)

This instrument is designed to assess the adaptive behaviour of students with intellectual and developmental disabilites ages 5 years -0 months through 18 years -11 months. It is individually administered. There is both a school and home version and either version takes approximately 20 minutes to complete. The following ten adaptive skills are assessed: communication skills, self-care, social skills, community use, self-direction, health, safety, functional academics, leisure skills, and work skills. There are separate norms for males and females and the school version includes individualized program goals, objectives and interventions for the 104 assessed items.

Achenbach Child Behaviour Checklist 6-18 (CBCL/6-18)

The purpose of this assessment instrument is to obtain caregivers' reports of children's (age 6-18) competencies and behaviour in a standardized format. It permits the examiner to get a measure of internal and external problems. *Internal problems* include social withdrawal, somatic complaints, and anxious/depression scales. *External problems* include rule-breaking behaviour, attention problems, and aggressive behaviour scales. The checklist takes approximately 25-30 minutes to complete.

AAMR Adaptive Behavior Scale, School Edition (The ABS-2)

This individually completed scale is used principally to aid in classification, placement, and general programming decisions for individuals age 3–18 years, 11 months with developmental delay by assessing their adaptive functioning. There is some evidence to suggest that this scale may also be helpful in assessing the adaptive functioning of students with autism spectrum disorders. The ABS-2 is divided into 2 parts: Part 1 focuses on personal independence and part 2 assesses social adaptation. The rater (test completer) can be the parent, teacher, social worker, etc. The scale takes approximately 30 minutes to complete.

The ABS-2 enjoys popularity with educators and health professionals who emphasize adaptive behaviour in assessing mental handicap. It is used most frequently to assess an individual's ability to thrive in a particular placement (independent, group home, etc.).

Asperger Syndrome Diagnostic Scale (ASDS)

This easy-to-use rating scale is designed to help determine whether a child has Asperger syndrome. It takes 10-15 minutes to complete by parents, teachers, or anyone else who knows the child well. It is designed to assess individuals 5-18 and provides an "AS Quotient," which can help determine if an individual has Asperger syndrome

Beck Youth Inventories–Second Edition for Children and Adolescents (BYI-11)

These inventories, designed for students between the ages 7 through 18 years of age, assesses symptoms of depression, anxiety, anger disruptive behaviour, and self-concept. They can be administered either individually or in groups. It takes approximately 5-10 minutes for each inventory.

The Behavior Evaluation Scale—Third Edition (BES-3)

The BES is a scale for evaluating behaviour in students K-12. It is filled out by the teacher or other adult, and covers areas such as learning problems, interpersonal difficulties, unhappiness, depression, etc. It takes about 15 minutes to complete and is useful for comparison purposes if it is completed by several significant adults in the subject's life. However, this or any evaluation scale should never be used as a sole determinant for identification or placement.

Beery-VMI (Developmental Test of Visual Motor-Integration)—5th Edition (VMI-5)

This instrument is designed to be a screening test to help detect visual motor deficits in students 2 to 18 years of age. It can be administered to either individuals or groups and takes 10-15 minutes to complete. It measures gross motor, fine motor, and visual and fine motor development. It is a culture-free test useful with students from diverse cultural and linguistic backgrounds.

Boehm Test of Basic Concepts, Third Edition ("The Boehm") (2000): The Psychological Corporation

A standardized individual or group screening

test of comprehension, quantity, and time concepts designed to assess knowledge basic to early academic success. If used to assess school readiness, it may help identify students at risk for learning difficulties. The grade range is K-2; it takes 30-40 minutes to administer and produces a percentile score.

Behavior Rating Inventory of Executive Function

This rating scale is used by parents, teachers, and day-care providers to rate a child's executive functions (e.g., working memory, plan/ organize, emotional control). It is designed to assess children between the ages of 2-5 years, 11 months, and takes about 10-15 minutes to complete.

Brigance Comprehensive Inventory of Basic Skills-Revised (CIBS-R).

An individually administered instrument, designed to assess pre-academic, academic, and vocational skills so that teachers can more easily define objectives and plan individual programs. The grade range is pre-school to 12; it takes 15-90 minutes to administer, and in some sub-tests produces a grade or age level score. Sub-tests consist of readiness, speech, listening, research and study skills, reading, spelling, writing, and math. (There are several other similar instruments by Brigance.) This edition contains both criterion-referenced and standardized assessment data.

The Canadian Achievement Test—3rd Edition ("The CAT-3")

A standardized, norm-referenced, and criterion-referenced group test to assess achievement. Grade range is 1-12; time to administer is flexible (depending on the number and combination of sub-tests). Produces percentile, stanine, scaled, and grade equivalent scores. The major content areas are reading, spelling, language, mathematics, and reference skills. The test is reasonably easy to administer. All norms are based on a representative sample of students across Canada in grades 1-12 and the test produces a detailed Student Diagnostic Profile (SDP) that can be very useful if personnel are prepared to take the time to interpret the results.

Canadian Cognitive Abilities Test Form K-1998 (CCAT-Form K)

This is a standardized, norm-referenced group test designed to measure cognitive abilities in the verbal, quantitative, non-verbal, and problem-solving areas. The grade range is K-12 (primary battery for K-2 and Levels A-H for grades 3-12); it takes 1-2 hours to administer and produces standard, percentile, and stanine scores for age groups, and percentile and stanine scores for grade groups.

The CCAT has high validity and reliability estimates and reviewers compliment it for careful norming and standardization. Supporters say it has better predictive value than IQ tests, although critics argue that cognitive ability by itself is not a straightforward entity to assess.

The Canadian Test of Basic Skills Form K 1998 (CTBS)

A Canadianization of the Iowa Test of Basic Skills, very popular in Ontario, the CTBS is a standardized, norm-referenced, group-administered achievement test for K-12 that produces mounds of data. The Primary Battery Form K is used for grades K-3.5, Levels 9-14 Form K are used for grade 3-8, and levels 15-18 Form K are used for grades 9-12. There is also a Survey Battery available (Levels 9-14, Form L) that assesses reading, mathematics, and language, but does not include science. It can be hand scored, although a computerized scoring system is also available. Scores range from percentile to scale to grade equivalent. Intra-class data as well as other, extensive comparative data can be made available. The test examines 7 areas: vocabulary, reading, language, sources of information, mathematics, maps, diagrams, and science.

The CTBS can be extremely time-consuming to administer but many educators say it is worth the effort. Validity and reliability data are generally good and the test is well-received by reviewers.

Childhood Autism Rating Scale (CARS)

This scale, appropriate for children over 2 years of age, helps clinicians and teachers identify and classify children with autism spectrum disorders. The scale is composed of 15 items and results in a total score that can assist in the determination of autism spectrum disorders and the category (mild to moderate or severe) in which the child may be placed.

Children's Memory Scale

This test is designed for students between the ages of 5-16 to assess their memory abilities (attention and working memory, verbal and visual memory, short and long-delay memory, recall and recognition). It takes 30 minutes to complete and the authors suggest that it is a good screening instrument for assessing possible learning disabilities and attention deficit disorders.

Comprehensive Test of Phonological Processing (CTOPP)

This test, appropriate for ages 5-24 years, 11 months, takes 30 minutes to complete and is designed to assess phonological awareness, phonological memory, and rapid naming. There are two versions, one for children age 5 and 6 and one for individuals age 7-24. Test results can help identify individuals who are significantly below in their age appropriate phonological ability.

Coopersmith Self-Esteem Inventory (CSEI)

This inventory measures attitudes toward self. It is composed of a brief self-report questionnaire with a school form appropriate for students 8-15 years of age and an adult form for those 16 years of age and older. It takes approximately 15 minutes to complete and is hand scored.

Detroit Tests of Learning Aptitude—Fourth Edition ("The Detroit")

This is an individually administered test designed to measure general intelligence and discrete ability areas. It is appropriately used for those in the age range of 6-17, and takes about 40 minutes-2 hours to administer. It produces percentile scores, standard scores, and age equivalents. The test purports to provide a thorough investigation of a person's cognitive functions.

Gates-MacGinitie Reading Tests ("The Gates-MacGinitie"), 2nd Canadian Edition

A standardized, norm-referenced, group test designed to measure silent reading skills. Grade range is K-12; takes 50-60 minutes to administer; produces grade, standard, and percentile scores. The Gates-MacGinitie is offered at nine levels and gives two basic measures: vocabulary and comprehension. They are pen-and-paper tests completed by the subject(s), usually in groups. These tests can be useful for determining broad comparisons and are often used for test-retest procedures because alternate forms are available.

Kaufman Assessment Battery for Children Second Edition ("The K-ABC-II")

A standardized, individual, norm-referenced test of intelligence and achievement for age range 3-18; it takes 30-70 minutes to administer and produces age level, standard, and percentile scores. Five scales, Simultaneous, Sequential, Planning, Learning, and Knowledge, are assessed in 20 sub-tests. The K-ABC-II is a complex and involved instrument requiring expertise, time, and patience in the examiner. A major claim made for the test is that it is an excellent instrument for the assessment of children of different backgrounds and with diverse problems. Draws heavily on neuropsychology and cerebral specialization theory, and whether or not a test based on these elements can be educationally useful is still uncertain.

Keymath Revised: A Diagnostic Inventory of Essential Mathematics-Normative Update (Keymath-R/NU)

This is a standardized, individually administered test designed to assess mathematics skills. Grade range is K-12. It takes 35-50 minutes to administer, and produces grade level and age equivalents, percentile ranks and stanines. It measures mathematical knowledge of numeration, rational numbers, geometry, addition, subtraction, multiplication, division, mental computation, measurement, time, and money, estimation, interpreting data, and problem solving. Keymath is easy to administer; diverse, colourful, and widely applicable.

(Note: at time of printing a newly revised edition, "Keymath 3," was due to be released.)

Kovacs Children's Depression Inventory (CDI)

The test is designed to help counsellors and clinicians detect symptoms of major depressive disorder in children and adolescents ages 6-17 years of age. It contains 27 items that ask the student to respond to statements that best describes his or her feelings within the previous two weeks. It only takes 5-10 minutes to complete and can be administered individually or in a group setting.

Leiter International Performance Scale—Revised (The Leiter-R)

A non-verbal test of intelligence and cognitive abilities measured by assessing areas such as reasoning, memory, and attention. It includes 20 sub-tests that measure both general intelligence and discrete ability areas. Scores are provided for the sub-tests as well as a composite IQ score. Often used for individuals with hearing and language difficulties, severe disabilities such as autism spectrum disorders or traumatic brain injury, and for non-English speakers. Directions are pantomimed and gestured. Age range is 2 years -20 years 11 months. There are no time constraints and the scoring is very objective. Subjects usually enjoy the test process. There is no leeway for partial scoring, which seems contradictory given there is no guarantee the subjects have fully understood the tasks, or are fully capable of responding. The Leiter-R is heavy and awkward to use and store, but is a popular and potentially useful instrument for certain subjects.

McCarthy Scales of Children's Abilities (The McCarthy Scales)

A standardized, individual, norm-referenced test of general intellectual ability frequently offered as an instrument to identify children with possible learning disabilities. Age range is 2.5-8.5 years; it takes an hour to administer and produces mental age, standard, and percentile scores. The McCarthy Scales include several verbal tasks appropriate for children with suspected learning disabilities and has good reliability support. Ironically, no children classified as exceptional were included in the norming sample!

Multidimensional Anxiety Scale for Children (MASC)

This assessment instrument is for use with individuals 8-19 years of age and is designed to assess the major dimensions of anxiety in young persons. It is composed of 39 items and takes approximately 15 minutes to complete. It is composed of the following scales: Physical Symptom scale, Social Anxiety scale, Harm Avoidance scale, Separation/Panic scale, Anxiety Disorders scale, Total Anxiety Index, and Inconsistency Index.

Peabody Individual Achievement Test-Revised-Normative Update (The PIAT-R/NU)

An individual, norm-referenced, standardized test designed to give a wide measure of general achievement, with particular emphasis on reading, spelling, and arithmetic achievement. The grade range is K-12, ages 5.0–22 years 11 months; takes 50-70 minutes to administer; produces age level, grade level, standard, and percentile scores.

The PIAT-R uses a multiple-choice answer format. It requires recognition of correct spelling and tests sentence comprehension as well as mathematical problem-solving skills. Provides a quick, overall, preliminary view, but should not be regarded as the last word.

Peabody Picture Vocabulary Test—Fourth Edition (PPVT-4)

A standardized, individual test of single-word receptive vocabulary of standard (American) English. The age range is 2 years-6 months–90 years. It takes 10-20 minutes to administer and produces age and grade based standard scores, percentile and stanine scores. The PPVT-R format presents pictures to elicit a response to a word; it is non-threatening. A good first test in a battery well-designed and normed. But not too much should be made of the results of a test of single-word vocabulary.

Raven's Progressive Matrices (The Ravens)

This test is designed to assess a person's intellectual and reasoning ability by the completion of progressively complicated visual analogies. It is entirely non-verbal, suitable for all ages from 6-adult and is available in Standard and Advanced levels. There is a coloured version for younger children. The Ravens can be used very effectively for a test-teach-test approach. Because it is non-verbal, it may reveal some cognitive strengths in poor readers.

Slingerland Screening Tests for Identifying Children With Specific Language Disability (The Slingerland)

Revised in 2005, this test is a non-standardized, informal group test of visual, auditory, and kinesthetic skills related to reading and spelling, designed to identify students with a specific language disability. The age range is 6-12; it takes 60-90 minutes to administer and it produces no scores but has guidelines for evaluating test performance.

The tests are strictly informal and permit a great deal of subjectivity. Some students become very frustrated during administration because extensive writing is required.

Stanford-Binet Intelligence Scale, Fifth Edition (The Binet)

Designed to assess intelligence and cognitive abilities for individuals 2 to adult, the fifth edition retains many features of previous editions with significant improvement in psychometric design. Its authors claim this edition, as in the previous one, is designed to help differentiate between mental handicap and learning disability, to identify giftedness, to understand why a student is having learning problems, and that the ability to measure ability is improved by having the difficulty of items tailored to the cognitive functioning of the individual completing the test. The test measures five factors of cognitive ability: fluid reasoning, knowledge, quantitative processing, visual-spatial processing and working memory.

Test of Reading Comprehension—Third Edition (The TORC)

A standardized, norm-referenced test for individual or group, designed to give a normed measure of silent reading comprehension independent of specific curriculum via nine sub-tests like paragraph reading, syntactic similarities, social studies vocabulary, reading the directions of school work, etc. The age range is 6 years 6 months—14 years, 6 months. It takes 1½-2 hours to administer and produces scaled (each sub-test) and standardized (total test) scores. The test has come to be used mostly at upper age ranges because of very specific, subject-based vocabulary. The sub-tests include general vocabulary, syntactic similarities, paragraph reading, and sentence sequencing. Several of these sub-tests measure abilities not taught in classrooms and therefore the value of the results for school purposes may be questionable.

Vineland Adaptive Behavior Scales, Second Edition (Vineland-II)

This assessment tool is designed to assist in the identification of children and adults (up to 21 years, 11 months) with developmental disabilities, autism spectrum disorders, and Asperger syndrome. It is composed of a survey interview and parent/caretaker rating form and teacher rating form which take about 20-60 minutes to complete. The scales identify abilities in personal and social skills needed for everyday living.

Wechsler Individual Achievement Test, 2ⁿᵈ Edition (WIAT-II)

This "achievement battery" is designed for students between the ages of 4–adult. The WIAT-II assesses achievement in reading, spelling, mathematics, and listening and can be of assistance in obtaining an understanding of discrepancy between academic achievement and intellectual ability.

The Wechsler Intelligence Scale For Children – Fourth Edition (WISC-IV)

This is an individual, standardized, norm-referenced test designed to offer an ability score (IQ) and to offer information about a subject's skills in a variety of areas. This version is a significant departure from previous editions of the WISC. Test results now give four individual index scores: Verbal Comprehension Index (VCI), Perceptual Reasoning Index (PRI), Working Memory Index (WMI), and Processing Speed Index (PSI), rather than the two (Verbal and Performance) provided in early editions. The Verbal Comprehension Index is composed of five sub-tests: similarities, vocabulary, comprehension, information, and word processing. The Perceptual Reasoning Index is composed of block design, picture concepts, matrix reasoning, and picture completion, The Processing Speed Index is composed of coding, symbol search and cancellation, and the Word Memory Index is composed of digit span, letter-number sequencing, and arithmetic. The Full-Scale Score (FSIQ) is derived from the four composite scores.

Classroom teachers usually do not administer a WISC, but they do (or should) receive results. Ideally, teachers will be given the sub-test results as well as the Full Scale and Composite Scores, for these may have diagnostic information on which a plan of remediation can be based.

The WISC-IV, like its predecessors, has wide acceptance as a clinical and diagnostic tool. Although the manual for the test states that the instrument is intended for use with people aged 6 years 0 months through 16 years 11 months, it is not uncommon for the test to be used with students who are older or younger. (Adult and older students should theoretically be tested on the WAIS-III, the Wechsler Adult Intelligence Scale, and younger children on the WPPSI-III, the Wechsler Pre-Primer Scale of Intelligence.) Reliability and validity coefficients are high; it is particularly well standardized, and can produce some useful diagnostic information. Testing time is approximately 1½-2 hours.

Wide Range Achievement Test—4 (WRAT-4)

Based on the previous three editions, the WRAT

4, is an individual, norm-referenced, standardized test designed to assess skills in reading (word recognition and sentence completion), written spelling, and arithmetic computation. Age range is 5 to adult; it takes 15-45 minutes to administer (depending on the age of the person being tested) and it produces grade level, standard, percentile, and stanine scores. This test is easy and fast in administration and scoring, and can be a fairly efficient first step in an assessment. It should never be used as the sole element in any evaluation, assessment, or admission procedure (but often is!). The arithmetic computation sub-test does not test ability as much as it tests what the subject's curriculum offered.

Woodcock-Johnson Psycho-Educational Battery—Revised (The Woodcock or the WJ-R)

An individual, standardized, norm-referenced test designed to measure cognitive ability, academic achievement, and interests over a wide range. The age range is 3-adult; it takes 1½-2 hours to administer and produces grade level, age level, percentile, and standard scores, along with scores the authors call "functional level" and "relative performance index." This is a busy and involved instrument, with a large number of sub-tests. Areas covered consist of measures of "cognitive ability" (e.g., analysis-synthesis; memory for sentences, etc.) as well as an achievement battery (e.g., calculation, dictation, proofing, etc.). Provides a large amount of information, but is difficult and time consuming to administer.

Woodcock-Johnson Tests of Achievement-III (WJ-III)

An individually administered, standardized test designed to assess cognitive ability, academic achievement, and scholastic interest. It is administered in three parts, with part I taking 60-90 minutes, part II taking 30-45 minutes, and part III taking 15-30 minutes. It is appropriately used with anyone from the age of 3 to 80. It assesses the following: letter-word identification, reading fluency, story recall, understanding directions, passage comprehension, calculation, applied problems, math fluency, writing samples, writing fluency, and spelling. An extended battery includes the following: word attack, reading vocabulary, quantitative concepts, editing, punctuation and capitalization, story recall-delayed, picture vocabulary, oral comprehension, academic knowledge, spelling of sounds, and sound awareness.

Woodcock Reading Mastery Tests—Revised-Normative Update ("The Woodcock Reading or WRMT-R/NU")

This is an individual, standardized, criterion, and norm-referenced test designed to measure a wide range of reading skills. The grade range is K-12; it takes 30-45 minutes to administer; and it produces a wide set of scores, including grade level, percentile, relative mastery, achievement index, and reading range.

This test offers six sub-tests covering letters, words, and passages. The word comprehension sub-test uses analogy, and the passage comprehension makes use of the cloze procedures, both highly regarded techniques. A useful concept is the "relative mastery," which provides a useful indication of what can be expected of a student. Another useful point is the concept of instructional range in which the test gives indication of where a student can be expected to perform. Reliability and validity data are very good.

Some General Terms Used in Testing (See chapter 7 for more.)

Age Norm (Age Score) A score indicating average performance for students classified according to chronological age

Base Level The level at which all items of a test are passed, just preceding the level where the first failure occurs. All items below the base level are assumed correct. Contrast with ceiling level.

Battery A group of selected tests administered to a student

Ceiling Level The highest item of a sequence in which a certain number of items has been failed. All items above the ceiling item are assumed incorrect.

Chronological Age (CA) Age from birth expressed in years and months; e.g., 7 years, 6 months

Correlation Coefficient (r) A statistical index that measures the degree of relationship between any two variables

Diagnostic Testing An intensive, in-depth evaluation process using formal, standardized tests and informal tests designed to determine the nature and severity of specific learning problems

Intelligence Quotient (IQ) An index of mental capacity, expressing a student's ability to perform on an intelligence test

Mean (M) The sum of a set of scores divided by the number of scores

Median (MD) The middle point in a set of ranked scores

Mental Age (MA) A measure of a student's level of mental development, based on performance on a test of mental ability and determined by the level of difficulty of the test items passed

Mode (MO) The score that occurs most frequently in a distribution. In the distribution 18, 14, 12, 11, 10, 10, 7, the mode is 10.

Percentile Rank A type of converted score that expresses a student's score relative to his or her group in percentile points. Indicates the percentage of students tested who made scores equal to or lower than the specified score.

Projective Technique A test situation in which the student responds to ambiguous stimulus materials, such as pictures, inkblots, or incomplete sentences, thereby supposedly projecting personality characteristics

Protocol The original record of the test results

Rank Ordering The arrangement of scores from highest to lowest

Raw Score The score initially obtained by scoring a test according to directions in the manual

Reliability The degree to which a student would obtain the same score if the test were re-administered assuming no further learning, practice effects, or other change

Scaled Score A score used to measure students' growth from year to year

Standard Deviation (SD) The most commonly used measure of variation. A statistic used to express the extent of the distribution's deviations from the mean

Standard Score Derived score that transforms a raw score in such a manner that it has the same mean and the same standard deviation.

Standardization In test construction, this refers to the process of trying the test out on a group of students to determine uniform or standard scoring procedures and methods of interpretation

Standardized Test Contains empirically selected materials, with specific directions for administration, scoring, and interpretation. Provides data on validity and reliability, and has adequately derived norms.

Stanine A weighted scale divided into nine equal units that represent nine levels of performance on any particular test. The stanine is a standard score.

Validity The extent to which a test measures what it is designated to measure. A test valid for one use may have negligible validity for another.

Ontario Legislation and Policies Affecting Special Education

The Education Act

Usually referred to as "The Act," it governs the operation of schools and school boards in the province. The requirement mandating special education is now found in paragraph 170 (1) 7. Section 1(1) defines exceptional pupil, special education program, and special education services (see Appendix Definitions and Categories above). Other sections deal with various elements, e.g., subsections 57(3), (4), and (5) deal with the Tribunal stage in appealing an IPRC decision. The obligations most immediately affecting day-to-day issues are usually covered in Regulations and Policy/Program Memoranda.

Key Regulations Affecting Special Education

296 Ontario Schools for the Blind and the Deaf relates to the operation of the Ontario Schools for the Blind and the Deaf.

298 Operation of Schools-General: Subsection 3(3) permits a reduction in the length of the instructional program for pupils with exceptionalities below the required 5 hours per day. Section 14 sets out qualifications teachers must hold to be placed in charge of or to teach in a special education program. Section 26 sets out the relationship between principals and professional support staff, including psychiatrists, psychologists, and social workers. Section 30 provides for special education programs for pre-school children who are deaf or hard of hearing. Section 31 sets out maximum enrollment for special classes.

181 Identification and Placement of Exceptional Pupils. (See chapter 6.)

306 Special Education Programs and Services requires each school board to maintain a special education plan for the delivery of special education programs and services

464 Special Education Advisory Committees governs the appointment to and operations of Special Education Advisory Committees (SEACs).

Policy/Program Memoranda

Policy/program Memoranda (PPMs) are statements on Ministry policy and often include information about the Education Act and regulations made under the act. The PPMs listed here contain information about the education of pupils with exceptionalities.

PPM 1 Ontario Schools for the Blind and Deaf as Resource Centres

PPM 8 Learning Disabilities

PPM 11 Early Identification of Children's Learning Needs

PPM 59 Psychological Testing and Assessment of Pupils

PPM 76C Alternative Educational Programs and Services for Deaf, Blind and Deaf-Blind Exceptional Pupils

PPM 81 Provision of Health Support Services in School Settings

PPM 85 Educational Programs for Pupils in Government-Approved Care and/or Treatment Facilities

PPM 89 The Residential Demonstration Schools for Students with Learning Disabilities

PPM 127 Provincial Secondary School Literacy Test in English-Language Secondary Schools—Accommodations, Deferrals

PPM 140 Incorporating Methods of Applied Behaviour Analysis (ABA) into programs with Autism Spectrum Disorders (ASD)

SUBJECT / CONTEXT INDEX

A

AAMD, 81, 223
ability grouping, 139
Aboriginal students, 51
absence seizures, 123, 182-83
academic achievement tests, 79
acceleration, 139
Achenbach Child Behaviour
    Checklist 6-18 (CBCL/6-18),
    115, 223
achievement tests, 101
acoupedic method,
acquired brain injury (ABI), 181-82
AD/HD, 102, 123-26
    see also behavioural disorders
Adaptive Behavior Evaluation
    Scale-Revised (ABERS-R), 223
adaptive behaviour, 150, 151
administrative support, 69
adventitious vision loss, 205
advocacy groups, 188
age norm (age score), 228
Aird, John Black, 5
albinism, 206
alcohol, see fetal alcohol syndrome
Alcohol-Related Neuro-develop-
    mental Disorder (ARNO), 157
allergies, 113, 185
alternative education, 51
American Association on
    Intellectual and
    Developmental Disabilities
    (AAIDD), 149
American Association on Mental
    Retardation (AAMR),
    see American Association
    on Intellectual and
    Developmental Disabilities
American Sign Language (ASL),
    192, 195, 197
Americans with Disabilities Act,
    10
Amethyst School,
analytic intelligence, 136
anoxia, 155
appeal process (IPRC), 15, 73

Applied Behaviour Analysis,
    170-71
apprenticeship pathway, 51
Aristotle, 6
arthritis, 180
articulation disorders, 215
Asperger, Hans, 167
Asperger's Syndrome Diagnostic
    Scale (ASDS), 223
Asperger's disorder (Syndrome),
    166
assessment
    alternative procedures, 81-83
    autism spectrum disorders,
        169-70
    battery, 78-81
    behavioural disorders, 115
    case study, 86-87
    components, 78
    developmental disabilities,
        159-60
    giftedness, 141-42
    hearing loss, 192, 198
    important terms, 82
    innovation, 84
    instruments, 222-29
    intellectual and developmental
        disabilities, 150-52
    issues, formal tests, 83-86
    keys to effective assessment, 80
    learning disabilities, 100-02
    parental involvement, 81
    process, 40-43
    purpose of, 75-77
    speech and language disorders,
        215
assistance, resource, 44
Association for Bright Children, 11
Association for Community
    Living, 11, 188
asthma, 185
astigmatism, 206
ataxia, 180
attention deficit, see AD/HD
Attention Deficit/Hyperactivity
    Disorder, see AD/HD

attention problems, 100
auditory training, 196
augmentative and alternative
    communication (AAC), 218
authentic assessment, 83
Autism Behaviour Checklist, 170
Autism Canada, 167, 168
Autism Diagnostic Interview-
    Revised (ADI-R), 170
autism spectrum disorders (ASD),
    26, 36, 113
    characteristics, 167
    definition, 165-66
    diagnosis, 169-70
    Intensive Behaviour
        Intervention, 171-73
    issues, 173-74
    misconceptions, 165
    pervasive developmental
        disorders, and, 166
    prevalence, increase in, 167-69
    strategies, 174-76
    treatment, 170-71
Autistic disorder, 166, 221
Autonomous Learner Model, 145
aversion therapy, 172

B

bands of confidence, 82
base level, 228
battery, 228
Beck Youth Inventories-Second
    Edition for Children and
    Adolescents (BYI-11), 223
Beery-VMI (Developmental Test
    of Visual Motor-Integration-
    5th ed. (VMI-5), 223
Behavior Evaluation Scale (BES),
    223
Behavior Rating Inventory of
    Executive Function, 224
behaviour disorders, 221
    assessment of, 115
    bullying, 110
    causes, 113-14
    childhood depression, and, 114

conceptual models, 118-22
conductive disorder, and, 116
increase in, 112
issues, 115-18
intervention styles, 85-87
mental health view, 111-12
misconceptions, 109-10
oppositional defiant disorder, and, 118
reactive attachment disorder, and, 115
strategies, 126-30
teachers' perceptions, 112
terminology, 111-12
video games, and, 120
see also AD/HD
behaviour intervention, 170
behaviour modification, 121, 125, 170
behaviourist theory, 112, 121
Betts, G.T., 145
bilateral hearing loss, 193
Bill 82, 5, 6, 159
   categories of exceptionalities, 33-34
   change and adaptation, and, 18
   elements of, 11-12
   implementation, 12-14
   IRPCs, use of, 48
   outstanding issues, 14-15
   passage, 11
biochemical intervention, 170
biophysical theory, 112, 119
Bleuler, Eugen, 167
blindisms, 212
blindness
   assistive technology, 210
   causes, 205, 206-07
   classifications, 205
   definitions, 205, 222
   educational implications, 209-10
   issues, 207-09
   misconceptions, 204
   placement, 211
   prevalence, 205
   strategies, 211-12
   vision problems, classroom checklist, 206
Bloorview MacMillan Centre, 8
Boehm Test of Basic Concepts, 80, 223
Braille Blazer, 210
braille, 204, 207, 210
Braille, Louis, 210

brain injury, *see* acquired brain injury
Brigance Comprehensive Inventory of Basic Skills-Revised (CIBS-R), 80, 224
buddy system, 201, 212
bullying, 110

C
Canadian Achievement Test-3rd ed. (CAT-3), 224
Canadian Association of the Deaf, 196
Canadian Attention Deficit/Hyperactivity Disorder Resource Alliance, 124
Canadian Charter of Rights and Freedoms, 16
Canadian Cognitive Abilities Test (CCAT-Form K), 80, 224
Canadian Hearing Society, 188, 196, 197
Canadian National Committee on Mental Hygiene, 8
Canadian National Institute for the Blind, 188
Canadian Test of Basic Skills (CTBS), 224
cancer, 185
Cascade Model, 47-48
case study, 86-87
cataracts, 206
categories, 32-34, 221-22
   autism spectrum disorders, 165-76
   behaviour disorders, 32, 109-30
   blindness, 204-12
   deafness, 191-02
   giftedness, 133-46
   intellectual and developmental disabilities, 149-63
   learning disabilities, 89-107
   neurological disabilities, 179-89
   speech and language disorders, 214-19
ceiling level, 228
central auditory dysfunction, 193
central auditory processing (CAP) disorders, 217
central nervous system disorder, 92
Centre Jules-Leger, 45, 196
cerebral palsy, 179, 180
checklists, 80
Child Behavior Checklist (CBCL), 115, 223

Childhood Autism Rating Scale (CARS), 224
childhood depression, 114
childhood disintegrative disorder, 166
Children's Memory Scale, 224
chronic conditions, 185, 187
chronological age (CA), 199, 228
civil rights movement, 9
classification, *see* categories
classroom strategies
   autism spectrum disorders, 173, 174-76
   behavioural disorders, 121-22, 126-30
   deafness, 201-02
   giftedness, 145-46
   intellectual and developmental disabilities, 161-62
   learning disabilities, and, 104-07
   neurological disabilities, 188-89
   speech and language disorders, 215
   Tourette syndrome, 184
   visually impaired, 207, 209, 211-12
classroom teachers, 67-68, 77
CNS disorder, 92
cocaine, 155
cochlear implant, 195
cognitive ability tests, 80
collaboration, 161
   see also school team
college connections, 51
colour deficiency (blindness), 206
communication approaches
   combination, 198
   manual, 197
   oral, 196-97
community mentor program, 145
Comprehensive Test of Phonological Processing (CTOPP), 225
computer-assisted technology, 210
computer software, 202
Computerized Test of Information Processing (CTIP), 84
conduct disorder, 116
conductive hearing loss, 192
congenital malformations, 185
congenital vision loss, 205
consultant teacher program, 145
content-area assessment, 82
Continuum Model, 47-48
convulsive disorders, 179, 182-83

co-occurring disabilities, 102
Coopersmith Self-Esteem
    Inventory (CSEI), 225
Co-ordinated Services Unit, 18
coprolalia, 179, 183
correctional facility, 46
correlation coefficient (r), 228
Council for Exceptional Children,
    55
credit recovery, 51
criterion referenced test, 82
cued speech, 160
cultural factors, 24-25,
curriculum-based assessment, 76,
    81
cystic fibrosis, 185

D
data collection, 34-39
    see also identification
deaf culture (community), 191,
    194
deaf, psychology of, 199
deafness, 1, 221
    classifications, hearing loss,
        193-94
    communication approaches,
        196-98
    degrees of, 193
    educational implications,
        199-200
    hearing aid technology, 198
    hearing loss, types of, 192-93
    indications, 192
    issues, 194-96
    misconceptions, 191-92
    placement, 196
    strategies, 201-02
decibel ratings, 194
demonstration schools, 45
Detroit Tests of Learning
    Aptitude, 225
development and readiness tests, 80
developmental coordination
    disorder (DCD), 189
developmental disabilities, 222
    assessment and placement,
        159-60
    causes, concern for, 155-56
    changes in definition, 150
    definitions, 150-52
    instructional implications,
        156-59
    issues, 152-55
    misconceptions, 149-50

strategies, 161-63
developmental period, 152
diabetes, 185
Diagnostic and Statistical Manual
    of Mental Disorders (DSM),
    109, 111, 123, 165, 166, 169
diagnostic testing, 228
diagnostic tests, 79
differentiated instruction, 28
diplegia, 181
Disabilities Act, 18
dopamine deficiency, 124
Down syndrome, 155, 156
DragonDictate, 210
drills, 162
drug therapy, see medication
Drury (Ernest C.) School, 45, 196
DSM, see Diagnostic and
    Statistical Manual of Mental
    Disorders
Duchenne MD, 181
dyslexia, 91, 97

E
Eaton vs. Brant Co., 16
echolalia, 167
ecological assessment, 83
ecological view, 11
Education Amendment Act,
    see Bill 82
Education for All, 18, 30, 36
education plans, see individual
    education plan
educational assistants, 14, 54-55,
    68, 185, 186, 212, 219
emotional disorders,
    see behavioural disorders
emotional intelligence, 138
emotionally disturbed, 111
employment training, 155
enrichment, 145
Enrichment Triad Model, 135-36,
    144
environmental theory, 111, 120
epilepsy, 179, 182-83, 187
Epilepsy Association 183, 188
epiloia, 156
Epi-pens, 185
episodic, 99
ESL students, 51
eugenics, 8, 9, 133
exceptional pupil, defined, 221
eyesight examinations, 171

F
facilitated communication, 172
feeble-minded, 6
Fetal Alcohol Effects (FAE), 113, 157
Fetal Alcohol Spectrum Disorder
    (FASD), 157
Fetal Alcohol Syndrome (FAS),
    113, 123, 157
fingerspelling, 197
fluency disorder, 216
formal tests, 79
funding, 25

G
Galton, Francis, 133
Gardner, Howard, 137-38
Gates-MacGinitie Reading Tests,
    225
gender, 141
genetic research, 158
giftedness, 222
    defined, 134-38
    issues, 138-41
    misconceptions, 133-34
    nomination process, 141-42
    organizational models, 143-45
    strategies, 145-46
    underachievers, 142
glaucoma, 206
Goddard, H.H., 150
Goleman, Daniel, 138
grade equivalent, 82
grand mal seizures
    see tonic-clonic seizures
grants, see funding
Gray, Carol, 173
guide dogs, 204, 210

H
hearing aids, 191, 195, 198
hearing loss, 191-202
    see also deafness
hemiplegia, 181
heredity, 89
Hippocrates, 6
Hoffman, Heinrich, 124
Hope Commission, 9
human Rights Commission, 9
hydrocephalus, 181
hygiene,
hyperactivity, see AD/HD
hyperkinesis, 124
hyperopia, 206

I

iatrogenic disorder, 117
identification, 26, 27, 40, 71-72
  behavioural disorders, 115
  developmental disabilities, 159-60
  giftedness, 141-42
  learning disabilities, 100-02
Identification, Placement and Review Committees (IPRCs)
  appeal from decision of, 15, 73
  assessment process, and, 42-43, 48, 71-72, 159
  data concerning, 34-35
  establishment of, 12
independent study program, 145
IEP, see individual education plan
incidence data, 34
inclusion, see integration
inconsistency, 99
individual education plan (IEP), 14-15, 16, 18, 76
  and school teams, 65-69
  chronic health needs, 185
  contents of form, 63
  development of, 62-64
  direction setting, 61-62
  drawbacks, 21-22, 65
  information gathering, 60-61
  implementation, 43, 64
  inclusions, 58-59
  IPRC, and, 59
  parental involvement, 65
  policy requirements for, 58
  preparation of, 59-60
  process, 21-22, 41
  review and update, 64
  roadmap, as, 58-59
informal tests, 78-79
institutions, 119-20
integration, 15, 16, 22-23, 47-48, 102, 154
intellectual and developmental disabilities
  assessment and placement, 159-60
  causes, concern for, 155-56
  changes in definition, 150
  definitions, 150-52
  instructional implications, 156-59
  issues, 152-55
  misconceptions, 149-50
  strategies, 161-63
intellectual functioning, 150

intelligence quotient (IQ), 79, 92, 134, 229
Intensive Behaviour Intervention (IBI), 171-73, 173
intervention focused assessment, 76
inventories, 80
IPRC, see Identification, Placement and Review Committee(s)
IQ tests, 79, 116, 134, 137, 141, 149, 150-51, 180, 196
Itard, Jean Marc, 7
itinerant teacher programs, 196

K

Kanner, Leo, 167
Kaufman Assessment Battery for Children- 2nd ed. (K-ABC-II), 225
Keymath Revised Inventory, 225
kind firmness, 126
Kirk, Samuel, 24, 91
Klinefelter's syndrome, 155
Kovacs Children's Depression Inventory (CDI), 225
Kurzweil Reading Machine, 210

L

labelling, 26
  see also identification
Lancet, 165
language impairment, 94, 113, 158, 214-19, 221
  see also speech and language disorders
language-processing deficiency, 94-97
Langue de Signes Quebecoise, 197
learned helplessness, 156, 158
learning disabilities, 24, 222
  assessment and identification, 100-102
  characteristics of, 94-100
  classroom strategies, 104-07
  definitions of, 90-94
  issues, 102-03
  misconceptions, 89-90
  school problems, 99
  strategies, 104-07
Learning Disabilities Association, 11, 92, 102, 188
learning enrichment service, 145
learning style assessment, 83
least restrictive environment, 15

legal blindness, 205
legislation, 229-23
  see also Bill 182
Leiter International Performance Scale, 225
Leon, Ponce de, 6
lip reading, *see* speech reading
lobbying see advocacy
Locke, John, 6
low self-esteem, 100
  see also self-esteem

M

Macdonald (W. Ross) School, 45, 196
macular degeneration, 206
mainstreaming, 15
malleable intelligence, 156
manualism, 197
maturation lag, 91
McCann, John Barrett, 7
McCarthy Scales of Children's Abilities, 226
Mcdonald, Ronald, 7
mean (M), 229
median (MD), 229
mediation, 17
medical information, 81
medical model approach, 11
medication, 118, 121, 125
memory, 97-98, 156
meningocele, 181
mental age (MA), 229
mental health theories, 111-12
mental retardation, *see* intellectual and developmental disabilities
mentor program, 145
Merrick, John, 7
metacognition, 98
mild intellectual disability, 222
minimally brain-injured, 91, 124
mobility assists, 210
Mobius syndrome, 184
mode (MO), 229
momentum, 162
monocular vision, 207
moral deficit, 124
morphology,
motor disability, 181
MRI technology, 92
multidimensional Anxiety Scale for Children (MASC), 226
multidisciplinary *teams see* school teams
multiple disabilities, 184-85, 222

multiple intelligences, 137-38
Multiple Menu Model, 144
muscular dystrophy, 179, 181, 185
mutism, 191, 216
myopia, 207

N

National Institution on Deafness and Other Communication Disorders, 195
National Joint Committee on Learning Disabilities, 93
Neuro Trauma Foundation of Ontario, 33
neurological disabilities,
    advocacy groups, 188
    classroom implications, 187, 188
    issues, 185-87
    misconceptions, 179-80
    needs, description of, 180-85
    strategies, 188-89
neurosensory intervention, 170
nomination process, gifted, 141-42
non-school settings, 45
noradrenaline deficiency, 124
norm referenced test, 82
normalization, 10, 153
norms, 82
nystagmus, 207

O

Ontario Institution for the Education and Instruction of the Blind, 7
Ontario Institution for the Education and Instruction of the Deaf and Dumb, 7
Ontario School for Crippled Children, 8
Ontario Student Record (OSR), 58, 60
open-fit hearing aids, 198
oppositional defiant disorder, 118
Optacon, 210
optic atrophy, 207
optical aids, 210
oralism, 196-97
organizational models, gifted, 143-45
outcome-based assessment, 83
overidentification, 103
oxygen tanks, 185

P

paraplegia, 181
parent nomination, 142
parent, defined, 5
parent/teacher interviews, 81
parental involvement, 13, 14-15, 65, 68, 81
Peabody Individual Achievement Test-Revised (PIAT-R/NU), 79, 226
Peabody Picture Vocabulary Test-III (PPVT-4), 226
peer nomination, 142
Pentagonal Implicit Theory, 137
percentile rank, 82, 229
perceptional handicap, 91
peripheral understanding, 98
peripheral vision, 207
perseveration, 158
personnel, see service providers
Pervasive Development Disorder (PDD), 166
petit mal seizures see absence seizures
phenylketonuria, 155
phonology, 216
physical development, 158-59
physical disabilities, 222
Picture Exchange Communication System, 172
placement, 27, 34, 71-73
    partially integrated, 45, 196
    regular class, indirect support, 43
    resource assistance, 44
    self-contained class, 45
    special schools, 45, 196
    specialized non-schools, 45-46
    visually impaired, 211
    withdrawal for assistance, 44-45
portfolio assessment, 83
positive attitude, 161
practical intelligence, 136
Prader-Willi syndrome, 155
premenstrual syndrome, 113
pre-referral intervention, 76
prevalence data, 34
primary gifted, 140
principals, role of, 66
privacy issues, 78
probing, 82
program planning, see individual education plan
progressive discipline, 112

projective technique, 229
protocol, 229
psychodynamic intervention, 170
psychodynamic theory, 111, 119
psychoeducational theory, 112, 119
psychological processing impairment, 92
psychological theories, 113-14
psychosocial theory, 111
Purdue Model, 145

Q

quackery, 103
quadriplegia, 181

R

RAD, see reactive attachment disorder
Rain Man, 174
rank ordering, 229
rating scales, 80
Raven's Progressive Matrices, 226
raw score, 229
reactive attachment disorder (RAD), 115
Regular Education Initiative, 15
regulations affecting special education, 229-30
Renzulli, J.S., 135
repetition, 162
research, 29-30
residential schools, 45, 196
resources, control of, 53
retinal detachment, 205
retinitis pigmentosa, 207
retinoblastoma, 205
retinopathy of prematurity, 205
Rett's disorder, 166
Revolving Door Model, 144
Ritalin, 184
Robarts (John) School, 45
Rochester Method, 198
rubella, 155, 205

S

Safe Schools Act, 112
Sagonaska School, 45
Saint Nicholas Thaumaturgos, 6
SALEP, see supervised alterative learning for excused pupils programs
scaled score, 229
schizophrenia, 113
school teams, 40, 41-42, 53
    collaboration, and, 68, 161

issues involving, 69
role of, 65-66
strength of, 61
team members, 66-68
Schools General, 58
schools, special, 45
Schopler, Dr. Eric, 172
scoliosis, 185
SEAC, *see* Special Education
    Advisory Committee
secondary schools, 50-52
seizure disorders, *see* epilepsy
selected mutism, 216
self-contained special education
    settings, 51-52
self-esteem, 100, 159
self-help skills, 159
self-injurious behaviour, 159
Seneca, 6
sensorineural hearing loss, 192-93
sensory disabilities, 32
sequencing, 98
seratonin deficiency, 124
service delivery
    formal versus informal
        procedures, 48-50
    inclusion models, 47-48
    placement options, 43-46
    referral process, 40-43
    secondary schools, 50-52
    service providers, 52-54
service providers
    deployment, 52
    multidisciplinary team
        concept, 53-54
    personnel involved, 52
    resources, control of, 53
    school team, 53
Shared Solutions, 49, 69
signal-to-noise ratio, 199
signing interpreter, use of, 197
signing, *see* manualism
Skinner, B.F., 170
skullbone-anchored hearing aid
    system, 195
Slingerland Screening Tests, 226
slow learner, 91
social adjustment, 158
social stories, 173
socioeconomic factors, 117, 142
Solon's law, 6
Special Education Advisory
    Committee (SEAC), 12, 14
Special Education Companion, 18
special education

legislation, 229-30
policy/program memoranda,
    230
special education program,
    defined, 221
Special Education Project, 28
special education services,
    defined, 221
special education teacher, 66
Special Education Transformation,
    16-17, 23, 35
Special Incident Portion (SIP), 25
special residential schools, 196
speech and language disorders
    articulation expectations, 215
    assessment, 218
    augmentative and alternative
        communication, and, 218
    central auditory processing
        disorders, 217
    definition, 214
    misconceptions, 214
    specialists, role of, 217, 218
    strategies, 219
    teachers and EAs, role of, 219
    types of, 215-16, 216-17
speech impairments, 113, 158, 221
speechreading, 192,
spina bifida, 179, 181
split half procedure, 82
standard deviation (SD), 229
standard error of measurement, 82
standard score, 229
standardization, 229
standardized test, 101, 229
Stanford-Binet Intelligence Scale,
    226
stanine, 82, 229
Sternberg, Robert, 136
stigma, 117
Still, George, 124
strabismus, 207
strategies, *see* classroom strategies
structure, importance of, 161
student success initiative, 50-52
sub-average intellectual function-
    ing, 150
supervised alterative learning for
    excused pupils programs
    (SALEP), 52
support personnel, 68
Supreme Court of Canada, 16
surgical implantation technology,
    195
sympathetic ophthalmia, 205

synthetic intelligence, 136
syphilis, 155

T
talent, 139
Talmud, 6
task analysis, 83, 162-63
TEACCH program, 172
teacher consultation, 40, 41
teams, *see* school teams
teamwork, 161
    see also school teams
technology, use of, 162
Terman, Lewis, 141
terminology, 152
Test of Reading Comprehension
    (TORC), 227
testing, *see* assessment
terminology, 37
    see also achievement tests;
        assessment; IQ tests
Thaumaturgos, Saint Nicholas, 6
three-ring model, 135
time management, 98
time to learn policy, 154-55
Tomatis method, 172
tonic-clonic seizures, 182, 183
Total Communication Method,
    197, 198, 200
Tourette Syndrome Foundation,
    188
Tourette syndrome, 124, 179, 180,
    183-84, 187
transition plan, 51, 64, 92, 155
Treves, Frederick, 7
Triad model, 135
Triarchic theory, 136-37
Trillium School, 45
tuberous sclerosis, 155, 184
tunnel vision, 207
twice-exceptional learners, 144

U
underachievers, gifted, 142
unilateral hearing loss, 193
*Universal Design for Learning and
    Differentiated Instruction*, 18, 28

V
vaccination, 165
validity, 82, 229
Versabraille II+, 210
video games, 120
Vineland Adaptive Behavior
    Scales, 159, 227

violence, 109
visual impairment, 204-12
   checklist, 206
   see also blindness
visual stimulation, 210
vocational training, 155
voice disorders, 215

W
Wechsler Individual Achievement Test (WIAT-II), 79, 227
Wechsler Intelligence Scale for Children (WISC-IV), 79, 141, 159, 227
Whitney (Sir James) School, 45, 196
Wide Range Achievement Test (WRAT-4), 227

Wolfensberger, Wolf, 10
Woodcock Diagnostic Reading Battery, 79
Woodcock Reading Mastery Tests, 228
Woodcock-Johnson Psycho-Educational Battery, 228
Woodcock-Johnson Tests of Achievement-III, 228
workplace pathway, 51

AUTHOR / RESOURCE INDEX

Adams, L., 70
Adams, S.M., 164
Adelman, H.L., 39
Agnew, C.M., 189
Akamatsu, C.T., 203
Akshoomoff, N., 176
Alaimo, D.F., 176
Algozzine, B., 28, 87
Alkin, M.C., 163
Allen, D., 146
Allen, J., 146
Almond, P., 88
Ambrose, D., 146
Anderegg, M.L., 31
Anthony, L., 220
Appleton, R., 189
Asher, S., 220
Attwood, T., 176
Aust, P., 131
Aylwards, E.H., 107
Bachor, D., 163
Bagnato, S.J., 87
Baldwin, T., 189
Bankson, N.W., 220
Barabasz, A., 131
Barabasz, M., 131
Baron, M.A., 220
Barton, L., 31
Bates, K., 107
Batshaw, M.L., 189
Battle, D., 220
Bauer, A.M., 70
Bauer, S., 176
Bauman Waengler, J., 220
Bavarette, L., 132
Bear, G.G., 31, 56
Beck, J., 163
Bender, W.N., 56, 107
Benner, S.M., 87

Bennett, S., 20, 30, 39, 56
Bernstein, L.E., 220
Berstein, D.K., 220
Bielinksi, J., 39
Bilkin, D., 31
Bishop, K.D., 56
Bishop, V.E., 213
Blum, R.W., 189
Blythe, T., 146
Bobrick, B., 220
Bocian, K.M., 39
Borich, G., 87
Borthwick-Duffy, S.A., 31
Brigance, A.H.,
Brimer, R.W., 189
Brores, J., 163
Browder, D.M., 163
Brown, L., 164
Brown, R., 70, 87
Brownell, M.T., 176
Bryde, S.M., 87
Bufkin, L.J., 87
Bunch, G., 20
Bursuck, W., 30
Butler, K.G., 220
Buyer, D.M., 189
Calandrella, A.M., 220
Calderon, R., 203
Carbone, E., 131
Carnevale, A.P., 163
Carrier, J.G., 20, 39
Cartledge, G., 132
Cattell-Gordon, D., 176
Cessna, K., 70
Chein-Huey, C., 213
Childs, K.E., 131
Choutka, C.M., 107
Cipanni, E., 163
Clarke, B., 146

Clarke, S., 131
Cohen, D.J., 176
Colangelo, N., 146
Cole, E., 70, 87
Coleman, M.R., 146
Colucci, S., 131
Connor, M.C., 189
Cook, L., 70
Cornell, D.G., 148
Craig, W.M., 131
Crealock, C., 20, 163
Crites, S.S., 132
Cronin, M.E., 163
Cummins, J.G., 131
Dalrymple, M.J., 177
Daly, T., 177
Danforth, S., 30
Davidson, I., 70
Davis, G.A., 146
Davis, P., 213
Deemer, S.A., 56
Deiner, S.A., 31
Del Prete, T., 147
Delisle, J.R., 146
Demchak, M., 56
Demorest, M.E., 220
Dennis, R., 30
Denny, R.K., 131
Deno, E., 39
DePaepe, P.A., 131
Deshler, D.D., 107
Dettmer, P.A., 70
Diament, S., 213
Dieker, L., 70
DiGangi, S., 131
Donahue, M.L., 108
Donley, P.R., 213
Donnellan, A.M., 176
Dormans, J.P., 189

Dowdy, C.A., 56, 164
Drew, C.J., 163
Dunlap, G., 131, 176
Duquette, C., 213
Dworet, D.H., 56, 131
Dyck, N.T., 70
Dyson, L.L., 107
Edelman, S., 30
Edwards, C.M., 107
Ellis, E.S., 107
Emanuel, E.J., 39
Epstein, M.H., 131
Erin, J., 213
Evans, S.B., 70
Faber, A., 131
Feher-Prout, T., 203
Feldhausen, J.F., 147
Feldman, D., 147, 163
Fetzer, E.A., 147
Filla, A., 220
Fisher, D., 56
Fletcher, J.H.M., 147
Fletcher, K.L., 108
Flint, L.J., 147
Flippo, J.R., 132
Foerter, J., 20
Ford, D.Y., 147
Ford, V., 70
Foster, J.F., 147
Foster-Johnson, L., 131
Fox, L., 176
Fox, S.L., 87
Francis, G.C., 164
Freeman, S.F.N., 163
French, N.K., 56
Freudenheim, D.A., 147
Frey, K.S., 131
Friend, M., 30, 70
Friesen, J.W., 147
Fuchs, D., 30, 70
Fuchs, L.S., 30, 70
Fujiura, G.T., 39
Furr, D.L., 131
Gailbraith, J., 146
Gainer, L.J., 163
Gajris, M., 87
Garderen, D., 107
Gardner, H., 146, 147
Gartner, A., 39
Gaty, J.C., 203
Gazelle, H., 220
Gentile, D.A., 131
George, A.L., 213
Gerlach, K., 56
Gersten, R., 107

Gesser, L., 132
Giangreco, M., 30, 189
Giuliana, G., 87
Glasow, A., 88
Goddard, H.H., 163
Goleman, D., 147
Gotez, L., 56
Graziano, A.M., 163
Greer, A.E., 203
Gresham, F.L., 176
Gresham, F.M., 39
Griffin, S.M., 31, 56
Grossman, H., 163
Gutkin, T.B., 31
Haigh, J., 87
Hallahan, D.P., 213
Hallenbeck, M.J., 107
Hankin, J.R., 163
Harris, J.J., 147
Harry, B., 31
Hatnes, W.O., 220
Heath, N.H., 56, 164
Heckman, K., 132
Hedge, M.L., 220
Heflin, J., 131, 176
Hemrick, M.A., 87
Henley, M., 131
Herman, K.L., 108
Herr, S.S., 164
Higgins, E.L., 107
Hill, E.W., 213
Hinchelwood, J., 107
Hirschtein, M.K., 131
Hitchcock, C., 108
Hofsetter, E., 108
Hogue, E., 163
Holahan, J.M., 147
Hollenbeck, K., 88
Holt, J., 203
Hontto, S.A., 203
Hopwood, V., 213
Hourcade, J.J., 189
Howell, K.W., 87
Hughes, C.A., 107
Hulit, L.M., 220
Hunt, P., 56
Huntinger, P.L., 189
Huntington, D.D., 107
Huntly, S.B., 146
Hutchinson, N., 30
Idol, L., 70
Itard, J.M.G., 20
Jack, S.L., 131
Jenson, W.R., 131, 132
Jitendra, A.K., 107

Johnson, D.R., 39
Johnson, L.J., 70
Jones, K.H., 31, 56
Jordan, A., 70
Kaiser, A.P., 220
Karchmer, M.A., 203
Kauffman, J.M., 131, 213
Kearns, J.F., 87
Kennedy, S., 87
Kirchner, C., 213
Kiyoshi, Y., 39
Kleinert, H.L., 87
Kliewer, C., 31
Klin, A., 176
Knowlton, E., 163
Kolloff, P.B., 147
Kozma, C., 164
Kubiszyn, T., 87
Kurlan, R., 189
La Blance, G.R., 220
Lambros, K.M., 39
Lantieri, L., 131
Lartz, L.M., 203
Lash, M.H., 189
Lenk, L.L., 56
Lenz, B.K., 107
Leuking, R., 39
Leutke-Stahlman, B., 203
Levy, N.R., 107
Lewis, M., 147
Lewis, S., 107
Lewis, T.J., 131, 132
Linder, J.R., 131
Lindsay, P., 132
Lipsky, D.K., 39
Litchfield, S.K., 203
Logan, D.R., 163
Longo, M., 203
Louis, B., 147
Lovaas, I.O., 176, 177
Luckasson, R., 20
Luckner, J., 203
Lupart, J.L., 20, 31
Lusthaus, C., 56
Lusthaus, E., 56
Lynch, P.J., 131
Maag, J.W., 132
MacDonald, I.M., 131
MacDougall, J.C., 203
Mack, M., 39
MacMillan, D.L., 39, 176
Madaus, J.W., 107
Maich, K., 131
Maker, J.C., 147
Makuch, R.W., 147

Marshall, W., 203
Masse, L., 147
Mastropieri, M., 164
Maté, G., 132
Matthews, D.J., 147
Maurice, C., 177
Mavis, L., 108
Mayer, C., 203
Mazlish, E., 131
McAnich, C., 88
McGee, G.G., 177
McIntyre, L.J., 164
McKenzie, R.G., 108
McKeough, A., 20
McLaughlin, V.L., 108
McLaughlin-Cheng, E., 177
Meltzer, A.S., 163
Mendler, A.N., 132
Meyer, L.H., 164
Meyers, A., 108
Miller, J., 132, 220
Mills, M., 70
Minke, K.M., 31, 56
Minor, R.J., 213
Mishna, F., 131
Mitchell, R.E., 203
Montgomery, W., 147
Moon, S., 147
Moore, R., 132
Moores, D.F., 203
Moran, M.J., 220
Morehead, M.K., 87
Morgan, C.R., 56
Morrier, M.J., 177
Morrison, J., 220
Morsink, C.V., 56
Mostert, M.P., 177
Munson, S.M., 87
Myles, B.S., 176, 177
Naidu, S., 203
Napier, E., 70
Neisworth, J.T., 87
Nelson, R., 189
Nevin, A., 70
Newcomer, L.L., 132
Nielson, A.B., 147
Nystul, M.S., 189
O'Shea, D., 70
O'Shea, L., 70
Oderkirk, J., 20
Olsen, K., 88
Orme, S.F., 70
Oseroff, A., 132
Oseroff, C.E., 132
Oswald, K., 132

Ownes, R., 220
Palmer, D.S., 31
Palmer, J.M., 220
Paolucci-Whitcomb, P., 70
Parette, H.P., 189
Parron, J.R., 163
Patti, J., 131
Patton, J.R., 56, 164
Paulson, P.R., 87
Pearl, R., 108
Peck, C.A., 164
Pellegrino, L., 189
Peplar, D.J., 131
Perret, Y.M., 189
Peterson, J.M., 31
Pickett, A.L., 56
Pierangelo, G., 87
Pindzola, R.H., 220
Pirto, J., 147
Polloway, E.A., 56, 164
Popham, W.J., 87
Powers, L.J., 132
Prizant, B.M., 177
Pugach, M.C., 70
Quill, K.A., 177
Quinn, M., 220
Rainforth, B., 189
Rapin, I., 177
Raskind, M.H., 107, 108
Rathgeber, A.J., 131
Rea, P.J., 108
Reavis, H.K., 131, 132
Reed, L.C., 87
Reid, R., 132
Reis, S.M., 147
Reiss, S., 164
Renzulli, J.S., 147
Reschly, A., 39
Resnick, M.D., 189
Reynolds, M.C., 31, 39, 56
Rhode, G., 97, 131, 132
Richardson, S., 108
Rimm, S.B., 146
Roberts, K., 203
Robinson, A., 148
Rogers, J.A., 147
Rogers, S.J., 177
Rose, D., 108
Rosenberg, R.L., 56
Rubin, E., 177
Ruble, L.A., 177
Safran, J.A., 177
Safran, J.S., 70
Safran, S.P., 70, 132
Salend, S.J., 87, 108, 203

Salisbury, C.L., 31
Salvia, J., 88
Sandler, A., 189
Sands, D.J., 164
Sarouphim, K., 87
Schein, J., 203
Schildroth, A.N., 203
Schirmer, B.R., 203
Schopler, E., 177
Schraeder, T., 220
Scruggs, T., 164
Secord, W., 220
Shaler, J., 213
Shames, G., 220
Shaywitz, B.A., 147
Shaywitz, S.E., 147
Shea, T.M., 70
Shekitka, L., 108
Sheridan, S.M., 70
Sherman, G.F., 108
Shippen, M.E., 132
Shipstead, J., 163
Shore, B.M., 148
Shores, R.E., 131
Shriberg, L., 220
Shu-Li, L., 190
Siegel, B., 177
Silverman, L.K., 148
Simpson, R.G., 132
Simpson, R.L., 177
Smith T.E.C., 56, 164
Smith, D., 20
Smith, V.L., 220
Smith, W., 56
Smith, W.J., 20
Snell, M.E., 164
Snook-Hill, M., 213
Snow, J.A., 31
Sparrow, S.S., 176
Speece, D.L., 108
Spooner, F., 163
Sprague, J., 132
St. Germaine, A., 189
Stanovich, P., 70
Stark, R.E., 220
Steckol, K.F., 220
Sternberg, R.J., 148
Stewart, D.A., 203
Stock, J.S., 164
Stockman, I., 220
Stodden, R.A., 39
Stoyko Deuel, L.L., 108
Strong, Scott M., 108
Sugai, G., 131
Swanson, H.L., 108

Taft, S.D., 30
Tedesco, M., 88
Thousand, J., 56
Thurlow, M.L., 88
Thurston, L.P., 70
Tindal, G., 88
Tobey, E., 203
Tomlinson, C.A., 31
Torgeson, J.K., 108
Treadway, P.S., 107
Turnbull, A.P., 190
Turnbull, H.R., 190
Tuttle, D.W., 213
Tuttle, T.N., 176, 213
Tyler, J.S., 190
Uslan, M.M., 213
Valenca, S., 88
Valeo, A., 20
Venn, J.J., 88
Vera, A., 131
Vergason, G.A., 31
Villa, R.A., 56

Vlachou, A., 31
Volkmar, F., 176
Volkmar, F.R., 176
Walberg, H.J., 56
Walker, H., 132
Walsh, D.A., 131
Walther-Thomas, C., 108, 176
Walton-Allen, N., 163
Wang, M.C., 56
Wang, P.P., 220
Ward, V.S., 148
Ward-Leeper, G., 220
Weber, G., 164
Weber, J., 88
Wehmeyer, M.L., 164
Welch, M., 70, 108
Westberg, K.L., 147
Westby, C.E., 70
Westling, D., 132
White, R., 131
Whittaker, C., 107
Whitten, E., 70

Wiener, J., 70
Wiig, E., 220
Wilcox, M.J., 220
Wilkinson, K.M., 177
Williams, K., 177
Wilson, D., 131
Windaman, K., 31
Wing, L., 178
Winner, E., 148
Winzer, M., 20, 31, 56
Wolery, W., 220
Wolfensberger, W., 20
Wong, B., 108
Wood, M., 31
Woolsey, M.L., 203
Wright-Strawderman, C., 132
Wynne, K., 20, 30, 39
Yantis, P.A., 220
Yewchuck, C., 20
York, G., 31
York-Barr, J., 189
Ysseldyke, J.E., 31, 39, 87, 88